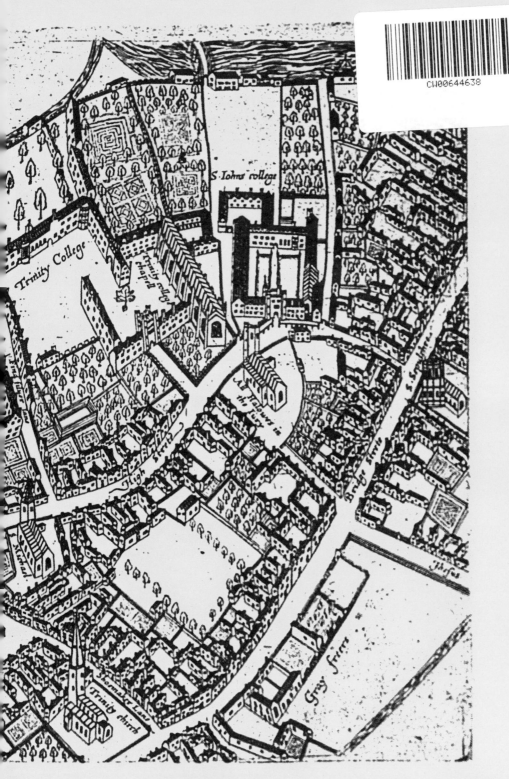

John Hammond of Clare Hall, 22 February 1592

Cambridge:
Treasure Island in the Fens

Cambridge:

Treasure Island in the Fens

The 800-year story of the university and town of Cambridge, 1209 to 2009

Nicholas Chrimes

Nicholas Chrimes

An imprint of Hobsaerie Publications

www.cambridgebook.com

Cambridge: Treasure Island in the Fens

Copyright ©W.N. Chrimes 2009

British Library Cataloguing-in-Publication Data.
A catalogue record for this book is available from the British Library

ISBN 978-0-9562382-0-7

Printed and bound by 1010 Printing International Ltd.

Cover illustrations briansanders.art@googlemail.com Text illustrations www.alicethomson.co.uk

The University Crest is reproduced with the permission of the University of Cambridge. The City Council has also permitted the reproduction of the city crest. Neither the City Council nor the University of Cambridge are responsible for the contents of this publication.

To my wife Narin and our children, Will, Katie, Ted and Emily. With loads of love and gratitude to each of you for making life so much fun.

Contents

List of Figures

Acknowledgements

As an outsider to Cambridge I have relied on the help of many people to gather the knowledge which has enabled me to write this book. Above all, I must credit the fine band of Cambridge Blue Badge Guides for inspiring my interest, as well as those among them who have shared their great knowledge of town and university so willingly.

Many members of the town and university have generously given of their time and knowledge. I am grateful to them all. The fact that those, like myself, from outside the university can reach into its heart, as I have been able to do in order to write this book, reflects the wish of many at the university to share its treasures with the local community. We who live close to the university in the twenty-first century have much for which to be grateful.

Special thanks to my editor, who returned some sense to the script following the dozens of alterations which I could not prevent myself from making right up to the last moment, and also to the friends who read the final version of the chapters. Their peer reviews were essential, although any faults which remain are my responsibility. I am also particularly grateful to those of my friends who were kind enough to allow themselves to be quoted on the book's dust jacket. Their supportive comments in no way imply that they necessarily share the opinions I express in this book.

Finally, I should mischievously thank the many graduates I know whose knowledge of the university and its history cannot match their love for the place; they inspired me in the first place to assemble this story. May this book fascinate and inform them.

Introduction

Acquaintance with Cambridge, whether the university or the old town, usually creates a great affection for the place. Such affection is, however, rarely matched by a knowledge of how such a magnificent place has been created and nurtured. This book fills in the background for those people whose love of Cambridge outweighs their knowledge.

Over the past eight centuries immense wealth and privilege have come together to create the magnificence that is found in Cambridge. The wealth has had many sources, but the privilege has come solely from the state. Two competing medieval universities, at Stamford and Northampton, did not secure the state's support and the privileges it could grant. They consequently perished. Then, as now, universities lived in a highly competitive world; Oxford University worried so much about competitors that up to the late fifteenth century it made its students take an oath not to study in Stamford. The story of why the state embraced only Cambridge and Oxford, rather than other seats of learning, is told in this book.

In developing into a institution of worldwide eminence, the university at Cambridge charted a careful passage through cataclysmic national events. The leaders of the university steered clear of the losing parties in the civil wars in the fifteenth and seventeenth centuries. There were battles to face in peacetime as well. After the Dissolution of the Monasteries in the 1530s, an act of parliament was passed which, if implemented, would have transferred much of the wealth of the university's colleges to the crown. Subtle leadership was necessary to survive these threats to the university's existence. There were also battles to be fought with the town to determine where supremacy lay in Cambridge; the university used a range of astonishing privileges to secure its domestic dominance.

These privileges stretched from the exceptional to the mundane. For almost 400 years the university sent its own Members of Parliament, elected by the university's graduates, to the House of Commons. It also controlled the town's weights and measures and the licensing of pubs and could appoint representatives to the town's council. The university vice-chancellor had the authority to lock up suspected prostitutes in the workhouse almost up to the twentieth century. It denied rights to the town – to stage plays or to travel by train from Cambridge on Sundays – which other communities in England already enjoyed.

In return for its privileges, the university has always been careful to follow the wishes of the state; it has long been a conforming place. The pronouncements of politicians in this century concern the university's leaders as much as did the pronouncements of a medieval king. It is the price demanded in return for the maintenance of exceptional privilege. From the beginning, the universities at both Cambridge and Oxford served powerful interests beyond their confines. In the Middle Ages, when illiterate knights felt their own career prospects were best linked to the strength of their sword arm rather than to their brain, scholars were recruited from society's lower social strata to provide a cohort of literate clerks who served both Church and state.

When either one of the two English universities did not perform as it was thought it should, the state interfered. Oliver Cromwell appointed himself Chancellor of Oxford University in the 1650s to reform an institution he thought dangerously wayward. There was good precedent for this, as the other Cromwell, Thomas, had made himself Chancellor of Cambridge University when he was Henry VIII's chief minister.

Later, the Victorian establishment was as inclined to interfere as had been the Tudor monarchs or the Puritan leaders of the Commonwealth. In the mid-1800s the Commission of Enquiry into the two ancient universities was set up by parliament because it was thought that they had become irrelevant to society: its brief was to examine 'the adaptation of those important institutions to the requirements of modern times'. Such meddling by the state has always been the practical reality behind Cambridge University's cherished, but nominal, independence. Although the status of each college as a charitable corporation gives legal independence, it is worthless if the university ceases to serve the interests of the state. Since the early twentieth century the state has added financial support to its gift of privileges. No matter that the university still provides half of its own annual income: half is not enough if real independence is sought.

Allied to the privilege enjoyed by the two most ancient English universities is their importance in the country's cultural life. They have transmitted the cultural values of the country's ruling class across the generations for centuries. With only two properly established universities in England between 1209 and 1832, when Durham University opened, Cambridge and Oxford have contributed immensely to the homogeneity of English society. Other European countries, with a greater number of regional universities, had less united elites.

This book seeks to provide an understanding of the path that Cambridge has travelled. The sights and customs which enthral so many are put in a historical context. The impact of the university on the country's culture through its customs, which even those with no connection to Cambridge may enjoy, is also discussed. The English vernacular is sprinkled with expressions derived from life in Cambridge, while the sporting life of this country owes a similar debt to the university; Cambridge University has played an astonishingly important role in the development of many competitive games. All these matters are addressed here.

Those with an interest in Cambridge fall chiefly into three groups – graduates, local people and visitors. Although they may sometimes mix together uneasily, they share an affection for the place. This book offers something to each. For the graduate, a mere seventy weeks spent in Cambridge over three years is sufficient to create an often unbreakable lifelong bond. A similar time spent at even the best of other British universities does not craft a comparable relationship. Friendship, social life and learning are the preoccupations of student days and consequently undergraduates have little time to acquire more than a passing acquaintance with the beauty and history of Cambridge. This book provides that background and will add another dimension to their return visits.

The local community's interest, pride even, in the university is seen in the way guests are proudly taken down King's Parade to be shown, with extravagant gestures and a not always very accurate commentary, the grand sites; yet the relationship with the university has always been complex. Local planning decisions in the 1950s, following the Holford plan, determined that further population growth in Cambridge would not be permitted. A policy to expand outlying communities was begun instead and the city (a status achieved only in 1951) has thus had a static population since this time. In the same period the numbers of undergraduates increased by 60 per cent and the staff at the university also grew significantly. Further large increases in student numbers are planned. In earlier times there had been two centres of power in

Cambridge and sometimes three in the days before the state mastered the Church. Since 1945 the university has overwhelmed the local community through weight of numbers as well as through privilege.

There are few cities of only 120,000 inhabitants which are familiar to people throughout much of the world. Those living in huge East Midlands conurbations are required when abroad to locate their home by reference to Cambridge, their much smaller neighbour. The university is now a source of pride for Cambridge people; it has put their town on the world map.

Yet in the past the success of the academic community embittered the relationship with the town. Cambridge townsfolk were swamped in the backwash of this great institution's advance. The physical expansion of the university displaced local people from the old centre of town. Townspeople must now live in distant suburbs, and one sad outcome of this townscape reorganisation is that centrally placed parish churches have struggled to survive. This book shows how the beauty of the city and university has been achieved at a cost to the people of Cambridge, even if the university has long been a source of employment and, most recently, has shared much of its cultural wealth with the townspeople.

Visitors to Cambridge reflect the wide cultural background of the town and university. Of the four million people who visit Cambridge annually in the twenty-first century, 35 per cent come from abroad. This international dimension to Cambridge is nothing new; academic communities have always been cosmopolitan. Strong and long-lasting links abroad have been built. For example, the close relationship which Britain still has with America can be partly understood through the development of this university.

People from many other countries, however, have also left a deep impact on Cambridge; Danes, Italians, the French and Germans, for instance, have all significantly influenced the shape of the town and university. Even the soul of the greatest symbol of Cambridge, King's College Chapel, is not English alone; it is European. The glorious portrayal of the Bible's story in twenty-five early modern stained glass windows is the outcome of the European Reformation and its Humanist philosophy. Fellow Europeans contributed to the chapel in a practical way as well: Italian, German and Flemish craftsmen worked there, while the beautifully carved limestone inside the antechapel came from Caen in Normandy. A narrow chauvinistic pride in the chapel – or in the university – is out of place.

So it continues into the twenty-first century. Alison Richard, the university vice-chancellor from 2003, returned from Yale University to take up her post. At the same time the Master of Trinity, Amartya Sen, an Indian Bengali, left Cambridge for an academic position at Harvard. The Alumni office is in touch with 144 overseas groups which represent 41,000 overseas alumni. Cambridge has derived so much from different cultures that it is fitting for its people to welcome so many international scholars and visitors. The debt Cambridge owes to those beyond its country's shores is immense.

The story of the university and town of Cambridge, its beauty and remarkable success, is told in this book. It is hoped that all those who read it will gain a deeper understanding of Cambridge, adding another dimension to their love of this great city and its university.

Chapter 1

The Beginning

Medieval Cambridge was surrounded by water. From the town's northern tip by the Old Quays the western boundary followed the River Cam southwards; to the east the boundary was marked by the 'King's Ditch'. The two waterways met up again at the King's Mill. The ditch has long since been filled in, but the town has remained an island in another sense, in that so much that has brought it fame has come from outside its boundaries.

The Cam, which curls up through the Fens, via the Great Ouse, to the sea, made Cambridge an easy place to reach and its people grew wealthy from trade. The town lay at the southern edge of the Fens, which spread north-eastwards for sixty miles to the Norfolk coast, and until they were drained in the seventeenth century it was necessary to travel through Cambridge when moving between eastern England and the north or the midlands. Travellers, too, brought wealth to Cambridge.

Cambridge was a good place to live. Its wealth and good communications have always attracted people – from Roman settlers, Viking invaders, Norman conquerors, to traders in quieter times and eventually scholars. There was good arable land to the south and west of the town; to the east there was an area of chalk uplands for grazing sheep. Even the Fens had virtues, as they were a good source of fish, fowl and peat for winter fuel.

The island analogy can be maintained: there was neither good building stone to be found locally, nor many trees, so that even the fabric of the town was brought in from outside. As Cambridge collected buildings shaped by fashions and inspired by architects from mainland Europe, so its academics accumulated treasures from overseas. People, too, came from outside the town: scholars from distant parts of Britain and overseas have long since found Cambridge enticing.

If there has been criticism of Cambridge it has been of its weather. Samuel Taylor Coleridge, who studied at Cambridge in the 1790s, wrote of the town as 'a very damp place – the very palace of winds'. A hundred and fifty years earlier the diarist John Evelyn described the town as 'a low dirty unpleasant place, the streets ill paved, the aire thick as infected by the fenns' – but then he was an Oxford man.

By happy chance there is an apposite salute to the town's prevailing weather in King's Parade. Directly opposite the main entrance of King's College stood for many years from 1825 the emporium of Isaiah Deck. He was a chemist, mineral dealer and seller of scientific instruments to the university community. Although the business at these premises has long since changed its trade, the doorway retains an instrument embedded in its right-hand doorjamb. It is a fine, though broken, barometer with its weather prediction forever set on the safe prediction for Cambridge of 'Wet or More Wind'.

Not much can be done about the weather, but through to the twenty-first century Cambridge has remained an attractive place to live. Although well connected to the outside world, it retains much of the style of a rural market town; yet at the same time it possesses innumerable treasures. Such attributes have a timeless appeal.

Early history

The history of Cambridge people reaches back far beyond the foundation of the university to at least the Iron Age. The earliest known areas of occupation were on the high ground around the castle mound to the north of the town and alongside St Bene't's Church by King's Parade; one was defendable, the other a good place from which to trade. Solid ground on either side of the river where Magdalene College now faces the modern Quays development provided a rare crossing point. This was where the first recorded bridge spanned the river, in the late ninth century AD.

A defendable fort beside a crossing point of a river navigable to the North Sea was particularly attractive to the Romans (and to subsequent invaders of eastern England). Within the province of Britannia, Cambridge was strategically significant; the Via Devana and Akeman Street crossed here, linking the town with the important Roman town at Colchester, with the north of the province and with the Wash and thus the North Sea. The Romans settled around the area of Castle Hill, to the north of medieval Cambridge. During the hiatus which followed the contraction of the Roman Empire in the fifth century, the town's significance greatly diminished, although fifth- and sixth-century burials outside the old walls hinted at some form of continuing occupation. At the end of the seventh century the Venerable Bede witnessed its neglect: he commented on the 'little ruined city called Grantacaestir'. Although re-established as a Mercian town during the eighth century, it was the Angles, the Danes and then the Normans who revived the fortunes of Cambridge. In due course its position in the richest part of medieval England, on a major river leading to the North Sea and the country's main trading partners, made it an important trading town. Where the river had once led invaders to the town, it now drew merchants. The majority of traded goods reached Cambridge by water along the Great Ouse from King's Lynn down past Downham Market and Ely.

For centuries Cambridge has been a place that people could, by the standards of the time, easily reach and leave. Such good communications would prove essential to building a university community.

The importance of Cambridge to the country's military network and trade attracted the attention of the country's kings. Soon after the Norman Conquest of 1066, William I had a castle built near the area once occupied by the Romans; its remains survive in Cambridge as the castle mound. In the early 1070s, William raised his standard at the castle before subduing Hereward the Wake in the fens.

Illustration 1.1: The site of the Roman fort and Norman castle is marked by the mound on Castle Hill; the castle retained a military significance until the 1650s.

By the early 1200s Cambridge had become an important trading centre from which the Crown derived customs revenue; that thirty-three medieval guilds were operating in Cambridge at this time provides some evidence of its wealth. By the fourteenth century the town possessed substantial leather and wool industries. Grain was collected and dispatched through King's Lynn to London and abroad; wine, salt, fish, timber and metals were typical imports.

Cambridge remained a significant inland port up to the 1700s. These were centuries when inland ports were crucial parts of the country's distribution network, as they were both safer from marauding foreigners and easier for English traders in central England to reach than were coastal ports. Cambridge was at the centre of a web of waterways which stretched through its rich hinterland. Centuries before logistics consultants theorised about optimal distribution networks, Cambridge operated as a distribution hub at the centre of the richest part of England.

This trading background explains what must be a mystery to many of those in modern Cambridge who notice the emblems within the city's shield of arms on the Guildhall in the Market Square. Drawn up in 1575, the charges on the shield include three ships in full sail with two enormous seahorses as supporters on either side. Such vessels would have been capable of navigating both the River Cam and the North Sea.

Illustration 1.2: The map of Europe turned on its usual axis emphasises how Cambridge was ideally placed to prosper from the country's main trading routes to northern Europe and Scandinavia in the more peaceful conditions which followed the chaos of the Dark Ages.

From the mid-1100s to the late 1400s, the majority of England's foreign trade was conducted from its east coast with the Hansa towns, along the north-west coast of continental Europe, and the Nordic countries. When the English went south in this period, it was as often to fight the French and Spanish as it was to trade with them. At this time the east coast was more peaceful. The benefit to the town of this trading pattern was similar to that which Liverpool derived in the nineteenth century from trade with America. This increase in prosperity, like its good communications, was an important factor in attracting a community of scholars to the town.

Cambridge and King's Lynn thus grew prosperous through international trade. The very name 'King's Lynn' (previously Bishop's Lynn) reflected the importance of its trade; by 1538, when Henry VIII took over the town and manor from the bishop of Norwich, it was the third largest port of England. Cambridge was the commercial heart of eastern England, pumping up goods along the Cam to its coastal partner and drawing down imports southwards in return.

The beginnings of the community of scholars

A town with a healthy pre-existing economic structure was an essential prerequisite for an economically unproductive group of scholars, in order that they had access not only to the necessities of life but also to the more esoteric requirements of their lifestyle, such as parchment, ink and clerical clothing. The wealth was important for another reason; it attracted monastic houses. The Benedictines had been in eastern England since the seventh century; they valued the tranquillity and isolation of the Fens, and built up substantial landholdings in this area after the Norman Conquest. Monasteries were established in the heart of Cambridge in the twelfth century, before the university existed. From 1092, the Augustinians took over the site in Cambridge destined, after occupation by the Benedictines, to become Magdalene College in the fifteenth century. In 1138, the Benedictines preceded the nuns of St Radegund in the area later adopted by Jesus College. By the 1230s, the Franciscans had moved into the area just south of the Round Church and the Dominicans had purchased space to the east of the old town. Carmelites, White Canons and the Friars of the Sack all followed by the end of the fourteenth century.

Some of the monastic orders, particularly the Dominicans and the Franciscans, had a tradition of teaching and there was a small community of monk-scholars already established in Cambridge before the Oxford scholars arrived. It is probable that some people in the medieval town visited the friars as much for instruction as for confession, even before the advent of the university.

Good communications, wealth and an emerging tradition of learning were all significant in ensuring that a successful university was established. Chance also had an important part to play, however. When the England of King John was under Papal Interdict, the burghers of Oxford were emboldened to try under civil law and hang two scholars for the rape of a woman by a third scholar, whom they could not apprehend. This was doubly illegal. Even had they apprehended the right scholar the civil authorities did not have the legal right to punish members of the university; scholars were obliged to take minor orders within the Church, giving them the legal protection of clergy. The Church alone thus held the right to try them and to determine their punishment under canon law.

The Oxford academic community left their town in protest at this action and the university closed for five years. Most of the scholastic community travelled to Paris, Reading or Cambridge, each of which had a tradition of learning. The educated elite in Europe were already itinerant in the thirteenth century. This influx of Oxford students to Cambridge in 1209 is generally accepted as the foundation date of the university, although there was certainly a self-constituted and self-governing community by that time which could attract and absorb the migrating scholars. There are, however, other credible foundation dates. It was only in 1233 that the Pope granted the scholars' community the status of a 'studium', a recognised centre of learning, but one without the charters which gave vital legal privileges. The more important status of a 'studium generale', which signified possession of several faculties with accredited masters teaching scholars from outside the immediate neighbourhood, was not achieved until 1318. It marked the transition from a loose association of local scholars into the equivalent of a recognised guild with a legally defined character and the full support of the Church. Degrees from Cambridge would henceforth be recognised throughout Christendom.

These are, however, less appealing dates to those raising funds for the university today. Eight hundred years later, the university used the 1209 anniversary to trigger a major fundraising effort. A foundation date of 1209 places Cambridge eighth, just after Oxford, in the list of the Europe's oldest universities. In 1233 there were thirteen European universities; by 1318 the number had risen to nineteen.

Among the universities of medieval Europe neither of the two English universities could therefore claim notable longevity or indeed intellectual leadership. English scholars were sensitive for centuries about the young age and modest reputation of both Cambridge and Oxford. Ludicrous claims about ancient lineage were made to counter these perceived weaknesses; for example, even in the 1550s one important member of the university, Dr John Caius, wrote that the Spanish prince Cantaber, a governor under King Arthur in the sixth century, had founded the university. Oxford's claims were equally farcical, among them the attempts to credit its foundation to Julius Caesar, as well as to some Greek professors who came to England with Brutus of Troy 'about the time, as it is written in the Book of Samuel, Eli was judge in Israel'. University foundation dates are often debatable matters.

State support

After the chance arrival of Oxford scholars, there was one further essential condition on which the long-term success of a medieval academic community depended: the ability of its leaders to attract the Crown's support. The country's rulers had long been aware of the military and trading significance of Cambridge, but for the place to become of intellectual relevance was a new challenge. It was still uncertain in the thirteenth century that Cambridge would secure the necessary support, as King John's interest in Cambridge was only commercial. He had granted licences for the renowned Garlic and Stourbridge Fairs of Cambridge, but made no significant impact on the scholars' community.

In addition, there were other rich and accessible places whose academic credentials rivalled those of Cambridge. Hereford, Exeter, Lincoln and York, as well as London, Stamford and Northampton, were such towns. Most of these also had cathedral schools of high repute. However, in medieval times neither Oxford nor Cambridge possessed a cathedral and this, perversely, helped attract monarchs' interest. During an era when there was no more critical issue than the balance of power between the supra-national Catholic Church and the state, the twenty-mile distance of Cambridge from the diocesan seat in Ely would have appealed to the secular rulers of the kingdom. Similarly, there was no tradition in the area of dominance by a feudal magnate who might have subverted a university's independence.

Even if the bishop was at some distance from Cambridge, academic communities could always be vulnerable to local traders and merchants who had more possessions and economic power. So, in order for a university to prosper, the monarchy granted privileges which, in the case of Cambridge University, permitted its academics to control rents, weights and measures, to own property which was exempt from death duties and to be responsible for law and order.

More concrete support for the scholarly community was forthcoming later in the thirteenth century. By the time that John's grandson, Edward I, had succeeded to the throne the need for educated clerics to run the state was recognised and in the 1290s Edward issued a charter confirming the secular privileges of the university. The next king, Edward II, supported the petition to the pope for recognition of the university as a 'studium generale' in 1318. A year earlier, this king had established the Society of King's Scholars, which Edward III later endowed as King's Hall. This was effectively a fixed branch of the itinerant Chapel Royal whose younger members, in return for lodging and education, helped tend to the spiritual needs of the king. The role of the Society in Cambridge was to train young court protégés, known as the 'Kyng's childer', the best of whom could in due course be royal and public servants. The idea of a community of scholars at Cambridge that could serve the country's interests had emerged.

Rivals and survival

Through to the fourteenth century Oxford and Cambridge still faced competition from other scholars' communities in England; Northampton and Stamford were the most threatening. Northampton had an established tradition of learning and attracted Cambridge scholars from time to time, occasionally in unfortunate circumstances. In 1260 a violent dispute between the townspeople of Cambridge and university members resulted in the hanging of sixteen townsfolk, while, in an early demonstration of how the university community was always to be treated differently, the twenty-eight students found guilty were pardoned. Some, nonetheless, decamped to join the academic community at Northampton. In 1261, despite Cambridge and Oxford pleading for it to be closed, Henry III recognised Northampton's academic community. Henry did close the university four years later, but only as a punishment for Northampton's support for the de Montfort insurrection; the town was forbidden in perpetuity to have a university within its boundaries.

It was not until 2005 that a university reopened at Northampton, and, astonishingly, serious consideration was given to whether there was an enduring legal obstacle from Henry III's perpetual ban. It was concluded, however, that the protection granted to Oxford and Cambridge was no longer needed and so the ban was irrelevant. Lingering doubts were dispelled by the pedantic argument that the university would in any event be located outside what would have been the town boundary of 1265.

Similarly, Stamford in Lincolnshire also contained a medieval community of scholars with the potential to rival Cambridge. The town had nurtured several monastic communities in the twelfth and thirteenth centuries. Both Oxford and Cambridge universities complained in the mid-1300s to Edward III that a university in Stamford would be 'to the disadvantage and dishonour of both (their) universities', demonstrating, along with the protests over Northampton's status, that even at this early stage in their existence Oxford and Cambridge were capable of closing ranks in defence of their elite status. Stamford issued degrees for only a short period in the 1330s and its main role may even have been as a cramming centre

Illustration 1.3: St Bene't's Tower was built between 1030 and 1050: the Carolingian detail of its interior suggests that Cambridge was well connected to the cultural movements of mainland Europe through its trade before the Oxford scholars arrived in 1209.

for Oxford and Cambridge. Despite its suppression in 1334 it concerned Oxford University sufficiently for its leaders to insist up to the late fifteenth century that all its scholars took an oath not to study at Stamford. In another echo from medieval England, Stamford tried in the 1990s to rekindle its academic aspirations through attempting to host the University of Lincolnshire; however, a site near Lincoln was chosen instead.

From the 1330s until the 1830s England had only two universities on which the benefits of royal protection were conferred; other European countries, less unified than England, had far more. Scotland had three by the late 1400s, with a fourth, Edinburgh, founded in 1582. The independent states within France, Italy and Germany each jealously protected their regional cultural identity through their own universities.

It was not until the nineteenth century and the ambition of Napoleon that the French system of higher education was nationalised in the manner in which the English had nationalised theirs in the Middle Ages; Italy and Germany had to wait until their countries were unified in the late nineteenth century for a national system of higher education. Regional universities on the continent were by then too deeply established for a place of higher education with the equivalent national dominance of Cambridge and Oxford to emerge. The focus of the English state on just these two universities played a significant part in their eventual emergence as the two most outstanding European seats of learning.

The peace and quiet of the Fens, the wealth of eastern England, the patronage of the Church and of the state were factors which combined to ensure that a university thrived in Cambridge. Nonetheless, there were occasions, such as the periods of religious revolution in the sixteenth and seventeenth centuries, when its prestige and existence were at stake. During the 1540s, for example, Henry VIII was only just dissuaded by advisors from purloining the wealth accumulated by the colleges; yet, after this traumatic period, Cambridge University flourished again during the sixteenth century, showing that as an institution it had truly passed into maturity and was able to handle the rough-and-tumble of the real world beyond its ivory towers.

Chapter 2

A Cuckoo in the Nest

The cuckoo places its eggs among those laid by the reed warbler. Once the eggs hatch, the louder cry of the cuckoo chick wins more food from the reed warbler than do those of the warbler's own young. Through the parasitism of its parent, the cuckoo chick grows strong at the expense of those among whom it lives. Reed warblers and the townsfolk of Cambridge, both native to East Anglia, have each struggled because of powerful incomers.

There was a struggle for dominance within Cambridge from the beginning of the university's existence. Only when that battle was won could Cambridge establish itself as a place of academic excellence.

The Church, the state and control of the town

When the Oxford scholars arrived at Cambridge in 1209, they found a prosperous town. The scholars rented lodgings from the townsfolk and bought their provisions from traders. The scholars possessed little bargaining power and were initially dependent on the hosts whom they would ultimately dominate. However, the need of both Church and state for well-educated clerks ensured that privileges for the university were soon forthcoming, an outcome hastened by the placements of Cambridge's own graduates in many of the most powerful positions at court and in the Church.

The pope's grant of studium status to the Cambridge academics in 1233 brought the valuable privilege of recognition of scholars as clerks, with membership of the Church. The Benefit of Clergy yielded privileges such as the right for disputes to be determined through canon rather than civil law. In addition, the right of 'Conusance' permitted the university chancellor to conduct the trial even if only one of the two parties involved was a member of the university. It was the disregard of this right in Oxford which had provoked the migration of scholars to Cambridge. Such disparity in legal protection between the two communities of Cambridge bred antagonism. However, the most significant privileges ultimately came from the state rather than the Church.

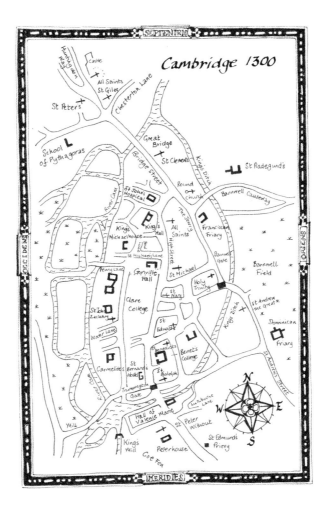

Illustration 2.1: The shape of the old town, sandwiched between the river and the King's Ditch, has barely changed over the last 800 years.

Time and again the monarch supported the interests of the university against those of the town. At the request of the university chancellor in 1270, Henry III forbade 'tournaments, tiltings ... or other warlike games' in Cambridge. The university was concerned with more than just inappropriate behaviour, however. In 1382 it secured from Richard II the control of weights and measures in the town. Henceforth it was the university's officers who set, for example, measures for the sale of butter in the town, which was sold by the inch from a yard-long mould rather than by weight. Butter was distributed around Cambridge in this manner up to the introduction of rationing during the First World War. Lest the university's authority in such matters be forgotten, on formal university occasions one of the proctors' constables still holds a leather instrument which, though not quite a butter measure, would have been suitable for sampling from top to bottom the quality of commodities sold in casks.

These were not temporary privileges, granted after moments of chaos in the Middle Ages and later withdrawn. The university's right to issue licences for the sale of wine was reconfirmed by the University Wine Act of 1743. Even as recently as 2003 a question was asked in the House of Commons by the MP for the Isle of Wight about the justification for the university's residual licensing powers.

Control of the town's trade gave the university considerable power; a power which was obvious to Daniel Defoe, who wrote in his *A Tour thro' the Whole Island of Great Britain* that 'the [Cambridge] tradesmen get their bread by the colleges … [and this is the means] by which they [the university] secure the dependence of the town and consequently their submission'. Using a term which carried distinctly religious overtones, the university would 'discommune' any town trader who earned its disapproval: discommuning prevented all university members from purchasing a trader's goods, causing his ruin. A trader's willingness to offer excessive credit to young scholars was one common way in which the wrath of the university could be incurred.

Hostility between town and university often caused violence. In addition to the riots of 1260, after which townspeople had been hanged, there was another significant uprising in June 1381. A rabble from the town burnt the university's documents, most of which were stored at that time in Great St Mary's Church; they also set alight the homes of the esquire bedell and other members of the university. Even the college founded by the townsmen themselves, Corpus Christi, was pillaged. The rioters, with whom it was later established the town mayor and bailiffs were actively involved, were perhaps emboldened by the events of the Peasants' Revolt, which had begun during May 1381 in the neighbouring county of Essex. The confirmation in 1382 of the university's powers over the town can be seen in the context of the Crown re-establishing its authority through a dependable institution such as the university had become.

These are but two instances recorded for posterity; there must have been many others which have not been chronicled. Like the Fen Ague provoked by the mosquito-ridden fens, violent disputes between town and the university were endemic in Cambridge for centuries.

Subjection and displacement

The university's dominance over the town went beyond a framework of regulations to the physical structure of Cambridge itself. The iconic views of Cambridge were created at the expense of those who occupied the town before the university grew so mighty. The most striking example is King's College. It is inspiring, today, to look from the Backs towards the west end of King's College Chapel. The golden Ketton stone of the south range of neighbouring Clare College is set ablaze when the sun shines; to the right is the tall upright chapel, whose brown limestone contrasts with the white Portland stone of the Fellows' Building on its other side. There are often cows in the water meadow and sometimes swans in the River Cam beyond. Punters glide along the river, separated from the college buildings by a sward of finely mown grass. It is an exceptional sight.

However, in this same area in the early 1440s many of the medieval townsfolk would have lived, worked, misbehaved and died. It was a place packed with hythes, wharfs, barns and homes. Cloth and iron imported from across the North Sea and corn from the rich hinterland around Cambridge were offloaded onto wagons destined for the town's workshops or for the mills up at Chesterton. The wagons would have rolled through the heart of the old town along Milne Street; the street ran from the King's Mill by Silver Street Bridge, past the old entrance to Queen's College, across the land on which King's Chapel was built and on through the parish of St John Zachary.

By 1449, the university had displaced the local people from this area and pulled down St John Zachary in order to expand King's College. The land was expropriated under the crown's right of 'domaine éminent', the medieval term (still used in the United States) to describe compulsory purchase. King's College Chapel was built across Milne Street; parts of this old thoroughfare remain on either side of the chapel as little dead-end lanes in front of Queens' and Clare Colleges' main gates.

The townspeople's dislike of the scholars must have been heightened by the power given to the first architect of King's College Chapel, Reginald Ely. After being cleared out of their houses in the 1440s, the townsmen were then forced, on pain of imprisonment, to assist in the building of the chapel; Richard III also granted the right to the master carpenter of the chapel to imprison those who stood in his way of finding craftsmen. The turbulence caused by the civil wars interrupted the flow of money to this building project, so it took over 100 years, which included periods when the area was little more than a deserted building site, to complete the college chapel. It was then 200 years before the next college building, the Gibbs Building, was constructed and a further 100 years before the south range of King's Front Court completed the buildings in the space where the townspeople had lived.

In the years following the foundation of King's College in the 1440s the central area of Cambridge became the heart of the academic quarter, its capture by the university showing just how effectively that institution had taken over the town. Besides the enforced acquisition of the land on which King's College stands, the local people were repeatedly inconvenienced in other ways as the university expanded. For example, the Kings Childer Lane, a road running from the river up into the town, was closed in the 1430s, around the time King's Hall commissioned the building of the King Edward Gate (usually referred to now as the Clock Tower). The creation of the vast Great Court at Trinity College around 1600 also caused disruption because one of the town's three main wells was situated in the centre of the new court. Good water in Cambridge was a rare commodity, but this fact seems to have been lost on the college authorities, as it took a riot to persuade them to fit a water pipe just on the public side of the main Trinity College entrance. A puny little tap marking the extension is still there, though it is now fitted with a laconic message which instructs that its water should not be drunk.

There are, too, more recent instances of the impact the university's expansion has made on the structure of the town. Two streets in modern Cambridge have fine ranges of townhouses, mostly from the eighteenth century, which extend down only one side of the street. They are King's Parade and Bridge Street; their opposite ranges were destroyed by, respectively, King's College in the 1820s and St John's College in the 1930s. Such change moved people out of the parishes of the old town to the suburbs and has had mixed results in terms of the townscape: in the case of King's, it has opened up magnificent views of the chapel and

Illustration 2.2: The Market Square: trade in Cambridge has long been an essential part of the town's culture; there is still a market each day.

the Senate House; St John's, however, constructed an unimpressive services building and car park. There is, perhaps, only one example where a college has encouraged people to live in central Cambridge: in the early 1970s, Jesus College sponsored blocks of flats in Malcolm Place and Manor Place near Jesus Lane, which are run by a housing association. In many instances, the creation by the university of buildings of outstanding

Illustration 2.3: The shields of arms of the university and town of Cambridge were drawn up in the 1570s. Both stressed their loyalty to the crown and ignored each other. Exceptionally, they are displayed side by side in the ceiling of the old Mortlock Bank (now Barclays) in Wheeler Street.

beauty has been possible only by displacing the descendants of the people who had once welcomed a group of itinerant and impoverished scholars.

The separation of the two communities was reflected symbolically in their shields of arms, both of which were drawn up in the 1570s. The main charges of the shield chosen by the town were ships supported by seahorses, but there was no allusion to the famous university, already almost 400 years old, in its midst. The university's shield of arms displays four lions to signify its connection to royalty and a book to indicate the importance of learning. There is no reference to the town. Both town and university drew attention to their loyalty to the crown, but neither acknowledged the other.

The people of Cambridge suffered in order that scholars and visitors may now marvel at the beauty of the university's buildings. Although the modern university now brings many economic and cultural benefits to the local community, the gains to them in earlier times were far less clear. Initially, local merchants certainly gained trade, but the prosperous community of thirteenth-century Cambridge had more to offer than it had to receive from the fledgling academic community.

This background provides a sharp contrast to the great English provincial universities of the nineteenth century, which were built with the co-operation of their local communities. Successful men of business, who wanted opportunities for self-improvement to reach the less privileged in society, played key roles in their foundation. Often of Nonconformist faith with liberal political views, they helped fund their local university and established the tradition whereby lay members of the community ran its administration. The names of some remain closely associated with the universities they helped found: Rathbone at Liverpool, Chamberlain at Birmingham, Wills at Bristol and Owen at Manchester each played a part without a parallel at Cambridge. The foundation of the small college of Corpus Christi by two Cambridge town guilds in 1352 and the influence of David Robinson, a local man who funded a Cambridge college at the end of the twentieth century, are not comparable to the depth of involvement by those nineteenth-century men of business.

Civic pride framed the close bond between a provincial university and its host city in Victorian England, whereas Cambridge University smothered the local community. Where one has been an imposition, the other was a cooperative affair without particular privilege. As the relationship between the university and town of Cambridge can be interpreted from their respective shields of arms, so too can those of the provincial universities with their cities: Liverpool University proudly displays the Liver Birds, while Bristol chose the sun and horse of the local Wills and Fry family crests.

Cambridge University's leading academics took care to support the monarchy in order to ensure that their privileges were not withdrawn. In 1530, for example, Henry VIII asked the university to consider the validity of his marriage to Catherine of Aragon. The vice-chancellor, William Buckmaster, then oversaw an explosive debate between members of Regent House, the university's governing body, into the king's 'Great Matter'. Conveniently, the university elders judged the marriage ungodly; shortly afterwards, Buckmaster received a remunerative fellowship at King's Hall and funds to continue the glazing of King's College Chapel were found. People sensitive to politics led the university and usually avoided attachments to dangerous causes which might attract the monarch's disapproval; the university has always had some members within its hierarchy willing to do the bidding of the state.

The university's acknowledgement of the state's support is well demonstrated in Trinity Great Court, where the statues of four monarchs are displayed. Inside the court are placed Edward III, James I besides Charles I as a child and, opposite the Clock Tower, Elizabeth I. Henry VIII stands outside the court, above the Great Gate facing Trinity Street. The town, notably, has no statues of monarchs.

When confronted by political change, some decisions were simple for those running the university. After the premature death of Edward VI in 1553 the Duke of Northumberland raised his standard in Cambridge on behalf of Lady Jane Grey's claim to be queen. Official support from the university was limited to a discreet dinner with a senior member of the university, Matthew Parker. Similarly, shortly after the first Hanoverian George I took the throne, Sidney Sussex College was offered the skull of its most famous member, the regicide Oliver Cromwell. The gift was declined.

Oliver Cromwell had caused the university difficulties of a more serious nature less than a century earlier, however. The Civil War and interregnum of the seventeenth century had been a challenging period for the university. As usual, it had supported the establishment; all but one of the sixteen colleges were led by men who declared for the Crown. These heads of colleges even made an unsuccessful attempt during 1642 to dispatch their college silver to the king in York. Thomas Eden of Trinity Hall, who represented the university in parliament over many years, led the one college which opposed the king's party.

The university had evidently reached a size where there was sufficient diversity of opinion among its senior members to allow the university the appearance of supporting whichever side emerged victorious from the conflict. Individual academics doubtless suffered by declaring for the losing side, but the university itself was mature enough to survive. Coping with shifts in power at the centre of the realm is an essential survival skill for an academic institution. Perhaps it was the small size of the academic community at Northampton which had made recovery after its backing of Simon de Montfort's insurrection impossible.

Thus, by 1645, despite the university once having had so many royalist leaders of colleges, the Long Parliament could support the motion that the university should 'continue in possession of their liberties and privileges they formerly used and enjoyed before these troubles began'. The motion went on 'to consider the Differences therein mentioned to be between the university and the town of Cambridge'. It did not seem to matter to the Parliamentarians that the university had predominately been royalist during 'the troubles'; after all, both Cromwell and his foreign secretary, the poet John Milton, were Cambridge men. The university had proved that it could extract protection from whoever ruled in Westminster.

With each new charter issued to the Borough of Cambridge there was always the condition that nothing should infringe 'the liberties, privileges and profits of the university'. The town's mayor swore an oath to this effect from the early 1300s until 1856. The university could always count on the state's backing to enforce this obligation upon the town. Such local influence was enhanced by the reservation of six of the thirty-six city council seats for the exclusive use of the university, a practice which lasted until the 1970s: a further indication of the university's power.

Town versus gown

Perhaps the greatest symbol of the university's superior power in its relationship with the town was its ability to imprison local people independently of the processes of civil law. Since 1314, two proctors appointed by the university have been charged to oversee its finances and the conduct of its junior members. They completed the latter task through their constables, referred to as Bulldogs. The town's police were specifically denied jurisdiction over university members; in contrast, the university's proctors policed both communities of Cambridge.

The proctors could authorise, for example, the arrest of townsfolk considered to be prostitutes – or, in the jargon of the time, those whom they suspected of 'incontinence'. Their suspicions were easily aroused, as the archives reveal. During the 1890s, they detained for ten days a girl called Daisy Hopkins for prostitution.

In the same decade, Proctor Horner Jackson was paid by order of the vice-chancellor 'For whipping ten girls – ten shillings'. From the 1600s to the end of the nineteenth century women thought to be prostitutes were imprisoned in the university's own gaol, known as the Spinning House, on the south side of St Andrew's Street. It had been funded in 1628 by Thomas Hobson, Cambridge's famous horse-hiring entrepreneur, as a Poor House. The role of Bridewell, or House of Correction, was subsequently added, eventually replacing its initial one. It was demolished in 1901 and a building on the old site was used as a police station until, more recently, it was taken over by a branch office of local government. The building is still named Hobson House.

The red light districts in medieval times were around the two dock areas: alongside the King's Mill in lanes not too dissimilar from St Mary's Lane and in the streets on the north side of Magdalene Bridge. By Victorian times these had moved to the north-east of Cambridge, around Barnwell Road near the modern-day Cambridge United football ground. The study of Victorian prostitution in Cambridge is less complete than for some other cities of the period, but the high number of prostitutes thought to have been working in the town must have reflected the absence of females at the university. The mid-nineteenth-century memoirs of a prim scion of the American Astor family, entitled *Five Years at an English University*, referred to colleagues who would invite him to visit prostitutes as casually as if they were inviting him for a drink.

A letter to the Secretary of State from the Coroner of the Borough of Cambridge, reprinted in the *Cambridge Independent Press* on 7 July 1845, reveals the deep resentment aroused in the town by the university's right of imprisonment. The coroner had sat at an inquest which found that one Elizabeth Howe had died of rheumatic fever caught at the Spinning House gaol – having been confined there by W.T. Kingsley, proctor of the university. He expressed his 'abhorrence of a system which sanctions the apprehension of females when not offending against the general law of the land and confining them to a goal unfit for the worst felons'. This particular privilege of – or rather abuse by – the university was stopped only in 1894, after some unescorted milliners of irreproachable virtue were arrested. The consequent uproar forced the university to yield its right of imprisonment.

Scholars were not so well protected elsewhere in Europe as they were in Cambridge. In the eighteenth century Heidelberg University solved the problems arising from student exploration of a town's leisure opportunities differently. It ran a prison, which can still be visited, called *Der Studentenkarzer*, specifically to detain students rather than the local people. The irritation of imprisonment was intensified by obligatory release to attend lectures. The university in Cambridge had a less respectful relationship with the community in which it lived, locking up the local people and dealing with its misbehaving students merely by confinement to college or, for more severe offences, through expulsion.

The interests of the town were subjugated to those of the university in other ways. The coming of the railway to Cambridge during the 1840s is a case in point. In the same way that Cambridge had been a hub for inland communications in ancient times, railway developers recognised the logic in making it a centre for regional railways. The university ensured, however, that the site for the station chosen from seventeen alternatives was the one furthest away from their fiefdom in the old town. There are not many towns of significance in England where nineteenth-century railway stations are situated over a mile away from the town centre. The dons simply did not wish to let the outside world come too close.

Their opposition also contributed to the delay in the railway's arrival at Cambridge for almost twenty years, from the time of the first survey's completion to the line's opening in 1845. The use of trains by undergraduates was then expressly forbidden in an act of parliament known as the Cambridge Railway Act; a power was even included in the act which permitted the officers of the university to detain a train and remove any person who 'shall be a member of the university or suspected of being such'. Oxford academics proved just as sensitive to the intrusion of the outside world: the terms of the 1844 Cambridge Railway Act were copied from the Great Western Oxford Railway Act of the previous year.

The remote location of the station was not the only inconvenience which faced local people. The university imposed a further astonishing restriction: No one – be they local resident or university member – could travel by train to or from Cambridge on a Sunday. This outrageous prohibition, which passed through parliament within the Cambridge Railway Act, specified a fine of five pounds to be paid by the railway company to 'the benefit of the Addenbrooke's Hospital or other County Charity to be decided by the university' for every passenger taken up or set down from the train on a Sunday between 10 a.m. and 5 p.m. at Cambridge station or for three miles to either side of it. Townspeople catching a train in Cambridge on a Sunday, up to the repeal of this clause in 1908, were breaking the law. For many Victorians, working six full days a week, an opportunity to catch a train on Sunday was a novel and liberating experience. It was an experience that the university community denied the people of Cambridge for as long as it could.

There were yet more restrictions upon the leisure activities of townspeople. The university's influence over the life of the local people was so wide that its power to ban theatres and play-acting within fourteen miles of Cambridge was confirmed by an act of parliament in 1844. Meanwhile, behind college walls, plays approved by the fellowship continued to be staged for private enjoyment. Even fast-food businesses took longer to spread through Cambridge than elsewhere in Britain – one of the earliest, in the late 1960s, was a fish and chip shop in King Street. The colleges, who own practically all the ground leases of the shops in the old town, were reluctant to lease property to such businesses, fearing that their students would desert their halls and eat in town. Colleges now deal with the threat of cheaper fast food by extracting advance payment for meals from their junior members through the Kitchen Charge.

Although there were two forces of law and order in Cambridge, proctors, porters and police generally worked in harmony with each other. College porters even played football matches against the police up to the 1970s. However, tensions could surface between them; during the 1970s the police made an arrest of a student drug pusher within college precincts. Permission to be on college property had not been sought by the police, nor had approval been given by the student's tutor for the police to speak directly to the student, each of which was required in law. Students 'in statu pupillari' or, in other words, with the 'rank of a pupil' were subject to the university's legal code before that of the state. Although there was by this time no longer any member of the staff who raised a formal objection, the point was still made that a university member's rights had been breached.

Antagonism between town and gown is not long passed, persisting until recently in perhaps unexpected ways. In the early 1970s, for example, female undergraduates still made up less than 10 per cent of the student population. Despite the bussing-in of girls from nearby teacher training institutes for the weekend's social events at the University Centre near Silver Street Bridge, there was still a superabundance of young male undergraduates. Thus on Saturday nights in term time the girls of the town were encouraged freely to join undergraduate parties, while the town's young males were denied entry at any price. Such rules did not foster good town–gown relations.

The end of the power struggle

In twenty-first-century Cambridge, it is cooperation, not dispute, which characterises the relationship between the two communities. Students no longer provoke riots with the townsfolk. There may perhaps be the occasional disagreement over commercial development within the medieval heart of the city, an excessive rise in rent or perhaps a dispute about how best to handle traffic. Even differences in opinion as to how the colleges can best defend themselves from the impact of the four million tourists who visit Cambridge each year may arise on occasion. Generally, however, it is a good relationship which now greatly benefits the local community.

Typical of the present rapport between town and gown is the cooperation over the magnificent horse chestnut tree that stands at the north-east edge of King's College Chapel, alongside King's Parade, precisely on the line which divides college from university property. A committee on which the university, King's College and the town are each represented is said to oversee the health of this magnificent tree. The tale might just be apocryphal; but that it is told illustrates the modern cooperative relationship between town and gown.

The trades of shops which once served the needs of local people have changed irrevocably. The locals have been moved away and colleges look after students' needs, so the shops instead serve the visitors who come to admire the university. Consequently there are now many coffee shops, art galleries and clothes boutiques. This causes exclamation from returning elderly graduates: whereas they can point with precision to their top-floor rooms within an unchanged old court, the shops in the street have no place in their memories. Apart from the supermarket in Sidney Street and the odd clothes shop such as 'Cult Clothing', the local shops are not of much interest to modern students either. There is little chance of the university needing to exercise its right, as it once did, to prevent the graduation of a scholar with personal debts to a town trader. Now the college only insists that students clear their college debts before graduation; were a stricture against wider indebtedness to be imposed in modern times, graduation ceremonies would be small affairs. Students now leave the university greatly in debt to the state, but their slates with the town's tradesmen are clean.

The dominance of the town by the university may appear at odds with some of the architecture of central Cambridge, as the old town still contains a charming variety of domestic buildings. They stand next to striking college and university buildings in an attractive weave of different styles. However, they are practically all owned by colleges, and have shops at ground level with flats above for students who cannot be accommodated in college courts. Changes in the ownership of central Cambridge properties are now typically between different parts of the university rather than between private individuals; for example, in 1982 the entire row of fine Regency houses in Park Terrace, alongside the west edge of Parker's Piece, was sold by Jesus College to Emmanuel College.

Illustration 2.4: The King's Mill, circa 1800, with Queens' College in the background and the old Silver Street bridge: the very name of this port area indicated the monarch's interest in this important trading town.

Management of much of the town's retail industry has also caused the town and university to cooperate. Similarly, the interaction between the university researchers and the knowledge industry companies which surround Cambridge has brought the two communities together.

This cooperation symbolises how the struggle for power is now over. Confident in its victory, the university has changed its behaviour towards the town. Townsfolk and visitors to Cambridge are welcomed at college chapel services. College land which supports sports amenities used by townspeople is leased out at modest rents. The Union Debating Society permits the public to visit its chamber, colleges participate in national open garden days and the University Centre for Graduates shares its facilities with the town's professional groups; it has even lifted its weekend ban on local young men. The university also offers a feast of educational and cultural opportunities to local people.

By letting the cuckoo into its nest, the town helped the university along its glorious path; in so doing the town paid dearly for centuries, but, it has to be said, now gains many advantages from living beside such an august neighbour.

Chapter 3

The Monastic Legacy

Misericords – the ledge beneath the choir seat in a monastery chapel – provided a chance for the monk to take the weight off his legs during the long hours spent in prayer. There are over 200 misericords in Cambridge, spread between King's, Jesus, Pembroke and Peterhouse colleges and one parish church, St Michael's. This is far more than in Oxford, London or the great cathedral cities of England. Their existence in such great numbers in Cambridge reflects the deep impression the monasteries made on the physical structure and customs of the university. They are a reminder of how the Cambridge monasteries succoured the scholastic community in its infancy.

Dissolution and profit

The monasteries existed alongside the university until England ceased to follow the Roman Catholic faith in the sixteenth century, and had been part of the town's appeal to the scholars fleeing from Oxford in 1209. Records of payment by the university for the rent of monastic properties for the scholars' oral examinations and the conferment of degrees proved its initial dependency on the monastic houses of the town.

In the fourteenth century there were as many as seventy blackfriars of the Dominican order in St Andrew's Street – hence the street's earlier name of Preachers' Street. Of the 600 to 700 scholars at Cambridge in the fourteenth century, probably a quarter of them were mendicant friars, mostly Franciscan and Dominican. Friars still made up 16 per cent of the scholars' community in the fifteenth century, although members of the friaries had never been permitted to matriculate into the university. Up to the Dissolution of the Monasteries in the 1530s, the colleges were all small institutions. Indeed, four of the five largest communities of scholars in Cambridge at that time were friaries – their only rival was King's.

Although Henry VIII benefited immensely from the opportunity for enrichment presented by the dissolution of the religious houses, for the university the Dissolution was, initially at least, a disaster. The closure of these foundations in Cambridge left an enormous gap within the academic community and the despondency of those remaining at the university can be imagined as college matriculations declined

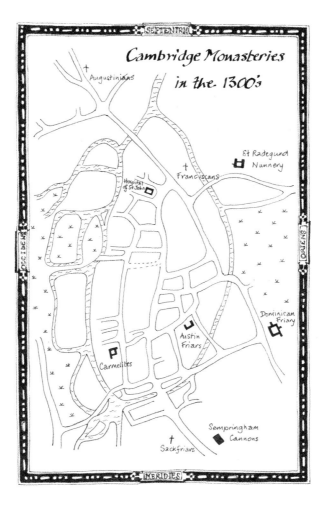

Illustration 3.1: Nine monastic houses were based in Cambridge by the 1300s.

dramatically. From 1542 to 1548 only 191 students were admitted to the colleges: in other words, an average of around two new scholars joined each college annually. It was not until the 1560s that matriculations regained the level of the years leading up to the Reformation.

In time the colleges did manage to benefit from the demise of the friaries. Certainly, the university's debt to the monasteries was swiftly forgotten as its leaders strove to profit from the new situation. Francis Mallet, university vice-chancellor and Master of Peterhouse, wrote to the king in 1536 that the monasteries had been 'unprofitable and pernicious to religion'. He pleaded that the university be permitted to take over the monasteries' properties, as it would make excellent use of them; he argued that 'as before, lazy drones and swarms of impostors were sent out of them, so now by these means men might be bred up in them to promote solid learning and the gospel'. The ungrateful leaders of the university had their wish. The colleges of Sidney Sussex, Magdalene and Emmanuel were established in the sixteenth century on ground previously owned by the monasteries. Even long-established colleges benefited: Queens', for example, expanded into neighbouring ground once occupied by the Carmelites.

St John's and Jesus had also been founded on monastic property in previous years; the former gained further endowments at the time of the Dissolution. Still others literally consumed the physical remains of the monasteries in Cambridge and East Anglia. Ramsey Abbey near Huntingdon, one of the biggest religious communities in England, was used as a surface quarry to expand the buildings of King's, Caius and Trinity colleges. The stones of the Franciscan monastery from the future site of Sidney Sussex were also used to construct the chapel at Trinity College; even the Catholic Queen Mary, who commissioned this chapel in the 1550s, could not prevent this use of monastic stone.

Long after the physical demise of the religious communities themselves, however, monastic values continued to be reflected in college life. These scholars' communities were led by teachers in holy orders who were sworn to celibacy and the worship of God remained at the centre of their lives. Like the monks scholars lived, whenever possible, apart from the town, worshipped independently, dressed distinctively and were protected by the Church.

The Benedictines had sited their early-fifteenth-century college for scholar-monks, Monk's Hostel (later to become Magdalene College), away from the temptations of the town to the north of Magdalene Bridge. However, an inn-cum-brothel soon opened immediately opposite the college main gate, which must have irritated the abbot in charge: records survive of instructions which required the young monks to report those of their peers who were tempted by the brothel. This attitude was carried forward into post-Dissolution university life, as colleges sought to limit the opportunities for recreation, a monastic approach to leisure which endured for centuries.

The rules governing the members of Christ's College provide a good example of this outlook. They were drawn up in the early 1500s under the authority of its patroness Lady Margaret Beaufort, and read like restrictions imposed on an order of monks rather than a guide to behaviour for young men starting their journey to the pinnacles of English society. At Christ's College, gates were to be locked at nine o'clock in winter and at ten in summer. Adult misdemeanours were punishable by fines, while younger offenders were to be beaten. Attendance at college chapel was required three times on Sundays – wearing, it was specifically noted, clean surplices. Only Latin was to be spoken in college. There were to be no drinking parties, no trading and no carrying of weapons. A long list of proscriptions followed: dogs and hawks were banned, as were cards or dice, except in the college hall at Christmas. The temporary relaxation of the rules at Christmas was some compensation for the scholars who lived too far away to return home in mid-winter. Christ's College rules were by no means exceptional among the colleges.

Oliver Cromwell, reputedly a boisterous youth, went up to Sidney Sussex College in 1616 to be confronted with similar prohibitions. 'Long or curled locks, great ruffes, [and] velvet pantaples' were not allowed. Activities such as bull-baiting, bear-baiting and bowling, together with visits to the town's taverns, were also all specifically denied to the young Oliver and his peers within the articles of his college.

The attitude which had led to Magdalene's position away from the fleshpots of the town also encouraged the university to maintain an overwhelmingly male culture for centuries. Only from the 1860s was the requirement for fellows to remain celibate dropped at some colleges: marriage was thought to detract from the loyalty of these less eminent members of colleges to the community, and the requirement of celibacy had been strictly enforced. Thomas Cranmer, who became Archbishop of Canterbury in 1533, was obliged to surrender his Jesus College fellowship around 1510 when he married his first wife. He moved to a more junior position outside the fellowship at Magdalene, until his wife's early death allowed him to rejoin his former college. Restrictions against marriage had not in fact applied to the heads of colleges since the university statues of 1559; Queen Elizabeth was content to let a master of a college marry or not 'as shall like him best' and in fact some latitude was also permitted for senior members who held a professorial chair or some other important university post. The queen's contentment was not in fact self-evident, as her thanks to the wife of Matthew Parker (the first master to marry) for some hospitality made clear: 'Madam I may not call you: and Mrs I am ashamed to call you: so I know not what to call you; but yet I do thank you.'

Dress and appearance

The earliest academic dress, if not exclusively monastic, was certainly determined by ecclesiastical tradition. Since scholars were ordained into minor clerical orders, they wore the appropriate dress as decreed by the Church. Clerical dress, with tonsures, for both master and students was specified in the thirteenth-century founding articles of Peterhouse. The square cap, known colloquially as a 'square', and more widely as the 'mortar board', also derives from the Church; it developed from the skullcap worn by all clerics, from cardinals downwards. This cap evolved first into the biretta, a soft three-pointed cap which can be seen in late medieval portraits of such people as Thomas Cromwell, Thomas Cranmer and Erasmus, before becoming the more familiar square.

In Tudor England, despite protests from the establishment, the Sumptuary Laws, which forced people to dress according to their rank, were increasingly ignored. At the university, vainer and richer scholars adopted furred robes lined with bright silk. Robes had more complex roles, however: various embellishments signalled college membership and rank, as well as social background – or at least the one to which the wearer aspired. Thus gown length, collar trimmings or fabric each carried a message; wealthier students would use ermine to line their cassocks, while the poorer made do with black lambswool. The gold embroidery on gowns distinguished the nobleman fellow commoner, the undergraduates of the highest social status, from those further down the social scale. The square was never worn by undergraduates even when in academical dress, although doctors of the university sometimes wear it with their gowns, instead of the black velvet bonnet, on formal occasions.

Despite this elaboration of strict ecclesiastical practice, for centuries academic clothing served to distinguish the university community from members of the town. Proctors continued to fine students for not wearing gowns into the 1960s and even more recently they had to be worn on a sufficient number of occasions – when dining in hall, after dark, to supervisions, in chapel – that it was generally less effort to wear them continuously than it was to keep returning to rooms to retrieve them. They are now worn only on exceptional occasions, such as when dining formally in hall or for graduation ceremonies. Outside those

Illustration 3.2: Two members of Peterhouse in academic dress within the secluded Old Court.

events and the beginning of terms, when the sheer influx of numerous similarly dressed young people make them conspicuous, it is difficult to identify a modern undergraduate.

The separation of the monasteries and colleges as communities from the town can be sensed even in their grounds. Just as the monasteries built walls round their properties, so did the colleges. The walls enclosed a community and could be breached only by passing through the imposing oak doors of their gatehouses; to this day they separate many of the colleges from the bustle of the town, as they have done for centuries, from when the university was in its infancy. The massive gatehouses showed plainly that here was a community to which some belonged, but others did not.

The private spaces of the monastic and college gardens were also practical resources used to provide 'all the necessaries', a phrase used by St Benedict to direct his order's communities towards self-sufficiency. The Sidney Sussex college gardens were founded on ground which had once held the Franciscans' malt house, a brew house, a mill house, a dovecot and a garner to store the monks' grain. There is still a sweet chestnut tree in the college gardens, whose predecessors would have yielded one of the monks' favourite winter foods. Another college, Jesus, nurtures medlar trees for their toffee-tasting fruit, which were also apparently enjoyed by monks. Emmanuel and St John's colleges have maintained the ponds that had served as a source of fish and duck for the monks, while Christ's has a reputation for its productive beehives. Bees were always closely associated with religious houses. St Bernard, after whom Queens' College was once

Illustration 3.3: The wall marking the boundary of Sidney Sussex College grounds alongside Sidney Street follows the boundary of the thirteenth-century Franciscan monastery.

named, is the patron saint of bees and is portrayed in the Queens' chapel with a beehive. Other colleges shared these and similar traditions, with Peterhouse even creating a deer park within their large grounds in the nineteenth century for the pleasure of their fellows.

The Fellows' Garden of Magdalene, behind the Pepys Library, is another place which retains the imprint of a monastery. It seems as secluded now as it must have felt to the scholar-monks. The garden slopes gently down to the river, occupying the same space used by the Benedictine monks in the 1400s. Academics enjoying a break from their work can still walk along the gravel path from the library towards the Cam; it is trimmed on either side with white periwinkle, just as it might have been when the Benedictine monks walked there 500 years earlier: periwinkle was thought to combat unseen powers of evil and was much cultivated by monks. College gardens are peaceful places connected to an ancient past; and through the degree of self-sufficiency they permitted, they became a symbol of the independence and separation which the monasteries and later the colleges cherished.

Monastic architecture

Besides the gardens, the academic costumes and the restrictive rules, college architecture also retains deep reminders of monastic life. Fifteenth- and sixteenth-century colleges were certainly influenced by the great country houses of that period. This is demonstrated by, for example, the grand gatehouses which many of them possess, but there was also an immense legacy from the monasteries.

Cloisters, chapels and courts of colleges would not have been out of place in a monastery. No college retains the feeling of a monastery as much as Jesus College, which occupies the space once owned by the nunnery of St Radegund, including the cloister court, chapel and chapter house of the old nunnery. Although the college has celebrated the quincentennial anniversary of its foundation, there are still reminders of the earlier occupants – twelfth-century Norman windows and thirteenth-century Gothic arches, for instance, survive in the college chapel.

In every century college architects have chosen to feature cloisters – covered walks framing a courtyard garden – in their building schemes. Queens' had a Cloister Court from its inception in the mid-fifteenth century. The seventeenth-century Nevile's Court, which incorporates the Wren Library, was built with cloisters down two sides. The university's Old Schools Building, built in the 1750s, also has arched cloisters on its ground floor. Even an accommodation building completed in 2009 at Selwyn College in Grange Road has a cloistered walk along its west and south façades.

As well as adapting the remains of ancient monastic buildings, colleges used the architecture of the monastic chapel within their own places of worship. As in the chapel of a monastery, college stalls run from east to west, whereas the pews of a parish church run across the nave, from north to south. From a stall, each communicant has an equal sight of the altar without the distraction of sitting behind other worshippers. Chapel stalls also permitted antiphonal singing, where the psalms were sung alternately from either side of the chapel. As in a monastic chapel, a college chapel has no pulpit; members of a college fellowship and scholars were already members of the clergy, so a pulpit was unnecessary. Furthermore, the template for a college chapel was established before the Reformation in a period when the importance of scripture, and hence the pulpit, was subjugated to the sacrament and the celebration of the Eucharist. Although pulpits were used in some churches during the fourteenth century, their dominant position in churches was generally a feature of the period after the Reformation. Through such internal architecture in their chapels, colleges reinforced the concept that they were, like monastic houses, communities independent from the outside world.

The cloistered monastery, which contained a chapel, a refectory, dormitories for the monks and perhaps an abbot's house, had an obvious influence in the design of college courts. Libraries were relatively late additions to the courts of both, because of the expense of purchasing books in the medieval period, but, where they existed, the chapel was often placed beside them. It was only later, as the college grew and the first chapel became too small to accommodate all members of the community, that larger chapels were built outside the court.

At some colleges there is more than just the shape of the court which yields an echo of the past. Within the south range of Magdalene's Old Court, opposite the chapel, are the Monks' Rooms, which remain more or less as they were when the Benedictines ran the college. There is a large central room with a wide fireplace and three small partitioned nooks, known as carrels, to the side for study where some scholars have left their names carved in the soft stone of the window splays. The central room, used chiefly by the senior monk, also had both a water closet and a piscina for washing. These were luxurious premises and, through the

Illustration 3.4: Corpus Christi chapel. All the oldest chapels have the internal architecture of a monastic chapel – stalls instead of pews and no pulpit.

investment they represent, underline the commitment of the Benedictines to the university. The only other surviving college lodgings from this era are the mean, austere rooms in the Old Court of Corpus Christi; the lesser investment which this secular college could afford suggests how dangerous was the sudden loss of the monks and friars to the university at the time of the Reformation. The monasteries had been both wealthy and committed to educating their scholar-monks in Cambridge.

College architecture continued to draw its inspiration from the concept of building and living around a court through the twentieth century. The women's colleges, Newnham and Girton, triggered some changes, such as the use of corridors rather than separate staircases, but Girton retained the concept of buildings around a court. It was Robinson College, in the late 1970s, which broke most dramatically with this tradition when it adopted the 'street' in place of the court as the axis linking the basic elements of a college. The new Education Faculty opened in 2005 alongside Homerton uses the same design concept. The departure of Robinson College from the ancient college template went still further: although a chapel was built, it has pews rather than stalls.

The deep connections between the university and religion stretch beyond the marks left on the physical structure of the university. Cambridge has prepared priests for the Church since its inception and although the Reformation removed the religious houses from the town, the university maintained strong links to the priesthood of the established church. College founders often sought to strengthen the priesthood; Bishop Fisher, who was eventually executed for opposing Henry VIII over the Reformation, had this objective in mind when he supported the foundation of St John's and Christ's. The founders of colleges such as Corpus Christi in the 1300s and King's in the 1400s, through to Selwyn in the late nineteenth century, also shared this motivation.

Since the secularisation of the university in the late nineteenth century, when dons were permitted to marry and the requirement for students to belong to the established church ended, training colleges for ordinands have been established. There are four theological colleges attached to the modern university, which prepare members for service to their church. They belong to different branches of the Protestant Church. Westcott House in Jesus Lane and Ridley Hall in Sidgwick Avenue were founded at the end of the nineteenth century as seminaries to prepare ordinands for the Anglican Ministry. Westminster College, on the corner where the Backs and Madingley Road meet, was built around the same period for Presbyterians; Methodists opened Wesley House, also in Jesus Lane, in the 1920s. Westcott House is thriving, but the Presbyterians and Methodists are struggling to attract recruits. There is also a Roman Catholic chaplaincy named after Bishop Fisher, just behind the Guildhall, near the Market Square. This was founded in 1895, shortly after Catholics were allowed back into the university to read for degrees after an absence of over 300 years, to buttress their faith against the overwhelmingly Anglican culture of the university.

The prominence of music within monasteries was also carried over to the university. Twenty-one of the thirty-one colleges offer organ scholarships; eighteen also offer choral exhibitions. It is generally the more recently founded colleges which have dropped this tradition; however, Robinson and Selwyn recruit organists. Even Newnham, founded near the end of the nineteenth century without a chapel, offers choral scholarships. The condition attached to these awards is usually that the student secures a place at college to study a standard degree course. Some minor financial reward, reflecting the nine or so hours of practice each week, accompanies the status of choral student. In view of such a modest commitment, it is not surprising that the hinges of the chapels' misericords have become stiff.

The all-male choirs of St John's and King's have long claimed a musical pre-eminence above all other colleges, although the mixed choirs of Trinity College, Caius, Jesus and Clare challenge their vaunted superiority. Unusually, Jesus College maintains two choirs: one, begun in 1849, is made up of boy choristers and adult male singers from the college, while the other, dating from 1982, is a mixed choir with its female members providing the top line.

Trinity College mounted a challenge to St John's and King's in 2005. Utilising its considerable wealth, it appointed Stephen Layton, a big name from the world of choral music, as its Director of Music;

this caused some disquiet among other leading music colleges. However, this competitive edge, which the colleges engender, has stimulated musical excellence at the university; for example, King's College alone has nurtured the composers George Benjamin and Judith Weir and the singers Mark Padmore and Gerald Finley.

The surviving legacy

The impact of the monasteries from centuries earlier survives in many parts of the university. The stark footprint of the old chapel in St John's First Court, the peace of the cloister courts at Jesus and Queens', the intimacy of Magdalene's Monk's Rooms and the stained glass of the old Franciscan chapel restored within Sidney Sussex's antechapel come directly from this tradition. Even the sometimes excessively introspective world of a modern college fellowship suggests parallels with a closed monastic community. Although the monasteries were destroyed almost 500 years ago both their physical and cultural influence persists.

The recent period of secular dominance has not washed away the monastic legacy. During the preparation for the May Balls, when students celebrate the end of their academic year, the thread connecting the university to the monasteries appears slightly worn. The twenty-first-century successors of devout medieval scholars prepare each year for a fortnight-long episode of conspicuous consumption. Medieval lanes are crowded with trucks disgorging electronic music equipment. Ancient pathways, such as the one through the Gate of Honour into Caius College, are thrown open as short-cuts through which vast speakers, cables and mixing desks are wheeled into place. Strobe lighting is placed in the nave of Caius' chapel to throw psychedelic images through the stained glass onto neighbouring ancient buildings. The shuddering spirits of ancient academics in holy orders can almost be sensed.

It will take a few centuries more for such ephemeral matters as these student parties to cut away the strong ties of the university to its monastic roots; the culture of the monastery remains in their bloodstream. Monasteries played an important part in attracting the first scholars to Cambridge; the beliefs and style of their monks cradled the young university. Their influence remains strong in many areas of university life.

Chapter 4

King's College Chapel and its Acolytes

Although it often took time for a medieval college to afford a chapel, its acquisition was a rite of passage for the fellowship. It was not until the late nineteenth century that a college, Newnham, opened without the express intent of acquiring a chapel. The chapel was simply the most important medieval college building. It is still the place where the souls of most colleges rest, where its members meet to honour its founders, where famous fellows and those killed in war during the twentieth century are remembered. These are important matters for the senior members of a college. However, chapel is now incidental to the lives of most undergraduate members. In the Middle Ages and during most centuries since, the very opposite was true.

The time spent in chapel by medieval scholars would astonish the modern student. In more modern times, Samuel Taylor Coleridge, when at Jesus College, wrote to his brother in 1791: 'we go to chapel twice a day – every time we miss we pay two pence and four pence on Surplice Days'. His letter continues, 'I am remarkably religious'.

College servants noted absence from chapel by sticking pins by names on a register; those missing were fined. Records at Magdalene show that undergraduates ran up large fines for non-attendance, which by the late nineteenth century had became a significant source of income to this relatively poor college. Chapel attendance at college generally had ceased to be compulsory by 1930; reflecting the importance of its 'non-attendance' income, Magdalene held out until 1933 before making chapel services voluntary.

The chapels' central role

Chapel was central to the scholars' lives: daily attendance was compulsory during the week, and more frequent visits were made on the many holy days and on Sundays. The time spent in chapel is reflected in the beautifully etched graffiti the scholars have left on some chapel stalls. The chancel was reserved exclusively for religious worship, while secular activities were (and still are) arranged in the largest of the college antechapels; thus the graffiti must have been completed during religious services. In Pembroke, for

Illustration 4.1: Meticulously carved graffiti from the late 1700s; the names can be identified in the Venns' records as pensioners admitted into Pembroke College in the 1700s and 1800s.

example, just a few feet from the alcoves in which the master and dean sat and in front of the back row of stalls where the dons had places, scholars have left their names deeply carved on the front stalls. The names and dates are clear, so there is no intimation that they feared their names being noted (always assuming they were carving their own names, that is). Neither does research into the scholars' names confirm that these were scholars from the highest social circles – noble fellow commoners or fellow commoners – whom the more socially humble dons feared to discipline; practically all of them are shown in J. Venn and J.A. Venn's *Alumni Cantabrigiensis* to have been admitted into college as pensioners.

As the membership of a college grew, practically all the colleges founded before 1600 either replaced their first chapels with larger ones or pushed out their chapel's east end. Only Jesus, Christ's and Magdalene chapels, each built around 1500, maintain the same chapel footprint as at the time their colleges were founded. The size of a chapel came to reflect the wealth of a college: wealthier colleges had more fellows and scholars and all of them had to attend religious services together.

Increasing student numbers in more recent years have in almost all cases outstripped the capacity of college chapels. In 1900 Magdalene and Trinity Hall had fewer than forty members each, totals which could be accommodated within these colleges' small chapels. Within a hundred years numbers had risen to 450 students at Magdalene and over 600 at Trinity Hall. By the twenty-first century only at King's could all the members of the college be seated at one time in their chapel – and then only if the antechapel was used.

It was necessary to secure permission from the pope to establish a private chapel before the Reformation; the first college to do this was Pembroke, which built its first chapel in the mid-1300s. Although damaged in the Civil War of the 1640s, it still stands in the north range of Old Court. The seventeenth-century plasterwork ceiling, designed by Henry Doogood, has flying birds sculpted into the ceiling; they seem so alive that it is as if they might not be there for a later visit. When the college chapel was replaced it became the college library; the library was in turn moved to a larger building in the late 1800s, since when the old chapel has been used as a meeting room. This journey of old college chapels to library and then, when it could no longer hold the college's books, to meeting room has been followed at Emmanuel. Queens' old chapel has yet to complete the full journey as it was converted into the Memorial Library during the 1990s and is used by undergraduates.

The smallest among all the college chapels, the chapel of Trinity Hall, was extended by an appropriately modest eight feet during the mid-1800s into the space occupied by the college treasury. The wall linings and stalls date from the eighteenth century, although the walls of the original mid-fourteenth-century building remain behind the panelling. It is one of the most moving places of religion among the colleges.

Gonville & Caius is another college whose expansion is reflected in changes to its chapel. Its first small chapel was built in 1393, within fifty years of the foundation of the college; the fellowship's priorities were clear, as it was another fifty years before the college built either a master's lodge or a dining hall. By the early 1600s, the chapel was too small for the 25 college fellows and 125 junior members and was lengthened by thirty feet. In the 1870s, Alfred Waterhouse was commissioned to extend the east end again. He added an apse brightened with bold Byzantine mosaic decorations depicting teaching scenes from the Bible.

The pattern of small extensions which in time proved inadequate was repeated at Pembroke, Sidney Sussex and Queens'. This last college had received a licence during 1454 for its chapel in Old Court. It was much altered and slightly extended in the mid-1800s by the architect George Bodley, before the same architect won the commission for an entirely new chapel. He worked there with the outstanding late Victorian church stained glass artist C.E. Kempe, whose designs filled the east and north windows. The interior of the chapel has a sumptuously decorated barrel-vaulted roof space into which is fitted one of the finest organ cases in the country.

Corpus Christi College used St Bene't's parish church for 200 years before building its own chapel in the sixteenth century, where the north range of New Court now stands. This first chapel was destroyed

Illustration 4.2: The east end of Jesus College chapel. It has been much altered, most recently by the Victorians, but retains parts from the twelfth-century nunnery chapel. It is among the most charming of places in Cambridge.

when the architect William Wilkins transformed the college in the early 1800s. Wilkins built the present chapel at this time, although within sixty years another architect, Arthur Blomfield, was commissioned to extend its east end.

Worship within Clare College has followed the same pattern of change. The first chapel was built in the early 1360s, probably on the ground now occupied by the college dining hall. It was destroyed in a major fire in 1521; a replacement was consecrated in the 1530s outside Old Court on the site of the modern chapel. It was left untouched by the Old Court rebuilding schemes between 1638 and 1714 and finally, by the 1760s, a larger chapel was built to the design of James Burrough, who was master of Caius and an amateur architect.

Although Jesus College's chapel remains where the nuns of St Radegund prayed in the twelfth century, it was much reduced in size and its style changed when it was taken over by the college in 1496. A shallower pitched roof was installed and parts of the aisles removed; at the west end, a section of the nave was converted to private accommodation for the master. A broad perpendicular Gothic window replaced five narrow lancet arches at the east end, three of which had probably been pierced as windows. A.W.N. Pugin was commissioned in the 1840s to recapture its medieval early Gothic style: a steep roof above the chancel and three narrow glazed lancet windows replaced the broader east window which the Jesus College founder, Bishop Alcock, had commissioned. Pugin, inspired by Chartres Cathedral, also designed the rood screen and the glass within the lancet windows. William Morris glazed the nave windows to the sketches of Edward

Burne Jones and the ceiling was also decorated under his direction. This chapel still feels like a place of ancient Christian worship yet, like so many of the college chapels, it has been reshaped to accommodate change at the university.

Despite the Reformation most college chapels retained the trappings of Catholicism. The chapel of Sidney Sussex reflects the importance of the Virgin Mary to the Roman Catholic faith: a picture of the Incarnation, painted by the Venetian artist Pittoni and given to the college in 1783, is behind the altar. A wooden statue of St Francis stands beside a Lady Chapel and there is a stoup for holy water at the entrance to the antechapel – all these details would be familiar to Roman Catholics. Unlike many churches in the town, most college chapels were, and remain, 'high up the candle'.

This is even more astonishing when it is remembered that Emmanuel and Sidney Sussex, each founded in the late sixteenth century, were known as 'Protestant' colleges. Both college chapels face south-east instead of due east; in part the axis of many college buildings had to accommodate the lines of existing buildings and streets. Yet there was also a point to be made in 'misaligning' their places of worship: the traditions of Rome were no longer to be followed blindly. At Emmanuel the first college chapel had actually been built on a north–south axis and, in a break with monastic tradition, was fitted with a pulpit. The college even put a weather vane on top of its second chapel which showed that the altar did not face due east but north-east, a moderate but significant deviation from the Roman Catholic compass. Besides veering from the traditional east–west orientation, both colleges also built their dining halls on top of the chapels of their monastic predecessors. To complete the confusion between Catholic and Protestant symbols at Sidney Sussex, the skull of Oliver Cromwell was offered for a second time to the college in 1960, when it was finally accepted; it is buried beneath the flagstones of the small antechapel.

The influence of the Wren family on college chapels

Matthew Wren, the uncle of Christopher, commissioned Peterhouse chapel when he was the college master in the 1630s. The chapel ended the use by college members of the neighbouring parish church, from which the college derives its name. The church was dedicated to St Peter when the college was founded in 1289; it was rededicated to St Mary in the mid-1300s and is now known as Little St Mary's.

As the positioning and design of the chapels at Sidney Sussex and Emmanuel reflected the break with Rome, so the reaction against the extremes of Protestantism in the 1630s was caught in Peterhouse's chapel. Church leaders like Archbishop Laud and Matthew Wren – who was Bishop of Ely after leaving Peterhouse – saw themselves as good Catholics who had corrected the errors of the Church of Rome. They wished to restore 'the beauty of holiness' – a phrase from Psalms 29:2 – through the restoration of Catholic rituals to the Anglican Church. Instead of using plain silverware for the celebration of the Eucharist, the chapel's silver plate copied the elaborate shapes of pre-Reformation chalices. A three-sided communion rail was installed and the altar was used as a communion table with elaborate frontal coverings. It earned the description of the 'Wren's Nest'.

The college's embrace of Anglican Catholicism reached a wider audience through the symbolism of its east end, which juts out into the sightline of those passing along Trumpington Street. It has stained glass

Illustration 4.3: The west end of Emmanuel College chapel, designed by Christopher Wren and completed in the 1670s.

within perpendicular Gothic window tracery, empty niches beneath ogee arches, an imposing pediment and octagonal turrets. These were Counter-Reformation flourishes brought together in the eclectic style of the Mannerists. The new chapel would have offended many in the Puritan-inclined Cambridge of the 1600s. Nikolaus Pevsner's comment on this chapel in his book *Cambridgeshire: Buildings of England* touches on the confusion its mixture of Gothic and Classical features has caused; he wonders whether this church was 'Gothic Survival' or the first example of 'Gothic Revival'. Whatever the answer, Gothic architecture was a symbol of the old Roman Catholic Church of England.

Wren was imprisoned by Cromwell for seventeen years because of his High Church beliefs. When he regained his freedom, he immediately commissioned his nephew Christopher Wren to build a new chapel at Pembroke College, where he had been an undergraduate. It was the first building that Christopher Wren designed. The new chapel was rectangular and crowned with a frieze and lantern, its Classical style contrasting with the Peterhouse chapel on the opposite side of the street. Its simple interior captures light in the manner of all this architect's churches. The ceiling has richly decorated plasterwork and the elder Cornelius Austin sculpted the swags above the stalls. This building is characterised by the beauty, proportions and practicality typical of Wren's genius.

Pembroke's full college membership at this time was eighty. By late 1881 the chapel could not accommodate the college's 128 scholars and George Gilbert Scott was commissioned to extend its east end. Yet, as with other chapels, its size was increased by only a few feet. The stonework of the original east end was reused, although the facing was removed on the existing walls to expose the underlying red bricks, so that the north façade now has a section in brick with the later addition in stone.

Wren won the commission for Emmanuel's second chapel from the college master, William Sancroft, a Cambridge graduate who went on to become the Dean of St Paul's in London and, still later, reached the See of Canterbury. Admiration of Wren's work in Cambridge must have helped him secure the commission to design St Paul's after the Great Fire of London in 1666. The Emmanuel chapel was designed in the Baroque style, with a hint of the flourishes and articulation which were to be the trademark of St Paul's. Its style contrasts with the plain Classical finish of Pembroke Chapel.

Wren, who disliked travelling, never visited the chapel at Emmanuel, but sent up a model of the proposed building. Externally, it shares the feature of open galleries at the west end with Peterhouse chapel. As at Pembroke, the chapel has white decorated plasterwork and woodwork by Cornelius Austin; Wren's plain glass was replaced at the time of the college's centenary celebrations in the late 1800s with stained glass and much of the interior was given an extensive Gothic overlay by Arthur Blomfield.

Blomfield, who also designed Selwyn College's chapel, even offered to replace Emmanuel's Wren chapel with a church in Gothic style at barely more expense, he claimed, than his alterations would cost. The more modest 're-ordering' actually commissioned from Blomfield by Emmanuel was reversed in an extensive project in 2005, and once more the influence of Wren predominates within this chapel, although the stained glass windows installed by the Victorians remain. In the windows of the north side are shown those who influenced the structure of the Church, such as Cranmer and Fisher; to the south are those who assisted its spiritual development, among them John Colet and William Tyndale. The name of John Harvard, a past member of college after whom the American university is named, appears in one window; there is no record of his features, however, and the portrait shown is reputedly that of his puritan Cambridge contemporary, John Milton.

Two statement chapels

The two richest colleges, Trinity and St John's, each built large chapels in their main courts; both replaced earlier ones. The scholars of King's Hall, one of Trinity's predecessors, had first worshipped in the old All Saints' parish church, almost opposite Trinity's main entrance. They then had their own small chapel from the 1470s. It was destroyed in order that the present chapel could be built over its foundations in the 1550s, during the reign of Queen Mary, but only the chapel's external walls were completed by the time of her death in 1558. Protestants therefore arranged its internal decoration during the reign of Elizabeth I. Its first stained glass windows were destroyed in the 1660s; however, subsequent Victorian stained glass maintained the Protestant bias through the Reformation Window, which depicts four Protestant martyrs – Latimer, Ridley, Tyndale and Cranmer – executed by the Catholics standing beside Edward VI and Elizabeth I. There are also two Catholic reformers: one is John Wycliffe, the dissident who founded the Lollards and whose body was burnt posthumously on the order of the pope; the other is Erasmus, whose advocacy of Humanism helped provoke the schism in Christendom.

The Protestants also decorated the outside of the chapel, which stretches out to Trinity Street: hence a large Latin inscription above the east window displays clearly to those in the street the words of Jesus when he threw out the money changers from the temple: 'My house is a house of prayer'. From the Protestant viewpoint a place of God should be a place to pray, rather than a place to celebrate the sacrament. This quotation made that point strongly, at least to those who could understand Latin.

These messages from college buildings, such as Peterhouse and Trinity chapels, are lost on most modern pedestrians. However, they would have certainly caught the attention of past members of the town's two communities as to what was, for the passing moment in any event, expected of them. They are proof indeed that part of architecture's role has always been to express a view of the social order.

Trinity's chapel reflects not only its Protestant heritage but also the soul of its college: the antechapel is full of statues, busts and plaques representing the famous among Trinity's alumni. Isaac Newton, Alfred Lord Tennyson and Francis Bacon, the father of modern science, are among those caught forever in marble. The less famous, mere Nobel laureates for example, simply merit a bronze plaque. The west wall honours the college alumni who fell in the Second World War; the fallen of the Great War are honoured at the east end. The antechapel is Cambridge's Pantheon to the Gods; following in their footsteps must, or at least should, be a little daunting for Trinity undergraduates.

The huge chapel at St John's College is connected only by the south tip of its antechapel to the east range of First Court. The ancient chapel and hospital, whose footings are still visible outside the chapel, were destroyed in the late 1800s to permit its construction. Its architect, George Gilbert Scott, was influenced by the thirteenth-century royal Gothic chapel Sainte-Chapelle on the Ile de Paris: both are massive and contain a decorated ribbed ceiling with an apsidal east end.

The vaulted timber ceiling contains effigies of the saints, clerics, martyrs and monarchs who supported the English Church. Several monarchs – Alfred the Great, Edward II, Henry VI – win a place, as do some college founders, such as John Fisher and John Alcock. It seems more than coincidental, however, that the men chosen to represent the nineteenth century, at the time the ceiling was decorated, had all studied at St John's. There are more heroes from among the college's graduates occupying niches along the outside of the chapel.

The chapel was designed with a modest spire, but a college graduate offered to fund the massive tower. He died before the work was paid for, leaving the college with a half completed tower and much debt, as the dons had apparently refused their bursar's pleas to insure the young donor's life. Since the early 1900s a tradition has been established of celebrating Ascension Day on top of the tower.

St John's also has marble statues of its heroes in the antechapel; there is one of William Wilberforce, while a statue of his mentor, a fellow Jonian, Thomas Clarkson, stands outside the chapel – these two men who exposed the evils of the slave trade were both nurtured in Cambridge. Seen from St John's Street on the north-east corner of the chapel, the figure of Clarkson holds a loosened pair of chains with a key at his feet.

The antechapel of St John's is set in a transverse position to the nave, a situation unique at Cambridge University, although seen more often in Oxford colleges. In its west window the Last Judgement is portrayed. The Latin dedication beneath the window records that it was a gift from the junior members of college; just above the inscription, bodies tumble down into the cauldrons of Hell. It was immediately

Illustration 4.4: The west end of Trinity College chapel. As with many other religious buildings, this one carried a political message: between the crenellations and the window the very Protestant exhortation 'My house shall be called a house of prayer' is carved into the stonework.

judged to represent the fate awaiting the idle scholars of the college. There could have been no such light-hearted interpretations of the scenes portrayed in stained glass windows of medieval date: in the England of the Middle Ages, living in the shadow of the 'Final Judgement' was a fearful reality about which there were no jokes. Hell had then been a vividly real deterrent against sinning.

The sense of a college being a quasi-religious community had weakened by the late nineteenth century. This change, together with the agnosticism of the founders of Newnham College, caused that college to be built without a chapel. In the twentieth century New Hall, two of the graduate colleges (Hughes and Clare Halls), Wolfson, Homerton, Lucy Cavendish and, initially, Churchill were all built without chapels.

A chapel at Churchill had not been part of the original plans, and agreement among the essentially scientific fellowship was difficult to secure. It is a small square building with narrow lancet style windows from the ground to the roof, built at the periphery of the forty-acre college grounds. There are odd large rectangular lumps on the otherwise flat lead roof, which bring light into its remarkably peaceful interior; from the outside it does not look like a chapel.

In an earlier age many colleges took financial risks in order to build their private chapels: the commission of the Selwyn College chapel in 1882 was in keeping with that tradition. It was a brave decision for an impoverished college. The college was named in honour of the Bishop of New Zealand in the 1880s and had an emphasis on religion which would have won the approval of any medieval college founder. The chapel architect Arthur Blomfield struggled with an inadequate budget and the neo-Gothic church is narrower than he intended. The Pre-Raphaelite artist C.E. Kempe interpreted Christ's Enthronement in the east window of the Selwyn Chapel and further stained glass windows were planned for windows on the north and south sides, but funds were insufficient for their execution.

The chapel at Selwyn was followed 100 years later by others at Robinson and Fitzwilliam. Among the modern college chapels that of Fitzwilliam is much admired; it is the college's only listed building. Designed by Richard MacCormac in 1990, the chapel ceiling is structured like the deck of a ship and two wooden staircases bend upwards from ground level as if against a curved hull; indeed, much of the chapel's design suggests a ship, presumably in a play on the word 'nave' (Latin *navis*, from which the word 'nave' derives, means ship). Another modern chapel has been built at Robinson. John Piper designed the stained glass behind the altar, which brings beautiful yellow and green light into the chapel. Standing in the building, it is easy to understand Piper's description of his work with stained glass as being like 'painting with coloured light'. These last few described chapels – those at Churchill, Fitzwilliam and Robinson, the first almost hidden from view and all rejecting the monastic chapel template – make an enormous contrast to the most famous chapel of all, King's College Chapel. It dominates the college and is a building of beauty and historical significance.

The king's chapels

The vast, pillarless chapel of King's was not the college's first place of worship. The building of a small college chapel had started in 1443, two years after the college's foundation, on the ground now set to grass between the north side of the chapel and the Old Schools. Before the foundations of the first chapel were complete, in an example of the inconsistent decision-making which was the despair of his contemporaries, Henry VI determined to increase the college community to seventy, the number of missionaries mentioned in the Gospel of St Luke (10.1). By the spring of 1448 Henry therefore commanded in 'my wille and myne entent' that another, much bigger, chapel be built as well. This is the building which is so admired today. It is possible that Henry himself came to lay this chapel's foundation stone in 1449; this is suggested by the research of Frank Woodman in his work *Architectural History of King's Chapel* (1986). Woodman also disproved the claim that the building of the second chapel began in 1446.

Those colleges who were still worshipping in town churches, such as Peterhouse and Corpus Christi, must have looked enviously at this college as it built two chapels simultaneously. Records prove that the smaller chapel was used for many years: for example, Henry VII celebrated St George's Day there in 1506. However, the fabric of the first chapel was neglected – doubtless as the prospect of the second chapel opening drew closer – and it collapsed around 1537. Always in the shadow of the great chapel, it can hardly have been much mourned; Dr Caius of Gonville Hall had described it in the late 1520s as a 'mean and inconvenient' building.

The building

Huge and magnificent structures such as the second King's College Chapel reflected the advance of building technology. The 1440s fell near the end of a long period of intensive cathedral building in the Gothic style throughout Europe. During the Renaissance the most gifted artists were drawn to oil painting; however, in the Middle Ages it was these cathedrals which attracted the best craftsmen and most talented artists. Their towering buildings, which supported massive weights of stone above vast expanses of glass, provided huge opportunities for master masons, who designed the buildings; for freemasons, who shaped the stone; for stone cutters, wood carvers, and artists who decorated the glass. Inside, huge spaces were filled with light and high ceilings drew the eye upwards towards Heaven.

Some claim that the dimensions of King's College Chapel are based on the precepts of 'Sacred Architecture' and symbolic geometry with which the Templars and Freemasons were associated. More prosaically, the twelve apostles in whose honour Henry had first determined to found a college community may explain the 288-foot length of the chapel. There are twelve bays in the chapel: however, twelve bays each 12 feet wide produced a chapel of only 144 feet in length. This was insufficiently grand; double that size was considered more appropriate, and the bays are thus 24 feet wide. Henry also doubled the number of oblates who were typically attached to a cathedral, so that there were sixteen rather than eight choristers.

The building took almost a hundred years to complete. The stonework of the chapel was finished by 1515, when Henry VIII ruled, but the stained glass work continued until 1547. Other cathedrals, such as the Anglican building in Liverpool and Gaudi's Barcelona, have taken as long, but it is unique for a building sponsored by the monarch to take so many years to complete. The extended period of construction was caused by the Wars of the Roses: five monarchs reigned while the chapel was built, and funding consequently proved very difficult. These conflicts began in 1455, only six years after Henry VI had laid the chapel's foundation stone. After a further six years, Henry was deposed by Edward IV, who chose to do little to assist this Lancastrian project. The next king, Richard III, was more supportive of the chapel during his short reign. By the time of his death in 1485, the first five eastern bays had been built and roofed over with timber. However, the next king, Henry VII, showed little interest in the chapel and twenty years of inactivity followed. With the building project abandoned, it must have appeared to the townspeople that the local people had been displaced from their homes to serve some incomprehensible purpose of the privileged academic community.

Illustration 4.5: King's College Chapel west end: with Clare College to the north and the Fellow's Building of King's on the other side, this is one of the best-known sights of Cambridge.

Both Henry VII and his son Henry VIII gave their support to the chapel project only when they could perceive personal benefit. Near the end of his life, Henry VII perhaps felt that association with this project of his uncle, the pious Lancastrian Henry VI, would boost the people's perception of the legitimacy of the Tudor dynasty. Or perhaps it was his religious mother, the great Cambridge benefactor Lady Margaret Beaufort, who coaxed funds from Henry to finish the final phase of stone building. In any event, from 1506 Henry did provide finance for the chapel project to resume. The costs of completing the chapel's external stonework still exceeded resources. When Henry died in 1509, his will instructed that a further £5,000, a huge sum, be given to meet the costs of completion. This bequest and a further supplement from the late king's executors ensured that the entire building was weather-tight, probably through the installation of a temporary flat timber roof and clear glass in the windows. The great vault ceiling, however, was but conjecture and the stained glass still required funding.

There were also eight heads of the college over this period, yet nonetheless an extraordinary unity of design was achieved. The buttresses, flattened arches, fan-vaulted ceiling and rectilinear window tracery make it an outstanding example of perpendicular Gothic architecture. This was the longest lasting (circa 1350 to 1530) of the three Gothic phases and the only one of the Gothic styles which originated in England. At a time when late Gothic architecture developed differently in several European countries, the English variety was characterised particularly by vast expanses of glass, in part because of the country's soft light and temperate summers. The harsh strong sunlight in southern Europe did not encourage the use of stained glass. The best stained glass artisans in Europe came from the Low Countries and England for the same reason. The virtues of this phase of Gothic architecture – strength, soaring verticality and magnificent stained glass – are easily appreciated when looking from the banks of the Cam towards the chapel's west end.

The Tudor imprint

The Tudors turned the religious project of a devout Lancastrian king into a propaganda exercise to mark the triumph of their family. Their heraldic devices were carved on the vaulted ceiling and on the walls, both within and outside the chapel, reflecting the lack of self-confidence of a family which had usurped the throne. It contrasts with the eastern portion of the chapel, whose plain walls were completed earlier. Where Henry VI's legacy is the scale and architectural style of the building, the Tudors gave the chapel its detailed character, through the stone decorations, the magnificent roof, the screen and the stained glass.

The erratic swings of fortune during the years of civil war are even reflected in the visibly different materials used at the east and at the west ends of the chapel. A good part of the five bays moving out from the east end were built while Henry VI reigned. They are constructed from expensive white magnesium limestone. The white stone forms a visible rectangle at the east end which gradually tapers down to ground level before rising twelve feet again at the west end. It shows how the medieval architect first had the entire footprint of the building laid out and then had the stones carried up with the minimum use of scaffolding. The lack of money after Henry VI's demise caused the white magnesium limestone from distant Yorkshire to be replaced by the cheaper and darker oolitic limestone from Clipsham, Rutland.

Inside the chapel, masons used a soft limestone from Caen in Normandy to carve the symbols of the Tudor dynasty; there are greyhounds and dragons, each holding a different posture, the stone worked as if it were malleable plastic. The varied poses of these creatures reflect the work of freestone masons, hence freemasons, who had some liberty over the shape and cut of their stone; 'rough-masons', who were lower down the artisan hierarchy, worked on the plain building blocks outside the chapel. The greyhound was the heraldic motif chosen by Henry VII's father, the Earl of Richmond, while the dragon was the symbol of the seventh-century King Cadwallader of Wales, the last king of the Britons. There are also Tudor roses, symbolising the end of the civil war, paired with the French symbol of monarchy, the fleur de lys, representing the English claim to the French throne. Portcullises, the badge adopted by the Henry's maternal relatives, the Beauforts, are as numerous as the roses.

The achievement that is represented by the building of the chapel – the lifting of so much stone so high in a period where such tasks were accomplished essentially by hand – is staggeringly impressive. It is the immense scale of the chapel's interior which first impresses the visitor entering the chapel. Even in modern times, when people are used to large buildings, it is sensational; the impact on medieval folk can but be imagined. Light filters through the stained glass of twenty-six windows onto the largest ever – 11,000 square feet – fan-vaulted ceiling, so termed as it appears to have the fine ribs and shape of a lady's fan. The ceiling was never decorated, even though a contract was issued in 1515 for the 'gildyng and payntyng of the great vawte'.

The architect was able to design huge spaces in the walls for windows, when only a few hundred years earlier a tiny opening within the tower of St Bene't's threatened the wall's integrity. It is almost as if the long walls of the chapel are made entirely of glass. Although the sculpted stonework and vast size of the chapel may first grip the imagination, it is the glass which fascinates and retains the attention.

The stained glass – the start

When the vault was finished in 1515, the glazing of the windows became the next and final project. Henry VI had probably foreseen a simple scheme of stained glass, perhaps displaying the familiar range of saints and Old Testament kings in the rigid postures of decorative Gothic architecture. However, the windows became a dramatic artistic representation of a new art style, the new religion and Tudor society.

Bishop Richard Foxe, an executor to the late King Henry VII, Bishop Fisher, the university chancellor, and Robert Hacomblen, the King's College provost, were appointed to oversee the design and installation of the glass, which was to take thirty years.

Stained glass requires a designer to determine the images to be used and a glazier to convert design into glass within the stone tracery of the window. Credit for much of the design, possibly almost half of all the windows, is given to the Fleming Dierick Vellert. However, some of the earlier designs are thought to be by an unnamed artist employed at Fairford Church in Gloucestershire, to whom Vellert may even have been apprenticed. The first glazier was Barnard Flower, a man from Antwerp who was probably of German extraction.

Funding throughout the thirty years of glazing was difficult to acquire. The first contract for the glass was issued in 1515. The first window glazed was the second window from the west end, above the north door. When compared to later windows, its figures are set in less colourful glass, without the action and humanity of scenes in later windows. Three others along the north side towards the east end were completed in the first phase of glazing. Funds were exhausted at the same time that Barnard Flower died, in 1517. The great window project was suspended.

Work resumed in 1526. Bishop Fisher had fought for the project but it took someone closer to the king, Cardinal Wolsey, to make funds available for further glazing. The cardinal's motives in helping the college are unlikely to have been altruistic; he may have hoped to win support in Cambridge from where, perhaps, scholars could be tempted to join his new college (now Christchurch) at Oxford; furthermore, if there was work to keep the itinerant skilled artisans in Cambridge, they could then more easily be moved on to the cardinal's Oxford college project. In any event, the 1526 contract specified a further six windows to be completed within a year and another twelve to be completed within six years. The east and west windows were included in this contract and Barnard Flower's successor was another Fleming, Galyon Hone.

The fall from power of both Wolsey and Fisher damaged the flow of funds for the windows and the scheme fell behind the dates laid out in the 1526 contract. In 1528 Edward Foxe succeeded Hacomblen as provost at the time Henry needed the support of the universities in his attempts to divorce Catherine of Aragon. The university's backing of Henry won new funding, largely through exceptional income the Crown derived from the break-up of the monasteries.

Typology and the stained glass

The design for the majority of the windows was typological, an art form of the late Middle Ages which related scenes from the Old Testament, known as types, to stories from the New Testament, anti-types. Typology reveals to the Christian how the events of the Old Testament foretold those of the New. This was the style of decoration which Henry VII had approved for his chapel within Westminster Abbey. The biblical scenes were taken from two sources, a mid-thirteenth-century bible known as the *Biblia Pauperum* and the early-fourteenth-century *Speculum Humanae Salvationis*. Both these illustrated manuscripts were works of popular theology aimed at the illiterate, in which the text was subordinated to the illustrations; they served as a pattern book for the stained glass at King's College Chapel.

There are some exceptions to this typological approach: the first two windows in the north-west corner are based entirely on stories from the Golden Legend, the collection of non-canonical stories about Mary, Jesus and the saints which have often played an important part in church iconography; and the entire east window is used to depict Christ's trial and passion. The west window, which is Victorian, deals with the Last Judgement. A further three windows were not completed until the 1540s, when religious priorities had changed: these, along the south-west wall, show scenes exclusively from the Act of the Apostles. Elsewhere the typology links the Old and New Testaments.

Events from the Old Testament appear in the top half of each window while those they presage in the New Testament are shown beneath. For example, the top half of the third window from the north-west corner shows the devil's temptation of Eve and her disobedience, which led to the downfall of mankind; beneath is the Annunciation scene where, through Mary, mankind was saved. In the next window eastwards, the top half of the window shows the Queen of Sheba presenting gifts to Solomon, while below are the Magi with gifts for the baby Jesus. In the top half of the eighth window along the north side Moses and his people, while fleeing from Egypt, are shown being fed with manna from Heaven; beneath, Christ feeds his disciples at the Last Supper. In the third window from the south-east corner a damp and bedraggled Jonah is shown emerging after three days in the belly of an ugly green sea-monster while, beneath, Christ is shown rising from the dead after three days.

There was a further significance in this extensive portrayal of scenes from the bible. Some, among them devout Catholics, believed that many of those in positions of authority within the Church were corrupt: practices such as simony, the sale of indulgences and pluralism were certainly widespread. It was believed by many that a more direct involvement by common people in religion through reading the bible would cleanse the Church, something which could be achieved only by the increased availability of the Word of God in English, so that it could be read by lay people without the need for the intermediary figure of a priest. Educated people were thus encouraged to make their own interpretation of the bible. The glass of King's College Chapel was installed at the same time as the king instructed that the Coverdale Bible, the first complete translation in English by the Cambridge graduate Myles Coverdale, be chained to a bookstand in every parish church.

Promotion of the new Anglican Church

The stained glass of King's is not simply an artistic representation of religious devotion. Its designs served a political purpose; the windows contained highly visible statements about the issues of the day, almost in the manner in which modern politicians use roadside posters. Churches were not unusual places for medieval publicity. This was why, a generation earlier than most of the political messages that were placed in the windows of this chapel, Martin Luther had nailed his ninety-five theses to the Castle Church in Wittenberg – although where Luther was inviting debate, the Tudor king wished simply to state the new truths.

The problem, from a retrospective position, is to distinguish between the intent of those responsible for the designs of the glazed windows and the interpretation which others have since drawn from them. This dilemma is by no means unique to King's Chapel. For example, it was unlikely that William Shakespeare intended his play *Richard II*, written perhaps only fifty years after these windows were completed, to be read as an overtly political message intended to uncrown a monarch. Yet so it was and the Earl of Essex procured its performance in 1601 just before his ill-fated uprising. It is possible to extract an overtly Protestant message from the fourth window from the north-west corner, regardless of the intent of the window's creators. It was completed around 1535, when Cardinal Wolsey had fallen from power and the English Reformation had begun, and shows King Solomon receiving presents from the Queen of Sheba. A few years earlier Hans Holbein had completed a woodcut with the same scene. Solomon can be interpreted allegorically as the Protestant Church; this ruler of the young Jewish kingdom accepts the obeisance of the Queen of Sheba, ruler of an ancient African kingdom. As Solomon ruled a young but powerful kingdom, so Henry VIII led a young reformed Church; the older kingdom of the Queen of Sheba pays homage to Solomon, as surely would the ancient Catholic Church bow to Henry.

The problem of interpretation versus intent is again evident in the window just to the east of the screen on the north side. Here, beneath the type of Jacob tempting Esau to sell his birthright, Christ is tempted in the desert. The devil is shown dressed as a friar, with cloven hoofs and a horn showing through his cowl. Despite the university having been full of Dominican friars but a few years earlier, by the 1530s they could be shown as devils. However, friars, although not priests, had been widely mocked throughout the Middle Ages – after all, it was in Chaucer's *Summoner's Tale* that the sick man farted in the face of the friar. Furthermore, it is thought that the window was completed by the English glazier Thomas Reeve in the mid-1520s, well before the break with Rome. Whatever the intent, however, there is little doubt about the interpretation put on the scene after the Reformation.

Similarly, in the next window to the east there is another symbol used by the sixteenth-century religious reformers. As he enters Jerusalem, King David holds a huge sword with the head of Goliath on its point. Late in his life, Henry liked to associate himself with the kings of the Old Testament; here, David is a symbol of the new Church and the slain Goliath represents the Antichrist who now resided in Rome. The sword was also the symbolic weapon used by the Protestant reformers and even appeared on the title page of the Coverdale Bible. This window was probably completed some time after 1536; it certainly contained very visible messages which those of the new religion could grasp.

The examples of religious and political messages continue: in the enormous east window Christ is shown, crucified, between the two thieves, the thief on the left appealing to Christ at the eleventh hour in a way that is manifestly repentant. Much of the new Anglican faith was based on the teachings of Martin Luther, who had stressed the value of repentance and a personal relationship with God; it was never too late to appeal directly to God. This depiction of a repentant sinner could be interpreted as a slight directed at Roman Catholics, even though the master glazier of this window, probably Galyon Hone, had signed the main contract for the window well before the break with Rome, in the late 1520s. Similarly, it has been suggested that in the window on the north side, again designed in the 1520s, the scene showing Moses leading his people out of Egypt could, later, have been read as a symbol for Henry VIII leading the English away from the Roman Catholic Church.

There is an almost undeniable political message in the second window from the north-east corner, where Jesus appears before Caiaphas, the Jewish High Priest, before being sent for trial. In the base of the monumental chair in which the priest sits is inscribed the legend: *Sic Respondes Pontificem*. The priest has expressed disbelief – 'Is that how you reply to a priest?' – that Jesus could respond in such a manner to the representative of the established religion. This scene demonstrated how the new religion would deal with the old. A similar interpretation can be drawn from the large red Tudor dragon positioned just above the head of Christ on the cross in the vast east window: the temporal placed above the spiritual. The king was now God's representative on earth.

The subject matter of the three windows to the west of the screen on the south side of the antechapel also promotes the new Protestant beliefs. Two of them, referred to as Nos 22 and 23, comprise eight scenes from the Acts of the Apostles dedicated to Paul alone. Paul was an important figure for the reformers and Luther particularly; he had come to God through direct conversion after a miracle, while Jesus had converted Peter and the other disciples. Furthermore, Peter, as the first Bishop of Rome, found particular favour with Roman Catholics, whereas Paul's Epistles were used by Luther as the foundation for his assault on the Roman Church. Images of Paul suggested modern, independent thinking without reliance on the interpretations of the established faith. Hence his character and adventures are given much prominence in these two windows. Peter is present in only one window and is in a sense symbolically surpassed by Paul. It is also interesting to observe that in window No. 21 Peter is portrayed doing 'Protestant'-type things – he is insisting on probity to Ananias, he preaches from the bible and heals the sick.

It was not just the stonemasons creating their dragons, greyhounds and portcullises, therefore, who reflected the political situation. The glaziers were also sometimes enrolled to this cause, even if subsequent Protestant interpretations perhaps twisted the original intent of the designers. Whether intent or interpretation drove the content of these magnificent windows, however, the king's glass became a mirror reflecting Tudor politics.

Even the west end window, in which the plain glass was not replaced with stained glass until the 1880s, was initially left out of the glazing scheme because of the political implications of the new religion. A portrayal of the Final Judgement had been planned for this window, but by the late 1540s it had become a tricky matter to display this scene. The Protestants had stood down many of the saints who might intervene on behalf of sinners in Purgatory. Purchasing a swift passage into Heaven was too close to the practice of selling indulgences. Furthermore, the very process of purification in Purgatory was rejected because it was not mentioned in the bible. In leaving plain glass in the window, this tricky doctrinal issue was shelved.

There is actually another Victorian window in the chapel; the bottom of the window in the south-east corner was 'blind' for 400 years, as there was an unachieved plan to attach another range of college buildings to the chapel in the place where William Wilkins eventually designed the screen in the early 1800s. The glass from the top level of this window was moved to the bottom in the mid-1800s; a new window to the design of George Hedgeland, and demonstrably of lower quality, was installed above.

It is only since the west window was decorated that visitors to the chapel have had the chance to admire the glass in the manner intended by the sixteenth-century glaziers. The subtle balance of coloured light necessary to appreciate the scenes would have been thrown completely out of balance by the huge amount of unfiltered daylight let in through the plain west window. Since the late 1960s, when the fan-faulted ceiling was cleaned, visitors have been even more fortunate, since conditions within the chapel were finally as the original craftsmen had intended.

Besides the religion and the politics, these windows portray the life of Tudor England. The priest in the fourth window from the north-west corner showing the Circumcision of Christ is wearing a pince-nez, which certainly was not an accoutrement of the biblical era. The rich colours and style of the clothes worn by the biblical characters are also those of Tudor England. The claim that the Queen of Sheba might be Katherine Howard is unlikely to be true, as the window was completed by 1535, several years before Katherine flowered briefly at the Tudor court. It is certain, however, that the face of Henry VIII has been used to portray King Solomon.

A Tudor view of nature is seen in the glass as well, from the numerous dogs, birds, plants and trees which fill the background, to trends in architecture. There is even a portrayal of a contemporary warship. The third window from the south-west corner shows the evangelising St Paul about to be rowed out to a large ship. This image also represents another significant departure from a coastline – that of Henry VIII, who left Dover in his warship, the Henry Grâce de Dieu, to meet the French king, Francis, at the Field of the Cloth of Gold in 1520, an event which was recorded in a painting that can be seen at Hampton Court.

Even the prejudices of the Tudor university are shown. The devil in the window above the north door is portrayed in the Garden of Eden scene as a very attractive woman draped round a tree; she has only one of the usual devilish accoutrements, a barely visible green tail. It is not unique to portray the devil as female – Michelangelo had adopted the same device a few years earlier on the ceiling of the Sistine Chapel – but the King's College Chapel's devil could be interpreted as making it clear to members of the misogynist academic community that all women should be viewed as wicked. In contrast, good men can be easily identified from a male devil, as the latter always had a number of helpful means of identification. These stained glass windows clearly portray more than simply biblical scenes; they are a record of Tudor life.

The ebb and flow of Henry's personal life, too, is marked in the chapel. The initials of one of the executed wives of Henry VIII, Anne Boleyn, are carved into the oak screen which separates the antechapel from the choir and sanctuary. The carving fixes the screen's date, as her tenure as wife lasted for three years from 1533. The initials A.S., standing for 'Anne (Boleyn) Sponsa', are entwined with those of H.R., 'Henricus Rex'. Not only are such reminders of Anne rare but, in a worrying sign to her successors, Henry had the initials of his subsequent wives carved separately from his own.

The initials of his fifth wife, Katherine Howard, are shown in the tracery glass above the main east window. Parallel with the head of the Tudor dragon above the scene of Christ's Passion in the east window are the initials of Henry VIII, his father and mother, and Katherine. This part of the huge east window was completed in the early 1540s, and the relief of the glazier can be imagined when, after Katherine Howard's eighteen-month grip on the king's affection ended, he discovered that her replacement shared the same Christian name. The device of Henry's son Prince Edward and the motto 'Ich Dien' also appear within the tracery on each side of the east window. The coat of arms of Henry's sixth wife, Katherine Parr, and a stained glass painting of his parents can be found in the side-chapels.

The scenes in these magnificent windows reflect the most fundamental events of Tudor England. Even as their artistic brilliance is enjoyed, the role of the glass in supporting the Tudors' efforts to legitimise their capture of the throne and to promote their religious revolution cannot be overlooked. These windows are a fascinating historical document.

Beyond the politics, religion and society of the Tudor period, the glass also reflects developments in art. Realism and perspective, the advances of the Renaissance, are evident throughout the scenes. The static human figures of the early Middle Ages, with their forms completely covered with drapes, are replaced by animated figures with exposed limbs. The ability to deploy perspective and to enliven the human form is seen everywhere, from the foreshortening of the table at the last supper to the scenes showing Paul fleeing down a rope from Damascus. The architecture visible in the background of some of the scenes, particularly those completed later on, marks the latest Renaissance style of building and, indeed, there are distinct changes in the buildings shown in the windows which reflect the development of architecture even over the short period of the glazing.

The King's College Chapel glazing is the finest possible demonstration of artistic skill from the early–mid sixteenth century, a time when chapels and cathedrals provided an important medium for the display of artistic ability. The dominant art form of the High Renaissance was soon to become painting, often with secular themes. The glass of this chapel caught the end of the period when art was still theocentric and focused on great religious buildings.

Threats to the glass

Although Cambridge churches and chapels suffered badly from iconoclasts during both the Reformation and the Civil War, these windows survived intact. The 'Parliamentary Visitor' William Dowsing, appointed in the 1640s to remove idolatrous imagery throughout the east of England, did considerable damage in Cambridge, but for reasons unknown, the glass was spared. Some suggest that the Puritans were more concerned with the destruction of more recently made images than those in the chapel, or even that the Christ's College graduate and Cromwell's Latin Secretary, John Milton, intervened to save them; either may explain their survival, but there might be other reasons. Dowsing's arrival at the chapel is recorded as being late on a winter's day, so it is possible that the depictions were not as clear as they might have been. There is also another, more mundane, possible explanation. Major General Crawford stationed some of his men and horses inside the chapel over the winter of 1644. The soldiers might have preferred to whitewash the stained glass rather than make their stay in the chapel still colder through destroying the windows. Evidence of the use of the chapel as barracks for Puritan soldiers was uncovered when the oak panoplies behind the stalls from the Stuart Restoration era were removed from the east end; a sketch of a prancing horse dated to this period can be seen clearly on the north wall near the altar. During the excavation to complete the changes at the east end in the late 1960s, the remains of charred chicken bones, dice and cards were also found.

The Second World War posed another threat to the glass. Members of Berkeley College, Yale, in New England met the cost of removing the glass, which was stored partly in the cellars beneath the neighbouring Gibbs Building and also in other safe underground places in Cambridge. The window spaces were filled with board and a small slit of clear glass to give some light; the chapel must have looked very dismal in those war years. The removal of the glass, however, did raise the question as to what would have been done with the glass had the chapel been flattened.

The glass was returned to the windows over five years following the end of the war, providing an opportunity to carry out restoration work in resecuring the glass and its fixings within the window tracery. One insurmountable problem was encountered: the face of the Virgin Mary shown in the Adoration of the Magi scene was somehow lost. In a startlingly different approach to conservation from that now current, the head of Saint Anne was removed from the window in the north-west corner and substituted for the lost face of Mary. The young Mary of the annunciation scene in the third window from the north-west corner has therefore aged dramatically by the time she is shown holding the infant Jesus in the fourth window. Without knowledge of this substitution, the casual observer might attribute the aging to the trials of childbirth in the Middle Ages.

The final and constant threat to the windows comes, of course, from their great age. The glass has been subjected to many bouts of restoration and repair; in particular, the fixtures securing the glass into the stone frequently require attention. Such ancient magnificence does not survive in such a glorious state without a huge and continuous programme of repairs.

The choir and change

The chapel's fame has spread from the brilliance of its architecture, stonework and stained glass to embrace its music. The organ above the screen separating the east and west ends of the chapel dates from the late 1600s; the first organ, installed in 1606, was dismantled during Cromwell's Protectorate. It has subsequently been refitted three times; the two gilded trumpeting angels which have adorned its top since the 1860s were an innovation of George Gilbert Scott's.

The famous Christmas Eve Festival of Nine Lessons and Carols started in 1918; it has been broadcast on radio since the 1920s and on television since the early 1960s, although the televised service is recorded several days before the concert on Christmas Eve. The boy who sings the solo opening verse of the first carol is not chosen until almost the last moment, apparently while the choir is gathering at the west end, in order to spread 'pre-concert nerves' equally among all the boys.

The choir sit in stalls along the chapel's long axis after the fashion of monasteries, reading their music by candlelight. The candles are now smokeless and will not contribute again to the blackening of the ceiling. The stalls and the misericords were installed in the early 1530s, as was the screen. The panelling behind the choir, which lines the north and south walls, dates from a hundred years later; the canopies above the misericords were put in a little later again, a few years after the Restoration of the Stuarts in the 1660s.

The appearance of the sanctuary has changed immensely since the late 1960s, when the Rubens painting of the Adoration of the Magi was placed beneath the east window. It was commissioned in the 1630s by a nunnery at Louvain in northern Belgium; purchased from the Duke of Westminster by Major Allnatt in 1959, it was later given to the college. It was one of those presents that should be feared for the expense which follows in its wake, as it made necessary a thorough redesign of the east end. The painting did not fit in the space between the base of the east end window and the floor; therefore, the floor was lowered. The seventeenth-century oak wall lining, which had stretched much nearer to the east end than it does today, had to be removed and new wall benches were required. Then it was found that the central heating system was incompatible with the timber on which Rubens had painted, so that too was entirely changed.

The reworking of the east end that the Rubens painting provoked has been much criticised: architectural purists argued that a Baroque painting had no place in a Renaissance chapel, while others more concerned with religion argued that great art was being favoured over correct liturgical practice. It is as well to remember that the internal architecture of the chapel, particularly the altar, the organ and the choir, has been changed many times. The alteration of the chapel sanctuary has a long history which stretches back to Edward VI in the 1540s. The chapel's original high altar above several steps in the chancel was installed in the 1530s when the country was still Catholic; the severely Protestant Edward VI in 1549 ordered the removal of the steps and altar; Catholic Mary authorised their return. They were finally removed and destroyed during Elizabeth's reign. Then, during the Commonwealth, the organ was dismantled. As at Peterhouse and Trinity chapels, the architecture of King's College Chapel reflected national events. The university has always eventually had to adjust to a ruling elite which has never, even to this day, been much concerned with the technical legal independence of the university and its colleges.

King's College Chapel and its critics

Every monarch since Henry VI has visited King's College Chapel: it is a building which could never have been built without the power of monarchs. Despite the taller towers designed by the Gilbert Scotts at St John's and the University Library, it still grasps the eye of the traveller drawing close to Cambridge. It has survived virtually as it was first designed – and astonishingly well, considering that the foundations of oyster shell and lime mortar barely reach five feet underground.

The chapel's expense and troubled initial history are forgotten when confronted with the magnificence of the building; indeed, it is so spectacular that some, like the Spanish philosopher George Santayana, who studied at King's in 1897, considered that 'the birds are not worthy of the cage'. This was not at all the point according to Abbot Suger, the twelfth-century French architect of Saint Denis. He wrote that 'The dull mind rises to the truth through material things': Cambridge students have unrivalled opportunities to cast aside their dullness. Yet, despite widespread admiration, the chapel has drawn criticism. Some, in reference to the pinnacles along the north and south walls, have dismissed it as a giant cradle, to others it is simply a huge structure decorated with pepper pots, while John Ruskin thought it more like a dining table turned on its back. William Burgess, an architect of the mid-1800s, considered it a 'wonderfully over-praised building', while a previous critic referred in the seventeenth century to the 'tedious repetition of roses which are but heavy and unpleasing ornaments'. Neither was the Victorian architect and designer Augustus Pugin overly impressed. He still thought it was 'a stupendous building', but it was of a Gothic style which had gone wrong, as it lacked pointed arches and a 'lofty groin' above its tall walls; he did not like the relatively flat fan-vaulted ceiling. To most people, these criticisms are incomprehensible; for them the chapel is simply a glorious achievement and the crown on top of Cambridge's fine gathering of architectural masterpieces.

The modern role of the college chapels

The medieval scholar viewing the colleges of the twenty-first century would be astonished by the physical changes to colleges and their chapels. Comfort drawn from the familiar external structure of the older chapels, such as Trinity Hall, Christ's and Magdalene, would be tempered by their altered interiors. Of the chapels built before the 1600s, King's would offer the least change, although its east end would shock.

Equally surprising would be the absence of chapels and chaplains from some colleges – Hughes Hall, New Hall and Lucy Cavendish have neither. There would be immense astonishment from scholars who had to sign up to the Thirty Nine Articles and the Act of Supremacy in the sixteenth century that three colleges – Churchill, Robinson and Fitzwilliam – have ecumenical chaplaincies.

The diminished role in the scholars' lives now played by college chapels would also be confusing. Certainly, the grand events of a college calendar, such as the commemoration of college benefactors and services to admit new fellows and scholars, are still marked in chapel. Weddings and baptisms, which would render speechless the celibate medieval scholars, are also celebrated and, since women have joined the colleges, some competition has arisen over access for wedding services. Delightful Evensong services are held throughout the week in term, as are other services of the canonical hours, such as Compline. The high points of the ecclesiastical calendar are also observed magnificently. Nonetheless, the chapels have undeniably been pushed to the periphery of the modern scholar's life. During past centuries they were central to the existence of the academic community, causing nearly all of them to be extended or rebuilt at some point. The pressure in modern times is just to keep them in good repair.

College chapels provided an opportunity to employ the country's greatest architects and artists; their work in stone and glass has been magnificent. Now artists must look beyond the college chapels or the towns' churches for patronage; opportunities to create masterpieces of stained glass are few now that colleges' appetite to change their chapels has disappeared. The great partnership at King's of Vellert and Flower, artist and glazier, has echoes in those more modern ones of Edward Burne-Jones and William Morris at All Saints, of George Bodley and C.E. Kempe at Queens' and of John Piper and Patrick Reyntiens, the stained glass artist, at Robinson.

It is now the college libraries, not the chapels, which are most likely to attract patronage. Graham Jones and Patrick Reyntiens' work at the Jesus Quincentennial library and the Von Stockhausen glass in the recent Pembroke library extension mark two recent occasions where high-quality stained glass art has been commissioned for such buildings.

Provided the maintenance bills can be met, it is difficult to imagine the chapels changing significantly over the next few hundred years. Their construction and alterations over centuries explain much about the past of the university and in some cases, as at Trinity College, Peterhouse and King's chapels, about the country. They will hopefully remain an inspiration to great music and as deeply moving places of religion. However, although historians have found reflections of the great issues which faced this country within them, it is unlikely that the chapels will reflect the issues of the future.

Chapter 5

The Medieval Soul

The town's medieval soul is perpetuated through its churches. They reflect the independent community which existed before the university; fifteen of them survive in the old town. Religious buildings, particularly cathedrals and parish churches of the Middle Ages, were constructed with the goodwill and involvement of the local community: they were, as the architectural historian Alain Erlande-Brandenburg has described, 'living concepts' which were at the centre of urban life. Victor Hugo popularised this theme in his 1831 novel *Notre Dame de Paris* through the idea that cathedrals and churches were 'social creations'; even in the twenty-first century, writers on cathedrals subtitle their books as biographies. Most religious buildings are an expression of the will, energy and wealth of the people; such was the case in medieval Cambridge.

A very different spirit had driven the construction of the college chapels in Cambridge. They were meant to reduce contact between the college members and the local people, and their construction reflected not the prosperity of the local community, but rather the wealth of the college patron. The building of King's College Chapel, for example, so nearly a cathedral in many respects, had caused deep resentment among the host community.

Besides reflecting the local community, the churches of Cambridge also nurtured national movements and witnessed events of historical significance. St Edward's, near King's Parade, was a haven for sixteenth-century reformers, while Holy Trinity Church was the hub of the nineteenth-century missionary movement. At other times Cardinal Wolsey and Oliver Cromwell each stormed up the nave of Great St Mary's to express their dissatisfaction with the religious affiliations of Cambridge folk.

In the Round Church and St Bene't's, Cambridge possesses two churches of great architectural interest. Still others, such as All Saints, Emmanuel United Reform Church and St Botolph's, have important nineteenth-century internal decoration. Simply the great age of two others – the Church of St Andrew the Less (once part of the eleventh-century Barnwell Priory) and the Leper Chapel, which are near Newmarket Road, on the east side of town – provide significant connections to the ancient past of this country.

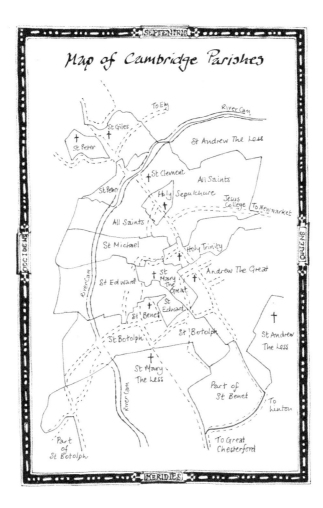

Illustration 5.1: Map of Cambridge parishes.

Churches of political interest

One of Cambridge's most significant churches, St Edward King and Martyr, is tucked into the alleyways between King's Parade and the Guildhall, the narrow passages which access it perhaps giving a flavour of how the medieval town might have appeared. Its dedication is to the young English king of the tenth century who was murdered by opponents within his family. The church passed from the diocese into the private ownership of Trinity Hall when the parish church of St John Zachary was pulled down to make way for the buildings of King's College in the 1440s. Trinity Hall, after paying Henry VI for the privilege, then shared the church with Clare College and the parishioners.

Illustration 5.2: The Leper Chapel: built in the early twelfth century, it is still clearly visible, as it was always meant to be, from the road (now Newmarket Road) leaving Cambridge to the east.

In 1446, Bishop Bourchier of Ely agreed that, as St Edward's was a private (or 'peculiar') church, divine services could be performed there 'without prohibition, molestation or contradiction from anybody'. This enabled Hugh Latimer, Bishop of Worcester, as well as other reformers such as Robert Barnes, Thomas Bilney and William Tyndale – men who were instrumental in the English religious revolution of the 1500s – to speak there against the corruption of the Catholic Church without risk of censure. Indeed, Latimer was mocked for preaching to 'butchers' at St Edward's. Corn Exchange Street, which was once known as Butchers' Row, is only a moment's walk away from St Edward's; its tradesmen, and those of Hog Hill (now Downing Street), probably did listen to Latimer. Eventually these reformers, together with Nicholas Ridley, who had been Master at Pembroke College, were each to die at the hands of Catholics for their beliefs. St Edward's still has the oak pulpit, with its fine linen-fold moulding, from which the reformers preached. It attracts a rent of a shilling per annum paid to its owner, King's College; a member of that college had found it in a scrapyard in the 1800s.

The first church on this site was burnt down in the great fire of 1197; the church now dates mostly from 1400, although by 1470 Clare and Trinity colleges had broadened the north and south aisles to provide space for their members. The building now appears in good condition, but its demolition was discussed in the nineteenth century as the building was then at the point of collapse. Repairs were effected, although the once-perilous angle of the northern pier of the early-fifteenth-century chancel is still obvious on entering the church from the west door. The carpenters who worked on the well-preserved wagon timber roof were evidently more skilled.

Great St Mary's, opposite the Senate House at the end of King's Parade, also witnessed events of national importance surrounding the religious upheavals of the sixteenth and seventeenth centuries. Cardinal Wolsey came to the church in 1521 to stamp out the spread of the Lutheran heresy: the works of Luther were burnt outside the church, attendance by local people at this spectacle being boosted through the supply of free ale. There have been other, similar, ceremonies here. One concerned the religious reformer Martin Bucer, a follower of Calvin and one of Edward VI's tutors, who worshipped at Great St Mary's. He was buried there but on the orders of Mary Tudor his remains were dug up and burnt outside the church in 1557; his ashes may have been collected in some manner, as a brass plaque on the south side of the chancel marks their supposed reinterment during Elizabeth's reign. Finally, around a century later, Oliver Cromwell ordered the burning of the Book of Common Prayer in the chancel to symbolise the imposition of puritan practices upon Cambridge people.

The university Senate met in the church to arrange the university's business until the 1730s, when the Senate House was built; hence it is also known as the University Church. The vocabulary used by the academics – meetings in Senate are still referred to as 'Congregations' and a motion put to the vote as a 'Grace' – reflects the close links of the university to the established religion.

As the University Church, Great St Mary's had a variety of other roles connected with the life of the scholars. For several centuries its bells rang from 9 p.m. until 9.15 p.m. every day to summon students back to their colleges, a custom which ceased only in 1939, when the mixture of bells and air-raid sirens was considered unwise. It is also the point from which the distance to students' dwellings is measured; a university statute, no longer enforced, requires that all its junior members live within five miles of the church. The strong room at the foot of the church tower housed the university chest which held its silver and records.

Great St Mary's was constructed in the late fifteenth and early sixteenth centuries on ground where a Saxon church, presumably built of wood, had been destroyed by fire during 1291 – plague, fire and riots were endemic in Cambridge, as in other towns, for centuries. Like its near neighbour King's College Chapel it is built in the perpendicular style, but more modestly. The resources the town could command were evidently less than those at the disposal of the Crown; the crenellated profiles of its north and south sides do not seize the eye as do the pinnacles of King's. In the early 1500s the aisles were redesigned and extended at the same time as the roof was constructed using oak trees presented by Henry VII. In fact, the king had had the trees harvested without permission from a forest at Great Chesterford owned by the Abbey of Westminster; the parish records contain a subsequent letter of apology from this parsimonious monarch. Later in the same century, Archbishop Parker approved a contract for an eighty-foot spire on top of the tower, which was never constructed. There was another plan, inspired by the artist-in-residence at Christ's, to place a spire on top of the tower to mark the university's 800th anniversary. Incorporating a 'camera obscura', it was to have been a temporary addition to the Cambridge skyline; the project was eventually abandoned.

Inside there are two organs, one at the east end and the other at the west. The latter, now known as the university organ, was installed in 1697. In the late 1800s, however, the university refused to contribute to its repair, prompting the parish to install a second organ; only then did the university fund repairs to the original organ. The pulpit is remarkable in that it slides on steel runners from the side to the centre of the nave: there are very few such pulpits in the country. The natural light in the church has been much reduced by the galleries which were fitted in 1735 to accommodate the members of the university; there are many references in the church archives before that time to 'scaffolds' and 'temporary galleries' being erected.

Churches of architectural and artistic interest

Other parish churches, while of less political importance, are of great architectural and cultural significance. One is St Bene't's, situated in Bene't Street, which leads to King's Parade. Its Anglo-Saxon tower was constructed between 1030 and 1050, although the other main parts of the church date from the fourteenth and nineteenth centuries. Part of the charm of the tower is the ease with which Saxon building methods can be understood. The tower, as it does at St Edward's, rises in three visible stages, diminishing in size with height. It displays that diagnostic Anglo-Saxon architectural feature 'long and short work', in which the quoins at each corner of the tower are positioned alternately vertically and horizontally.

The tiny round openings at the top of the tower demonstrate the Saxon concern that openings in walls compromised the integrity of a building. The holes, which let in owls hunting mice, are worked out of single pieces of stone to minimise the stress to the tower's façade. They are also high in the tower, so that the weight above them was the slightest possible. The two lancet windows directly beneath the round holes are from the thirteenth century, while the double-arched larger openings, one on each side of the tower, were added at the time of the Reformation in the sixteenth century to allow the sound of the bells to reach out into the parish.

A plaque of 1931 inside the tower marks the restoration of the church bells and the 300th centenary of Fabian Stedman's birth. Stedman was parish clerk here in the 1670s and has traditionally been considered as the inventor of a system of change ringing known to campanologists as the Stedman Peal. Since then, however, it has been acknowledged that a different Fabian Stedman – one from Herefordshire – is probably the person responsible for this bell-ringing innovation; the plaque however, remains. There are six bells in the tower, the oldest dating from 1588. As is often the case, each bell has a charming inscription: bell number three, which dates from 1603, carries the message: 'Of all the bells in Benet I am the best. And yet for my casting the Parish paid the lest'. Its tonality is now thought to be poor but perhaps its jaunty claim was once justified.

Between the tower and the nave there is a Romanesque arch with mouldings of two fearsome beasts. This was the style of architecture used within the Carolingian Empire of Charlemagne; that such architectural features could be found in Cambridge during the eleventh century shows how well trade had connected the town to the culture of mainland Europe. Even before the arrival of the scholars, Cambridge had been no cultural backwater.

Illustration 5.3: The Round Church, built between 1113 and 1140: it is one of five remaining medieval round churches in England.

Steps reach down five feet from modern Bene't Street to the Saxon street level and church graveyard. An old parish water pump stands alongside the graves, and water filtered down into the well below through bodies buried in the graveyard, a situation that reflects the level of medical knowledge in those times. The small patch of grass between the pump and the gravestones also happens to be the most central piece of grass in Cambridge on which visitors may stand without provoking apoplexy in a college porter.

In the early twelfth century the Normans built a round church dedicated to the Holy Sepulchre at the junction of St John's Street and Bridge Street. It marked the northern boundary of the medieval town; travellers would have offered thanks there for a journey safely passed, or prayed for a safe one to come. Although initially built as a wayside chapel for travellers, and maintained by the monks of the nearby St John's Hospital, it later became a parish church.

This church is one of five such round medieval churches in England – the others are the Temple Church off Fleet Street in London, St Sepulchre's in Northampton, St John the Baptist in Little Maplestead, Essex, and one, now ruined, in Ludlow Castle. Round churches were favoured by the crusading orders the Knights Hospitaller and Templar, probably because the shape replicated that of the Church of the Holy Sepulchre in Jerusalem, constructed by the Emperor Constantine over the tomb of Jesus. As a circle has neither beginning nor end, so a round church symbolises the eternity of God. In this case, however, the Round Church appears to have been constructed by a local guild called the Confraternity of the Holy Sepulchre, who may have had some connection with the Holy Land.

Like St Bene't's, it is of great architectural interest. The entrance has the deep zigzag ornament which is typical of Norman architecture. It is a thick-walled building, barely half the height of the

Anglo-Saxon tower of St Bene't's; the Normans used the thickness of their walls to compensate for their inattention to foundations.

In the fifteenth century the church was extended to the north-east, and a taller octagonal tower, with a crenellated top, was constructed above the Norman church. In the 1840s the height of the tower was reduced and the present conical roof and bell turret were added in an attempt to recapture its medieval appearance. More restoration of the Round Church was required in 1942 after the east end of the fifteenth-century extension, along with the Union building behind, was damaged by incendiary bombs.

As at St Bene't's, the visitor is required to step down from the street level of twenty-first-century Cambridge in order to enter the church. Inside there was probably an altar in a small apse opposite the west door at which travellers prayed. Heads, carved in stone, stare impassively down from the stonework above eight massive stone columns barely four feet apart with small windows above. Sadly, sketches from the 1800s reveal that the faces are not those of long-dead Norman people; they date only from the church's Victorian restoration, suggesting that the original ones had deteriorated beyond repair. There are some rare carved wooden angels from the fifteenth century in the beams of the north aisle timber roof: rare because of the efficiency with which Cromwell's puritans destroyed such 'idolatrous' imagery.

The Round Church is the second most visited place in Cambridge after King's College Chapel; it has also attracted an enthusiastic evangelical congregation which outgrew the church in the 1990s and moved to the then redundant St Andrew's the Great, opposite Christ's College. As a result, the Round Church is now a heritage centre, with some excellent displays about the country's religious history.

The third church whose architecture captures attention is All Saints in Jesus Lane. Built in the 1860s, it is opposite the entrance of Jesus College and was, therefore, long referred to by Jesuans as 'St Opps'. The decline of active membership of the Church of England combined with the expansion of the two neighbouring colleges of Sidney Sussex and Jesus into the domestic buildings near to the church made survival for All Saint's too difficult. It was declared redundant in 1973.

An earlier All Saints Church had flourished for many centuries at the west end of the parish, in St John's Street, but by the mid-1800s it was considered too small for its parishioners. The old All Saints graveyard in Trinity Street has been kept as a small park, which is often used to host craft fairs. A memorial cross designed by Basil Champneys has been left there to mark the original church and the neighbouring alleyway linking Trinity Street with Sidney Street is still called All Saints Lane. This part of medieval Cambridge was once the Jewish quarter. It was also where Thomas Cranmer, when a fellow at Jesus College, came during the 1520s to romance Black Joan, his first wife and the daughter of the landlord of the Dolphin Inn.

The Victorian architect G.F. Bodley built the new church of All Saints, an outstanding Gothic Revival church, on a small patch of land in Jesus Lane given to the parish by Jesus College. Bodley felt that suburban churches should be part of the community, so the church was placed right up to the pavement, although given the size of the plot there was little alternative. He also wished to give the impression of a church which had evolved within its community over centuries; hence the south aisle might once, he attempts to suggest, have been the nave of a smaller church before its extension to meet the needs of a growing parish. This is why there is no 'balancing' north aisle, and why the tracery in the windows of the south aisle has the detail of the early Gothic period. The main nave is much taller, with decorated window tracery, suggesting

Illustration 5.4: The west end of All Saints Church, drawn from inside the court of the theological college Westcott House.

it was added later, and to add a final touch of authenticity the tracery of the windows in the spire is of a style from the very end of the decorated period. Unusually, the tower is placed directly over the chancel, and, in order to give adequate width inside the church, is actually rectangular rather than square, though a single pinnacle disguises its asymmetry. The tower, with the prominent ribbed spire above, has made the church a Cambridge landmark. There are very few spires in Cambridge; Oxford is the university of spires. The specialities of Cambridge are solid imposing towers and small practical pinnacles which help hold a building upright – perhaps in keeping with the generally serious and practical nature of the Cambridge academician.

Funding for the new church was difficult to obtain and the internal decoration took more than thirty years to complete. The total cost mounted to £5,000. Nonetheless, the interior stuns visitors who are accustomed to the decorative restraint of post-Reformation English churches. The old All Saints had been an Anglo-Catholic church and these practices were taken to Jesus Lane; the new internal decoration fits the 'high church' beliefs of the Tractarian movement. The ceiling and walls are a mass of vivid colour in a variety of designs, decorated as if they were of a Catholic church of medieval England. The artisans even used medieval methods of decoration to increase the appearance of authenticity: the glass of the east window and the windows by C.E. Kempe were completed using the rediscovered medieval 'silver-stain' method of glazing, which permitted a wider variety of colour. The portrayal of Christ in Majesty painted above the main rood screen by Wyndham Hope Hughes used the tempera technique (pigments mixed with egg yolk), which had been used in the Middle Ages before the discovery of oil-based paints. Paintings using the tempera technique, which change less over time than those executed in oil colours, appealed to these craftsmen of the Pre-Raphaelite movement, who wished to capture the permanence of medieval culture.

There are two rood screens in the church: the one in the south nave was inserted to give the impression that it had once led to an altar in this supposedly earlier part of the church. A pulpit designed, with his trademark attention to detail, by Bodley was beautifully decorated by Hope Hughes in 1875. William Morris, Edward Burne Jones and Ford Maddox Brown all contributed to the design of the glass and the decoration of the walls and roof. The east end window, which portrays Christ in Majesty surrounded by the saints, combines the work of each of them. The faces of the saints are intensely human; they symbolise the link between craftsmanship and humanity, which this group of artists sought to shelter from the onslaught of the Industrial Revolution. The portrait of St Peter, holding the keys, is a likeness of William Morris himself. His company was so busy at this time that it reused the cartoons of the common figures, and there are supposedly over seventy portrayals of St Peter with the features of Morris around the country, all made in his workshop; so many, indeed, that he was perhaps at odds with the Pre-Raphaelites' hostility to the mass-production methods of Victorian England.

William Morris designed the wall decorations, which were then executed by his company and local craftsmen from the Leach Studio. Those on the long north and south walls are stencilled, but the black pomegranates placed against a richly red background on the west wall were completed by hand. Pomegranates feature in many Renaissance religious paintings; when shown cut open with the seeds exposed, as in this church, they represent the suffering and resurrection of Christ. The floor tiles come from Minton and Hollins, a frequent supplier to Bodley; their manufacture, too, was inspired by medieval techniques, using pigments mixed with beeswax and keyed into the tile through heat. As with tempera paints, these encaustic tiles were made to last.

Bodley, Morris and Burne Jones also helped restore Jesus Chapel, on the other side of the road from All Saints, some fifteen years later. The work of Burne Jones in the chapel's nave windows displays a more mature style, using far richer colours and greater movement in the figures than is seen at All Saints. It is a further fascination of Cambridge that there are two places so close together where the evolution of the Pre-Raphaelite style can be observed.

All Saints' Church shares with other famous Cambridge buildings, including King's College Chapel, a remarkable architectural consistency despite the length of time each of these projects took to complete. In contrast, however, to the chapels of King's or, indeed, Trinity, both of which were started and finished by different patrons with opposing faiths, the building of All Saints was guided consistently by the beliefs of the Tractarians and the principles of the Pre-Raphaelites.

After the church was declared redundant, it deteriorated badly. Before it was rescued by the Redundant Churches Fund in 1981, its nave was almost replaced by an office block and, after that project was thwarted, it was suggested that the entire church be converted into a college library for Jesus. It is now in excellent condition, with the official designation of 'redundant' belied by the many secular and religious activities which take place there.

Bodley, along with the local craftsman F.R. Leach, also decorated the interiors of other parish churches in Cambridge. One of them is St Botolph's, built at the Trumpington Gate on the western edge of the old town, where Silver Street now meets Trumpington Road. Like the Round Church to the north, it was a place of prayer for travellers: St Botolph, a seventh-century East Anglian saint, was a patron saint of travellers, and a dedication to him is common for churches placed at the gates of an old city. London once had four such named churches at its gates; one survives to greet those using Liverpool Street Station near Aldgate. It, too, like St Botolph's in Cambridge, welcomes East Anglian travellers.

As with other ancient churches in Cambridge, it is probable that a church of Norman or perhaps even Saxon date stood on the same site. Parts of the present building are particularly old; the nave and aisle date from the 1320s. Neighbouring Corpus Christi College first supported the church, but patronage passed to Queens' College in the 1400s. The rood screen of St Botolph's is the oldest in Cambridge; it was installed in the fifteenth century, although the paintings on the screen were not completed until the nineteenth century. There is also a rare baptismal font from the 1600s, which was designed in the manner approved by Archbishop Laud to restore beauty to acts of Anglican worship. The church bells were installed in 1460.

St Botolph's Church has stained glass, mainly from the Victorian era, of the highest quality. In the 1880s C.E. Kempe completed a window in the north aisle depicting the Crucifixion, beneath which is a portrayal of the Pelican in Piety, in which the bird is shown pecking at its own breast to feed its young. This allegory of the body of Christ and the Crucifixion is also the emblem of the neighbouring college, Corpus Christi, although the presence of this particular image in the church probably reflects a relationship to the medieval guild of Corpus Christi, rather than link to the college that had formerly supported the church. A decorative 'B' in the Kempe window marks this church's collegiate loyalty to St Bernard, who is associated with Queens' College. The quality of the Kempe window contrasts with a less impressive window a few feet away, which was completed in the same period by a local company, W.H. Constable. Constable still trades in Cambridge, but now focuses on the artistically less demanding business of double glazing.

Bodley also worked in this church; he rebuilt the chancel in the 1870s. Chancels often required rescuing in Victorian times as, after the Reformation, this domain of the priest had often been abandoned while church services were moved into the nave of the church. The focus has been on the pulpit and meeting table rather than the altar. Abandoned chancels, some even bricked in, often came near to collapse at this time in English churches. At St Botolph's the roof has been conserved in recent years and further efforts to preserve the church's beauty are now being led by some of the members of neighbouring Corpus Christi College. Although the west door to its bright interior is usually open, visitors to Cambridge too often ignore this beautiful church, lured away by the sight of King's College Chapel and the Senate House further up King's Parade.

Oases of old Cambridge

There are yet other Cambridge churches which witnessed the cultural turmoil of this country's past. On St Mary's Lane, just outside the old town boundaries and beyond St Botolph's, stands Little St Mary's church. The Parliamentary Visitor, as the official Puritan iconoclast William Dowsing was known, 'did brake down sixty superstitious images' in this church alone in the 1640s, but his visit has been shrugged off and its Anglo-Catholic soul rediscovered. Now it is, and this within a strong field of candidates, the most Catholic of all the places of worship in Cambridge.

Kempe worked here as well, designing the west and east windows; the east window, which shows the Annunciation, is judged among the very best of this artist's work. A small stained glass design was added in the twenty-first century on the north side: a beautiful modern depiction of the Eucharist by Caroline Benyon. There is a bell from the early 1600s above the north door, now hidden from view within a wooden structure, which carries the practical admonition in Latin that it 'tolls not for the souls of the dead but the ears of the living'.

The wilderness garden in this church's cemetery is a peaceful enclave seemingly far from the hubbub of Trumpington Road. The narrow street alongside which the church lies once led down to the wharves by the River Cam and the old church and the terraced houses have a similar feel of medieval Cambridge as do the alleyways around St Edward's.

The Pre-Raphaelites also worked within the Emmanuel United Reform Church, which stands across the lane opposite Little St Mary's. The firm of William Morris completed the glass windows to commemorate six prominent puritans associated with Cambridge, among whom were Milton and Cromwell.

These beautiful old churches survive only by the efforts of small bands of dedicated supporters. Only one, St Peter's up near Castle Hill, has fallen into disuse, although it is cared for by the Church Conservation Trust and retains the feel of a small village church in a rural setting. Its structure dates chiefly from the eleventh and eighteenth centuries.

The three redundant churches of Cambridge are All Saints, St Peter's and St Michael's. The Church Conservation Trust is working successfully to re-establish the place of All Saints within the Cambridge community and also cares for St Peter's, while St Michael's in Trinity Street has been reborn as a pleasant city-centre café. Religious services are still conducted in the chancel of this church, while the nave provides a delightful contrast to the anodyne coffee-chain franchises which surround the Market Square.

The founder of Michaelhouse College, one of the predecessors of Trinity College, paid for St Michael's to be rebuilt in the 1320s. The chancel is large in relation to the nave because the church was designed to serve both a college and a parish; until Gonville Hall had its first college chapel in the 1390s, its members also worshipped there. The choir is fitted with misericords from King's Hall's chapel, which was closed at the time of Trinity College's foundation. St Michael's was restored and redecorated in the late 1800s by George Gilbert Scott the younger and F.R. Leach: fine examples of their decorative scheme are now within

Illustration 5.5: St Peter's Church on Castle Hill, the road leading north out of Cambridge. It is another of the surprisingly rural corners which can still be found in the centre of Cambridge.

the Ladies' and Gentlemen's lavatories. The latter even has a tombstone of a lady from the eighteenth century embedded above the urinals, as if her spirit is ensuring nothing untoward takes place there.

Those looking after some other churches have also had to be flexible in order to ensure these buildings' survival. For example, the maintenance of St Clement's in Bridge Street is now shared between the Anglican Church and the Greek Orthodox Church. The church was once in the patronage of Jesus College although St John's College acquired most of the property around it; the survival of the church was then made more difficult by the college's destruction of a large number of good townhouses on the south-east side of Bridge Street in the 1930s to provide an ugly service access area to the rear of their North Court, at a stroke displacing much of the church's congregation.

The evangelicals

Two churches on the evangelical wing of the Anglican community are thriving in Cambridge: they are the Church of the Holy Trinity, to the east of the Market Square, and St Andrew the Great, opposite Christ's College. They have the robust support of active congregations.

An outstanding evangelical, Charles Simeon, ran the parish of Holy Trinity for fifty-five years from the late 1700s, inspiring students to devote their lives to missionary work in the East. He studied at King's College and was then appointed as a young man to Holy Trinity against the wishes of the parishioners. At first, the pew holders locked their box pews, refusing to attend. (These pews have long since been removed by the Victorians; however, his teapot and umbrella – the latter is claimed to be the first seen in Cambridge – are kept in the vestry.) Eventually, however, his goodness won over the local people. The pulpit on which this modest man had had carved the words from the Gospel of St John 12:21, 'Sir, we would see Jesus', has not survived; the words were to remind him whom it was people came to find. However, he is remembered through a modest memorial in King's College Chapel; near the west door his initials and the date of his death, 1836, are embedded in the stone floor. He was the spiritual father of Henry Martyn, who had been a student at St John's in the late 1790s and later worked as a missionary in the Far East.

The impact of Simeon is possibly still felt in Cambridge, as the town retains a reputation for the size and robustness of its evangelical congregations. That there are fifteen parish churches crammed into the confines of the small medieval town may also have a hand in explaining why Cambridge has not experienced the dramatic decline in church attendance that has affected the rest of the country.

Since the Anglican monopoly on worship at the university was removed at the end of the nineteenth century, choice of religious worship is just one more course in the cultural feast set before the fortunate modern students of the university. Centuries ago the building of private chapels by the colleges reinforced their isolation from the townsfolk; indeed, an undergraduate hearing Charles Simeon preach at Holy Trinity in the early 1800s invited the offensive taunt of being a 'Sim'. Today, without compulsory chapel attendance, some of these churches are providing a connection between town and gown, as they did in the university's earliest days. For those young students seeking certainties in a chaotic age at an unsettled time of their lives, the evangelicals at Holy Trinity and St Andrew the Great have much to offer and both churches draw large numbers of students. The conservative end of the theological spectrum, which offers firm boundaries determining both behaviour and belief, has proved attractive to young members of the university. Conversely, college chaplains offer a more liberal, less certain, approach to Christianity. The electoral roll of Holy Trinity parish provides another example of the university's domination of the old town, as for many years now none of the roughly 150 communicants who qualify for the Parochial Church Council have lived within the parish boundaries.

The disappeared

The spirit of the church of St John Zachary, which had stood in the way of Henry VI's grand plans for King's College in the 1440s, survives; its destruction and replacement by the peculiar church St Edward's ensures

– ironically, through the latter's cultural importance – that the earlier church is remembered.

Lost territory of two other parishes is recalled through the striking of the bells of Trinity College Clock Tower in Great Court. This famous court was crafted out of territory once claimed by the parishes of All Saints and St Michael's. The Clock Tower, before it was moved back twenty yards in the early 1600s to create the Great Court, stood on the boundary between the parishes. The boundary between the two parishes remains etched on the stonework of the west-facing side of Trinity's Wren Library. The double chime of its bells was introduced, however, only at the time of the overhaul of the clock in 1726. William Wordsworth heard these bells from the neighbouring college of St John's and used his autobiographical poem 'The Prelude' to record his own memory of them:

> Near me hung Trinity's loquacious clock,
> Who never let the quarters, night or day,
> Slip by him unproclaimed, and told the hours
> Twice over with a male and female voice.

The town's medieval soul

The parish churches are eloquent witnesses of the medieval town. Their number and quality reflect the great wealth of this part of England as well as the existence of a community which was independent of the university. Before the colleges could afford their own chapels the churches were a touching point between town and university, but now, in the mesmerising glare thrown out by the beauty of the university's buildings, the parish churches can be overlooked; yet they merit a place of their own.

Architecturally, these churches provide examples of practically every phase of English architecture over the past thousand years. Some have provided a canvas on which this country's Victorian artists worked; still others framed momentous historical events. Above all, these churches reflect the medieval life of the town. They show the extent to which religion dominated medieval life, where physical reminders of the threat of Hell and promise of Heaven were rarely far from the gaze of the people. At the opening of the fifteenth century, Cambridge boasted several monastic chapels, fifteen parish churches and eight college chapels. The melody of their bells on holy days must have been awe-inspiring. Although Gerald Manley Hopkins' description of a 'bell-swarmèd' place refers to nineteenth-century Oxford, it could equally have described medieval Cambridge.

Some of the town's churches are hidden away and difficult to find, or are open at unpredictable times. Huge secular edifices overshadow others. Yet the parish churches are worth seeking out. They are a fascinating part of the Cambridge story.

Chapter 6

The 'Unfinished Fabrick'

Nature bestowed little that is spectacular on Cambridge: its glories are man-made. The flat wetlands of the Fens were not a promising backdrop for the creation of so much beauty. While the land is certainly fertile and fascinating to wildlife enthusiasts, it does not offer much support to builders of great monuments, and the transformation of this damp windy island alongside the Fens in the cause of religion and learning has been remarkable. The Fens had their uses – they provided food, peat, roof thatch and, later, clay for bricks; but decent building stone was not among these resources.

Almost every notable aspect of Cambridge, from the people that settled there – whether armed invaders, traders, monks or scholars – to the stone which helped made the place so appealing, derives from outside the region. Even the huge numbers of trees now spread through the college gardens and town's parks are not, in the main, indigenous and, despite the best endeavours of town and university, Cambridgeshire still has the fewest trees of any English county.

Variety and competition

The nearest source of decent building stone, the Jurassic rock outcrop which runs from Portland on the south coast north-east through Oxford and Northampton to Yorkshire, bypasses Cambridge. Only clunch, a hard chalk, is found locally; it is an inferior building material.

The absence of good-quality local materials has contributed to the wide variety of stone used in Cambridge. The creamy Portland stone of the Senate House, the dark Ancaster stone at Caius and the golden hue of Clare's Ketton stone are mixed with buildings of red or yellow brick to make it a place of interesting contrasts. This variety, together with the diversity of architectural styles, contributes to the distinctive charm of the town.

The gathering of so many different architectural styles and materials has been possible because the community has been rich for so long; always one college or other has had the funds to indulge in the latest architectural fashion. Most cities in Britain, with their more ephemeral moments of glory, were able to

Illustration 6.1: The Senate House at the top of King's Parade, with the façade of Old Schools Building alongside. Both were completed in the first half of the eighteenth century using the then fashionable Portland stone.

purchase but one single style: places such as Stamford or Liverpool, for example, are defined architecturally by only one period. The wealth of the university ensures, as was noted by a fellow of Clare College in the late 1660s, that Cambridge will always have an 'unfinished fabrick', which is constantly renewed.

Another characteristic of Cambridge architecture is the tolerance that has been shown towards earlier buildings. There have been a number of grand building schemes which could have imposed a single style throughout the centre of town, but either the controversy they provoked or, more usually, the lack of funds for their execution meant that these plans came to naught. Instead, little pieces of Cambridge were reworked and new buildings were shaped to fit round those from earlier times.

Competition between colleges also provoked variations in the style, shape and size of buildings. The Gonville & Caius buildings of Tree Court, which stand at the junction of the Senate House Passage and Trinity Street, designed in the 1860s on a scale which challenged the restrained Classicism of its neighbour, James Gibbs' Senate House. It is even suggested that the tall, sculpted tower at the south-east corner of the court was added only so that it would reach above the tower of Great St Mary's. Similarly, the dimensions of St John's nineteenth-century chapel were not unconnected to the size of the older chapel of neighbouring Trinity College.

The competitive instinct over buildings was not limited to the university, however. When the town's Nonconformist community moved their place of worship in the 1870s from Downing Street, near Emmanuel College, to Trumpington Street, the brief to the architect was to design a tower which would exceed the height of its neighbours, Little St Mary's and Pembroke's Wren Chapel. Similarly, when the Catholic church of Our Lady and the English Martyrs was built in the late 1880s, its spire was designed to be a few feet higher than the one Bodley had placed above All Saints' Church. In more recent times, the modern tower of Addenbrooke's Hospital has outreached them all.

Transport costs, which for builders in Cambridge were always significant, often caused the use of different types of stone. Its most striking impact was the shift from the lighter stone (from Yorkshire) to the cheaper darker stone (from nearer Northamptonshire) at King's College Chapel. White Portland stone reached Cambridge only after the British navy controlled the channel from the early 1700s; before then, shipment from the south coast to King's Lynn was too hazardous to be economical. Similarly, the development of the railways added to the diversity of Cambridge building by making stone from the land-locked quarries of the South West accessible. The Pitt Building in Trumpington Street, which opened in the 1830s, was the first in Cambridge to use Bathstone.

The difficulty in obtaining stone also caused abandoned buildings to be used as surface quarries. Stone from Cambridge castle went to King's College Chapel in the late 1400s; a century later, Barnack stone from both Ramsey Abbey and Barnwell Priory was used to build Caius Court. In the mid-sixteenth century the Franciscan monastery was dismantled to build the chapel of Trinity College before the land itself was taken over by Sidney Sussex. The chipped edges on stones knocked out from the Franciscan monastery and the occasional exceptionally wide strip of mortar which made up for a stone slightly too small mark the places where materials had been found a second home.

The manner in which the different stones age has added still further variety. The Portland stone of the façade of King's Fellow's building facing the Backs retains its cream appearance, but on the side opposite King's Parade it is more black than cream. This 'golden stain of time', to use John Ruskin's reverential description of the imprint of pollution, is valued by some. King's Fellows – who once filled the bachelor premises within this building, but by 2009 were reduced to only three – recently voted down a proposal to clean the building, as the appearance of the restored Portland stone of neighbouring Senate House and Old Schools was considered rather vulgar.

Nature, of course, shaped Cambridge through the river beside which the medieval town grew up. Threading its way past several colleges, it dominates in a way which the River Cherwell does not in Oxford. Although nature may have deprived Cambridge of good building stone and provided only flat and relatively featureless terrain, the river has provided both an excuse for some attractive bridges, as well as an outstanding setting for the building projects of the riverside colleges.

The original river crossing was at the point where Magdalene Bridge now spans the Cam; its earlier name of the Great Bridge dated from the era when the fenland to the north was impassable and it was the town's widest and strongest bridge. Cromwell destroyed that bridge in the 1640s; the present one dates from 1823.

The only bridge Cromwell left standing was the then newly constructed one of Clare College, which is therefore the oldest and, many would claim, the most attractive. It was built by Thomas Grumbold; his relative Robert Grumbold built the three-arched Kitchen Bridge of St John's, so named because it lay in the path of an old medieval way, Kitchen Lane, another town thoroughfare consumed by a college. The design of this bridge is attributed to Christopher Wren.

St John's commissioned Henry Hutchinson in 1831 to build perhaps the best-known of the town's river crossings – the Bridge of Sighs. It connected their old courts with the new accommodation buildings on the other side of the river. Though it cannot compete with the beauty of, for example, the Venetian Ponte dei Sospiri, it adds charm to the river – and has provided a challenge for students: that of suspending various objects from its structure.

Illustration 6.2: The Bridge of Sighs (in the background) and the Kitchen Bridge (in the foreground); the latter leads to St John's Third Court.

The only bridge which might compete with the renown of the Bridge of Sighs is Queens' Mathematical Bridge, which was designed by William Etheridge and built in 1749 by James Essex. The present version was built in 1902 and certainly contains the nuts and bolts without which some claim the original was built. Its name probably derives from its geometric shape and may well be the source of the other canard about this bridge – that it was designed by Isaac Newton. In fact, Newton died before this bridge was first built.

A further bridge of interest, which was designed by Sir Edward Lutyens in 1959, crosses Silver Street. Records show that bridges, often two separate ones, spanned this part of the river by the King's Mill back into medieval times.

The absence of readily available stone has resulted in many buildings of brick in Cambridge. Whereas the budget of a king might run to stone, that of a monarch's consort reached only brick; Queens' College therefore used bricks while King's, also founded in the 1440s, purchased limestone. The bricks for Queens' were imported from the Low Countries, which, having geology similar to that of East Anglia, had already developed a more advanced brick industry than England possessed. The external south range of Queens' Front Court, facing Silver Street, has some of the earliest patterned brickwork in the country. Darker bricks make up lozenge patterns, referred to by architects as diapers, near the pavement. Along with the bricks, Cambridge imported Flemish building styles, such as Dutch gables and Flemish bond brickwork, which alternates header and stretcher bricks. However, by the time St John's was built fifty years later it was possible to use English bricks.

Examples also exist of poorer colleges choosing brick rather than stone. The Brick Building at Emmanuel College was commissioned from John Westley in the early seventeenth century. Forming a wing off the south of Emmanuel's Front Court, it has stepped and curved Dutch gables with attractive stone dressings. While the fellows of Emmanuel College made do with red bricks, richer colleagues at Clare College chose Ketton stone from Rutland for its Old Court, the east range of which was also designed by Westley.

Red bricks, so reminiscent of Tudor and Stuart England, fell out of fashion by the turn of the nineteenth century, and lighter-coloured bricks, which could be made from the local Gault clay, became modish. Many of the university's small administrative buildings, like those in Trumpington Street and Tennis Court Road, as well as the dons' villas beyond the Backs, use this material. It was not until the end of the 1880s that architects such as Alfred Waterhouse and Basil Champneys brought red brick back into fashion.

Twentieth-century buildings in Cambridge more often use brick, concrete or glass as their main building material, rather than stone. Nonetheless, Ketton limestone was used at Emmanuel's Queen's Building, which was designed by Michael Hopkins and finished in 1995; in the seventeenth century the college chapel had been built with the same stone. Two years earlier Quinlan Terry, one of Prince Charles's favoured neo-Classical architects, chose Bathstone for Downing College's library. More recently, limestone has been used at Caius' accommodation building in West Road, which opened in 2008.

Fittingly, the range of brick and stone used throughout Cambridge is captured in the Museum of Earth Sciences, which opened on the east side of Downing Street in 1904. The building was designed with forty-eight types of stone to make it, like Cambridge itself, a monument to the geology of Britain; the exterior is also an interesting example of the combination of stone with brick.

The domestic theme

Over centuries, the link connecting the style of Cambridge architecture was domestic, albeit with a distinct monastic influence. College communities, the most consistent patrons of architects, were, after all, places of domestic life as well as of learning, and the grand college entrances would have been recognisable to anyone familiar with the country homes of the medieval nobility.

College architecture retained the domestic theme up to the 1930s. Edwin Lutyens followed this tradition in designing Benson Court at Magdalene College in 1932. It was built opposite the main college entrance behind a row of sixteenth- and seventeenth-century buildings. Lutyens used hand-made red bricks in deference to the style of the college's First Court and also chose staircases, rather than corridors, in the manner of all the old courts. The building comprises one range of five sections, virtually identical both inside and out. Only the newel posts supporting the handrails at the bottom of each staircase distinguish one small entrance hallway from another. They carry carvings of different animals whose different shapes have served generations of Magdalene scholars to find, when too tired and emotional, the light switch.

Lutyens completed only one range of the three-sided court which had first been envisaged; another range had been planned along the south side of Magdalene Street, which would have destroyed the best example of medieval domestic buildings in Cambridge. Fortunately, college funds proved inadequate. If completed, the resulting court would have been exquisite, but another delightful footprint of old

Cambridge would have been lost. Lutyens' building is attractive, although, in one of those mystifying phrases which architectural critics employ, Nikolaus Pevsner described it as 'a little too convinced of itself'.

G.C. Drinkwater also designed an attractive brick building in the mid-1930s. Built for the undergraduates of Queens' College on the corner of the Backs and Silver Street, it was the first college building at the university to have bathrooms and lavatories on landings near the students' rooms. Although the university has always possessed domestic-looking buildings, the details of domesticity had, previously, been much neglected. Such innovation provoked jealous comments about the dominance of sanitary engineering over aesthetics. It began the removal of sleepy students trudging across old college courts in the early hours to communal bathrooms, which had been part of the scholar's rite of passage since the earliest days of the university.

Drinkwater used red brick to give the building a character appropriate to its setting in Queens', a college where this material dominates. The curved contour of the building actually follows a medieval tributary of the Cam; the latest piling technology was necessary to construct a secure building above such ground. Similar preparation had been required for the building of Wren's library at Trinity, which also borders the river.

Clare College, which commissioned Memorial Court, possesses an Old Court with a strikingly different architectural style – or rather styles. It was built over eighty years, from 1638 to 1707, by two architects, John Westley and Robert Grumbold, using Ketton stone. At first glance, because of its Classicism, symmetry and use of perspective, it appears to be almost Palladian. However, it is a collection of several styles: Mannerism is evident in the eclectic detail of the range containing the main college entrance and, through its swirls and arches, the Baroque influence is also clear. Its two gateways with Roman Classical arches even have the fan-vaulted ceilings of the perpendicular style of English Gothic. Now that neighbouring Trinity Hall has cut down some trees in its master's garden, the surprising nature of the north range of Clare's Old Court is evident to those walking across Garrett Hostel Bridge. Its extremely irregular profile, which dates from before Westley and Grumbold's work, is made of brick. It was probably left untouched when Old Court was built because the college had constructed a new hall, lodge and kitchen there after the college was devastated by fire in 1521; rather than rebuild relatively new buildings, the north-facing side of this range was left unaltered while the south-facing side was Classicised and used as the datum point from which to construct the much larger Old Court.

The challenge to domesticity

The link with domestic architecture was challenged in the 1930s by the construction of the University Library and Clare's Memorial Court. University buildings of earlier centuries, among them the Senate House, the Fitzwilliam Museum and the old University Library in Senate House Lane, cannot fairly be described as domestic; however, their scale and even their style fitted the domestic building tradition of colleges. These buildings of the interwar period clashed with that tradition. Neither building had any pretension to domesticity and, through their vast size, dominated the Backs.

Across the Backs, Clare's Memorial Court, a large building in a neo-Georgian style, was designed by Giles Gilbert Scott in the 1920s to cope with the increase in students who came up to Cambridge at that time. The vast triumphal arch that forms its entrance dwarfs its occupants, who are lodged in rooms in the three storeys of the building. It was the first move, much criticised at the time, to build beyond the Backs; but it proved a sensible decision which all the riverside colleges have followed. The building has proved very successful and is more attractive than many of the buildings the colleges erected a generation later to deal with the university's expansion following the Second World War.

Gilbert Scott also designed the University Library. Following the style of the Monumentalist and Brutalist schools, it proved controversial. At the opening ceremony in the mid-1930s King George V, struggling to find words of praise, referred to the tower rising high above the library's entrance as 'a fine erection', a comment which caused much amusement. Like others of Gilbert Scott's buildings, the interior works well for its users but the exterior attracts few admirers. Some compare his buildings to the vast buildings built by Communists in the capitals of Eastern Europe, while still others suggest that Gilbert Scott's design of the much-loved classic red 'K2' phone box in 1924 influenced the style of the library tower. Even the then headmaster of the Perse School wrote that 'the sight of such a building would deter a student from paying it a visit'. In fact, the building's narrow Roman bricks and Italianate roof, along with other pleasing architectural details, do reduce its severity, but it remains a very institutional building.

The grandfather of Giles Gilbert Scott, George, had also strengthened Cambridge's reputation as a place of towers in the 1860s with his design of St John's College's chapel. Neither of these towers attracted admirers – one denigrator wrote of the latter as being best appreciated during a day of thick fenland mist.

Giles Gilbert Scott's library seemed to release the inhibitions of those at the university who chose architects for the new building projects. The main building projects at that time were commissioned by the university's faculties and they, rather than the colleges, have fashioned the university's post-Second World War architecture.

With the old town unable to provide space for new building, the post-1945 expansion of the university has been to the west of the town. Many of these buildings are unseen by visitors, who congregate in the medieval town. Not only are they up to a few miles from the centre, but they often cannot even be seen from the roads leading into the town. The masterpieces of earlier centuries – the Senate House, King's College Chapel – can, in contrast, be admired from afar.

The university had taken centuries to expand westwards across the Cam. Although Magdalene College in the fifteenth and St John's New Court in the early nineteenth century had been built on the far side of the river, they were each barely a punt's length from the riverbank. It was not until the 1880s, when Newnham and Selwyn Colleges had been placed along the western edge of Cambridge near Grange Road, that the university made significant moves westwards away from the medieval town. By that time much of the area had been colonised by the academic staff, who had recently won permission to marry; but now the villas built for the academics have mostly been demolished to accommodate buildings of the late twentieth century.

Both Selwyn and Newnham Colleges lack that defining characteristic of old colleges – architectural variety. The buildings of colleges established from the end of the nineteenth century generally belong to one era and use one type of building material. These new colleges burst upon the university community. They were built to a complete, preconceived plan and immediately housed hundreds of scholars. Many consider these modern colleges to be less attractive than their predecessors because they are constructed in one style and generally did not have opportunities to recycle older buildings.

In contrast, the older colleges had grown slowly, opening with only a handful of scholars and barely any buildings. They often acquired existing buildings and then adapted or built around them. The Great Court of Trinity College, for example, is not a perfect square for this reason. It comprises buildings from five centuries and incorporates the remains of the two colleges which preceded it. Just inches behind the glass of the fourth top-floor window in the range to the west of Edward III's Clock Tower, there is ancient brickwork. It is the remains of the fourteenth-century King's Hall, around which Trinity's buildings have been woven. The college simply built over the buildings which it inherited. With similar flexibility, Jesus College adapted the nunnery's buildings. In another example, there are buildings from five centuries around Walnut Court in Queens' College. First there is a clunch wall from the 1400s just past the passageway from Old Court. To the west of this is the early-sixteenth-century Master's Lodge, while to the east is Walnut Tree Buildings, completed in 1616; a fire caused the top half of this building to be reconstructed 150 years later. On the north side is the chapel Bodley designed in the nineteenth century and then, finally, the Erasmus Building, designed by Basil Spence in 1959.

The tradition of building around old buildings or improving and adapting them is typical of Cambridge. The term 'palimpsest' is sometimes used to describe the university's physical structure: its original meaning refers to the way in which the ancients of the Classical world reused their parchment after scrubbing away the original writing: hence its application to Cambridge is clear.

Old Addenbrooke's Hospital in Trumpington Street provides another example of such recycling. During the mid-1990s the architect John Outram was engaged to convert it into the university's Institute of Management Studies. Its multi-coloured façade, which is still striking despite the even more colourful wishes of Outram being toned down, hides a stunning interior. There are numerous brightly decorated staircases in its main hall, which cross randomly in the space above; pillars reach up to a wooden ceiling, which is decorated as if it were a forest canopy above the vast tree trunks which carry the building's services. The library of Peterhouse, too, has been adapted from an earlier function: this building, on the edge of the Cam, was first a vinegar warehouse. It was then transformed by Basil Champneys into the University Museum of Archaeology, acquiring its nickname of the Ark, before its present incarnation as the college library. Gonville & Caius' library also started its life by combining the role of Geology Museum and research library for the university, before the English and Law Faculties kept their books there.

Architecture's big names: creating and funding new buildings

For centuries either the colleges or the university have employed the foremost architects of the day. Indeed, architects are keen to have a Cambridge building in their portfolio. Only a few of them, however, have received the ultimate accolade of having their building named after them. There is the Wren Library at

Illustration 6.3: The Fitzwilliam Dining Hall, designed by Denys Lasdun Associates in the 1960s.
The design combined the idea of a lantern opening above a dining hall with an allusion to monastic architecture made
through the parabolic arches.

Trinity College and the Essex Building at Queens'. King's has the Gibbs Building, while its Bodley Court is named after George Bodley. Magdalene has the Lutyens Building and Peterhouse the Burrough's Building.

Leading architects are still retained – as witnessed by the work of Edward Cullinan, Norman Foster, James Stirling and Quinlan Terry – but excellent buildings by the somewhat less famous have also been built in recent years. The firm of Allies and Morrison completed the Criminology and English Faculty buildings in 2004, which stand in the shadows of Norman Foster and James Stirling's Law and History buildings. The Education Faculty building constructed by the Building Design Partnership alongside Homerton College in Hills Road is another attractive new building, as is the curved Hawking Building in West Road designed by Donald Insall Associates for Gonville & Caius, which opened in 2008.

The university community also acknowledges its past heroes – be they benefactors or famous graduates – through buildings. The university's Pitt Building in Trumpington Street, Nevile's Court at Trinity College and the Queens' Erasmus Building are but three examples of this. Still other buildings, such as Addenbrooke's Hospital, the Fitzwilliam Museum and Caius Court, are named after significant donors.

At the more vulgar end of this naming game come those dedications which are purchased through the funding of a college or the acquisition of a building by a benefactor. New buildings have a price tag when it comes to dedications: Selwyn's Ann Court, the building of which began in 2007, is so named after the wife of the major donor. Similarly, the rededication of New Hall in 2008 twins the name of Rosemary Murray, the university's first female vice-chancellor, with the name of a rich donor to create Murray Edwards Hall. The delightfully lop-sided building (its incline is due to its being built on top of the medieval King's Ditch) at the junction of Free School Lane and St Botolph's Lane was a little disfigured in 2008 by a large plaque which records the graduate of Pembroke who funded its acquisition for his old college.

The 800th Anniversary Campaign website in 2009 detailed precisely what donations of £1 million or £500,000 will achieve: the former will support major research initiatives, whereas the latter will support and name a faculty position for fifteen years. Unwelcome as this may be to some, such procedures do attract donations; it is also, undeniably, an ancient university practice.

Post-war architecture in Cambridge

The Second World War and post-war austerity interrupted the flow of new building projects at Cambridge and the library remained the university's most modern major building for some twenty years. When building projects were recommenced, the break with the university's domestic architectural tradition was confirmed through the competition won by Hugh Casson to design the Faculty of Arts in the late 1950s. It was built on what became known as the Sidgwick Site between West Road and Sidgwick Avenue.

Using the principles of the French architect Le Corbusier, Casson designed the main building with a flush façade, standing above the stilt-like pilotis which form a court at ground level. The roof is flat, leaving (unrealised) potential for another key feature of Le Corbusier's work, the roof garden. Some, like Webster and Howard, in their *Cambridge: an architectural guide*, get carried away in writing of the building's 'New Empiricist style'; they refer to the 'Brutalists' erroneous chastisement of this type of building. It is, these critics add, a timid and over-polite construction. Such comments will be lost on the students using the building, who complain of excessive heat gain in summer and heat loss in winter. Casson expected to design seventeen similar buildings in the same area but only seven, mostly along the Sidgwick Road edge of the site, were commissioned.

Other eminent architects besides Casson, such as Leslie Martin, Denys Lasdun and Basil Spence, worked in Cambridge in that period. Basil Spence was commissioned to design the Erasmus Building at Queens' in 1959. Like those of Hugh Casson, its design is derived from Le Corbusier's work, although some critics consider that it lacks the 'plasticity and clarity of expression' typical of that seminal architect; others simply regret that a building at such odds with the ancient buildings along the Cam should have been placed there at all.

A decade later Denys Lasdun provoked a similar reaction at Christ's College. Architectural critics have assigned to his building there some diverting and rather incomprehensible descriptions: 'the incredible single-mindedness of the megastructure concept is breathtaking', yet it is apparently 'tyrannised by its own internal logic'. The profile of the building steps backwards with each successive floor, hence its nickname of 'the Typewriter'. The first-year students accommodated there mention the wafer-thin walls and ill-kempt hessian wall coverings. It seems at odds with its setting: it is situated at the back of college grounds, and approached past the ancient buildings of Christ's Third Court; the ugliness of its aspect from King Street caused disquiet before it was infilled with shops. The building design was to have been replicated along King Street: it is uncertain whether it was lack of admiration or funds which defeated this intention.

Leslie Martin, who took the first Chair of Architecture at Cambridge in the 1950s, was another of these well-known post-Second World War architects to win a commission from the university, designing the modernist building known as Harvey Court in West Road. It is an inward-looking building with a virtually solid brick wall facing West Road: in this, Martin had maintained the tradition of seclusion and exclusion in Cambridge architecture. A harsh exterior was presented to the local people, contrasting with the pleasantly stepped southern range overlooking the college gardens.

These concepts were repeated at Robinson College as late as the 1970s. The college, built like a citadel, is approached through an entrance which clearly symbolises a drawbridge. It even has small slit windows, like the loopholes of a castle, facing out onto Grange Road. College members can see out; passing members of the hoi polloi cannot see in.

After Casson, the Sidgwick Site was used from the 1960s to host three particularly significant buildings. The designs of two were so at odds with the traditions of Cambridge architecture that they generated immense controversy.

James Stirling won the first commission, from the History Faculty, in the early 1960s. The building, which has an exterior made up of red tiles and glass, presaged an era in British architecture where glass was used as the dominant building material, notably in the City of London. The influence of Stirling on British architecture has been huge; architectural students come to admire this ground-breaking building. His acolytes in the profession award the Stirling Prize for British Architecture to such monuments as the City of London's glass-clad gherkin building. Although architectural critics may praise 'the radical inventiveness of its form and tectonic daring', Stirling seriously misjudged the ability of technology to service the building. Its shortcomings – heat gain and loss, excessive sound transmission, condensation – have caused endless expense to the faculty. Condensation from its glass roof even gave the impression of flooding during its opening ceremony.

A feature of the building is a glass roof set at forty-five degrees from its apex to the ground, which significantly reduces the usable space above its footprint. Small meeting rooms oblige its history students to hear their lectures in the neighbouring buildings. It is even a challenge to find the tiny entrance; the grand entrances of the old colleges can never be missed.

Norman Foster was the next architect who worked on this site. His Law Faculty building, opened in 1995, stands opposite the History Faculty. It, too, has its critics, who amuse themselves by talking about the dangers of mixing dons cut off from normal life with the huge egos of celebrity architects. Like Stirling's building, it used materials in a style which was unusual at the time; broad facades of steel and glass join in a sharp angle at the entrance. Like many of Foster's buildings, it has a visible supporting structure of tubular steel. It prompted one critic to refer to this corner of the Sidgwick Site as the point 'where plant-house meets aircraft hanger'. The building is not unattractive, however; after dark, when its lights shine out through its huge glass façade, it is particularly appealing.

Edward Cullinan's Faculty of Divinity building is the least outlandish and most recent of these three iconic buildings on this site, and is reputedly pleasant to use. It is formed around two drums, the larger of which contains a library at the top of the building.

Between the Foster Law building and the Casson building, the Estates department of the university has recently planted a row of *Ginkgo Biloba*, one of the oldest existing tree species. There is some irony to be enjoyed in their placement, as an extract of this plant is said to improve brain function and delay the onset of senile dementia –useful in a place of aging academics.

The medieval buildings of a college supported the feeling of a community living together. Some of the early college buildings of the university could have been mistaken for grand domestic dwellings, while others were clearly more influenced by the monastic background of the university. The sharp-cornered modern Law and History Faculty buildings, however, are to many eyes brutal and unwelcoming, and do not at all belong to the domestic collegiate style. They represent another dramatic challenge to the traditions of Cambridge architecture.

Seclusion from the local community was a typical aspect of university architecture in the past. Hence high walls and buildings with few outward-looking windows are commonplace. The college gates, which once could shut out the plague and rioting townsfolk, still offer protection against 'the madding crowd's ignoble strife'. Appropriately, it was the eighteenth-century Cambridge don Thomas Gray who penned this superior phrase.

However, this tradition too has been challenged. The English Faculty building on West Road, by Allies and Morrison, was completed in 2004. It is a sensible building. In a surprising contrast with the past, it even has lecture rooms into which the passer-by can gaze from the pavement. The Institute of Criminology, another occupant of the Sidgwick Site that was also opened in 2004, was built by the same firm as the English Faculty and in the same open style.

These two buildings may reflect the university's attempts to appear less exclusive. While the intellectual elite must still be nurtured carefully, this can now be done within buildings to which students and those contemplating study at Cambridge can relate. They are not signature buildings by 'name' architects with big egos, but practical, useful and pleasant buildings in which scholarship can progress unhindered. In the same vein, Allies and Morrison also completed the much-admired auditorium at Fitzwilliam College in 2004.

The psychological power of architecture has long since been acknowledged. John Ruskin wrote in the nineteenth century of the twin roles of buildings: to provide shelter and to speak to the soul of those who live in them. Messages are picked up through architecture: moving around such buildings as the university possesses may cause the clever or well-connected to feel superior. Indeed, some claim that the inward-looking style of college courts is not unconnected with the introspection of some college fellowships. However, the modern efforts of the university to be more open and less exclusive have been reflected in the architecture of its modern faculty buildings.

Other modern buildings have attracted praise. Edward Cullinan's practice designed the Centre for Mathematical Sciences in Clarkson Road, near Churchill College, in 2003. It is a striking collection of ten buildings in a landscaped setting. The centrally positioned social centre has the shape of a low aircraft hangar, on whose soil-covered roof flowers and grass are grown. The roofs of the perimeter buildings have

Illustration 6.4: The Centre for Mathematical Sciences: the lanterns, more old-fashioned examples of which were invariably placed on top of college dining halls, dominate the skyline of the Centre for Mathematical Sciences. The centre was designed by the architectural practice of Edward Cullinan (MA Cantab, Queens' College) in 2000.

the lanterns which also sit on top of most college dining halls. Where the dining hall lanterns appear as an atavistic connection to times of the medieval monasteries, those on these buildings make a futuristic impression. This collection of striking buildings is an antidote to those who might believe that either the university is stuck in a medieval timewarp or it cannot commission great modern architecture. Both architectural and building industry awards have been won by architecture commissioned by the university. Sadly these buildings must be sought out and cannot be casually admired from afar: their builders, unlike those of earlier centuries, did not have carte blanche to flatten every private home for hundreds of yards around to improve their buildings' settings.

The costs of some modern buildings

The use of the best-known architects has not spared the university from massive problems with some of their buildings, however. Every Regius Professor of History of the last forty years has wanted to pull Stirling's History Faculty down because of its crippling maintenance costs. Destruction would now be difficult as, to the despair of many, the building has been listed and must be preserved. The Sackler Building at the Fogg Museum of Harvard University, also designed by Stirling, has met similar problems and is likely to be pulled down. It is perhaps telling that none of Wren's buildings have ever come close to being destroyed because they were thought not to work. Beauty and convenience were the marks of Wren's genius.

Each summer, during the long vacation, certain Cambridge buildings are cocooned in plastic sheeting behind scaffolding; frequently they are the post-War Modernist buildings. Older buildings, often left by anonymous architects, soldier on with much less attention. The very newest are particularly frugal consumers of resources. Maintenance costs of buildings constructed in the second half of the nineteenth century amount to £200 for every £1 of initial investment, whereas the cost of the newest buildings and those planned for the future is forty times less, at £5 per £1 invested over the assumed thirty-year economic life of the buildings.

On an environmental basis as well as on aesthetical grounds, the quality of new building since the early 1990s has been praised. Buildings such as the Fitzwilliam College auditorium and the Caius accommodation and conference building in West Road are vastly superior to many buildings from the earlier post-War period. The traditional materials that have been used in these buildings do not jar with older neighbours and they are in theory very ecologically correct. They are energy efficient, typically, for example, using recycled power from computers to service the building. The windows, blinds, lights and doors at the Centre for Mathematical Sciences even 'talk' to each other, causing automatic adjustments in light, heat and air circulation as necessary. As has often been the way, however, this is not always appreciated by the building's users. Students complain of how, when locked in a brown study over their books, they can be disturbed by window blinds mysteriously rising and leaving them dazzled uncomfortably by the sudden arrival of sunlight. Delicately balanced mechanisms are in practice compromised by students through such gestures as the jamming of blinds. These quibbles aside, much of the recent architecture at the university is of outstanding quality and has shown that there is a way between the Modernists' rejection of all tradition and the staleness of neo-Classical architecture.

A remarkable man-made landscape

The university has filled Cambridge with glorious buildings. It was once the pinnacles of King's College Chapel which caught the eye of the traveller approaching Cambridge from the west. Then, for a while, Gilbert Scott's St John's Tower held centre stage before the edifice of his grandson at the University Library took over.

It is now enormous cranes which stand out, hovering permanently over the city and periodically shuffling around the university's building sites. The scaffolding of medieval times must have been similarly ubiquitous; there can scarcely have been a time when the sight of building activity did not greet the traveller to Cambridge. From the days in the 1440s when Reginald Ely commissioned his master masons to construct King's College Chapel, building at the university has always been important to the economy of the entire region. In the twenty-first century almost 10 per cent of construction revenue in the entire East of England is generated in the small area of land occupied by the university.

There is hope, too, for the future. To judge from twenty-first-century commissions for university faculties, the reasons for the success of some twentieth-century architects, such as Lutyens, Drinkwater, Hopkins and Cullinan, have been appreciated. These architects respected the cultural context in which they were building.

The colleges have been able to import the best styles and the best materials onto their island. The eclectic styles of building derive from centuries of great wealth, as well as the paucity of local building materials and the competitive instincts of colleges. The university undoubtedly caused occasional hardship when people were moved forcibly, their streets blocked and access to drinking water denied: it used its power and wealth to push the town's inhabitants around. Nonetheless, when confronted with the beauty which has been created, it is impossible not to admire what the academic community has achieved over the past 800 years. It is also certain that the fascinating 'fabrick' of Cambridge remains incomplete.

Chapter 7

The Charm and Contribution of Colleges

'Pray at King's, dine at Trinity, study and sleep at Jesus' is the advice within a chronicle of King James I, recorded following his visit to Cambridge in 1615. He added the further uplifting note: 'stool at Magdalene'.

Each college still has its own individual charm, deriving from the pre-college history of the land a college occupies, the buildings it knocked down, retained or commissioned, its famous alumni and the intellectual, cultural or sporting traditions which undergraduates maintain. Together they combine to form the special character which distinguishes one college from another.

The laconic observations of James I regarding colleges' reputations still hold good. Among the smaller chapels, such as Trinity Hall, there are some deeply moving places which invite prayer; yet, as James I recorded, no place transmits the power of religion better than King's College Chapel. Trinity's reputation for a good table endures, while the atmosphere encouraging study at Jesus College remains powerful. Its spacious grounds, the slight distance of college from the town's diversions and the still-beating soul of St Radegund's Nunnery create an unparalleled tranquillity. As for Magdalene, the king simply missed what else was on offer at this enchanting college.

The origins of colleges

Before the first college was founded at the end of the thirteenth century, members of the university lived in hostels or private houses; for centuries many continued to do so, as the colleges which were established accommodated very few scholars. The masters, who were licensed by the university to teach, regulated the conduct of university members; in this, the university was much like a medieval guild. In the very earliest days of the university less experienced teachers would gather round a more renowned master, but these were ephemeral groupings which rarely outlived their leader. More permanent college communities became possible only when the monarch, aware of the advantages a university could bring to the state, was persuaded to grant certain groups of scholars legal recognition. This gave colleges the crucial right to hold

Illustration 7.1: The Entrance Court of Christ's College, which faces on to St Andrew's Street. It contains the chapel, the master's lodge, the dining hall, accommodation and, initially at least, a small library. Uniquely among colleges in Cambridge, the lawn is oval-shaped.

property in mortmain. Mortmain, meaning literally 'dead hand' (as mortgage means 'dead pledge'), allowed property to be passed in perpetuity to a college without incurring death duties.

This single right underpinned the survival of a college. First, it encouraged groups of academics to accumulate wealth for their college in the knowledge that it would be shielded from tax liabilities. Secondly, the evident permanence of these new communities encouraged the rich to leave their worldly goods to colleges in return for masses said for their souls: colleges came to be perceived as academic chantries. As far as the living were concerned, the colleges brought stability to the academic community; they were the means through which the university grew strong. Such academic communities were well established on the continent, particularly in Paris, before they emerged in Cambridge.

Hostels and the earliest colleges

It surprises those from outside the university when they learn that the university and colleges have separate legal identities. They each have their own privileges and rights which are jealously guarded against infringement by another college or by the university itself. Where the university has provided the structure for the academic community, the colleges provided the domestic comforts which to this day enhance the lives of their senior members. Examinations, teaching in 'schools' or faculties and managing the relationship with the state are the responsibility of the university. Its most senior positions – such as the vice-chancellor or the chancellor – and indeed the university's ruling bodies have, however, been filled by academics who were also members of a college.

The foundation of the colleges, one at a time, followed that of the university. They were primarily domestic conveniences designed to make the lives of the fellows both more congenial and more secure. Initially only a few scholars joined a college, almost as servants. Those that were admitted initially came from the poorest backgrounds and would complete domestic tasks for the fellows in return for tuition and a roof over their heads. Once it was realised that the money to be made from taking scholars into college outweighed the disadvantages of living in proximity to them, colleges determined to provide accommodation and teaching for larger numbers of students. Its tuition, however, was always complementary to, not in place of, the university's teaching.

All scholars were – and still are – required to matriculate into the university, literally meaning to be signed on to the roll, from the Latin *matricula*, a list or register. It indicated an acceptance of the university's statutes and ordinances. The scholar would then seek lodgings in a hostel or admission into a college. A college was a much more permanent institution, through its endowments and special tax status, than a hostel; above all, a college provided an opportunity for a scholar to study under a particular tutor.

Peterhouse, founded in 1284 by Hugh de Balsham, Bishop of Ely, is the oldest college of the university. Its small community of scholars moved to Trumpington Street from the opposite end of town, where accommodation had been shared with the monks of St John's Hospital (later to become St John's College). The initiative which led to the next college, King's Hall, came through Edward II in 1317. Nonetheless, the founder and foundation date of this college are generally given as Edward III and 1337. Meanwhile, Michaelhouse had been founded in 1324 and University Hall in 1328 (refounded as Clare Hall in the 1330s). The Hall of Marie de Valence (known later as Pembroke Hall) was founded in 1347. Another three colleges, Gonville, Trinity Hall and Corpus Christi, were founded over the next five years. These eight colleges were sufficient to provide a permanent college-based structure for the university.

It took time for their impact to be felt throughout the university, however. The heart of the university remained the Old Schools, which are now behind the Senate House. Individual colleges were small communities, often with insignificant numbers of undergraduates; King's Hall was the only medieval college to have a significant number in residence. The majority of scholars over the first 200 years of the university's existence lodged in hostels.

In the fourteenth century there were over thirty hostels, with names like Oving's Inn, Tyled Hostel, Garret Hostel and St Gregory's Hostel. Some were substantial enough to possess dining halls and have a formal link to a parish church. Others were more temporary arrangements, where a Bachelor of Arts, perhaps studying for a doctorate, might lease a property and rent out rooms to younger pupils. The memory of two hostels still lingers in modern Cambridge: one is commemorated in Garret Hostel Lane, which runs towards the river, separating Trinity Hall buildings from those of Trinity College; the other in a small court at Trinity College called Bishop's Hostel. Hostels were licensed and inspected by the staff of the university chancellor. However, without the legal rights of a college, they could be short-lived communities.

Colleges sometimes formed partnerships with hostels. Queens' was closely tied to St Bernard's Hostel, as was Corpus Christi to St Mary's Hostel and Gonville to Physick Hostel. Membership of a college was even possible while belonging to a hostel, the former providing accommodation and instruction, the latter only lodgings. Many in the twenty-first century face, in a physical sense, the same situation; a student enrolled at Clare can be lodged half a mile away in college-owned property at The Colony in Castle Street, beyond Magdalene Bridge.

The colleges soon joined the university and the longer-established friaries as the three centres of power within the early medieval academic community. While the hostels sought alliances with colleges and the friars were vying for influence within the university, the burghers of the town had become wealthy through trade, and retained some authority within the town. Medieval Cambridge was a pluralist community in which the university was not yet the dominant force.

During the hundred years following the mid-1400s, colleges admitted more scholars. A college was funded through its endowments; added to these, lodging and education fees paid by scholars eased the lives of the fellowship. Living in proximity to scholars became, and no doubt remains, a tolerated inconvenience for the fellows. As far as the scholars were concerned, hostels merely provided food and lodging; a place in college offered, in addition, access to teaching, greater stability and the possibility of election to the fellowship – an appealing prospect to some young students.

The impact of colleges

The move by scholars into college was accompanied by the employment by colleges of salaried 'lectors'. This marked the beginning of the shift from teaching at the centre of the university. Disputations and oral examinations continued in the lecture rooms at the Old Schools building, but instruction in college lessened the need to attend. Indeed, through to modern times lectures remain an optional extra to the less diligent student. Colleges gradually took over the lead in teaching from the university and developed their own academic syllabi. By the Reformation they were more important than the university's lecture rooms as places of learning.

Even after the rise of the university's faculties in the nineteenth and twentieth centuries, the colleges' influence on undergraduate education was maintained through their fellows' role as supervisors to a small number of students. An undergraduate attends, normally on his own, a weekly 'supervision' with his supervisor, during which an essay is surrendered. A student also has a Director of Studies in his college who will advise on the choice of courses. Finally the student is allocated a tutor, who has a role somewhat akin to that of a guardian: at Oxford this position is described as a Moral Tutor. In some Cambridge colleges the role of personal tutor is now combined with that of Director of Studies. Whether this is the case or not, this level of personal attention is exceptional and an immense privilege, but it also places considerable pressure on the student. There is no hiding place for anyone struggling or distracted from their studies. Cambridge University has a relatively high number of students suffering from stress and depression, which the outside observer might connect to its exceptional tuition system. While the brightest and most talented, at whom the Cambridge education is aimed, will thrive, the less gifted may struggle – but will probably not drown, as the colleges employ nurses and welfare officers, as well as maintaining a university counselling service for staff and students. This is a support structure which is perhaps paralleled only at Oxford.

As a result parents living out their dreams through their children now do a huge disservice to their child if they seek a string to pull – or even fund intensive additional tuition prior to admission – in order to secure a place in a college. It is certainly no longer accepted practice at either Oxford or Cambridge – indeed, when in 2002 two senior fellows of the relatively poor Oxford college of Pembroke were exposed discussing such terms they were both forced to resign.

The college-based supervision system, as an intense one-to-one form of instruction, was revitalised by the arrival of women into the university in the early 1870s. The unequal access to lectures enjoyed by women, which continued for some time after they were accepted into the university, was compensated for by close personal tuition from which female students derived great benefits. Such instruction also made up for the often inferior academic preparation they had had before their arrival at the university. It was soon recognised by all colleges that this system was a very effective form of instruction. It also pulled the fellows into a close involvement with students' progress, reducing the risk of withdrawal into their research.

Colleges made it possible for communities of scholars to live separately from the town. As soon as funds were available private chapels, lodgings for a master and fellows, dining halls and libraries were all built behind vast forbidding gates. As the colleges matured into a framework through which control might be imposed over students via their division into small groups, their impact stretched even further. This has been subtly achieved, as the colleges have always generated immense loyalty from their members.

They also introduced into the university the key element behind advancement in most societies, namely competition. From the master wishing to attract the cleverest student or fellow to the desire to possess the most beautiful buildings, colleges have always competed over many things. Chapels are more glorious, the libraries larger and the fare at top table better as a result of this competition.

Another benefit, incidental to the motives of those who first caused colleges to flourish, has been to underpin the independence of the academic community. The domination of legally independent colleges by outside interests such as the Church, or more recently the government, has always been difficult. For instance, politicians currently seek to influence the candidates which Cambridge accepts; they press for a change in selection procedures in order to implement positive discrimination in favour of social groups underrepresented at the university. However, the present admissions system, in which each college exercises its independence in determining whom it will admit, frustrates these ambitions: it would be simpler for these politicians if the current system were replaced by a central admissions office. Allied to this individualistic approach to admissions is the fact that many of the academics who now interview prospective students come from outside Britain and are perhaps less sensitive to the subtleties of the English class system or the political pressures brought to bear from government. They are more likely to select on academic criteria alone and to disregard the nuances of class background.

The origins of individual colleges

Two of the earliest colleges, Peterhouse and University Hall, met a particular need of the university community at the time of their foundation. The independent community at Peterhouse reduced the influence of the Augustinian monks by removing its scholars from St John's Hospital; indeed, the foundation of the college represented a marked advance in emancipation, as it established the idea that a university education need not be confined to those destined for a monastery or those intending to take holy orders. University Hall provided a home of more permanence to the university's teachers. With each new college, both the members of the university and, in consequence, its reputation grew.

Whatever the needs of the university, conditions in the wider world influenced colleges' foundation. The Plantagenet monarchs, for instance, saw the need for an educated cadre. Such necessity made the earliest colleges possible, as it led to the grant of such crucial privileges as the right of mortmain. Thus, for colleges to be successfully established, a meeting between the domestic interests of the Cambridge academics and events in the wider world was required.

During the fourteenth century these circumstances helped two rich widows, Elizabeth de Clare and Marie de Valence, the benefactor behind Pembroke, to play a significant part in the foundation of two more colleges. Unselfish motives must to a large degree have prompted these women, but their actions brought personal benefits, such as the saying of prayers for their souls to hasten their passage through purgatory. Such intervention at this early stage of the university's existence by those from the highest social circles demonstrated that the leaders of the academic community already had the ability to secure patronage.

By the 1350s different circumstances led to more colleges being founded: the Black Death of the mid-1300s affected Cambridge very severely and the town's burghers resented the increased costs of church ceremonies brought about by the shortage of surviving clergy. Three colleges were set up in the wake of this plague: Gonville Hall, Trinity Hall and Corpus Christi. The articles of the last of these obliged its graduates to practise locally for several years after graduation, in the hope that the laws of supply and demand would reduce the cost of baptisms, weddings, burials and other religious services.

The intellectual awakening of northern Europe at this time also contributed to the foundation of a large group of colleges. Increased interest in education followed in the wake of the westward movement of scholars with their libraries after the fall of Constantinople in 1453. Several colleges were founded in this period at Cambridge: the Monks Hostel, which ultimately became Magdalene, was opened by the Benedictines in 1428 and God's House (refounded as Christ's) in 1438. King's and Queens' Colleges followed in the 1440s, and St Catharine's, Jesus, Christ's, St John's, Magdalene, Trinity and Gonville & Caius were all founded by 1557. This phase of rapid expansion ended with the two 'puritan' foundations, Emmanuel and Sidney Sussex, in the late 1500s.

A variety of motives lay behind the foundation of these disparate colleges. Henry VI's foundation of King's, for example, was aimed at providing the Church with men whose young minds had been trained to serve the established religion. To that end, he founded Eton College in early spring of 1441 and then came to lay the first stone of his King's College on Passion Sunday, 1 April, in the same year. Henry's plans for the college were initially modest – it was to be a community with just twelve scholars – but within a few years he decided to greatly increase the college membership, to seventy. His choice of Cambridge rather than Oxford was probably influenced by two factors. First, Wycliffe's Lollards had left a taint of heresy over Oxford, whereas Cambridge appeared orthodox in its religious practices. Secondly, Henry's foundation of Eton and a Cambridge college could counterbalance the established partnership of Winchester College and New College, Oxford. The King's College statutes were drawn up to ensure that sixty of the seventy scholars studied theology and took holy orders within three years of graduation. The college visitor, invariably someone of eminence who acted as a final judge of appeal in the event of internal college disputes, was the

Bishop of Lincoln, rather than the Bishop of Ely, whose proximity to Cambridge might have led to excessive church interference. Henry also ensured 'peculiar' status for the college chapel, so that the authority of the Archbishop of Canterbury did not hold sway over events there.

Queens' College was also founded in the 1440s, the one peaceful decade of Henry's long reign when, between his minority and his insanity, he was almost in charge of his kingdom. This shows how new colleges emerged only when appropriate conditions existed beyond the university, as the thirty years of civil war which followed ensured that the next college foundation, St Catharine's, did not take place until Edward IV was firmly installed as monarch in 1473.

After the establishment of Sidney Sussex in 1596, there was a gap of 200 years before the next college, Downing, was set up. In that period England endured a civil war and then spent much of the eighteenth century locked in wars of succession on the continent. The country was also almost permanently at war with the French around the globe. Reflecting these distractions, the university itself was in a state of decline during much of the eighteenth century. Far from needing new colleges, the university saw its membership decline. The position at Oxford was similar to that at Cambridge as, discounting the refoundation of Gloucester College as Worcester College in 1714, no colleges were founded there for a period of over 160 years from 1624.

Cambridge University lost its way somewhat in this period; the state of its mismanagement can be glimpsed from the appointment in 1764 of a Dr Samuel Ogden, fellow of St John's and once vicar of the Round Church, as the Woodwardian Professor of Geology. It was a sinecure, as indefensible as those filled by Catholic priests before the Reformation. Ogden held the post until his death in 1778; he never gave a lecture in geology, as he openly admitted that he had absolutely no knowledge whatsoever of the subject. Regrettably Odgen's behaviour was not exceptional, as very few of the university's professors performed any of their supposed functions in these times: for example, no lecture was delivered by any Regius Professor of History at Cambridge between 1725 and 1773. These were poor conditions for new colleges.

The impact of the Industrial Revolution, the need for educated men to run distant parts of the British Empire and the wish of some to correct the injustice of women's exclusion from higher education led to another phase of college building for men and women in late Victorian England. Men fashioned within the Oxbridge mould were useful to fill the Empire's outposts; 'Blues' who ruled 'Blacks' could generally be counted on. Syllabus changes and new colleges met the need for more and better-educated graduates. At Cambridge alone two colleges for women and seven others were founded in the last thirty years of the nineteenth century.

World Wars and the Depression accounted for another gap of over fifty years in college foundations before the next college, New Hall, opened in 1954. Again, its foundation reflected pressure from wider society, in this case to offer greater educational opportunities to women. Another five colleges, ending with Robinson, opened by the late 1970s. Opportunities to extend co-education, the need to strengthen the country's scientific base and the wish to extend the privilege of higher education to many hitherto excluded prompted their foundation.

In the twenty-first century there is talk of three more colleges. No matter that an academic community's prestige is no longer measured by size and that many within college fellowships may feel they have endured enough expansion – politicians want both more places in higher education and a reduction in the perceived social exclusivity of Cambridge. In the past, the university has been unable to resist such outside pressures; it is unlikely to be able to do so in the twenty-first century.

College founders

Although college foundations have reflected events in society beyond Cambridge, credit for their foundation has generally been given to individuals. Statues and plaques adorn the physical environment of colleges and feasts are held annually in founders' honour. The romance associated with medieval monarchs and aristocrats beats the alternative of acknowledging the more mundane circumstances which actually caused the foundation of a college. Dining in honour of the Civil Service at King's Hall or at Trinity College, the Black Death at Corpus Christi, Social Justice at Fitzwilliam or the Cause of Science at Churchill would be far less fun.

There is an interesting variety among the 'founders' of colleges. Four claim monarchs or the wives of monarchs as founders: Edward III at King's Hall, Henry VI at King's College and Henry VIII at Trinity College, while Queens' College had three medieval royal consorts as patronesses. Clerics, in particular bishops, founded another six colleges: Peterhouse, Gonville, Trinity Hall, God's House, St Bernard's College (later Queens') and Jesus College. Remarkably, women played an important role in the foundation of seven of the most ancient colleges: Clare, Pembroke, Queens', Christ's, St John's, Sidney Sussex and Buckingham Hall were each the outcome of female influence. Setting to one side the qualification that some founders were semi-detached from their foundation, aristocrats can be credited as the founders of seven colleges, while courtiers, usually the monarch's chancellors, set up a further seven.

The degree of the official founders' connection with their college varied: some were closely involved, such as the rich widows of medieval England and Henry VI, while others, such as Henry VIII at Trinity and Thomas Audley at Magdalene, were mere figureheads. Audley and, probably, the three queens of Queens' College were simply powerful intermediaries who could secure the monarch's blessing and the delivery of vital privileges to a new college. Support from those who could manipulate the Tudor patronage network was essential. Audley, for example, gave nothing to Magdalene beyond its name and access to these, admittedly indispensable, privileges; he even denied the poorly endowed Magdalene College any share of his wealth after his death.

There were almost invariably less exalted people behind the figureheads which colleges claim as their founders. It was, for example, Andrew Docket, a priest and member of the university, who really provided the impetus to found Queens' College; Margaret of Anjou, wife of Henry VI, was simply the first patroness. Likewise, a Welshman, John Hughes, did much to secure the support of Thomas Audley for the conversion of Buckingham Hall, previously the Monks Hostel, into Magdalene College. Similarly, it was Bishop Fisher who fought to establish both Christ's and St John's in the early 1500s, even though Lady Margaret Beaufort, the mother of Henry VII, was more involved than some founders. John Redman, Warden of King's Hall and Tudor courtier, as well as Katherine Parr, the last wife of Henry VIII, did more to ensure the foundation of Trinity College than did Henry VIII.

More surprising than the role in college foundations by priests and kings is that eight of the oldest colleges – King's Hall, Trinity College, King's, Michaelhouse, Clare, Pembroke, St Catharine's and Corpus Christi – were founded through lay influence. University education on the continent had to wait until Napoleon for such secular involvement. Since the late nineteenth century, 'committees' rather than individuals have been behind the foundation of new colleges. Nonetheless, individual generosity can still secure a personal dedication: Downing College (1800), Wolfson College (1973), Robinson College (1977) and Murray Edwards (previously New Hall) in 2009 were each named to reflect rich benefactors.

The college template

Over their 700-year existence Cambridge colleges were built to the same template. When wealth permitted, all colleges up to the late 1800s built a home for the head of college, a library, a dining hall with kitchens, a chapel and scholars' accommodation. They were also constructed around a court, even if it took time to acquire this feature. Gonville Hall, established in 1348, did not complete its first court until the late 1400s and it took 150 years to create the Great Court of Trinity.

Girton (founded 1869) and Newnham (founded 1871) broke with this tradition. Newnham operated without a chapel and neither college arranged their first buildings around courts. In the 1970s Robinson College also challenged the ancient consensus behind college architecture. Not only was it built along the axis of a street, but it was the first college designed from the beginning to accommodate members of both sexes. It is probable that, if new colleges are built to the west of Cambridge, they will between them share catering facilities and a place of worship. However, the biggest difference from the old colleges remains the modern belief that a college should open with a full complement of buildings and a large number of junior members.

Many of the idiosyncrasies of the university flourish through the colleges. The college heads have an array of different names. The most common is 'master'; as the title used within many medieval guilds, it was the natural form of address for the heads of the earliest colleges to assume. Among the colleges which survive from before 1600, only King's and Queens' do not use the term; such variation probably derives from the view that there could be no master of a king, while, equally, no one other than a king could master a queen.

A 'provost' took charge of King's, while a 'president' ran Queens'. Five other colleges, four of them founded in the 1950s or later, have followed the lead of Queens' and appointed presidents. Newnham and Homerton use the term 'principal', Girton has a 'mistress', while Robinson appoints a 'warden'. The title of warden is actually an old one in Cambridge; King's Hall, before its subjugation by Trinity College, was led by one.

There are in all twenty colleges out of the full complement of thirty-one which opt for the title of 'master'. The titles have not been adapted to reflect the sex of the office holder; when Sidney Sussex elected Dame Sandra Dawson as its master in 1999, her title of office was left unchanged, just as it was when Girton appointed a male vice-mistress and St Catharine's a female master. Similarly, no adjustment was thought necessary when Dame Mayhew Jonas was appointed provost of King's in 2003.

Illustration 7.2: The entrance gate of Robinson College in Grange Road. Although the college was designed by the Scottish architectural practice Gillespie Kidd & Kola in 1977, it retained the medieval notion that even a late-twentieth-century college should have a gatehouse protected by a tower and a quasi-drawbridge.

Other variations exist within college vocabulary; besides each college dining hall there is a Combination Room where the fellows 'combine', or mingle, before or after their meal. However, Emmanuel and Pembroke choose to meet in a room referred to as the parlour, a term which, since it derives from the Latin *'parlatorium'*, suggests a place in which to talk. Whatever their names, these rooms were and perhaps remain the place where masters fear that the bursar, dean and fellows meet to meddle with the delicate balance of power within a college at the expense of the master.

The majority of the pre-1800 colleges derived their names from aspects of the Christian faith; for example, the college names of Emmanuel, Corpus Christi, Jesus, Magdalene, St Catharine's, St John's, Trinity Hall and Trinity College reflect the close ties that bind education to religion. It is therefore not surprising that all those college names, give or take the odd vowel or apostrophe, are used at both Oxford and Cambridge universities. In contrast, the naming of modern colleges has usually been driven by secular influences.

Most colleges' full names – those recorded in their foundation articles – are longer than those generally used. The full name of Trinity College, for example, is 'The College of the Holy and Undivided Trinity', while Trinity Hall is 'The College of Scholars of the Holy Trinity of Norwich'. King's is properly referred to as 'The King's College of Our Lady and St Nicholas in Cambridge', whereas its neighbour is correctly known as 'The Queen's College of St Margaret and St Bernard in the University of Cambridge'. The dedication at King's to St Nicholas was determined by Henry VI's birth on 6 December 1421, the feast day of this saint, which is still celebrated in the college.

Illustration 7.3: The Chimney entrance to Jesus College. The three-storey brick gate tower was erected in the early 1500s. It contains two crosses on either side of the top windows in the tower, which record the approval of Queen Mary's Catholic inspectors of the college's religious practices. The range to right and left was only two storeys high until the 1720s, when a third was added; the entrance gate until then was very similar to those of Queens', Trinity and St John's Colleges.

The longest official college title is 'The College of the Blessed Virgin Mary, Saint John the Evangelist and the glorious Virgin Saint Radegund, near Cambridge'. This college's more commonly used name, Jesus, was taken from the first dedication of a chapel on the site. Grand-sounding names were otherwise cut down to size by common usage; the College of Corpus Christi and the Blessed Virgin Mary in Cambridge' was known as Bene't College until the old name was revived when the New Court of William Wilkins was built in the 1820s.

The variation in spelling between those colleges whose names are shared between the two universities has also been a source of esoteric interest to those who know Oxford and Cambridge. The names of three Cambridge colleges, Queens', Magdalene and St Catharine's, vary slightly from their cousins at Oxford. The use of the apostrophe in the first of these examples denotes the singular at Oxford, the plural at Cambridge, but it was not always so; in the early 1500s the scholar Erasmus of Rotterdam wrote in the singular of the 'Collegium Reginae' at Cambridge. The idea of shifting the Cambridge apostrophe came much later; it was moved in the early 1800s as a piece of rather contrived etymology to acknowledge the association of the three queens with the college's foundation. There is no overlap between Oxford and Cambridge in royal patronesses; the queen after whom Oxford's Queen's College was named was Philippa, wife of Edward III.

The variation between Magdalen (Oxford) and Magdalene (Cambridge) was also established only in the mid-nineteenth century, when the Oxford college removed its final letter. There is a legend, unsupported by any evidence, that at a meeting of both colleges an agreement was reached to differentiate the spelling. Another variation exists between the fifteenth-century St Catharine's College at Cambridge and the twentieth-century St Catherine's College of Oxford.

The pronunciation of Magdalene as Maudlyn, which dates from at least the 1500s, also causes comment. With the usual medieval imprecision on such matters, various spellings including Maudeleyn, Mawddelayn and Mauddelayne are found within college documents. The affinity of Maudlyn, in terms of spelling and pronunciation, to the name of the college founder probably prompted its choice by Audley himself. He was a vain man who even the normally scrupulously polite *Dictionary of National Biography* condemned as 'simply a man of low moral tone'. It is certainly not the case that the pronunciation of Magdalene was changed to flatter its founder; nor was there any particular connection between Mary Magdalene and the Benedictine monastery which had occupied this site earlier.

There is an odd twist to the issue of the letter 'e' and this college. As the college gained an 'e', its founder lost one. Thomas Audeley spelt his own name with a second letter 'e', which historians no longer use; indeed, his black granite tomb, which he designed himself, in St Mary's, Saffron Walden, remembers him as Audeley. The country house and village of Audley End appear to have loaned their 'e' to Magdalene College.

College reputations

Colleges have garnered reputations for excellence in different academic fields, usually through the pre-eminence of particular academics; some of these have endured for centuries. It is, however, by no means proven that such repute should be the basis for the scholar to choose a college. An academic's reputation is based on published works and research; the ability to impart knowledge is altogether a different skill. Despite this, Gonville & Caius has long been known as the place to study medicine, a reputation acquired from that of its refounder, Dr Keys. Keys, who had 'Latinised' his name to Caius (though retaining the English pronunciation) while studying medicine in Padua in the 1540s, used the wealth he later gained practising in London to salvage the poorly endowed Gonville Hall. William Harvey, who identified blood circulation, was also at this college in the 1600s and a reputation for cultivating medics has endured in the wake of these men. Similarly, Trinity Hall has a reputation for law, while Trinity College has one for science and maths, Jesus for architecture and St Catharine's for geography.

Despite these reputations, none of the colleges chooses to stress in their pitch to potential students a particular academic discipline to the exclusion of others. Most colleges offer almost thirty subjects, known as Triposes, to study. Indeed, they are keener to stress their mission to encourage more women and state school students to apply for admission than to attract students of a particular academic discipline. Doubtless among the colleges there remains, hidden from view, strong competition to win the brightest of students in every academic discipline.

Churchill is one exception to this generalist approach, as its founding statutes of 1960 require that 75 per cent of its students study scientific subjects; yet even there the modern student can study Anglo-Saxon, Norse, History of Art or English. The requirement imposed by Henry VI on the majority of King's scholars to study theology has long since been dropped.

Reputations outside academic study have also endured for centuries. Although much of the pithy summary of James I still holds good, Magdalene acquired an additional reputation. From the late 1800s the college was viewed as being as much a gentleman's club as an academic institution; it was caricatured as a depository for Etonians after King's ceased to take its students exclusively from Eton in the late 1800s. Its ambition to be perceived as a more socially liberal community was not helped by it being the last college to embrace co-education, in 1988. Despite setting the highest price in 2009 – £180 per head – for its May Ball and being the only college still insisting on white tie for the occasion, its 'Hooray Henry' image has waned considerably.

Most at Magdalene prefer its reputation as the literary college. Samuel Pepys bequeathed his library to the college, since when authors such as Thomas Hardy, Rudyard Kipling, E.M. Forster, C.S. Lewis and Seamus Heaney have each had strong ties with the college; on a perhaps less highbrow note, a Magdalene English graduate, William Donaldson, penned the diverting correspondence of Henry Root. Like the Fitzwilliam Museum, whose recent director has also been Master of Magdalene, the college succeeds in sharing its interests with those outside. The college has links with schools to encourage creative writing, runs a programme of public reading to which everyone is welcomed and is usually home to a writer-in-residence.

In 2009 Magdalene evidently took pride in its ancient history. The college website at that time offered a century-by-century summary tracing its fascinating evolution. Other colleges, such as King's, display a practical website facing forwards not backwards with little mention of illustrious college members or regal connections; the briefest of historical notes are hidden beneath a page on chapel and music. The 500-year umbilical link with Eton College, a school still considered the epitome of privilege, is barely mentioned.

At the same time, Trinity College preferred to put forward a grander image suited to its original role as the nursery of the 'Kyng's Childer'. The depth of the college coffers and its imposing buildings, combined with the exposure it gives to its illustrious alumni, must permeate the skin of even its least deserving modern student. The college website of 2009 displays some detailed college history, but not as readily as it shares its connections to grand figures of the country's cultural heritage, providing, for example, extracts from Chaucer quoting his reference to 'Soler Halle' (King's Hall) in the *Reeve's Tale*. It also lists its twenty-five

Olympians, its thirty-one Nobel laureates and the number of MPs who were its graduates after each general election (typically over thirty in the second half of the twentieth century). Its list of eminent graduates did, however, include the odd error – for example, it claimed as a graduate Thomas Nelson, the American who signed the Declaration of Independence, when Nelson had in fact been admitted into Christ's College.

The college with the second highest number of Nobel laureates is Gonville and Caius. Many would place it first for eloquent modesty as the Caius website referred to the undesirability of listing its famous graduates, stating that 'by concentrating too much on "famous" people, one risks forgetting those who have made, and still make, the college a vibrant community'. Most other college websites also leant towards modesty though Trinity people might have contended that they had much to be modest about.

St John's shares both physical proximity and character with Trinity. These two ancient colleges are the richest at the university and the jealousy of siblings has seeped into their souls. Even the bells of Trinity's Clock Tower have gently fuelled the rivalry; the tower is on the northern edge of Trinity's Great Court, so close to St Johns that the chimes can be heard clearly in both colleges. They sound out twice at every hour in order, as the old joke goes, first to wake up the sleepy dons and a second time to tell them the time – which college's dons it is that require wakening depends upon college loyalty .

Selwyn, with little more than a hundred years to celebrate, offered through its 2009 website a far lengthier college history than did St John's. In common with the older colleges, Selwyn also has bells to ring; the Gladstone family donated the larger of its two bells in the late 1800s. W.E. Gladstone was the uncle of the first Selwyn College master; he had also sent one of his daughters to Newnham College, which is on the other side of Sidgwick Road, which runs between these two colleges. Selwyn makes much of its gardens, describing scenes from every season with a summary of future gardening plans.

Fitzwilliam College is evidently proud of its foundation as the poorer man's college. It may not have achieved full college status until 1966, but Fitzwilliam can trace its roots back to 1869, and still takes a smaller proportion of its undergraduates from the private sector than is the case at other colleges. Two of Fitzwilliam's clubs, the Mornie Onions for drinking and the Vikings for rugby, support the robust sporting culture attached to this college. However, as a focus on the arts at Magdalene replaced its once rather uncultured reputation, so the master of Fitzwilliam's encouragement of music in recent times has bested its more unrefined traditions. There is a string quartet 'in residence' at Fitzwilliam, and two singing groups, The Barbershop Singers and The Sirens, are run. With its new auditorium, opened in 2004, the college has a claim to possessing the music hall with the best acoustics in Cambridge.

Christ's students, for the moment, have a reputation for more serious study. Appropriately, its seventeenth-century alumnus John Milton was known for his quiet studious demeanour and pallid skin. 'Some people', Milton wrote, when an undergraduate in the early 1620s, 'have lately nicknamed me the Lady. But why do I seem to them too little of a man ... because I have never had the strength to drink off a bottle like a prize fighter ... [or] ... showed my virility the way those brothellers do'. The college maintains a strong interest in cultural matters. It has been much preoccupied in 2009 with celebrating the centenaries of its graduates John Milton and Charles Darwin and has also retained for some years Issam Kourbaj as artist-in-residence, awarding him, in good Cambridge college fashion, a 'rank and number'. They have made him a bye-fellow, a status which gives him some, but not all, of the privileges of a fellow.

Although Christ's numbers the popular comedian Sacha Cohen, alias Ali G and Borat, Kazakhstan's famous reporter, among its alumni, it is presently Queens' which enjoys a reputation for diverting entertainment. Its 2009 website passed over its 500-year history in two small paragraphs, stressing rather the multiplicity of student pastimes and, as with so many of the colleges, its twin commitment to academic excellence and social diversity.

Threats to colleges

The survival of the colleges over the past several centuries, during which time each developed character and accumulated a delightful weight of history, has not always been easy. It was not just a matter of college heads navigating through national political storms. Money – its lack at some colleges and its super-abundance at others – at times attracted unwanted and threatening attention.

During the 1530s, for example, the pillaging of Church property raised huge wealth for the Crown; but within a few years Henry VIII had either spent the money on his French wars or given it away to men like Thomas Audley in order to secure support for the religious revolution. Endowments, which funded masses for the dead, proved an irresistible target for the king. As Protestants could find no biblical proof that Purgatory existed, places such as chantries, which were funded by people trying to ensure that their souls passed quickly through Purgatory, were placed in a difficult position. Henry could, therefore, cover his greed with some appearance of doctrinal justification. An act of parliament was therefore passed in 1545 to dissolve chantries, colleges and other religious foundations. It was probably Henry's intention to remove the chantry land from the colleges rather than to close down the colleges themselves but many colleges had received large endowments in return for the perennial recital of masses. The implementation of the act as it was passed in parliament would have gravely threatened the Cambridge colleges and the university. After it received the Royal Assent, a commission of senior Tudor courtiers undertook a survey of college wealth; as if by coincidence, many of them happened also to be Cambridge men. John Redman, for example, who was both warden of King's Hall and the royal chaplain, was a member of the commission, as was the master of Corpus Christi College and future Elizabethan Archbishop of Canterbury, Matthew Parker; William Mey, the president of Queens', was another member.

Their report to the king certainly understated their wealth, amid observations of proper management and appropriate religious adherence to the new faith. Most colleges carefully presented deficits from small incomes. The king commented, 'he had not in his realm so many persons so honestly maintained in living by so little land and rent'. It is doubtful if Henry was fooled, but colleges were subsequently expressly excluded from the act dissolving the chantries. In fact, one college was identified by the commission as having expenditure which did not exceed income. This was Magdalene, certainly the poorest college at the time and also, it would appear from its honest reporting, the most naïve. The commendable solvency of the impoverished Magdalene fellowship does nonetheless support the adage that living within an income is, above all, a state of mind.

Adroit use of its past graduates' and fellows' influence at the heart of government has long been a key survival skill of the university. It was only eighteen months after the passage of this act through parliament that Henry VIII agreed to the foundation of Trinity College; John Redman was its first master. However, the foundation of Trinity College revealed that a greater threat to a college's existence could sometimes come from other colleges within the university, as it caused the closure of two colleges, Michaelhouse and King's Hall. These ancient and proud colleges, as well as seven hostels, were subsumed by Trinity College at the time of its creation in 1546. Ironically, given the parliamentary statute of two years earlier, much of the wealth to fund the college came from dissolved monasteries. It was indeed well endowed; at its inception its wealth was four times that of the combined wealth of the two colleges it replaced.

Henry died early in 1547. As his effigy dominates the Great Gate of Trinity College and had secured a niche in the screen of King's College, a few hundred yards away, so his memory has always stuck closely to the university and Trinity College in particular. However, anything Henry did for the university was done for selfish motives. As his support for the glazing of King's College Chapel had depended on the university's support for his divorce, so his interest in Trinity College was doubtless related to his desire to pass quickly through Purgatory and onwards to Heaven: despite the break with Rome, Henry had retained his belief in Catholic doctrine. He was only ever a patron of the university when it served his own interests.

Despite the temptation presented by college assets to avaricious monarchs, it has been poverty which has more typically proved a threat to colleges. Some schemed to absorb others, usually citing a neighbour's lack of wealth as the excuse. Hence poorly endowed Trinity Hall was the occasional target of its rich neighbour, Clare College. Similarly, Gonville Hall, a large part of whose property was adjacent to that of King's Hall, almost became the third college swallowed up in the wake of Trinity College's foundation. It managed to survive, however, until re-endowed by Dr Caius.

In refounding Gonville Hall, Dr Caius specified in the new articles that 'the deaf, dumb, deformed, chronic invalids and Welshmen' be excluded from the college. The exclusion of Welshmen might be an incorrect transcription of the Latin for Frenchman, a slip between Wallicum and Gallicum. (In those days Welshmen were generally found at Magdalene, as John Hughes, an important figure when the college was refounded in 1542, came from the principality.) Given Dr Caius' medical interests a reference to the French could, then, have implied his wish to bar students carrying the contagious sexual disease known as Morbus Gallicus, otherwise referred to as syphilis. Ironically the paraplegic Stephen Hawking is one of this college's senior fellows and it can only be hoped that the presence of this famous man within the Caius fellowship causes some discomfort to the soul of the doctor.

Lack of funds continued to be a dangerous threat to colleges into the modern era; for instance, in the early 1800s financial pressures, which proved temporary, prompted discussions of a merger between Emmanuel and Christ's. In the late 1800s King's needed more accommodation for its students at a time when the financial resources of its neighbour, St Catharine's, were thought too weak for it to remain independent. King's came near to persuading that college to submit to its embrace. Some non-collegiate foundations – Fitzwilliam Hall, Ayerst Hostel and Cavendish Hall – were set up from 1869 for poor students, but Ayerst and Cavendish were dissolved through bankruptcy by 1896. Some modestly endowed foundations, such as Selwyn, Fitzwilliam and Homerton, did, however, manage to survive.

Through Ayerst, Cavendish and Fitzwilliam, the university hoped to widen social access to the university by reducing the cost of an undergraduate degree. The average age of matriculating students had risen from fourteen in medieval times to nearer eighteen by the nineteenth century. Since the age of sixteen generally marked the end of secondary education for the less privileged outside the public school network a matriculation age of eighteen further reduced the likelihood of the under-privileged accessing higher education. These non-collegiate students were therefore admitted as junior students at seventeen and graduated at twenty. Their academic year was divided into four terms to avoid the expense of a long vacation. In 2005, the government made a remarkably similar proposal to condense an undergraduate course into two four-term years, the objective again being a reduction in the cost of a university education.

College size and growth

Older colleges had generally started as very small communities and grew through the gradual acquisition of adjacent plots near a central building. Their development of symmetric ranges of buildings and orderly square courtyards, and their acquisition of hundreds of scholars, took centuries. The dramatic appropriation of several acres of central Cambridge in the 1440s to accommodate the new community of seventy scholars at King's College was an exceptional approach.

Peterhouse, in contrast, opened in 1284 with a total membership of less than twenty and colleges generally remained small by modern standards for centuries. Even in the late eighteenth century there were only 1,000 students at the university, spread among the sixteen colleges: an average of sixty-three scholars in each college. Trinity Hall still had only twelve fellows and twenty-five undergraduates at the end of the eighteenth century. In the 1830s the number of undergraduates admitted to Pembroke was between nine and fifteen a year; postgraduates, undergraduates and the fellows could fit cosily within the boundaries of their Old and Front Courts. In contrast to the slow pace of development of the older colleges, their modern successors have burst onto the university scene.

Very few of the sixteen pre-1600 colleges have been allowed to avoid the burdens of expansion. Over the twentieth century Magdalene, for example, has moved from educating forty undergraduates at any one time to nine times as many. This expansion changed the ancient balance of college life. It took time for college building to catch up with the increased numbers – in the 1930s it was usual for undergraduates to spend two years in 'digs' with private landlords, almost a reversion to the times when medieval scholars lived in hostels. By the twenty-first century junior members were living in college-owned colonies, although often at some distance from their college, for the duration of their undergraduate studies; the length of Grange Road, to the west of the backs, is stuffed with accommodation for students who cannot be squeezed in the 'Old Courts'. Some parents, and doubtless employers as well, have been known to remark that three years cocooned in college, be it in Old Court or The Colony, is perhaps not the perfect preparation for the Cambridge graduate's transition to the outside world.

The average number of undergraduates in each college in the early twenty-first century is around 400. Among the undergraduate colleges, Peterhouse and Corpus Christi are the smallest, each having fewer than 400 junior members (under- and post-graduates), but Trinity College has almost 1,000 junior members.

Generally, college size has been determined by wealth. The two richest colleges, Trinity and St John's, have been the two largest for centuries; Caius, King's and Jesus, ranked among the richest colleges, are also among the biggest. There are exceptions to these generalisations: Homerton, recently awarded collegiate status, has marginally exceeded the numbers at Trinity College, yet it is certainly among the poorest colleges. Similarly, Emmanuel and Peterhouse are placed firmly among the wealthiest colleges but have remained small; only the postgraduate or mature-student colleges of St Edmunds, Hughes, Lucy Cavendish, Clare Hall and Darwin are smaller than Peterhouse.

Despite the rapid increase in college size, they remain the emotional focus of their students, even though influence from the centre of the university has grown significantly. The university oversees the examinations and faculties, handles the vital financial relationship with government and funds many sporting and cultural activities. The key to its growing influence is the rising influence of faculties and the research agenda.

The contribution of colleges

The colleges have benefited the university in a number of ways. They have underpinned the independence of the academic community – the domination of a university with a number of separate colleges by an individual academic or group of politicians will always prove difficult. They, or at least new colleges, have also been drivers of change. The concept of a college has provided the university with a template to respond to new social pressures which had been ignored by the long-established colleges content with the status quo. In early times, Peterhouse secured the independence of its scholars from the Austin Canons, while in later centuries Fitzwilliam and Cavendish Halls opened Cambridge to the less privileged and Girton, Newnham and New Hall drew women into higher education.

Colleges have also provoked academic excellence through vying for the best scholars and fellows: academic standards have been raised through competition between colleges to secure such accolades as the Wrangler mathematics prize. In more recent times, the Tompkins table achieves a broader impact through measuring the academic ranking of colleges. College fellowships perhaps like to consider themselves above such charts but those such as Emmanuel, who presently do well, announce their positions in their promotional material. Other colleges, such as Peterhouse, are mute on this subject.

Wealth has come into the university via the colleges. A Tudor aristocrat could secure a more individual acknowledgement through a gift to a college than would otherwise have been possible had 'the university' been the beneficiary. A means of bypassing Purgatory may not be a concern today, but names can be given the sort of immortality within colleges which evidently appeals to some donors. The colleges have also been an outstanding means of securing the loyalty and financial support of the university's graduates. Both wealthy unmarried dons and past students have been far more ready to support their college than would have been the case had there only been the university to receive their gifts.

However, the hold of the colleges over almost everything at the university is now challenged. This has partly come about through the university's commitment to research. Although most colleges take two or three research fellows each year, the vast majority of research is undertaken by postdoctoral researchers – 200 to 300 across the university at any one time – who are contracted to the faculties and are isolated from colleges. The colleges often try to recruit some of them for supervisions (although their prime responsibility is research, the college offers in return payment and access to the benefits of college membership). Most of them, however, remain isolated from colleges. Mixing in college with contemporaries from other academic disciplines had been one of the traditional benefits of collegiate life to both the university and individuals. This is denied to increasing numbers of academics. In fact, young researchers in many science-based disciplines probably now benefit academically more from each other, and 'virtual' contact internationally with their peers, than from a college fellowship. Outside working hours, the luxuries appreciated by those within the university – be they nourishment at the top table, sports facilities or private rooms for study – are college-based, and are only accessible through college membership. Life at the university is a little cold outside the college embrace.

There have been two further blows which have undermined the colleges' role as bastions of the university. First, most of the funding from government, for either undergraduate education or research purposes, goes through the centre to faculties, bypassing the colleges. Secondly, postgraduates – who now account for one-third of the 18,000-strong student body – are admitted to the university through faculties and not colleges. Indeed, after the exhausting process of securing the support of a faculty and obtaining finance, the final stage of allocation to a college does not generally excite the postgraduate and their relationships with their college do not approach the emotional commitment which the younger undergraduates usually offer.

Fortunately for those who support the collegiate system, colleges still bring advantages to the university. They have enabled the university to deal with the huge expansion since the 1950s without denying its students the intimate experience of college life. They keep a balance in the lives of their senior members between teaching and research through the supervision system. The college is also the conduit through which graduates give emotional loyalty, as well as financial support, to the university. Furthermore, they provoke competition within the university, which, while being deadly serious, is generally conducted within agreed rules and is extremely productive to the university as a whole. Finally, the fellowships' determination to guard their independence provides a real, albeit convenient, barrier to undue pressure from outside political forces.

Those who direct the university appreciate these benefits of the college system, and it is evident from the conduct of the 800th anniversary fund-raising campaign that there is no wish on the part of the university to undermine the power of the colleges. Vice-chancellor Alison Richard stressed during the campaign that the colleges and university are partners. She even spoke of the dangers of leaving a large body of researchers adrift outside the college embrace.

Colleges will stay at the heart of university life for a long time yet. They shaped Cambridge from the fifteenth century onwards and contribute immense charm which is enjoyed by their members, townspeople and visitors. They remain delightful places.

Chapter 8

In Praise of Study with Dumb Teachers

Sharp questions and blunt punishment sometimes accompany the transfer of knowledge to a scholar from the living teacher. A book, in contrast, is invariably a kindly provider of knowledge. To the loss of scholars from the Middle Ages up to the mid-1800s, these dumb friends played only an indirect role in students' education.

Books were then scarce and too expensive for most scholars to possess. Collections of books certainly existed, but they were, like much else in colleges, for the benefit of fellows rather than undergraduates. Individual reading and private study played only a small part in the education of scholars. Rather, it was conducted face to face, the focus being on the spoken word, both for learning and examinations. A scholar's oral skills, honed through the study of rhetoric, were crucial – even reading was a communal affair. Paper, for either the printed word or for writing, was too expensive for casual use.

This bias against the written word was reinforced by the design of books. Up to and even past Johannes Gutenberg's development of the printing press in the late 1400s the words themselves had to compete with the stunning images in illuminated manuscripts. By the late fifteenth century new printing techniques had much reduced the role of image in education and religion. Reading gradually changed from a communal affair to a silent, private pastime; attention shifted to the line of argument. It was at this time that Cambridge acquired its first libraries.

For centuries instruction and examinations were conducted in Latin as oral disputations, during which a student was expected to defend a position against opposing views. The limitations of this method were sharply exposed in mathematics examinations. By the 1770s they were dictated to examinees, who would submit written responses; fifty years later printed examination papers were in general use.

The importance of books to the culture of the academic community, if not to the individual scholar, was acknowledged in the university's shield of arms, which was granted in 1572. Its principal charge was a book, as it had been within the Oxford University shield of arms drawn up a century earlier. However, where the Oxford tome is open, that of Cambridge is closed. Depending on where one's loyalties lie, the variation suggests that the Cambridge scholars have yet to open the book, or that scholars at Oxford are stuck on one page, too baffled to read further.

No matter the rumours that are peddled in Oxford, the Cambridge master would certainly have instructed scholars with his book open, most probably while seated in a chair, a symbol of religious and therefore educational authority throughout Europe. Pronouncements from the Church and particularly from the pope came '*Ex Cathedra*' – '*cathedra*' being Latin for chair. Its symbolic value was carried over to academic life; as Jesus preached his sermon on the mount from a chair, so did the academic master deliver his lecture seated. The position of the senior professor of a faculty from earliest times was referred to as the chair in English and 'la chaire' in French. (The French use the same word for a pulpit and professorial chair, reflecting their Church's close involvement in medieval education.) In college, too, the chair has especial significance. Up to 1875 only the master at Jesus College sat in a chair when dining in hall; every other member of college perched on a bench.

Medieval professors and dans

Although the university had always been led by masters, it took until 1502 for the first professor's chair, the Lady Margaret Professorship in Divinity, to be founded. Lady Margaret Beaufort's grandson, Henry VIII, added the Regius Professorships of Divinity, Civil Law, Physic, Hebrew and Greek. Since then over 100 permanent chairs have been created, besides a number which are given on the grounds of individual achievement.

The concept of a salaried academic profession emerged around the same time as these early chairs were founded. Endowed lectureships, which had began in southern Europe during the thirteenth and fourteenth centuries, took until the fifteenth century to reach the two English universities. In the late fifteenth century God's House, Queens' College and King's Hall created a few endowed teaching positions at Cambridge and the university itself established three lectureships in the late 1480s. The availability of such posts encouraged staff to stay longer at a university, promoting the concept of an academic career.

However, inadequate remuneration left the university short of teachers; the shortage was dealt with through the 'Necessary Regency System', whereby every newly qualified Master of Arts or Doctor who was requested to do so had to stay on two years to teach the younger scholars. Teaching in the Middle Ages, particularly before the introduction of endowed lectureships, was more often an obligation than a career choice; it was viewed as a stepping stone to social advancement for people from modest social backgrounds, rather than as a vocation. Perhaps as a consequence, a perception that many university teaching positions offered a mediocre occupation endured for centuries; even in the Victorian period, a clergyman, George Faber, wrote of how: 'A fellowship is an excellent breakfast, an indifferent dinner, and a most miserable supper'.

The venerable grey-haired Victorian dons captured in sepia photographs, with interminable service records matched only by the length of their beards, had few equivalents in the early centuries of the university's existence. A teacher earned the title of master at graduation after his oral disputations had been judged successful and thus were often almost the same age as their students, a situation which persists

Illustration 8.1: The carved ends of the chancel stalls within Jesus Chapel, some of which date back to the early fifteenth century, emphasise the importance of the chair as a symbol in both Christianity and within college.

to some degree today. The colloquial term 'don', still used for anyone holding a teaching position at the university, was a Victorian twist on the more ancient term 'dan'; the Oxford English Dictionary gives their origins as the Latin for master, *dominus*.

A lecturer at Cambridge in the late Middle Ages was supposed to give 140 official lectures annually, a number reduced to 100 if he held weekly disputations. Tips as payment for lectures, which could last as little as fifteen minutes, were expected from students. Richer lecturers would sometimes waive this fee; doubtless such largesse irritated the poorer lecturer, whose greater mastery of the subject could be overshadowed by a neighbour's free tuition.

Consequently, the quality of education varied considerably. Many graduates would lecture while they looked for careers outside the university and would have made reluctant teachers. Within the university, roles such as Keeper of University Chests, proctor or writer of university letters could prove appealing alternatives to instructing scholars. A more attractive career move for many fellows within the university was to secure a headship of a college or to act as a principal in one of the better hostels.

Teaching by the newly graduated continues into the twenty-first century. A significant proportion of undergraduate supervisions are completed by postgraduates, although the amount of such work a postgraduate can undertake is limited to about a day a week. Paid at around £25 per hour of teaching (which includes preparation and marking) in 2009, this amounts to modest but welcome extra income for the modern postgraduate.

Some fellows in earlier centuries acquired such strong reputations that it was they who determined a parent's choice as to where their son was educated. In the manner in which some parents might choose a public school by the quality of a particular housemaster, the parents of medieval scholars chose both the university and the college by the fellow. The father of the poet John Milton chose Christ's College in the 1620s because he shared the Arminian beliefs of its tutor William Chappell. Fellows were almost, in one sense, in private enterprise, charging fees according to their reputation and to the circumstance of the families whose sons they educated. Records at Christ's College from Milton's time show payment being received by a tutor in tobacco. Some fellows also clearly did better than others – two tutors in the 1620s at Christ's tutored half the college's junior members. The fellow's chamber remained the basic unit of college accommodation, with scholar and teacher sharing a main room up to the mid-1600s, after which time partitioning was introduced. It was only later that tutors acquired private rooms.

As paid positions became standard from the early 1500s, the Necessary Regency System declined, although the obligation on graduates to teach was never officially abolished. This process was also hastened by the impact of the printing press: once printed texts were more readily available the need for young graduates to teach students from scarce hand-written material diminished.

The process through which the university acquired students was always carefully controlled. Both teacher and scholar benefited from the privileges which came through being treated as a member of the Church. It was, for many of the less privileged, the first step in a career which could lead to the heart of the establishment. There was even a term, 'vagabond scholars', to describe those who had not joined the university properly. A Royal Ordinance of 1420, reconfirmed in the Elizabethan Statutes of 1545, decreed that all attending Cambridge must matriculate formally and swear an oath to uphold the university laws. Even more importantly, the scholars had to declare their support of the belief system, whatever it was at the time, condoned by the state; from 1613 those graduating had to sign a declaration 'willingly and ex animo (heartily)' that they supported the three basic articles behind the Anglican Church. Hence from the Reformation up to 1856 no Catholics could obtain a bachelor's degree without signing their approval of the Thirty-Nine Articles and the Acts of Supremacy and Uniformity. The Test Acts from the late 1600s also ensured that a series of penal laws kept Nonconformists, Jews and Catholics away from the university. The Tests prohibiting non-Anglicans remained in force for theology students and heads of colleges until 1870;

prejudice must have lingered, as there were still barely a hundred Catholic undergraduates forty years later at the start of the Great War.

Matriculation, the trivium and the quadrivium – and Mr Tripos

There has always been a formal ceremony of entry to the university during which the scholar's name was entered on a master's roll. Before official entry students faced the Previous Examination, which identified the scholars with an academic grounding insufficient to complete an Honours degree course. Referred to as the 'Little Go' from the eighteenth century, the exam survived until the early 1960s. The final examination for the Bachelor of Arts was known as the Great Go. The term 'Greats', used at Oxford, derives from the term 'Great Go'; it now describes the Oxford Classics tripos, the *Literae Humaniores*.

The university matriculation ceremony, in which all scholars involved were presented to the vice-chancellor, was dropped in the 1950s. The requirement of the university's new members to subscribe to the tenets of the state then passed to the Praelector of each college (who is charged to ensure both that college junior members are properly matriculated and that adherence to the ceremonial aspects of university life is maintained). He collects signed declarations that each student will, among other things, abide by the Ordinances of the university.

Education at Cambridge and indeed in medieval universities across Europe required seven years of study by the scholar before graduation as a Bachelor of Arts. This process began with the Trivium, a three-year foundation course which comprised Grammar, Logic and Rhetoric. It was followed by a four-year Quadrivium during which Arithmetic, Geometry, Astronomy and Music were studied; Astronomy was the most important of these subjects, in part because the feast days of the ecclesiastical year were calculated through the movement of the stars and planets. Like Thomas Cranmer, who began his studies of the Trivium in 1503 (possibly at Jesus or, more probably, at one of the hostels), most scholars came up aged fourteen. Candidates for degrees encountered an examiner who sat on a stool; after the Greco-Latin word for a three-legged seat, he was referred to as Mr Tripos, a name from which the term for the examination itself is derived. This also explains why an undergraduate degree course is known as a Tripos and, indeed, why examination results are published on a Tripos List, which was until 2009, pinned to notice boards on the south-facing side of the Senate House.

Twenty-first-century students argued that such public display of their academic worth was excessively traumatic. The promise was therefore made by the university in 2009 to replace this long-established custom with email communications. It is doubtful that the modern student would have coped with the excitement of an even older communication method: up to the late 1940s the Tripos List was read aloud in the Senate House, after which copies were scattered down from the gallery to the assembled students below. At first, only two classes were displayed on the Tripos List, Senior and Junior Optimes; the word Optime extracted from 'Optime Disputasi', from the days when the 'Bachelor of the Stool' conceded that a scholar had 'argued very well'. Then the category of Poll Men, from the Greek *hoi polloi* (common people), was introduced; these had merely passed. The most dismal among these common scholars were prevented from graduating through being, in Cambridge terminology, 'plucked' from the list.

At the same time as the method of oral examination was replaced by written papers, Mathematics, regarded at the university as the pinnacle of academic learning, became the first specialised tripos. Civil Law was added in 1816, the Classical Tripos followed in 1824, Theology in 1843 and Natural and Moral Sciences in 1851. Law, History and Theology Triposes were possible by 1900. Much of this academic expansion resulted from the recommendations of the Royal Commission of 1850, which was set up to modernise the university. There are now around thirty Triposes, which each offer a further diverse range of subjects to study; the two most recently added, in the late twentieth century, have been Fine Arts and Education.

The impact of book acquisition

The printing revolution did more than weaken the oral basis of education. It led to the acquisition by the university of so many books that their storage became an issue. The earliest books at the university had been stored in chests. Their value ensured that a book chest had a number of locks with different key holders; in fact, they were generally so valuable that college members could take out loans from the university against books left as a deposit. Loan defaulters doubtless added to the university's collection. Storing books in chests must have been inconvenient and their use until the mid-1400s, 250 years after the foundation of the university, suggests both a low number of users and a small quantity of books.

The building of the first libraries reflected the wider use of books at the university. The first one was above the ground floor of the Old Schools Building, opposite the front gate of Clare College. Its construction began in 1420. Remnants of the building were hidden in the 1750s behind the white Portland façade alongside the Senate House. Now, there are around 120 libraries in the university. New ones are still being built, while old ones are occasionally stood down or merged with others. This huge number is less surprising when it is remembered that every college, faculty and museum of the university establishes a library. Many colleges, even some of the newer ones, have old and new libraries.

The Old Schools was a two-storied rectangular building in courtyard form. Three sides of the first floor were dedicated to libraries, while the fourth, on the north side, was a chapel. The western range contained the 'New Library', completed in 1457; the Common Library took up the first floor of the south range from circa 1470; while in the east range was 'The Library of our Lord Chancellor', built in 1473, to which access was particularly restricted. The most valued books, the *'libri concatenati'*, would have been chained to the bookshelves, while those designated as *'libri distribuendi'* could remain in circulation among senior members of the university. The university would rarely have purchased books; nearly all those in its possession would have been received as bequests.

There are no complete records of the books held within the Lord Chancellor's library, but more than half of those in the Common Library are thought to have been works of theology. Canon law was, naturally, well represented. Evidently access to the Common Library for undergraduates had been possible at the beginning, as by the 1470s the right of admission for an undergraduate had been specifically removed unless they were accompanied by a graduate. Prejudice against the medieval scholars was reflected by a bishop of Durham with connections to Cambridge. They were, this cleric wrote in 1333, with the timeless prejudice against youth, likely to deposit 'catarrh from a running nose, spittle from a mouth engaged in too much idle chatter, fragments of cheese and fruit, or doodle in the margins and take naps with their heads on books'.

The printing press was to undermine the book's role as a pledge and loosen the restrictions over their access by students. Books remained expensive but printers were devising ways to reduce costs; the 1458 Bible of Johannes Gutenberg was printed with forty-two lines per page rather than the thirty-six of earlier editions and vellum was gradually replaced by thick paper, which in due course was produced more thinly. Cheaper books spread ownership.

The new technology had another impact in Cambridge, however. Books had, traditionally, provided a wide range of jobs for local people. Bookselling increased but, book binders apart, there was less employment for those associated with the book trade: opportunities for copying scribes, parchment dealers and limners, who illuminated scripts, became limited. Book-related employment extended to the colleges. Trinity Hall retains records of payments to 'book-bearers', presumably for humping the generally heavy tomes of their masters from college to lecture hall and back. The University Library still employs 'book-movers' and 'book-fetchers'.

It was at this time that the university began its journey towards becoming a vast depository of books. About five million books were printed in Europe before the close of the fifteenth century; from these incunabula (the term for books printed before 1501) there remain about 4,500 in Cambridge. They constitute an outstanding collection. They were collected slowly, however, as can be judged from the progress of Caxton's career. Despite devoting the last twenty years of his life to printing, he had only produced around 100 different books by the time of his death in 1491.

The university licensed sellers of books to work from 'fixed stations', initially in churches or outside their north and south walls. Theirs was one of the few stationary trades and was therefore superior to those of itinerant peddlers. The Latin word '*stationarius*' had been used to mean a trader with a fixed place of business. Booksellers secured this term for themselves: the guild formed to protect their interests became known as the Stationers and ultimately gave rise to the word 'stationery' – the 'e' was an eighteenth-century deviation from the original spelling. The association of books with churches has led to old bookshops, such as the Cambridge University Press (CUP) bookshop by Great St Mary's or those near St Paul's in London, being sited close to churches. When a bookseller outgrew his fixed station he naturally moved across the street to more permanent premises. Books have been bound and sold from the premises now occupied by CUP since the 1580s.

The Stationers' Guild, founded in 1403, controlled printing in fifteenth-century England. Printed books, produced in previously unimagined quantities, could be turned to support dangerous causes in those times. The guild, with which the government kept in close contact, ran the licence system for printing. The university received its first licence to run a press in 1517; in 1534 the king strengthened the university's printing authority by a Royal Charter which granted the power of censorship to the university, together with the right to license three printers.

The first printer in Cambridge was John Siberch, who ran a press from his home opposite St Michael's Church in Trinity Street, roughly where the porter's lodge of Gonville & Caius now stands. Siberch's return to Germany in 1522 caused printing to cease in Cambridge until 1582, when Dr Thomas, a fellow of King's College, was appointed university printer.

It is remarkable that a place of learning such as Cambridge University did not exercise its right to print during this sixty-year period, during which hungry European minds were being fed with the ideas of the Renaissance through this revolutionary technology. The explanation lies in the restrictive practices of the London Stationers' Guild. This guild acquired considerable censorship power, which had been strengthened by its legally recognised status as a corporation in 1557. Despite the king's actions of 1534, they did not wish printing to resume in Cambridge following Siberch's departure. When it was clear that Dr Thomas intended to start a press, members of the Stationers' Guild, with the backing of the notoriously conservative Bishop of London, John Aylmer, seized the Cambridge 'presse and furniture'.

As a fellow of Queens' College, Bishop Almer knew Cambridge and he feared the books which the puritan interest in Cambridge would print. His involvement indicated how the rapidly changing religious background made book publishing a dangerous practice, particularly when watchful authorities supported the restrictive trade practices of the Stationers' Guild. Nonetheless, the university reclaimed, through the university chancellor, their equipment and the freedom to print. Fortunately, their chancellor was also Elizabeth I's chancellor, William Cecil, Lord Burghley. He had studied at St John's and was chancellor of the university from 1559 to his death in 1598.

Cambridge bookshops

This interest in books at the university has rubbed off on the town. Since the sixteenth century Cambridge has never been short of bookshops. It was the seventh town in Britain to respond to the Public Library Act in 1850, which encouraged communities of over 10,000 people to raise money to establish a library. An impressive library, well lit through an elegant domed cupola, was built in Wheeler Street, off the Market Square. However, rather like the college libraries, its uses have varied: once a suitably impressive reception hall for tourists seeking advice about Cambridge, it was converted into a restaurant in 2009. The present town library nestles amid the shops of Lion Yard and the Grand Arcade.

Trinity Street, since its conversion to a street of business in the nineteenth century, has been good territory for bibliophiles. In the 1851 census there were four booksellers in the street, among them Alexander Macmillan, who, with his brother, founded the Macmillan Publishing Group; their bookshop, opposite Great St Mary's, later became Bowes and Bowes. By the end of the 1990s, there were two bookshops left in the street; CUP, and Heffers at No. 20. With occasional relocations, new arrivals and closures, the town now supports around twenty-five bookshops. They are mostly pressed into an area around Trinity Street, St Edward's Passage, Green Street and Sidney Street. Recently, more bookshops have opened in Mill Road, to the east of Parker's Piece. There was even a celebratory little rhyme about Cambridge bookshops which scans well to the tune of 'Frère Jacques':

> Heffers bookshop, Heffers bookshop
> Bowes and Bowes, Bowes and Bowes

Galloway and Porter, Galloway and Porter
Deighton Bell, Deighton Bell

The shape of bookselling in Cambridge has changed recently. The Bowes' business died in the 1980s and Heffers then swallowed Deighton Bell, being taken over in its turn by the Oxford-based publisher Blackwells in 1999. Although they still trade as Heffers at two premises in Trinity Street, their branches in King Street, the Grafton Centre and Sidney Street have been sold. Waterstones took over the old Dillons premises in Sidney Street in 1999.

Cambridge also has some second-hand bookshops of which it can be proud. The quality of David's, in the charming quarter of St Edward's church between the Guildhall and King's Parade, places it above all competitors. Its labyrinthine depths, reached through narrow corridors, unfold seductively before the browser. Second-hand books can also be bought at The Haunted Bookshop nearby, to which the Frenchman David first moved after leaving his stall in the Market Square; it is a tiny shop which now specialises in second-hand books for children. Stalls in the Market Square, which are positioned less than a stone's throw from the ancient fixed book stations which were once attached to St Mary's, sell old books, while bin-ends – that is, end of print runs – can be imbibed at Galloway and Porter near Sidney Sussex. Nearby on the same street Oxfam runs a second-hand bookshop, selling books of an erudition appropriate to this university community, while Browne's second-hand bookshop operates from Mill Lane.

The quarter of St Edward's has a particular significance for the book trade in Cambridge. As well as being home to two fine second-hand bookshops, for seventy years the Society for Promoting Christian Knowledge, which was founded in 1698, sold bibles from premises marked today only by the ornament above a door which now leads to accommodation for King's College students: a pediment in the form of an open book resting on top of a closed one. Sadly the SPCK's bookshop, having moved from this long-term home to Sussex Street, finally closed in 2008. It was the brave revolutionaries who came to preach at St Edwards in the early 1550s who made the business of selling bibles possible and the spark that set these Englishmen alight also reached Cambridge in the form of a book: the ninety-five theses pinned to the door of the Württemberg church by Martin Luther came to Cambridge as printed words. It is thus appropriate that this little corner of Cambridge is still devoted to books.

A variety of libraries

As religion provided a reason to build beautiful chapels, so books eventually provided a similar incentive to outstanding architecture. Book collections, largely through bequests from graduates and bachelor dons rather than by purchase, reached a size where chests became a hopelessly inadequate means of storage, and entire rooms were needed. There 'Old' college libraries (this prefix was imposed on them by the advent of their much younger and larger successors) have remained as a remarkable record of scholarship from earlier centuries; most of them still have their books stored in their original book stalls.

Illustration 8.2: St Edward's Passage, which connects the Market Square to King's Parade. The memory of books is kept alive opposite the church where the Protestant revolutionaries were first inspired by the Word through the two second-hand bookshops in this alley and the pediment above the door.

One of the oldest was established in the early 1500s at Jesus College. The original glass, which survives in the first-floor windows along the west range of Cloister Court, contains an image punning on the name of the college founder, Bishop Alcock: a proud cockerel standing on a globe. The contents of the library, too, are noteworthy, including: Archbishop Cranmer's signed copy of Erasmus's translation of the New Testament, as well as the works of Coleridge and Thomas Malthus, who were both members of the college. There is also a rare collection of John Clare's works. The 9,000 books are stacked within bookcases made in 1662. It is a delightful place, charmingly untouched by anything modern and zealously guarded by a fellow nominated as its keeper.

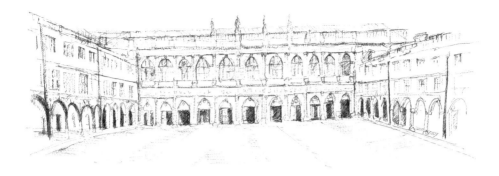

Illustration 8.3: The Wren Library, which was completed by 1690. It is a naturally well-lit building with books around the entire internal lengths of its walls. The open arches beneath the library lead to the stoa; the ranges leading upto the library form part of Nevile's Court and pre-date Wren's building by sixty years.

The oldest libraries occupied a central place in the courts of colleges, just as they had done within the cloisters of monasteries. Jesus Old Library adjoins the Master's Lodge. Trinity Hall Library, built in the late 1500s, even had a doorway in its south wall leading directly across an elevated walkway to the Master's Lodge opposite. The Master's Lodge at Clare also led directly into the college's old library. Such direct links between master and library stand as a symbol of the importance of books at the university in the Middle Ages.

Renaissance libraries such as those at Trinity Hall, Trinity College and Jesus were always placed on the first floor to benefit from the strongest light available. Indeed, so important was the issue of light that the long axis of most old college libraries ran from north to south so that the long sides of the building could draw in the light of the rising or setting sun. Scholars sat on the west side in the morning as the sun rose on the opposite side, moving across to the east after midday.

The use of candles and the consequent risk of fire was also reduced through the better natural light of the first-floor library. Furthermore, books stored above ground level were less likely to be damaged by flooding, ever a risk in Cambridge as most of the old colleges were built on low-lying land close to the Cam. Wren utilised the classical device of a stoa, or open colonnade, in order to protect his library at Trinity College from floods. In modern times Trinity's stoa is merely used for summer drinks parties or as a beautiful setting for the college May Ball bar rather than the philosophical discussions of which the Stoics would have approved. Only in the twenty-first century has a riverside college, Trinity Hall, risked building a library at ground level. Care was taken to ensure that its 'Jerwood Library', set within inches of the river bank, had exceptional protection.

A first-floor location for libraries was also preferred because of the great value of books. Inside the library books were chained to the book stalls – examples of this mechanism can still be seen in the Trinity Hall Old Library. A chain fixed to a metal bar was attached to the fore-edge of a book rather than to its spine and the book was then stored with the spine away from the fingers to avoid damage when the book was pulled from a shelf. The scholar read the book from a lectern, which was usually part of the bookshelf.

Even if the book could be prised free, a library on the first floor made it less likely that books could be stolen. Many of the modern libraries are also designed to hold books on the first floor for the same reason; indeed, not only were the bookshelves of the 1990s library at St John's placed on the first floor, but the windows were even designed not to open in order to prevent college members launching books through the windows to accomplices below.

There was agreement over the internal architecture of old libraries just as there was over their position in the college court. Bookcases with lecterns attached were set either side of a central aisle at right angles to the long east- and west-facing walls. However, the scarcity of books ensured that the library was more a place of quiet study than a place for extensive research or reading. There were barely 200 books within the Jesus library almost 100 years after it was founded; Peterhouse listed 302 books by 1418, with Queens' recording 224 and King's 175 by the 1470s. In contrast, the new Jesus Quincentenary Library opened in 1996 with almost 48,000 books.

The expansion of the colleges required changes not only to chapels; the old libraries, too, were often classed as inadequate to cope with either the quantity of books accumulated or fellows' perception of their college's prestige. Although the designs of medieval times had been driven by the need to protect and create the best conditions for study, libraries sometimes reflected the vanity of the college fellowship.

Types of libraries

Two distinct types emerged – the 'monumental' library and the 'collector's' library. Three stand out as examples of the first group: the Wren Library at Trinity, St John's old library, commissioned by the bishop of Lincoln in 1623, and, finally, the current University Library, built in the 1930s by Giles Gilbert Scott. Into the second category come the libraries of Archbishop Parker at Corpus Christi, Samuel Pepys at Magdalene and Viscount Fitzwilliam at the museum that bears his name.

Isaac Barrow, Master of Trinity College in the 1670s, revealed the motivation of some fellowships when he described the new library venture to potential donors as a facility which would 'yield much ornament to the university and honour to the nation'. The project was certainly not about books alone. Barrow chose his friend Christopher Wren as architect, who provided his services *pro bono*. Donors who financed the building were rewarded with their shields of arms at the end of the bookcases by that master of wood carving, Grinling Gibbons.

In commissioning buildings of great beauty to store books, no college has surpassed the library of Trinity College. Wren's first wish had been to design a domed circular library. His similarly shaped Sheldonian Theatre at Oxford had been finished the year before he discussed the commission with Trinity and he proposed a similarly shaped specification. The college fellows preferred an elongated pavilion. It is a beautiful, classically simple building. Whether from inside, from within Nevile's Court or looking from the Cam, it is stunning.

Wren's building replaced a library in Great Court between the Master's Lodge and King Edward's Tower and became the fourth range of Nevile's Court, which had been built sixty years earlier as a three-sided court. Like the medieval libraries, it was built on a north–south axis, with its single floor at first-floor level.

The arches beneath are partly filled in, giving the appearance of a two-storied building; the arches give the inward-facing side of the building a soft intimate appearance, while the openings on the side facing the Backs appear harsher.

Wren, like Abbot Suger, who was the architect of St Denis Cathedral in Paris, valued light greatly. In the twelfth century Abbot Suger had written of 'the power of light on the mind' and how it was 'the closest substance to God's true essence'; this was a concept which Wren understood and, as in his churches, he filled the inside space of this library with light. The bookcases, which conceal iron ties supporting the floor, are below the windows rather than between them. The windows, as well as the bookcases, can therefore stretch the length of the building. There is another benefit to scholars from the positioning of the windows way above their heads: the distractions of life passing by outside are hidden from view. This crucial consideration was to be neglected in some twentieth-century university libraries.

Within the library, Wren's seating arrangements and the storage of books were radically different to those of medieval times. Book stalls had once been placed between windows, but it was no longer unusual for architects to include a huge expanse of glass within walls. Bookcases could therefore run along the entire wall beneath the windows, extending out intermittently towards the centre of the library like a castle's crenellations. Between the bookcases Wren designed tables and chairs for scholars who had hitherto been expected to perch at a high lectern.

A statue of Lord Byron by the nineteenth-century Danish sculptor Bertel Thorvaldsen stands in a central position at the south end of the building. Bryon's admirers had commissioned the statue for presentation to Westminster Abbey, but the dean considered that Bryon's lifestyle made him ill-suited to such a distinction. His old college was less censorious. The library also has a stained glass window by Giovanni Cipriani at its south end which depicts Isaac Newton being presented to George III while another Trinity scholar, Francis Bacon, records the scene. In the nineteenth century a curtain (since removed) was positioned over the window, to be drawn when female visitors were present to cover the bare breast of the female figure portrayed in the stained glass. On permanent exhibition are Newton's own annotated copy of *Principia Mathematica* and manuscripts of A.A. Milne's *Winnie the Pooh* and *The House at Pooh Corner*. Milne had studied at Trinity. Not only were books stored there: before museums opened in Cambridge, Wren's library was considered the most appropriate place to store a variety of anthropological artefacts, astronomical instruments and even inscriptions from Hadrian's Wall which fellows had brought proudly to their college. This practice continued until the university's museums were built in the nineteenth century.

As the first monumental library, Wren's building was filled by acquisition; the Parker Library at Corpus Christi was, in contrast, constructed *after* the acquisition of its books. It is the most famous collector's library. Matthew Parker was personal chaplain to Anne Boleyn and then Henry VIII; he was master of Corpus Christi College in the 1540s before Queen Elizabeth made him Archbishop of Canterbury in 1559. He was in an outstanding position to collect the books which the monasteries were no longer able to protect, but in part his quest for books was to uncover justification for the break with Rome. He believed that with the arrival of Saint Augustine on the Kentish coast in AD 597 had come the papal intent to create an independent English church: an intent which had been thwarted by the Norman invasion and the centralising reforms of Pope Gregory VII in the 1070s. King Alfred's translation of Gregory the Great's

Pastoral Care, the Gospels of St Augustine and biblical texts written in Old English helped those arguing that the break with Rome was a restoration rather than a revolution. Even the library's unguarded ownership of bibles in English was a dramatic change, as Parker and his contemporaries had lived through a time when their possession had been a capital offence.

Parker must have also loved books for their own sake, however. The quality of his collection is stupefying: in addition to the books of Alfred and Augustine, it contains rare Romanesque bibles, the oldest version of the *Anglo-Saxon Chronicle* and books written by Bede and Chaucer. It was also through Archbishop Parker that Cambridge colleges became the depository of choice for many subsequent collectors of illuminated manuscripts; there are, spread between the Fitzwilliam Museum, the University Library and the colleges, around 3,000 such manuscripts in Cambridge. It is a collection which is rivalled only by that of the Vatican.

The Parker is the one library in Cambridge in which the quality of books palpably outweighs the architectural interest of the library building itself, which was designed by Wilkins in the 1820s and occupies the first floor of the south side of New Court. The books are unique and fascinating; perhaps no architect could have designed an adequate sanctuary. Indeed, the value of the collection was reflected in the complexity of Parker's will: he tied three Cambridge colleges together in a revolving contract which enforced an audit of the books each year on 6 August by the Masters of Gonville & Caius and Trinity Hall. Missing books would incur a fine; if the fine remained unpaid the custody of the books, and his silver plate, were to be handed over to Caius. Should that college not meet these obligations, Trinity Hall was to take over the library. In the event of their failure to meet Parker's criteria, the books were to be returned to Corpus. The college was evidently provoked into exemplary care, as no books were lost and the annual inspection has long since ceased.

The Pepys Library at Magdalene College is another outstanding example of a collectors' library. The building is an attractive amalgam of Tudor and Classical styles; its front façade, with its Classical logia and windows, has much in common with the façade of the Old Schools designed by Stephen Wright. The reverse of the building, in red brick, is strangely domestic given its grand front façade. Surprisingly, neither the precise age of the building nor the architect's name are known, although it was presumably completed by 1688, as it appears in Logan's engraving of Cambridge of that date.

Pepys' books arrived in 1724, twenty-one years after his death; as he had no children, his college was the obvious choice as the custodian of his library. This date is recorded in the central arch of the Pepys Building, along with the legend *'Bibiotheca Pepysiana'* and Cicero's motto, *Mens cujusque is est quisque* – 'The mind's the man'. Pepys, who had originally entered Magdalene as a sizar, a student whose fees were paid by the college, had determined to limit his collection to 3,000 books, holding the curious notion that the accumulated wisdom of the world could therein be adequately represented. Once the limit had been reached, a book was discarded for each new one that was acquired. The books are still arranged according to height, as Pepys had instructed, on oak shelves built at his command by an Admiralty Master Carpenter in 1666; they too came to the college.

Pepys' will was almost as complicated as that of Archbishop Parker's a hundred years earlier and it is tempting to think that the archbishop's legacy may have inspired Pepys' own: each exhibit the neuroses of bibliophiles who worry over the fate of their collection after their death. Pepys, who had been an undergraduate at Magdalene College in 1650, left his books to the college, but in the event of the college declining his gift, he specified that they be offered to Trinity College. If Magdalene accepted his bequest, an annual inspection by Trinity College was required and any losses or poor handling was to result in the collection's transfer to Trinity. There is no record of the inspection by Trinity ever have been carried out. Nonetheless, in the nineteenth century Magdalene felt it should secure Trinity's agreement to move the books from the library to the Master's Lodge, a change which was never implemented.

In fact, not quite 3,000 books arrived at Magdalene; five volumes on loan at the time of Pepys' death were never recovered despite the efforts of John Jackson, Pepys' nephew and a Magdalene graduate. A further three volumes have gone missing, two before 1819 and another prior to 1899. Subsequent quincentennial audits have declared no further losses. His bequest also contained the manuscript of his famous diary, which was left unread at Magdalene, its contents concealed by a coded short hand, until 1825. As Viscount Fitzwilliam required that his pictures never leave the Fitzwilliam Museum, so Pepys forbade the lending of any of his books.

This literary connection with Pepys triggered the college's interest in many of the country's greatest writers. The City Council has even acknowledged this connection by moulding black and white bollards in the pavements near the college in the shape of an old-fashioned fountain pen; they stretch either side of Bridge Street from the Round Church up to Magdalene College. Sadly, it is probable that this gesture is wasted on the keyboard-focused modern student.

There have been other significant literary bequests to colleges; in the seventeenth century William Sancroft, Archbishop of Canterbury, left 5,000 volumes to Emmanuel, while the bishop of Lincoln gave his collection to St John's later in the same century. In the next century George I directed that the library of the bishop of Ely be presented to the University Library. The seventh Viscount Fitzwilliam, who, like Pepys, stored his books by height, left his collection of 10,000 books to the museum he founded. It is a tradition which continues: in 1943 Newton's old library was donated to Trinity College and in the 1950s Lord Rothschild's collection of English literature was presented to the same college.

The Wren and other old libraries had been designed to serve the fellows of the college community. However, during the nineteenth century part of the north wing of Trinity's Nevile's Court was converted into a library for an hitherto neglected group of readers: its purpose was to give students, rather than just fellows, access to books. The idea of libraries serving only fellows and researchers, rather than undergraduates, nonetheless lived on for some time after Trinity's new library. Even in the 1930s the University Library was conceived as a place for research rather than a place of study for undergraduates.

The new libraries

During the latter half of the nineteenth century the university's hunger for books had caused them to occupy all the buildings on the Old Schools site – the Registry, the heart of the university's administration, which now occupies these buildings, was then sited in St Andrew's Street opposite the town's main Post Office. Since 1837 the university had also had its own library, designed by Charles Cockerell, which lay alongside Senate House Passage. Both resources proved inadequate by the 1930s and as a result the university commissioned the present building, which opened in 1935.

The library is one of five copyright libraries in the British Isles; Trinity College, Dublin, runs a sixth. They are each entitled to receive a copy of every book published in Britain. The Cambridge University Library chooses to accept almost 100,000 books each year from those it is offered. Although the University Library runs two other small libraries in Cambridge it is uniquely compact among copyright libraries, a factor contributing to its extremely efficient book-retrieval service. Those running the library now cheerfully admit to the dubious decisions of their predecessors, such as the rejection in the 1800s of the works of Jane Austen and Beethoven, but acknowledge no more recent errors.

The University Library publishes some diverting statistics. In the medieval chests which stocked the first library when it opened in the 1420s, there were possibly 200 books. In comparison, the present library holds six million books, stored on ninety-two miles of shelving; every week more than 1,500 books and 2,000 periodicals are delivered to its premises. Book acquisitions now require more than two miles of new shelving to be added every year.

The library extension, started to the rear of the building in 2004, is designed to store nineteenth-century books in ideal conditions while freeing space in the older building. The shift in the nineteenth century from printing on paper made from rags to printing on paper made from wood pulp means that a book from the late Victorian period, which is full of chemical residues, is at much greater risk of decay than one printed in Tudor England.

Libraries have taken over from chapels as excuses for colleges to commission fine architecture, but modern architects have been liberated from the restrictions their predecessors worked under through building services technology. Library design and usage have changed irrevocably. The Wren Library used to shut for three months of the year because of the cold. Modern libraries are open all year and in some cases twenty-four hours a day. Books can now be stored on the ground floor and on bookshelves along the central axis of the building with readers, not books, placed towards the outer edge – often glazed – of the building. An immense variation in design is possible, which is fully reflected in the modern libraries of the university. Unlike the medieval libraries, each of their successors is different.

In the library in Chapel Court at St John's, designed by Edward Cullinan in the 1990s, the students sit around the edge of the building; books are stacked centrally. The building stands opposite the huge west end of the neo-Gothic college chapel and the building echoes its religious partner in this court. It is almost church-like, with its cruciform shape and pointed gables with columns that would suit any neo-Gothic structure. Inside it is light and the space is broken up into interesting nooks for nest-building by students, overlooking on one side the austere Chapel Court and on the other the luxury of the master's garden.

The Jesus library, which opened in 1996 to celebrate their quincentennial anniversary, is another example of a college making a statement about its pride and wealth – although in this case it perhaps reflects the wealth of its old members, as it was funded entirely from their donations. It is a magnificent building and the architectural prizes it has won make note of its low building costs. Externally its Georgian proportions and windows seem a little severe; inside, however, its fittings are opulent and it works brilliantly as a place of study. The ground floor is dedicated to computers and offices, so that, in keeping with tradition, its books are stored on the first floor and above. It is a vast barrel-vaulted space with a broad staircase on the central axis; white walls reflect the light which comes down through the skylight above. The statues, the pictures and the stark whiteness of the walls against the deep-pile lilac carpet might suggest to the casual visitor that he has stumbled upon a private museum rather than a library. Upstairs there are book-lined alcoves with plants on central galleries; books are mostly stored on the outside walls.

New Hall's library, built in the 1950s, is again different; modern conveniences such as electric light have enabled the building to be built along an east–west axis. Indeed, daylight is acknowledged there as the enemy for its impact on valuable manuscripts. The roof on this building therefore overhangs the walls to reduce the ingress of light. Inside there is a single vertiginous central staircase which runs steeply from the ground floor to the third floor. Reflecting the symbiotic relationship between college chapels and libraries, it appears almost like a gothic church, with a barrel-vaulted nave and pillars on both sides; ironically, New Hall is one of the few colleges built without a chapel. Book stacks fill the external walls of the building, with an open area left on the ground floor for study.

These new libraries have enormous capacities; Trinity's, for example, holds 250,000 volumes. As recently as the 1970s a collection of only around 20,000 books was generally thought appropriate for a working college library. They differ from their predecessors in other ways, too: technology has given architects the ability to devise new shapes for libraries. The Newnham Rare Books Library, designed in the 1980s by Van Heyningen and Haward, is a barrel-vaulted multi-coloured brick building. Its shape matches that of the medieval chests in which rare books had once been stored.

Variety in form is also characteristic of the modern libraries of Trinity Hall and Clare. Trinity Hall barely had an undergraduate library until the 1990s, when the ground floor beneath its Old Library was set aside for undergraduates. It was tended, not untypically in the era of late-twentieth-century college libraries, by the wife of a fellow and was open on only two afternoons a week. Then, in the late 1990s, Freeland Rees Roberts were commissioned to build the Jerwood Library. The building completely altered the dynamics of the college, as it was sited in the depths of the relatively small college grounds alongside the Cam, where few members in the past had bothered to go. The attractive half-timbered brick building now draws people into numerous discreet spaces within its five storeys. It is an intimate and pleasant place in which to work. A lesser concern with theft than at St John's is reflected in the students' freedom to open its windows.

Clare Library was designed in the 1980s; the architect Philip Dowson was inspired by Brunelleschi's Florentine Pazzi Chapel. The octagonal building faces the University Library, with its back to the centre of the college; it is almost as though it is paying homage to the grand depository of books in whose shadow it stands. As a free-standing circular building, it is uncertain whether the library acts as the final range to Memorial Court or as an object in its own space. Intriguingly, Wren's first, circular, design for the Trinity Library was rejected over precisely this dilemma of orientation. The Clare library works well internally; it has a double-height octagonal entrance hall which echoes the college's elegant antechapel. Books are placed around the outside walls, with work space located centrally.

Security remains a problem for libraries both modern and old, although modern books, unlike those of medieval times, are not particularly valuable. In the Middle Ages there was a better tradition of guarding books because they were immediately of value. The type of care taken of books in fifteenth-century England

Illustration 8.4: Newnham's Rare Books Library, alongside Sidgwick Avenue. It connects delightfully the storage of precious books in the twenty-first century with the book chests of medieval Europe.

might have prevented the plundering of the University Library by a Jesus graduate in the twentieth. Two original editions of Newton's *Principia* and a work by Galileo went missing; the culprit was imprisoned in 2002. These are not the only priceless works to have been lost to the university: it was another Jesuan, James Halliwell-Phillips, who allegedly removed manuscripts from the Wren Library when a postgraduate at Trinity in the late 1800s; rather bizarrely, it is said that he later presented them to the British Library, where they remain. In the confusion around the allegations the British Library first removed and then restored his Reader's Ticket. In any event, the guarding of books in Cambridge is a huge task at which the university has not always excelled; it was once famed in the rare books trade for its reticence over its losses.

Another type of library, the faculty library, was developed more recently to complement the medieval, the monumental and the collectors' varieties. They developed as the academic focus moved away from colleges back to the centre of the university, where it had been in medieval times; they are therefore mostly twentieth-century creations, although the first History Faculty library opened in 1807.

The necessity for extra space for their books often resulted, as we have seen, in colleges developing grand free-standing buildings in addition to the modest libraries they already possessed. Similarly, faculties have used libraries to express their own ambitions. The History Faculty, viewed by some as a backward-looking and conservative faculty, was the first to commission a provocatively modern library. Its physical form could not have contrasted more strongly with the Wren Library, also a ground-breaker in its day. Where Wren used the form of his structure, through its size and window shape, to make his building work, the Seeley Historical library, covered with a skin of glass and metal, works only through a total reliance on building services technology. Unlike the readers in Wren's library, whose eyes have little opportunity to wander, occupants of the Seeley Library sit facing a glass front which opens out onto the main open space of the Sidgwick Site, where students mingle.

The library, which occupies three-quarters of the building, certainly tackled the issue of book security; the book-stacks radiate out from a point in line with the librarians' desks, like the ribs of a lady's fan, so that all the bookshelves can be seen at once. However, beyond security, it ignored many of the established design criteria of a library; it lacks intimacy and its role as a study centre could have been addressed more successfully. It feels as though its users are under constant surveillance; indeed, architectural guides describe it as a 'Benthamite panoptican'.

Another faculty library equally dependent on technology is the Squire Law Library, within Foster's faculty building and opposite the Seeley on the Sidgwick Site. Like the History Library it, too, moved from more central premises. The library occupies the top three floors alongside the glazed barrel-shaped north-facing side of the building; students sit near the glass with views out through the pipes which adorn the inside and outside of Foster's building. Books are stored centrally; air movement, humidity and temperature are all mechanically controlled and, after some initial problems with excessive sound transmission, the building has been acknowledged as technically efficient. Its power requirements, however, combined with the decision to open all day every day has made it a particularly high consumer of energy. Both this and the Jerwood Library alongside Garret Hostel Bridge look delightful when lit up at night but the merits of such huge energy consumption merely to accommodate a few late-working students are questionable.

This variety of libraries in Cambridge, from university to college to faculty, must entail a considerable duplication of books, particularly of the most popular ones. Librarians acknowledge that a substantial majority of the books are little better than wallpaper, never leaving their shelves. In this sense, the libraries are, as they were in medieval and Jacobean England, primarily places for study where, coincidentally, books are stored. Darwin College has been honest in calling the space in which it stores books a 'study-centre'. It offers quiet corners looking out across the Cam to Laundress Green for study or personal reading; the books that line the wall which faces onto Silver Street are more suited to the down-time reading of the decently educated student rather than to postgraduate research.

The future of libraries in Cambridge

Belief in the future of books and libraries in Cambridge remains strong. Since 1980, Clare, Newnham, Jesus, Trinity Hall, St John's and Homerton have each opened new libraries and work began in 2007 on two more, at Selwyn and Corpus Christi. The books in the new Corpus library will be kept above a student bar and party room; books at this college, and also at Sidney Sussex and Magdalene, were once stored above sixteenth-century college chapels. It is as if a college's books are always close to its focal point, be it the chapel of a medieval college or the student bar in the twenty-first century. Certainly, some colleges try to emphasise how books are central to their culture: Trinity College and Clare have a book-signing ceremony for each year's new undergraduates to mark their admission to college and the membership of their libraries. It is usually combined with a party in the library or the Master's Lodge. It is a symbolic event which underlines the importance of books and the privilege of having access to them – and which in a way replaces the university's matriculation ceremony.

Books have provided excuses for some magnificent, as well as some controversial, architecture. The oldest of the libraries, such as those at Trinity Hall or Jesus, are time capsules from medieval England, while that at Trinity College reflects the culture of the late eighteenth century, after which time no further books could be squeezed onto its shelves. Similarly, the Fitzwilliam Museum Library reflects the tastes of a cultivated English gentleman in the early 1800s.

Many of the libraries, particularly the Parker, the Pepys and the Wren, hold unique manuscripts and books which reach to the heart of English culture. Had it not been for the erudition of men like Matthew Parker at Corpus Christi, many of these books, which reflect this country's culture through their brilliant illuminated texts, would undoubtedly have been lost in the troubles of sixteenth- and seventeenth-century England. The libraries of Cambridge colleges have thus been outstandingly successful in fulfilling a university's central obligation to pass a country's cultural values from generation to generation.

The story of Cambridge books and libraries began in small chests in the thirteenth century and moved through modestly sized college libraries and the grand libraries of Wren and Cockerell to the monumental libraries of the twentieth century. On that journey, books of huge cultural value have been captured in Cambridge and kept in beautiful buildings.

In a throwback to the bookless scholar of the Middle Ages, information technology may be causing a decline in the importance of books to undergraduates; the reflex reaction of the researching student is now to go onto the Internet rather than to reach for a book. Similarly, the Internet can be blamed for a reduction in the number of books written by academics; briefer articles are circulated on the World Wide Web, leading perhaps to the neglect of deeper research. As with Gutenberg's press, the eventual impact of information technology through, for example, virtual books will take time to be measured.

Conventional libraries are still being built, even if the consensus over their design has been lost. E-books have, so far, made only a small impact. Perhaps with the pace of technological change, all that has been achieved is the introduction of uncertainty over the future. Not only does the use of e-books lack the serendipity of browsing along bookshelves, but the very pace of technical change makes it difficult to choose any one new technology on which to focus. Cambridge's reputation as a place of science may yet impact directly on the business of book storage, of course: a spin-out company from the university's Cavendish Laboratory, Plastic Logic, is a world leader in flexible electronic-paper display technology, launching its 'eReader' onto the market in 2009. The present Cavendish Professor, Sir Richard Friend, and Henning Sirringhaus, who is head of Microelectronics and Optoelectronics at the Cavendish, sit on its board.

Despite such intimations of change, those running the University Library declared in their Long Term Plan of 2006 that they expect 'no significant reduction in the output of traditional paper-based publishing'. It leaves the hope that future students will still derive comfort from these dumb teachers, as well as the expectation that libraries will retain the role, hitherto fulfilled by chapels, of inspiring architects to increase the sum of magnificent buildings in Cambridge.

Chapter 9

The Gathering of Wealth

The Cambridge academic community has always excelled at gathering wealth into the university. Its members have never been as isolated from the less cerebral world of money-making as their background might suggest. Indeed, professional managers from the world of business, who come to assist the university in managing its affairs, are generally astonished to find how 'finance' is on the mind of every academic. Money has always been at the heart of the university's culture.

How successful it had been in accumulating riches over 800 years became clearer following the election of the Labour Government in 1997, when the colleges and university were finally obliged to make full disclosure of their assets. The declared figures reach far beyond the point to which most people can relate. Furthermore, the accounts of university and colleges are very complex; a rummage within the detail reveals that simplistic definitions of riches do not apply, as some assets are excluded from the calculations and others are subject to a variety of special accounting rules. Operational and non-operational buildings are measured under diverse rules, while there are also trust assets, endowment assets and other classes of asset, such as historic buildings and art treasures, each of which is treated differently.

Assessment of income is a no less complicated issue than the analysis of assets. New definitions of income have been devised, which bear little relation to those associated with modern personal taxation. There are many income sources, each requiring different accounting procedures. For example, there is corporate internal income derived from renting out facilities and corporate external wealth from endowments, as well as investments held on trust for specific purposes. There are, moreover, numerous binding restrictions on how income can be spent.

Whatever is left in or taken out, however the wealth is recorded and wherever it is spent, the simplest conclusion to draw is that the university and the colleges are extremely rich.

Wealth comparisons and exceptional demands

Reliable comparisons of wealth between universities are difficult to make and recourse to broad conclusions is, again, the safest option. Leading American universities, notably Yale, Stanford and Harvard, are far richer than Cambridge. Other British universities, apart from Oxford, are much poorer. In the pre-credit crunch days of 2008, and at an exchange rate of $1.5 to £1, Harvard was generally credited with endowments of £25 billion, Yale £15 billion and Stanford £11 billion. Those of Cambridge University and its colleges were estimated at just under £5 billion, Oxford coming a little behind. After Oxford and Cambridge, the next richest in Britain are two of the long-established Scottish universities, Glasgow and Edinburgh; they each record endowments of a value less than half of those revealed at Cambridge.

Until quite recently, colleges derived most of their income from agriculture. Revenue was thus a simple matter: the value of the harvest less its costs. To protect their long-term interests, represented by the land, college statutes sensibly directed that capital could not be sold to finance current expenditure. However, colleges now have many diverse assets and capital appreciation, rather than income, is often an investment objective. The determination of income, as well as deciding how assets should be valued and classified, has therefore become much more complex. Some universities, including Cambridge, now measure both income and capital at the beginning and end of a period, weighting the values of several years through complicated formulae with the objective of smoothing out variations. Income can then be redefined as a percentage of the total value of assets and may perhaps prove to be higher than previously.

Predictably, universities have devised different formulae to calculate income. Harvard uses 'total return', Cambridge 'total value' – equally sophisticated but a little different. This is why inter-institutional comparisons have become so difficult. Two Cambridge colleges, Caius and Jesus, have adopted the 'total value' approach chosen by the university's trustees. Other colleges have debated the issue, but perhaps because 'total value' does not always increase present income, have so far declined change. Definitions of wealth and income are very important because they affect current expenditure. This needs to be remembered when any of these financial comparisons – within or without the university – are discussed.

In any debate about wealth, it is essential to acknowledge that although the university and its colleges are rich, the demands on their resources are vast. They are major custodians of the country's heritage; collections of rare books, artefacts and outstanding paintings demand expensive care. There are nine university museums full of such valuable objects, quite apart from those in colleges, and miracles are required to finance additions to these collections or sometimes merely to ensure their maintenance. King's College Chapel is glorious, but it consumes cash. A college's illuminated manuscripts may stimulate scholarship, but their protection troubles college bursars. The financial subsidies from government and the university for these collections barely amount to more than life support.

College buildings also need exceptional protection. Most buildings which make up the country's national heritage are carefully isolated from the impact of daily use; in contrast, Cambridge students roam through their colleges' ancient buildings, increasing maintenance bills with every footfall. The conversion of medieval buildings, erected centuries before mixed-sex education or health and safety requirements, has also been hugely expensive. Even the cost of new building in Cambridge exceeds the expense faced by most other universities. A provincial university can construct buildings which are practical but possibly unattractive in order to meet a modest budget. Planners in Cambridge, however, demand a much higher, and more expensive, aesthetic standard in order to match the architectural heritage established over the past 800 years.

Teaching costs at Cambridge in proportion to the number of students are also far higher than elsewhere, as its renowned supervision system requires a remarkably high ratio of tutors to students. Even if some of the teaching burden is off-loaded onto postgraduates, figures suggest that the 18,000-odd students (undergraduates and postgraduates) are tended by a body of approximately 7,000 academics. Among the latter, however, there will be some academics whose research pursuits leave very little time for tuition. Reliable figures are difficult to provide and, indeed, the issue of 'contact hours' between student and teacher has become a matter of concern at a number of universities. It is probably safe, however, to assume a ratio of around four students to one teacher at Cambridge; in contrast, a ratio of twenty-eight to one is generally thought applicable elsewhere in Britain.

Costs of academic courses vary – from those of medics and vets to the philosophers who barely consume pens or paper. The average costs of teaching in 2008/9 were estimated at around £14,000 per student. Students' fees and the government contribute £9,000. The colleges and university are left to make up the deficit of £5,000. The total shortfall rises in proportion to the number of students the university educates – and the university is expanding rapidly. The provision of pensions for the large staff has also become a huge liability – the days have passed when elderly dons in holy orders could be quietly moved on to one of the many livings which were in the gift of the colleges.

This is why the finance men at Cambridge, as well as those at other universities, seek political approval to impose higher charges on students. They also look enviously at the £22,000 annual fee which Harvard charges. All universities, however, even Cambridge, will have to do more to convince potential students that the prospect of considerable debt justifies the university experience.

In addition to the exceptional demands on the wealth of Cambridge described above, the university needs also to be able to continue to compete with the world's best universities. Top academics must be attracted to Cambridge. The university trades on the prestige and charm of working in Cambridge as much as it dares, but still cannot drift too far from the salary benchmarks set by rich American universities. Likewise, its facilities, such as those for sport and music, require considerable investment if it is to compete successfully for the best international scholars.

International competition now extends also to securing the very brightest students. It is no longer a question of whether Oxford or Cambridge, Trinity or King's, secures the brightest young people. American universities use their wealth to offer tempting bursarships and scholars have always been itinerant. Cambridge uses its bursary schemes energetically to ensure no one is put off from applying because of financial considerations; so far, this has been aimed at the relatively impoverished. The future use of bursaries may be to ensure that the brightest, regardless of their financial profile, come to Cambridge.

A host of factors – a unique heritage, college-based education, competition from other universities and a role supporting the knowledge industries – demands exceptional wealth. This is the basis of the university's pleading for additional funds to the country's rulers – and such pleading is a skill Cambridge academics have honed over centuries. Their success in securing funds is self-evident. The university's ancient buildings appear in good condition and new ones are still being opened. Colleges build new libraries, conference centres and concert halls. Yet 500 years after all the colleges but Magdalene reported trading losses to Henry VIII's commissioners, most of the colleges still post net operating losses in their annual accounts. It may be a desperate struggle to match demands on their wealth to their resources, but they manage somehow.

The assets of most other universities are controlled centrally. This is not the case at Cambridge, where the colleges, particularly the older ones, own much of the wealth. Of the almost £5 billion of assets across the entire university, roughly two-thirds are owned by the colleges. The university itself possessed little wealth, aside perhaps from the treasures it held in the Fitzwilliam Museum, until the start of the twentieth century. From this time funding from government for both undergraduate teaching and research work, fed in through the university rather than the colleges, became increasingly significant. The growth in state funding, combined with the contributions from activities such as the University Press, its Examination Board and its own fund-raising foundation, has created a more even balance of wealth ownership and power between colleges and university.

Wealth accumulation

The thirteenth-century Oxford scholars who settled in Cambridge arrived with little more than a few chests to contain their possessions. Now the wealth of just one college, Trinity, merits a position, after the Crown and the Church of England, as the third-richest of the country's institutions. The ways in which the academic community brought – and continues to bring – wealth into their colleges makes an interesting story.

The first fundamental achievement of the university in the cause of wealth accumulation was the securing for its colleges of the special taxation status which the right of mortmain brought. The colleges could then become the conduits through which wealth reached into the academic community.

College archives record the donation of chests containing cash, property deeds or perhaps books from those outside the university community. The motives behind the gifts probably ranged from the altruistic wish to support education to the securing of some favour within the college's gift or the promise of prayers for their soul. The 'Chest' remains a powerful symbol of the university's wealth. An ancient chest on wheels with seventeen locks, which replaced one burnt in the Peasants' Revolt of 1381, remains in the Old Schools Office of the Registrary, the university's senior administrator. It conjures up an image of university money being carefully counted in and cautiously handed out before the key-holders bang the chest shut.

Another external source of wealth was the Roman Catholic Church. Over thirty years before the Dissolution of the Monasteries, in 1496, Bishop Alcock removed the two remaining nuns of St Radegund – about whom the slander was spread that one was loose and the other absent – and took over their premises to found Jesus College. A few decades later, Lady Margaret Beaufort used the wealth of the dissolved Creake Abbey in Norfolk and the nunneries of Bromhall (Berkshire) and Higham (Kent) to fund St John's and Christ's colleges. Then, through the gift of monastic land in the 1530s, the colleges of Magdalene, Sidney

Sussex and Emmanuel were founded. Others, such as Queens' and Trinity College, either received monastic land and endowments or took the very stones of monasteries to extend their own colleges.

By the mid-1500s an important new source of wealth had appeared: the dons and graduates themselves. The university's contribution to the kingdom had grown through its members securing powerful positions in Church and state. These Cambridge men grew rich. Some, particularly those who retained teaching positions at the university, were of necessity unmarried and without legitimate heirs. Their old college was the natural ultimate depository for their wealth.

Cambridge has benefited consistently from those it nurtured. Priests such as Gonville and Bateman at Trinity Hall, or Docket at Queens', played pivotal roles in colleges, but their contributions were inspirational rather than financial. After the fifteenth century, its graduates began to contribute financially. In the mid-1550s Dr Caius used the great wealth he had acquired as a successful London doctor to support the indigent Gonville College. A generation later, Archbishop Parker left valuable plate, an unrivalled manuscript library and his vast collection of printed books to Corpus Christi College. There are examples of huge generosity to many colleges. Thomas Nevile, a rich cleric who held the Mastership of Magdalene and then of Trinity College, funded the building of Nevile's Court at Trinity; during his Mastership of that college, he had also been instrumental in the transformation of the Great Court.

Charles Beaumont, a fellow of Peterhouse in the early 1700s, provided masters of Peterhouse with an impressive home. It stands alongside Pembroke College on the opposite side of Trumpington Road to the main entrance of Peterhouse. Later in the same century a vice-master of Trinity, Richard Walker, gave five acres besides Free School Lane to the university. It became the first Botanic Garden in 1762. At the beginning of the twentieth century Dr Glashier, a fellow of Trinity College, left his ceramics and porcelain collection to the Fitzwilliam Museum. The munificence of departing dons is not just confined to the past: when Professor Grierson, Senior Fellow of Gonville & Caius, died in 2006 he left a coin collection valued at up to £10 million to be shared between his college and the Fitzwilliam Museum.

Men no longer dominate this channel of wealth into the colleges as they once did. As is so often the case in Cambridge, ancient traditions continue into modern times with a slight twist. There are now rich unmarried women who leave their wealth to the university. Spinsters have taken the place of the celibate male don. A shortage of men after two World Wars, perhaps compounded by the male fear of a superior female intellect, has left an above-average number of spinsters among Newnham and Girton graduates. As a result, women's colleges enjoy a substantial flow of wealth from spinsters' legacies, as the medieval colleges once did from those of unmarried men. A survey undertaken by four British universities in 2007 suggested that clever spinsters will remain a source of wealth, concluding that for each sixteen-point rise in IQ a man's chance of marriage rose by 35 per cent, while a woman's prospects fell by 40 per cent. In any event, whatever the sex of the deceased, legacies are welcomed by bursars – in many cases they are probably more welcome than gifts from the living, as live donors tend to be more difficult to deal with.

Illustration 9.1: The Peterhouse Master's Lodge, built in 1701 initially as a private residence for Dr Charles Beaumont, a fellow of Peterhouse, who left it to his college in 1725.

Comparative wealth of colleges

The success of the colleges in attracting wealth has varied. Trinity College, endowed initially with wealth transferred by Henry VIII from the monasteries, has been the richest since its foundation. However, had Queens' College managed to keep hold of the endowments provided by Richard III, which were removed by Henry VII, it might have challenged Trinity's position as the richest college.

In the twenty-first century Trinity is the richest by far; so wealthy, indeed, that it can fairly be described as a vast educational charity whose wide responsibilities happen to include running a Cambridge college. Gross annual income runs near to £30 million, with endowments of almost £800 million. With barely 25 per cent of Trinity's wealth, St John's is second in the college wealth league; its riches are on a par with the richest Oxford college. The least well-endowed college at Cambridge is the postgraduate community of St Edmunds, established in 1896 for Catholics with financial support from the Duke of Norfolk.

The disparity in wealth is partly addressed at Cambridge through a Colleges' Fund. Trinity College presently contributes almost £2 million annually to this fund, the aim of which is redistribution of money to the less wealthy colleges. The colleges have been divided into three groups according to their wealth, defined in this instance by their non-operational assets. In the top group, which contributes most to the fund, are Trinity, St John's, Emmanuel, King's, Caius, Jesus and Peterhouse. In the middle group are Clare, Christ's, Churchill, Downing, Girton, Magdalene, Newnham, Pembroke, Queens', St Catharine's, Sidney Sussex, Trinity Hall and Corpus Christi; none of this group contribute significantly. The poorest group, who are net beneficiaries, include St Edmund's, Hughes Hall, Clare Hall, Wolfson, Lucy Cavendish, Darwin, Robinson, Selwyn, Fitzwilliam and New Hall. The college missing from the above summary, Homerton, has so far been excluded from this mechanism since it was only in 2009 that it moved from the status of 'approved society' to that of a college. The determination of a college's relative position requires interminable hours of debate: the decision to move King's College from its place in the poorest segment in 2005/6 directly to a place among the plutocratic colleges the following year is a case in point. A change in the method of calculating wealth, from a system based on income to one based on assets, apparently caused this unfortunate improvement in the college's fortunes. Trinity College offers further subsidies within the university; in 1988 it established the Newton Trust, which makes substantial peer-reviewed education and research grants throughout the university.

Disparities in college wealth have also derived from each college's relative success in managing its resources. Outstandingly successful investments have been made, which added immensely to the riches of the colleges. In the early twentieth century, before the container port was developed, Trinity College purchased 4,000 acres of property around Felixstowe; the rumour spread by other, perhaps envious, bursars was that the Trinity man had merely enjoyed the fishing there. This move was followed by Trinity's development of 130 acres to the east of the town into the Cambridge Science Park. Equally astute has been Trinity's development of a 96-acre business park at the Ashford 'Chunnel' entrance in Kent. Bursars' office staff and their gardeners also work hard at a more mundane level to attract conferences and businessmen to their enchanting facilities out of term time and, increasingly, within term as well.

The rising contribution of the state

There was a healthy plurality within these sources of wealth. Dependence on a single source would have compromised the university's independence. The fact that this wealth was spread between the determinedly autonomous colleges improved this situation even further for the university. Up to the twentieth century, however, the state barely contributed financially to the University. Although Henry VIII used the riches of the Catholic Church to fund Trinity and the Edwards II and III had endowed King's Hall, direct involvement by the government of the day in the gathering of wealth at Cambridge had hitherto been limited.

Each monarch, from King John onwards, might have argued, however, that the granting of special privileges to the university – licences to hold profitable fairs, the holding of land in mortmain, special protection from the town – amounted to financial support. Furthermore, their wives (at Queens'), their mothers (at St John's) and their fathers (at King's) also contributed. Yet, within the scheme of Cambridge wealth, these were modest gifts. The inescapable conclusion is that for centuries the state has had its servants educated at Cambridge cheaply; some might suggest that it still does.

It was the steep academic decline within both Cambridge and Oxford during the eighteenth century that provoked a greater state involvement in the university's finances, initially with the Royal Commission of 1850 into the two universities. The gap between the science taught at the universities and the needs of the burgeoning industrial structure was damaging the country's economic advance and the commission proposed reforms to university management and an expansion in the range of education offered. To defray some of these costs a Commission on Grants to University Colleges was established by parliament in 1889. It resulted in relatively modest sums being paid by government to the university, thus establishing the principle of direct state support.

The next trigger for the state to assume a more significant role in financing Cambridge was the First World War. A total of 14,000 former students and staff fought in that war; 2,500 of them were killed, which was almost equivalent to the entire Cambridge student population at any one time in the pre-War years. Their names are recorded in the college chapels. Both teaching and income – much of which came from the depressed agricultural sector – were severely disrupted. The level of financial support from the state consequently increased significantly from 1919.

Sustenance from the state came at a price; it was conditional on another enquiry into university resources and organisation. This led in 1919 to the establishment of the University Grants Committee, which in the cases of Cambridge and Oxford paid grants to the university rather than the colleges. The flow of wealth to the university, which controlled the faculties, rather than to the colleges, gradually shifted the influence over the academic agenda towards the centre. Furthermore, although Cambridge and its colleges retained a formal independence, their position in truth became increasingly similar to the state-controlled universities of Spain, France and Germany. It is principally in the United States that long-established and eminent universities have remained truly independent of central government.

Various other such national funding bodies followed in the course of the twentieth century. In the 1980s the Conservative politician Kenneth Baker founded the University Funding Commission, a body with two important new characteristics: it contained a majority of non-academics and was accountable to the Ministry of Education. The Higher Education Funding Council of England (HEFCE) was then created in 1992 to provide a single channel of government finance to both polytechnics and universities. It was Margaret Thatcher's Conservative government, while intent on denationalisation in many areas of public life, which did most to extend governmental control over the academic community.

Further increases in government funding have been necessary for two more reasons beyond the need to repair the damages wrought by the Great War. First, the enormous expansion of the country's higher education sector was not simply a matter for other universities; Cambridge was expected to play a full part. In the Cambridge context of slow self-funded growth over centuries, modern expansion has been at a pace with which its own resources could not cope. In terms of quantity, its role is still rather modest as, with around 12,000 undergraduates, it is among the country's smaller universities. However, the relative expansion was still very significant and numbers of postgraduates also increased; there were almost 6,000 in the academic year of 2007/8. They make up a third of the total student body.

The second pressure on the university has been the requirement to serve the economy through research projects to which the government has attached importance. Cambridge has led other universities in its response to this obligation from government and the country's research endeavours are closely woven into the fabric of the university. Most of the funding for the huge body of research conducted at Cambridge comes from the half-dozen or so Research Councils, such as the Biotechnical and Biological Sciences Research Council, the Medical Research Council and the Engineering and Physical Sciences Research Council. The mechanism which secures funds is controlled centrally. First, civil servants announce that cash is available in certain areas of study deemed relevant to the funding bodies' priorities. Researchers guided by a professor within a faculty may then apply to one of the research councils through which the funds are channelled.

The degree of outside influence over the direction of intellectual effort at the university has never before been so great. Pure research certainly continues in Cambridge – the Genome Research Foundation, which is independent of but closely allied to the university, the work of academics such as Stephen Hawking and the university team studying high energy particle physics are significant examples. Yet there is pressure to pursue applied research at the expense of blue-sky thinking.

Where medieval monarchs required an elite to apply their trained intellect to the service of the state only after leaving the university, modern government requires an immediate practical contribution from academics while still at Cambridge. Periodically, in order to ensure that value for money in terms of research is extracted, a 'Research Assessment Exercise' (RAE) is carried out in universities across the country. Cambridge came out top in the 2008 RAE results (the last review in its current form); the review rated 71 per cent of the 2,040 research staff at the university as being world-class. Of the faculties, computer science and engineering fared best, while linguistics was judged the weakest. The RAE is used to distribute £1.5 billion of funding to universities, but many universities are left out altogether, as of the 159 institutions that participate in the exercise, 29 received 82 per cent of available funding. Some politicians regard the disproportionate support that Cambridge receives via the RAE as an excessive indulgence of a particular academic elite and believe that research expenditure should be spread more evenly among universities; it is possible that such a change in policy would cut £10m annually from Cambridge's research budgets.

The plurality of funding which underpinned intellectual freedom has thus been largely replaced by state-funded research projects and grants towards undergraduate education. Over 50 per cent of the university's annual income presently derives from a government run by politicians who still dither between unabashed development of an elite and their beliefs in equality. The international pre-eminence of Cambridge University will suffer through such uncertainty.

New sources of finance

In 2008/9 the university's income was around £676 million, excluding £310 million income of colleges, trust income of £20 million, the contribution from CUP of £187 million and that from Cambridge Assessment (its examinations and assessment department) of £222 million. The largest portion of university income came from sponsored research (£243 million), with another £136 million reaching the university through HEFCE; the same body contributed a further £68 million towards teaching. Students, or more usually their families, paid £74 million – still barely 10 per cent of the university's income. Investments yielded £41 million, leaving £115 million to be categorised as 'other income'. The average college – though there is really no such thing – received 44 per cent of its income from investment and donation, 30 per cent from residential and catering charges, and 17 per cent from fees, leaving 9 per cent as 'other'.

The university's income has grown at a striking pace since the late nineteenth century. Even in the mid-1990s, it barely reached £300 million *per annum*; in the twenty-first century it has maintained a compound average annual growth rate of 8.5 per cent to reach the 2008/9 level of £676 million. The growth in income has been matched by the expansion of capital investment. In the 1990s the university invested around £20 million annually in land and buildings, conserving the university's heritage and purchasing new equipment. In the current decade capital investment rose to £100 million annually. A walk around the New Addenbrooke's Hospital and the West Cambridge Site, a glance at the new faculties of English, Criminology and Education or a study of the plans for the Sainsbury Laboratory at the Botanic Garden show where this investment is directed. Plans for the New Museum site behind Free School Lane, expansion to the north of Cambridge and the prospect of new colleges suggest that the new level of investment will be maintained.

Those who manage Cambridge, as well as the state itself, are keen to find new sources of finance to reduce dependence on central funding and the university is developing two increasingly significant sources of independent income. One is the exploitation of its own academics' intellectual property; the other is donations from its richest members, who are encouraged to give a greater share of their wealth to the colleges which once nurtured them.

The opportunities open to academics for financial enrichment, while remaining attached to the university, have grown. Until recent times academics generally had to leave their university to become rich. In medieval times, for instance, once away from the university they could pursue a career in the Church, become a court physician or provide some other rewarding service to the monarch. More recently, in the late 1960s, the Oxford historian A.J.P. Taylor was one of the first academics to market his intellectual skills. Other historians have followed Taylor; among the best-known have been Andrew Roberts and Norman Stone, both graduates of Gonville & Caius, David Starkey of Fitzwilliam and Simon Schama of Christ's. Starkey is now a Visiting Fellow at Fitzwilliam. Evidently Cambridge does not excel exclusively in the sciences.

Wealth accumulation by academics has now gone far beyond the amounts which could be earned by 'standing to camera', as A.J.P. Taylor and his fellow historians have done. In particular, science and mathematics are now delivering serious riches to academics. The new potential of mathematics is symbolised in the contrast between the old and new facilities for mathematicians. Until 2002 the old Mathematics Faculty occupied the nondescript buildings behind the University Press in Trumpington Street; its faculty building was an architectural orphan in a city where some of its peers in the liberal arts had long since been known by their architect's names. Indeed, the most prized attribute of the mathematicians' former unloved lair was its proximity to Fitzbillie Cafe's chocolate buns across the road. There was, as the historians may have mocked, no money in maths. Its practitioners were the university's paupers. Life for mathematicians has changed, however. They have moved to new territory alongside Madingley Road. Their relocation might have denied the mathematicians their Fitzbillie cakes, but in exchange they have received the most up-to-date facilities imaginable. The names of the departments, centres and institutes operating there indicate not only the investment they have received but also how the old boundaries between scientific subjects have broken down: computational biology, quantitative finance and mathematical biology are studied there. The interdisciplinary Centre for Nanoscience on the neighbouring West Cambridge Site links them all together intellectually. Of the sciences, only the chemists have stayed in the centre of town.

The Cambridge connection to the 'knowledge economy' is well established; the university draws in high-tech enterprise as once its college chapels attracted the faithful. Professors lend their names and time to fill non-executive and executive roles in businesses which exploit the university link, as well as starting new companies themselves. Examples abound: in 2002 Dr Sydney Brenner, a Fellow of King's College and a Nobel laureate for work on genetics and molecular biology, launched a company called Population Genetic Technologies. Based in Cambridge, it provides mass population analysis at a fraction of the cost of other current technologies; the application of its work to DNA analysis attracted investment from the Wellcome Trust. A Selwyn fellow founded the company Arakis to develop new uses for known drugs; it was sold in 2005 for £107 million. Alan Munro, a Cambridge immunologist, left the university in 1989 to found Immunology Ltd, later Cantab Pharmaceuticals; he returned as Master of Christ's in 1995. Cambridge Display Technology started within the physics department of the university; it raised $30 million on the Nasdaq stock market in 2005.

It was individual academics, rather than the university itself, who initially benefited from this creation of wealth, but in 2005 the university's governing council proposed that the university should no longer remain excluded from a share in this new-found wealth. The university, after all, provides the facilities, the training, the opportunities to network and often the postgraduates who work as foot-soldiers in the early research. Furthermore, it had not become one of England's richest institutions by passing up such opportunities for enrichment. The university has therefore established Cambridge Enterprise Ltd and its subsidiary Cambridge University Technical Services Ltd to assist university inventors in bringing their ideas to the market. Raising money on the American financial markets for Cambridge Display Technology Inc. was its first major success.

Without too much controversy a formal proposal was voted through Senate at the end of 2005 to tap into this potential source of wealth. It gave the university primary control of patents, copyrights and design rights which had resulted from the work of academics in its employ. Cambridge had previously had one of the most liberal policies on intellectual property, which essentially meant the academic paid no dues to the university when discoveries made within the confines of the university were subsequently exploited. Some argued that such a policy stimulated technology transfer, yet indisputably Cambridge was losing an opportunity to accumulate wealth which other universities had taken.

Roughly expressed, the arrangement permits the academic inventor to retain most of the first £100,000 of surplus made; after that point, the academic's cut is reduced to a third of the surplus. Managed properly, such an arrangement could help both sides: the university should acquire cash while the academics should benefit from the experience Cambridge Enterprise gains in extracting commercial benefit from intellectual property. The university is already managing intellectual property through directing the licensing procedures and providing new businesses with financial and consultancy support. Income to the university from licences in 2003 amounted to £1.8 million; typically, about twenty-five new companies are established each year. The university's annual accounts now list the spin-off companies in which it has tangible net assets.

Such developments as these in both the arts and sciences expose the mythical gap between 'doing' and 'donning'. Cambridge dons were in fact closely caught up in worldly matters from the beginning. The number of them who became chancellors, archbishops or leading diplomats in the service of medieval kings makes this point clearly. It was also true for many less prominent academics as well: the medieval masters could be closely involved with world affairs, with an academic post often being viewed as a stepping stone to another career. Given the involvement of the state in the university, it is hardly surprising that its leaders were, in turn, so tied to matters of state outside the university. However, it has not been until recently that so much money could be made by academics from marketing their intelligence while at the university.

Another source of income which could yet yield greater returns is charitable giving. The university's appeals for monetary donations are a relatively recent innovation; rather in the style of the gifted amateur who does not have to try too hard, it was felt that wealth from the university's members and friends should flow in naturally. The first general appeal was launched in 1897; many felt it a humiliation that such a great university should be required 'to beg for guineas'. The Master of Emmanuel inspired the campaign on the grounds that many modest gifts from graduates, rather than a reliance on gifts from millionaires, was the way forward. By 1899 £10,000 had been raised, almost £900,000 in present values; remarkably, half of that sum was contributed by dons. The constant barrage by colleges soliciting modest donations from its members is now a well-established ritual; junior members of college are often employed by the college foundation office to accost graduates by telephone for this purpose.

Neither are the millionaires neglected; strong personal links are developed with those who either run or own successful businesses. Relationships are nurtured carefully, typically by the development director of the college foundation office, which each college has established; predictably, the last college to consider such an office necessary was the wealthiest, Trinity. The philanthropy of rich men has had an immense effect on the university: for example, Gordon Moore, the founder of Intel, paid for the new Mathematics Library; Bill Gates of Microsoft is making a huge impression through direct investment in buildings and projects. Business leaders such as the ex-BP Group chief executive John Browne, once of St John's, are sought out when they are powerful; such people are the decision-makers within companies over the direction of research budgets. That neither Gates nor Moore graduated from Cambridge demonstrates how the university can also attract support from outside its own domestic constituency.

Eminent graduates also have their own contacts which can serve the university well. When it was thought that the Gulf states might be persuaded to assist the funding of the new Mathematics Park, the ex-Foreign Secretary and Trinity College alumnus Douglas Hurd took advantage of a visit to Kuwait to speak on the university's behalf. Other universities, with less illustrious members, cannot so easily generate such support; nor do they often get the opportunity to try.

The colleges, in particular, are an outstanding means of capturing financial support from graduates. One advantage of wealth from this source is that plutocratic graduates rarely compromise independence in the manner which state finance sometimes can do; the graduate's influence is short-lived, probably limited to the occasional flattering reception in college and rarely stretching beyond a name carved on a building. The generous bequests of past scholars stretch back over a long history: from the eighteenth century alone, the names of John Addenbrooke (St Catharine's), Samuel Pepys (Magdalene) and Viscount Fitzwilliam (Trinity Hall) recall three famous graduate-donors. Such generosity, though, did not always ensure gratitude. The official history of Addenbrooke's Hospital dismisses the founder as having made 'no contribution to medical science' and declares that it was 'unlikely that he would have found his place, modest though it is, in the history of medicine if he had not had the wit to found the hospital'. It is an unnecessarily mean epitaph, which might cause some concern to potential Cambridge donors.

Those who once studied at Cambridge remain a major source of wealth for the university, one the full potential of which has yet to be realised. Cambridge certainly continues to benefit from its most wealthy graduates – most recently, Dr John Taylor, an Honorary Fellow of Corpus Christi, made the highly visible gift to his college in late 2008 of the spectacular Chronophage Clock on the corner of Bene't Street and King's Parade. It cost £1 million and the mechanism is apparently set to run for over 200 years, although, unfortunately, it has already been withdrawn a number of times for repairs. The donor, who made his money from the thermostat switches used in kettles, gave another £2.5 million more quietly to finance the new college library behind the clock. Most colleges have benefited similarly from its plutocratic members; it is, however, the less wealthy, but more numerous, from whom more is sought.

There is much that Cambridge can learn from the American universities about such matters; they are better at extracting cash from their past students. In the United States graduates are handled more subtly; donors are also closely involved in subsequent expenditure. Private institutions such as Harvard and Princeton are able, through their accumulated wealth, to guard their independence zealously. They have raised sufficient funds to avoid dependence on state handouts. Their graduates help in this process; they are encouraged by both lower taxes and better tax breaks for donors.

Only 10 per cent of British Cambridge graduates give money to their old university, while for the American Ivy League universities the comparable figure is 40 per cent. With a similar-sized graduate base as Harvard, Cambridge raised around £65 million in 2003; in the same year Harvard raised £230 million ($558m). Generally, the oldest American universities expect to raise seven times more from their graduates than do either Oxford or Cambridge. The different culture behind giving in the States is seen in the money raised from the 12,000 American Cambridge graduates, who amount to 8 per cent of the graduate

Illustration 9.2: The Fitzwilliam Museum in Trumpington Street: the treasure house of the university. It was designed between 1835 and 1875 by three different architects. The first, George Bassevi, fell to his death from scaffolding at Ely Cathedral; the second, C.R. Cockerell, died 'in office'. It was completed by E.M. Barry.

body; they contributed 20 per cent of the income gifted to Cambridge University in 2003. Cambridge is trying to do better, however. There are now fifty staff employed by the appeal office in Quayside, off Bridge Street, and a further twenty in New York. This amounts to one collector for every 600 American Cambridge graduates and one for every 2,750 non-American graduates. Bristol University, in contrast, has one per 8,000.

Harvard also makes it clear, in a manner unthinkable in Britain, that the children of significant donors, even if perhaps near the bottom of an acceptable range of academic ability, will be given preference over those of marginally greater ability. This is not considered iniquitous. It is accepted that the wealthy donor enables a number of other young people from much less privileged backgrounds to gain access to a superlative education.

Although Cambridge clearly has some way to go before it can match the performance of the American institutions in terms of fund-raising, contributions from a wider cross section of the 175,000 graduates are now sought with greater sophistication. As the university expands, the graduate base increases. However, there is one problem – or possibly two problems. First, although it is the college which is the most effective means of attracting money from old members, it is the university which generally requires the money – for new colleges, better research facilities and improved faculty and social resources, as well as support for its museums and central library. The warm feelings of past scholars for their college, which might just induce a donation, do not extend so readily to the 'university'. Secondly, wallets were sometimes opened in the past in the expectation of 'favours to come' – for example, a place at the old college might be extended to a graduate's own child in time. Since such linkages have been broken, the college must lean on the graduate's gratitude for their Cambridge education.

Although there is more to collect from the students of the past and the benefits from the university's intellectual property have so far barely been touched, just how the members of the university have excelled at gathering wealth since their arrival as penniless itinerant scholars from Oxford cannot be overlooked. Over the centuries they have gathered immense treasure onto their island.

The 800th Anniversary Campaign Fund and beyond

The role of the university has been a new dimension of the twenty-first-century campaign to gather wealth into the university at the time of the anniversary celebrations. The campaign has stressed the partnership between colleges and university, but hitherto it has generally been the colleges alone which have led the acquisition of wealth. However, power and wealth in the twenty-first century are drifting away from colleges to the university.

Indeed, some argue that it is from the centre that existing college wealth must be managed to achieve a return which would meet professional standards. Ironically, even where there have recently been good performances at individual colleges, such as at Peterhouse, which relies heavily on its London-based property portfolio, professionals would probably have built a more balanced portfolio – albeit one which might have decreased returns. Excessive bias towards property is a common criticism which professional advisors make of their college clients; it is an inevitable legacy of their ancient landed wealth. The movement of a share of college wealth into the stock market, for example, is generally made reluctantly. Another well-endowed college, Jesus, held 90 per cent of its wealth in property as recently as 1976. By 2005 property had been reduced to 60 per cent, but was still far above the preferred property weight of 37 per cent. The nature of the property which makes up this wealth is also changing; there is less emphasis on East Anglian farms and Cambridge property and more on commercial property in other parts of the country. In 2007, the concern that financial matters could be handled more professionally prompted the vice-chancellor Alison Richard to appoint a chief investment officer, whose role is to oversee central funds and to create pooled investment vehicles for colleges to join.

Illustration 9.3: Clare College Old Court, with the domed cupola over the chapel's antechapel in the background. Both the lantern over the dining hall and the cupola are crowned with gilt-painted pineapples – an eighteenth-century symbol of wealth. There are many pineapples above the pavements of Cambridge.

The vice-chancellor herself would have observed how differently financial matters were dealt with when she was an academic at Yale University. There, and at other American universities, far greater use is made of debt financing; several hundred such institutions have credit ratings from the credit rating agency Standard & Poor's, which are used to raise debt on more competitive terms. In Britain only the universities of Bristol, King's College London, Nottingham, Sheffield and Lancaster have secured Standard & Poor's ratings.

The Wellcome Trust, which has invested so significantly in the Genome Centre, just outside Cambridge, has set a precedent for rich charitable institutions which Cambridge might yet follow. Without an appreciable impact on its triple A credit rating, Wellcome has used its wealth to issue bonds, the money from which will be used to achieve returns beyond the cost of the debt. Cambridge has assets which could be used similarly to raise more debt.

The pressure to develop financial expertise at the centre of the university, rather than in thirty-one disparate colleges, reflects the wealth being gathered there rather than in the colleges. The need for better financial performance in colleges has also been reflected in the appointment of financially trained bursars. Until quite recently 'amateur' bursars came exclusively from the fellowship – albeit such amateurs included Maynard Keynes as the King's bursar in the 1930s – but over time the 'typical' background of a bursar has moved from ex-diplomat through ex-military to ex-financier: the prefix attached to this last group, however, may be dropped in the pressure to achieve top results. These must match those achieved by financial professionals in the City of London and elsewhere. Since accounts must be published openly, any inadequate financial performance would lead to pressure on the under-performing college to transfer its financial management to the Chief Investment Office.

Much of the £1 billion which the '800th' organisers determined to raise during the three or four years leading to the end of the 2009 anniversary year will be controlled centrally rather than by the colleges. The university will direct £300 million of the funds raised to improving staff pay; the same amount will be channelled through a bursary scheme to assist less wealthy students who might otherwise be deterred by top-up fees. A further £200 million will support the art collections and architectural heritage of the colleges and university. The remainder of the funds raised will go towards promoting research.

It is through this last objective – the provision of funding for research – that the university will perhaps liberate itself from excessive reliance on government. It is likely that Cambridge will do all it can to increase the research it undertakes at the behest of private industry rather than the government. Those at the university responsible for managing the transfer of technology will also ensure that the university benefits from its academics' contribution to industry. Should some 'Microsoft'-like jackpot emerge, the university will profit; indeed, it may already have uncovered a dramatic means of enrichment. In 2009 the university announced its development of new light-emitting diode bulbs which can last up to sixty years and provide brilliant light while reducing electricity bills by 75 per cent. They may cost as little as £2 each. The expectations for this project are, understandably, huge. Whatever the future of the Cambridge light bulb, income from businesses in which the university has a stake will be increasingly important. Certainly, no university in Europe is as well placed to benefit from the expansion of the knowledge economy and industry through its scientific discoveries.

In future, the university will also become considerably more effective at raising money from graduates. Colleges will remain crucial to this challenge as they retain an unrivalled grip on the emotions of graduates, even though their days of leading both the acquisition and the consumption of wealth at the university have passed. Links with the great and the good, who have riches to spare, will also be nurtured. Huge efforts will be made to ensure that relationships with such businesses as the Microsoft Corporation remain productive to both parties. Should all these different avenues succeed in directing new wealth to the university, it would restore plurality to this great university's finances and thus strengthen the university's independence.

Yet so important a university can never be absolutely independent from the state. It never was truly sovereign at its beginning, nor was it during its journey through to the twenty-first century, despite all the college charters which grant a nominal legal independence. Nonetheless, given the requirement to support the state and the Established Church, there was generally freedom for its academics to travel the paths along which their intellectual thirst drew them. Over the last 100 years the government's contribution has become so important that this intellectual freedom is perhaps at times vulnerable.

The real independence of the university and colleges of Cambridge will only ever be a practical proposition with the blessing of the state. Charitable donations, dividends from their intellectual property, student fees and direct links to industry could replace the HEFCE funding but, should the Government divert its research funding as well, independence would be unsustainable. As the situation currently stands, the government's wish to manage higher education's contribution to the knowledge economy and to use access to the university as a means of building social mobility is too strong for real independence to be an option.

However, a reduced dependency on central funds remains an important objective of both university and government. The government chooses to contribute as little as it can get away with, while funds from other sources would assist the university's governors' resistance to the more nonsensical demands of politicians. The sourcing of adequate finance will remain a major task, a significant distraction from academic pursuits and a topic of conversation from the high table in college to the postgraduate in the town pub.

Chapter 10

Walled Gardens and Open Places

There are over 200 acres of gardens and parks near to the centre of Cambridge: a remarkable amount of green space for a town of modest size. Those open areas that belong to the town are known by names which evoke their medieval past. Two spaces are known as Butts Green; there is Lammas Land, a Laundress Green, Donkey's Green, Coe Fen and a Sheep's Green. The victims of medieval plagues were buried beneath Coldham's Common, near the present-day Cambridge United football ground; those of the Great Plague of 1665 were buried under Midsummer Common. Near the Leper Chapel, on the edge of town, were the Stourbridge Fields, where the famous fair was held. They each preserve a memory of the times when Cambridge people lived and worked in the centre of the town independently of the university. They are another reminder that the university's founding scholars came to a thriving community.

The appearance of the town's spaces in modern Cambridge is reminiscent of their fenland origins. Much of the flat land is still crossed with small streams which water nearby willow trees, while cows still roam a few of the greens. The use of the land by the townspeople once reflected the practicalities of survival in the fens. The rights to pasture, to collect wood, to dig turf on the common land, to wash clothes and to fish in ponds were guarded jealously. Since the townsfolk have left central Cambridge, the communal spaces have only to be mown and kept clean. The 'pieces' and 'greens' have few practical uses apart from grazing for the occasional cow, and certainly no arrows are shot at butts. Beyond recreation, they serve mainly as pleasant short cuts between parts of the old town for bicyclists and pedestrians on their ways to work.

The land tended by the colleges is no longer needed to supply food, in the manner of the monasteries, to the master's table. Instead, colleges have developed secluded gardens and landscaped areas which are far more manicured than the town's equivalents. The Cam's streams have been drained or diverted and the ground has been landscaped. Exotic trees and plants have been planted behind college walls. Yet the taming of the tributaries of the Cam which run, for example, through the gardens of Robinson and around three sides of Clare's Fellows' Gardens cannot really disguise the land's earlier function as water meadows.

The variety of Cambridge gardens

As almost the entire history of English architecture can be explained through the buildings of the university and town, so the same claim can be made for English gardening. Furthermore, as architectural fashions pursued in Cambridge sometimes reflected political events, so too at times did the style of its gardens. The adoption of the Dutch gardening style of clipped hedges and topiary could signal support for the Glorious Revolution of 1688 and by the mid-1700s landscape gardening was adopted by some of those opposed to Walpole's administration and the Hanoverian kings. Each of these styles can be found in Cambridge.

Topiary, the art of creating sculptures from trees and shrubs, was the first recognised garden style practised in England, through the influence of the Romans; it was later reintroduced from the Netherlands in the early 1700s. The art of topiary is well displayed at Madingley Hall, the university's college of further education to the west of Cambridge, where yews have been shaped with an evident sense of fun and eccentricity. After the Romans left Britain, there is little evidence of gardening until the monastic orders came to this country, bringing their *herbaria* with them. Monasteries strove for self-sufficiency and thus played an important role in the development of medieval horticulture; the Rule of St Benedict was 'Ora et labora' – 'ora' in their churches and 'labora' within their private gardens. The gardens of the nine medieval monasteries within the town ensured that the development of gardening was reflected in Cambridge. Indeed, the gardens of Emmanuel, Magdalene and Sidney Sussex are each on land once worked by monks.

Anglo-Saxon culture in Cambridge is directly represented by St Bene't's Church: but at Lucy Cavendish College there is a herb garden which also indirectly represents this period. Only plants which flourished before 1066, such as woad and pimpernels, are grown there; they help show how the English once flavoured foods, made their medicines and extracted perfumes and dyes. The plants were sourced in the 1980s, under the direction of the archaeologist Lady Renfrew, and chosen from the tenth-century Benedictine monk Aelfric's *Colloquy* (*Nominum herbarum*).

While monasteries still thrived, the use of gardens by, particularly, aristocratic women emerged; gravelled walks and covered arbours of pleached trees, with their branches bent and interwoven overhead, formed a 'pleasance'. It is probable that Lady de Clare and Marie de Valence walked through such enclosed places at their colleges during their visits; indeed, such gardens were identified in the medieval period as feminine spaces. Madingley Hall has a pleached walk in its Walled Garden and there is still a similar walk at Pembroke named after Bishop Ridley. The small and enclosed spaces within colleges were ideal for the *hortus conclusus*, the enclosed garden.

In the Tudor period more formal knot gardens which were designed to be viewed from the first floor of the house became popular with the elite. These were divided into different areas: they had scented flowers for nosegays, as well as separate areas for medicinal herbs or plants which yielded dyes for clothes or colours for illustrated manuscripts. John Hammond's map of 1592 shows knot gardens along the Backs as well as orchards. They are now rare in Cambridge although Emmanuel created one within New Court during the 1960s.

In the late seventeenth century the Dutch style of gardening flourished after William of Orange took the English throne. The use of aromatic evergreens, topiary and trees, combined with the diminutive

Illustration 10.1: Clare Gardens, with the DNA double helix symbol in front of Memorial Court, commemorating the attachment of James Watson to the college.

geometric beauty and crafted fussiness of the garden spaces, was embraced by a number of colleges. The watery landscape of Cambridge made the colleges natural venues for this horticultural fashion, in which canals and moats played an important part; indeed, Erasmus remarked in the early 1500s how walking in the water meadows opposite Queens' reminded him of his home town of Rotterdam. Jesus was then also famed for its topiary conceits, which it still fashions, while Peterhouse indulged in evergreen obelisks.

The reaction against the geometric style was expressed through the work of many eighteenth-century garden designers. A transitional style termed by garden historians 'late geometric' was promulgated by designers such as Charles Bridgeman, before landscape gardening in its most famous form followed in the mid-eighteenth century. Inspired in part by the experiences of English gentlemen on the Grand Tour, these naturalistic landscapes were designed to suggest the landscape paintings of artists such as Lorraine and Poussin; vistas of grass, trees and water were characteristic of this phase. Its proponents modified the natural landscape to create an 'ideal' prospect, a method referred to as consulting the 'genius of the place'. William Kent and Capability Brown exemplified this period.

It is thought probable that Brown designed St John's Wilderness Garden, a space which had previously been laid out with walks in the pattern of the nave, transepts and chancel of a cathedral. Bridgeman was commissioned to reshape King's 'Scholars' Pieces' across the Cam while James Gibbs was designing the Fellows' Building. The garden plans, which were never implemented, envisaged wide gravelled paths across Front Court by the chapel with views up to a raised temple beyond the Backs. The bridge from that period, the mounds of which are still visible, lay in line with the central arch of the Fellows' Building. Despite the rejection of the combined scheme at King's, Bridgeman and Gibbs did work together at Wimpole

Hall, eight miles south-west of Cambridge. Robinson College, which amalgamated the gardens of nine villas behind Grange Road, is an homage to this phase of English gardening, where nature was both humoured and tweaked.

It was during the eighteenth century that the colleges developed their reputation as fine keepers of mown grass. Areas of land close to buildings, which previously had been indistinguishable from pastureland, were dedicated to nurturing swards of grass. Cows, the master's horse and meadow plants such as camomile or thyme were displaced in perpetuity. Such care has led to a mentality where a boundary between college and university property can be marked by the direction of the lawn stripes: along King's Parade, the King's College gardeners mow from south to north, whereas the university has its grass mown from east to east. The division in ownership is always clear.

Selwyn College gardens exemplify the Victorian reaction to previous fashions, which is epitomised by the work of the Victorian garden designer John Loudon. The Victorians thought that the focus on nature had caused the neglect of horticulture and so brought flowerbeds back into fashion. Selwyn gardeners have always maintained a huge Victorian flowerbed. Two ranges of Old Court have flowerbeds at their base, another Victorian feature not often seen in a Cambridge college. One of Loudon's typical touches was to grow ivy, as in Selwyn Old Court, on the facades of buildings. The Victorian style of gardening required the application of technology to grow plants in green- and hot-houses, as well as the wealth to build and run them. Colleges were well placed to run such gardens. Loudon worked at Christ's and also in the town at the Nonconformist Histon Road cemetery grounds, which opened in 1843. The cemetery has a central flowerbed like a roundabout; the large circular flowerbed in Trinity's Fellows' Garden, around which visitors may walk, has the same influences.

In the late nineteenth and early twentieth centuries the Arts and Crafts movement gave rise to a new style of gardening which is reflected in the gardens of Robinson College. The college took over land which had once been part of several nineteenth-century villas behind Grange Road. The gardens' established feel provide a surprising contrast to the harshness of the college's late-twentieth-century red brick buildings. The Bin Brook tributary of the Cam, which flows down to St John's College, has been restrained and now follows a flower-lined path into a small lake bordered by shrubs and a woodland area. Curiously, the garden is entered via an obscurely placed 'Alice in Wonderland'-sized staircase. Once inside, one of the villas, Thorneybrook, catches the visitor's eye beyond the lake. The college may own the space, but the gardens still seem to stretch out to the once-private villas for spiritual support. Clare's Fellows' Gardens, inspired by Gertrude Jeykell, with its separate 'rooms', is another example of the Arts and Crafts style.

By the 1950s, contemporary garden style was reflected at New Hall gardens. The buildings and garden complement each other here, but it is the built structures which are the drivers behind the gardening style; sunken gardens and water channels surround the gleaming white college buildings.

Practicality and profit

College grounds, which are now so beautifully tended, were viewed for centuries as a practical resource rather than as an opportunity to create beauty. David Loggan's late-seventeenth-century drawing of

Cambridge shows that, for example, although Pembroke College had a bowling green and an orchard with espaliered fruit trees, the majority of its grounds was used for the supply of herbs, honey, fruit and vegetables, as well as for nurturing carp and pike in the ponds. Only a small portion was left to provide sedate walks.

At Magdalene, Loggan depicted an orchard near the Master's Lodge, but the area which now contains the Fellows' Gardens is shown as a plain field. College records of the 1570s contain some diverting complaints about cows, which grazed in college grounds. Animals which meandered into the dining hall evidently irritated the Magdalene fellows, although their successors might now prefer them to tourists. Cows grazed in Jesus College grounds during the nineteenth century before the area was turned over to hay in the early 1900s; hay continued to be cropped from the lawn to the west of First Court until the 1930s. The last tenant with grazing rights over the Jesus cricket ground did not surrender them until 1919.

The writings of both Shakespeare and Johnson show that the term 'garden' was in wide use during their lifetimes. However, Loggan in 1688 chose to use the word 'Piece' (still a familiar word in Cambridge) to describe much of the college territory – a term defined by Samuel Johnson, writing not long after Loggan made his map, as a 'patch of land'. Thus the beautifully cultivated college gardens of today are a more recent phenomenon: gardens were the pastime of the very rich, who had confidence in their survival and money to spare. Both were sometimes in short supply at the university's colleges.

Aside from use as a source of food, college grounds were occasionally also utilised in various unsuccessful attempts to make money. Records from the 1370s show that Peterhouse had a large area dedicated to the cultivation of saffron, grown for its uses in cooking and dyeing; *crocus sativus*, also known as the Saffron crocus, was a speciality of the region, hence the name of the local town Saffron Walden. King's Hall shared this interest of Peterhouse and in the 1450s Pembroke also records crocus cultivation for 'the public advantage of the college'. Since over 4,000 *crocii* blooms were required for a single ounce of saffron, it was probably not the best use of college space. Similarly, Christ's, Emmanuel and Jesus each planted a large number of mulberry trees, partly through the encouragement of James I, who wished to develop an English silk industry. This opportunity to turn their gardens to financial profit floundered, as the wrong variety of mulberry tree was selected; *Morus nigra* was planted instead of *Morus alba*. The same mistake was made in the grounds which later became the gardens of Buckingham Palace. Two trees from this original planting survive in Cambridge, one each at Jesus and Christ's. It is said the Christ's tree was planted in 1608, the year of John Milton's birth, and that he studied beneath its branches when a student at the college twenty years later. Peterhouse used their land to nurture a deer park from the 1860s to the interwar years, but the deer were more for the delectation of dons than for profit. The animals were sometimes housed in the college's abandoned real tennis court, which was situated beside the wall separating college land from the river.

It was the same practical approach which determined how Gonville & Caius used their land to the south of Harvey Court, between West Road and Sidgwick Avenue. Dame Anne Scroop gifted this area of meadowland to the college in the early 1500s. For centuries the college preferred the land's rental potential to any garden development. The property was let as farmland until the nineteenth century, when houses for dons were built there. They have moved on and the once private gardens are now linked together, providing a fine outdoor setting for the students living in these outposts of Caius.

Emmanuel's modern Knot Garden in New Court, where herbs are grown alongside the college kitchens, is a rare modern example of a college using the horticultural potential of gardens to their advantage. Similarly, fruit and vegetables are rarely grown, although a few apple trees have been planted in New Court at Jesus: fending off unofficial harvesters proves difficult. There are also a few apple trees around the sunken pond at Clare, but these are pruned for shape rather than for nurturing apples. The loneliness of the Maid of Kent apple tree, planted in front of Newton's rooms by Trinity Great Gate, is symbolic of the loss of such plants and the decline of the practical use of these gardens.

The Botanic Garden

Even the Botanic Garden, sited since the late 1840s in forty acres between Trumpington Road and Hills Road, was designed for the pursuit of 'Physick' before Botany. The garden had first opened on five acres of land where the New Museums site now stands, behind the Cavendish Science building in Free School Lane: a small triangular piece of ground marking this first site is still tended beside the lane. The vice-master of Trinity College, Richard Walker, had given the plot to the university in 1762, with the intention that the gardens would be a practical affair concerned with the pursuit of knowledge; flowers, which he adored, were mere 'amusements'. Cambridge had been slow to acquire a Physick garden; Oxford developed theirs in the 1620s and the most renowned Physick gardens on the continent, of Pisa, Padua and Heidelberg, dated from the sixteenth century. In an age when medicine was still made from plants, medical students had to learn which herbs would reduce a fever or banish colic. Cambridge established its Chair of Botany in 1726 to support the Chair of Physick, which, tellingly, had been one of the five original Regius Professorships set up in 1540. Other natural sciences, such as zoology, had to wait until 1869 before they were considered a sufficiently serious subject for a chair and a full degree course.

The original site of the Botanic Garden, hemmed in on three sides by houses and polluted by the smoke from its neighbours' fires, was not ideal; among other hazards, jackdaws nesting in nearby chimneys stole the plant labels to build their nests. These problems were left behind in 1846, when Professor Henslow moved the garden to its present site and oversaw a more disciplined study of plants; 150 beds were planted using the theories of systematic classifications developed by Carl Linnaeus and Augustin Pyramus de Candolle in the eighteenth and nineteenth centuries. All the varieties listed by Candolle are systematically planted and meticulously maintained in the Cambridge Botanic Garden.

The planting of the Botanic Garden also reflected the work of another Cambridge man, John Ray, 200 years earlier. He was a fellow at Trinity College from 1649 until his refusal to sign the 1661 Act of Uniformity caused his resignation from the university. Acknowledged as the father of English natural history, his basic scheme of classification is still used by the world's botanists. He divided plants into two groups, monocotyledon and dicotyledon, depending on whether their embryos possessed one or two seed leaves. Thus at the Botanic Garden, monocots were planted centrally within the flowerbeds.

The motivation behind the Botanic Garden was certainly highly practical; it was intended to support learning at the university, and still does so, as the Faculty of Plant Sciences is based there. The garden's original twenty acres was doubled in the 1950s; the original area still reflects the early interest in plant classification and diversity, while the later area focuses more on ecology and genetics. Plant biology remains highly significant at the university: an £80 million investment funded by the Gatsby Charitable Foundation and begun in 2007 is establishing a research laboratory within the Botanic Garden. It will include a building designed to accommodate over 120 scientists, most of whom will be studying plant diversity.

The modern uses of gardens

The importance colleges attach to their gardens now varies considerably. Caius nurtures little of horticultural interest at its site in the heart of town and, equally, Downing and Churchill can lay claim to no prizes in this area. At Churchill, grass is used as a setting for the display of modern sculpture. Clare, Trinity and Jesus also promote this art form; Jesus hosts a biannual sculpture exhibition. In 2005 the Jesus Fellowship welcomed the vast masterpiece 'Excavation', by Kate Whiteford, onto the grass of Chapel Court. It was meant to focus the mind on the continuous human occupation of college space from the time Romans lived in the area along Jesus Lane; after they had been forced to dig up the lawn, the minds of the college gardeners were simply focused on how they could repair the resulting damage within their gardening budget. Statuary makes the gardeners' work difficult. One permanent sculpture at that college, the bronze horse in First Court, is also a tempting prop for student misbehaviour, although the rumour of a scale of punishment dependent on the degree of student abuse is officially denied. The only harm so far caused to the horse resulted from the tomato sauce with which some students once smothered it; the vinegar in the sauce damaged the copper.

The development at many colleges of outstanding gardens in the modern era has been partly justified by their role in securing additional income. The perfect lawns and tended beds are an ideal site for the smart marquee and help to justify the high prices extracted from the commercial enterprises renting college facilities. In the same way, the gardens also provide an enviable setting for the undergraduates' May Balls. Otherwise, it is unlikely that the substantial budgets currently granted to the gardens would have survived the innumerable college financial reviews. Most colleges spend between £100,000 and £250,000 a year on the maintenance of their vast grounds, of which often over 80 per cent is consumed by wages. The gardens, beautiful and apparently ancient, follow the hard-headed tradition of the university whereby much of its beauty has been created with a purpose which is not always immediately obvious to the charmed visitor.

However much the gardeners may resent the distraction of statuary exhibitions and May Balls, their jobs must have some attraction. The head gardener of St John's retired in 2005 after twenty-seven years' employment; Clare have only just hired their third head of gardens since the Second World War; and examples of service records over fifteen years – as at Newnham, Jesus and Trinity – are common. College gardeners, however, are the only group at the university who do not have a pan-university union. Many groups, from bursars to housekeepers, nurses and heads of colleges' spouses, spend hours in sometimes mutinous debate about the burdens they must bear on behalf of the academic community. The gardeners have tried to build a similar professional camaraderie but, interestingly, it has not survived.

The college garden which deserves particular attention belongs to Clare. This college, which is famed for the beauty of its main court, had once been referred to as 'The Jewel in the Jungle' because of the

Illustration 10.2: Emmanuel College gardens: the Fellows' Gardens lie beyond the small wall and include a magnificent 200-year-old Oriental plane tree. Wendy Taylor's statue 'A Jester' has been placed directly over the space on which the sixteenth-century tennis court was constructed.

neglected state of its gardens. However, a happy confluence in the late 1940s between Professor Nevill Willmer's twin interests of colour perception and horticulture with the opportunity for garden design removed the basis for that insult. He used landscaping and colour in the Fellows' Garden to create the impression of a space greater than the two and a half acres that actually exist. For example, the device of a series of different steps from the Clare Causeway down to the sunken pond garden gives the impression of a pond sited more deeply than is the case. Similarly, separate and distinct spaces such as the scent garden give an overall impression of greater size. The walk between the old kitchen garden wall and Garret Hostel Lane has only white flowers, which exaggerates its length; by reducing the main lawn from its broad width by the Cam to a narrow point up by the Backs, the apparent length of the lawn is stretched beyond its real size. Along the path parallel to Queen's Road the yews vary in height and the path in width to give the impression of much greater length from one direction than from the other. Strong-coloured plants set in the foreground of large beds, with plants of lighter shades at the back, give the illusion of greater depth, while herbaceous borders which contain only plants with blue and yellow flowers are a testament to Willmer's interest in the perception of colour by the human eye. From its sunken pond garden, which was inspired by a visit Willmer paid to Pompeii, to its commitment to keeping its wind-scythed but healthy medlar and Judas trees, the Fellows' Garden has an unmatchable charm.

Although reminders of these landscapes' fenland heritage are, generally, firmly hidden away, some college gardeners do now promote biodiversity in a variety of forms. Indeed, two colleges, Jesus and Trinity, have recently won regional biodiversity awards – the former for its woodland and preservation of newts, the latter for the protection of voles. More modest contributions are also made: the gardeners of King's leave untended a section of ground by the main college gate; Churchill College leaves the earthen mounds which screen the students' rooms from Madingley Road unmown; and, at Westcott House, opposite Jesus College, half their attractive court is given over until the autumn to a wilderness of long grass and wild flowers. The autumnal disarray is slightly shocking in a place like Cambridge, where there is on the whole so much discipline and good order. Generally, however, the formality of many college gardens makes them fairly incompatible with wildlife; it is the riverbanks of the Cam and its tributaries which offer the last opportunity in central Cambridge for the natural world to flourish.

The great walls of the colleges in the most central parts of the old town, like those of Sidney Sussex, have helped keep the bustle of the modern town at bay. A hint of the Sidney Sussex gardeners' skills comes from the glorious wisteria whose flowers hang over the college wall opposite the Sidney Street junction with Green Street. In the far corner of the gardens is a secluded grass tennis court, which competes with those of Clare College, near Trumpington Road, for the accolade of being the best-maintained among the many which the colleges possess. The Sidney Sussex gardens contain an archaeological treasure, too: a surviving section of the town's 'King's Ditch' dating from the 1200s.

Christ's gardens, also in the centre alongside St Andrews Street, are equally impressive. There is another lovely wisteria, which wraps itself round the heraldic stonework on the Master's Lodge in First Court and flourishes beside an outstanding *Magnolia grandiflora*, a tree which is ubiquitous in Cambridge colleges. Unusually for Cambridge, the lawn of this court is oval shaped. The fellowship of the college is fortified by the long tenure bees have enjoyed here; uniquely among colleges, honey is one of the perks its members enjoy, although the bees swarmed in 2008 and stung the head gardener so severely that he had to be treated in hospital. An opportunity for fellows to improve their health through exercising in their eighteenth-century pool is now sadly denied to them, however, as the pool has been declared unsafe. In past years, the cold plunge was claimed to provide protection against the vapours and impotence, though concern with the latter should not have been uppermost in the minds of the celibate dons. Enthusiasts for cold-water swimming have indeed emerged from Cambridge: for example, the Jesuan Lewis Gordon Pugh swam in the Arctic in 2007 to highlight the issue of global warming. It is heartening that the tradition of bathing is maintained at one college at least: fellows at Emmanuel College may still swim in their seventeenth-century pool, although its popularity is limited as the pool exists in more or less its original state, the modern comfort of artificial heating having not been provided.

Emmanuel also nurtures a little wildlife, in the form of its ducks. In the earlier life of these grounds, when they contained a Dominican monastery, the monks fed themselves on the fish and ducks they raised in their grounds. Ducks waddle throughout the gardens today and even force the dons to share the hallowed turf of Front Court; they bring an air of informality to Emmanuel. Indeed, the college is generally thought of as less formal than some of its peers. It makes a great play of the ducks; they feature in college publicity and have their own page on the college website. The master feels it necessary, however, to write in the college prospectus that the ducks are neither culled nor eaten by the fellows; indeed, duck is rarely served in hall. Perhaps the Emmanuel master had in mind the libellous verse directed at St John's, whose fellows enjoy the rare privilege of being permitted to dine off unmarked mute swan. This privilege seems to have been acquired by the college from Edward IV in the late 1400s; swans are reserved for the monarch, although the Dyers' and Vintners' guilds may harvest swans, whose beaks they mark, on the Thames. St John's right to eat unmarked swans is unique, but it is not known how the college acquired this right. Of that college's swans, an irreverent versifier wrote:

> There was a student of St. John's
> Who wished to make love to the swans.
> Out stepped the loyal porter and said
> 'No, take my daughter instead'
> The swans are reserved for the dons.

Alongside the Emmanuel swimming pool in the Fellows' Garden there is a great Oriental plane tree with branches which reach down to the grass and then sweep up again. It is listed among the most remarkable trees in Britain and was grown from seeds a group of Cambridge scholars picked up while visiting Thermopylae in Greece in the early 1800s. A twin of this tree survives in the Fellows' Garden at Jesus; at eighty-two feet, it is now taller than their chapel tower. A seedling of the Emmanuel tree has been planted outside the Addenbrooke's research laboratory, as it was supposedly in the shade beneath such a tree that Hippocrates passed on his knowledge of medicine.

Newnham's gardens have a charm which fits well with the country-home feel of its buildings; rarely among colleges, it has no grass which is out of bounds to the undergraduates. They nurture an oak tree given by the Liberal prime minister W.E. Gladstone to celebrate the college's opening. A Tory vandal tore out the first one and it is a replacement sent from Gladstone's home at Hawarden which flourishes today.

Across the road from Newnham, Selwyn College accepted a different gift from the Gladstone family: a huge bell for its chapel. It can be heard in their enchanting gardens, which are now judged to be some of the best among all the colleges. Its vast flowerbeds evoke the Victorian age in which Arthur Blomfield completed the design of the main buildings in Old Court. In this court a flowerbed of New Zealand shrubs, such as *Hebe* and *Pittosporum*, is maintained in honour of the New Zealand bishop George Augustus Selwyn, after whom the college is named; Selwyn was a much admired cleric and graduate of St John's who rowed in the first Boat Race, in 1829. The college has also imported some fine trees: examples include the Pocket Handkerchief Tree planted in the lee of the chapel and an enormous holm oak on a mound made from the spoil of their pond.

Some gardens provide links to the giants of Cambridge. The open space facing Trinity Lane was once the private walled garden of Isaac Newton. The Maid of Kent apple tree growing there is genetically related to the trees at his Lincolnshire home which helped him to explain his theory of gravity. There is no hope of watching an apple fall from this cankered tree, although it is not unknown for a small apple to be attached

Illustration 10.3: Jesus College gardens. A very Cambridge moment in the Fellows' Garden of Jesus College, when the 200-year-old plane tree, which has a twin at Emmanuel, was orated in Greek by the university orator and sung to in Latin by one of the college choirs in 2004.

by a prankster to a withered branch in autumn. There are sister trees in the Master's garden, the Botanic Garden and by the Isaac Newton Centre on the Mathematical Sciences Faculty, which appear more healthy.

Many of the colleges provide a particularly sheltered environment and reflected warmth from their walls allows such trees as the medlar, Judas and mulberry to flourish at the limit of their habitat in this part of Europe. Pembroke even cultivates a Chusan Palm tree, usually more at home in sub-tropical Asia, and Clare, amid much publicity, has recently grown bananas in its little tropical garden. In support of the notion that fellows inhabit another planet to normal folk, it seems that the colleges have created their own climate within college gardens.

The extent of the areas tended by college gardeners in central Cambridge is staggering. Newnham cultivates seventeen acres, Jesus twenty-seven, Trinity nearly forty, though a few gardens, like those of Darwin and Hughes Hall, are squeezed into tiny areas. In the case of Darwin a delightful strip of land is cultivated above the Cam near the Mill Pond by Queens' College. The open spaces of many colleges have been reduced slightly in order to satisfy the demands of student expansion. Across the Backs, the colleges of Caius, Clare, Trinity and King's have built in corners of their gardens and the gardens at Jesus have had to absorb the buildings of North Court. Yet these are mere nibbles; it is difficult to imagine anything other than a thriving future for these enchanted spaces around the colleges. No matter that the gardens' origins were largely practical and that their apparent age is deceptive. At last perhaps Voltaire's valedictory advice in Candide, seemingly so apt for academics, can be followed in Cambridge. His character Pangloss suggests withdrawal from a difficult world: 'Il faut cultiver nos jardins'. Of course, Cambridge academics were far too practical to heed such advice until the benefits of pleasure gardens to colleges were clear.

The town's spaces

Of those open spaces in the care of the town, none can compete with the beauty of the college gardens, but Christ's Pieces is the leading contender among them for horticultural praise. There are some charming gardens attached to parish churches; the outstanding one is the churchyard of Little St Mary's, between the river and Trumpington Street. A timeless, 'secret garden' sort of a place, it is maintained by those living along the old medieval lane opposite. It offers a place of sanctuary away from the bustle of modern Cambridge. The garden and graveyard of St Botolph's, across Trumpington Street, are equally charming. St Peter's, up on the hill near the old castle mound, is also set in an attractive wild garden.

The town's largest open places – Parker's Piece, Midsummer Common, Christ's Pieces, Coldham's Common, Sheep's Green, Lammas Land, Jesus Green and Coe Fen – surround the university's medieval heartland. Lammas Land lies between Fen Causeway and Newnham Road towards Newnham village. The word 'lammas' comes from the Old English *hlaf maesse*, meaning loaf mass: this was the first harvest festival of the year, after which the land was given over to common grazing until the ground was ploughed up again.

Lammas Land, now covering less than two acres, has been enclosed since the 1920s and is used as a recreation area. Next door, across a branch of the Cam, is Sheep's Green; the sheep have long since departed and it is more usual to see cows grazing there. With its old trees and the small Cam tributaries on both sides, Sheep's Green, which runs up to Coe Fen by Trumpington Road, still has the look of ancient fenland.

Coe Fen was truly fenland until the 1830s, when, as it was thought to be a severe threat to public health, the cost of its draining was met by public subscription. It stretches over thirteen acres from the junction of Brooklands Avenue and Trumpington Road along behind the Leys School and up to Peterhouse. The word 'coe' might come from the call of the jackdaws which once rested there, perhaps in between their flying missions to steal labels from Professor Walker's first Botanic Garden – but, equally, it might be a corruption of 'cow'. The wall beside Coe Fen encloses the gardens of Peterhouse. An ancient water gate survives in the wall from the time that bishops of Ely, official Visitors to the college, would have come by water from Ely to the college. At the end of this area, near to the Mill Pond by the back of Darwin College and the university's graduate centre, lies Laundress Green, an area once used by the townsfolk for washing clothes. The right to graze horses there was held by the parishioners of St Botolph's and Little St Mary's. It is now the territory of sunbathers and traditionally a place where students unwind after their examinations.

Further on from Laundress Green across Silver Street Bridge are the Backs: with their lime trees lining Queen's Road, they frame the most attractive views of the riverside colleges. Despite their visual domination by colleges they are actually owned for the most part by the town. They stretch up to the land opposite Trinity College, an area once referred to as Long Green. Trinity acquired this part of the Backs from the town in the early 1600s; it was traded, along with some cash, for Parker's Piece.

Jesus Green and Midsummer Common complete the circle of town open spaces around the edge of medieval Cambridge. These ancient-sounding names were not attached to the area until the late 1890s, when Victoria Avenue split it in two; in the twelfth century it was known as Greencroft. Jesus Green is to the west of that road and incorporates an open-air pool. On the east side lies Midsummer Common. Tradition has it that between Old May Day and Old Candlemas Day cows and horses could be grazed there. More significantly, from 1211 it was the site of the famous Midsummer Fair. Travellers from all over the country came first to trade horses and then in the eighteenth century it became famous for its china auctions. In modern times the fair is organised during June by the Showman's Guild of Great Britain. In the corner of this common near Maids Causeway is an area once known as Butts Green, where the men of Cambridge would in times gone by have been obliged to hone their archery skills shooting at the butts; a second Butts Green once occupied part of the land within Clare's gardens, but this name has not been applied to it for many years.

Parker's Piece has a variety of claims to fame. It has been the town's cricket pitch since the 1830s and was the nursery of the great English cricketer Jack Hobbs. In the same decade a massive feast was held there to celebrate the coronation of Queen Victoria. Balloonists cast off from the Piece in the 1840s; before the First World War the French aviator Blériot landed his plane there.

Confusingly, Christ's Pieces, which occupies the area behind Christ's College on St Andrew's Street, was once owned by Jesus College and was sold to the town only in 1886. The town purchased a rough field and converted it into an attractive park. Where Parker's Piece attracts the town's field sportsmen, Christ's Piece is more a place of gentle leisure, where bowls can be played, tennis balls exchanged across a net and people can meet in idle leisure. It is the most attractive of the town's places, with fine trees, well-tended flowerbeds and grassed areas which are kept immaculately tidy by the council's staff, who clearly take an immense pride in its upkeep. It contributes much to the lives of Cambridge residents.

At the other side of Christ's Pieces is New Square. It has attractive small townhouses around its edge, whose appeal is even greater now that the square has been reclaimed after its use for over fifty years as the town's car park. Further east lies Coldham's Common, by Coldham's Lane, with the twelfth-century Leper Chapel nearby: this was the base of the Stourbridge Fair. Two further delightfully named spaces are Empty Common and Donkeys' Common, though neither now amount to more than a tiny patch of grass. Empty Common occupies a small rectangular space opposite Coe Fen and alongside Brooklands Avenue; Donkey's Common is near Gonville Place and Mill Road. This was where a town gaol, which was opened and closed within the nineteenth century, was built.

Illustration 10.4: Christ's Pieces.

The town is well endowed with green land, but it has struggled to guard it against the greater power of the university. Where they could, a pinder, a fen reeve or another paid agent of the town, such as a beadle, a hayward or a woodward, ensured rights over common land were not abused, but they arbitrated merely between the townsfolk. The university and colleges could never be constrained by these modestly ranked servants of the local community. Although the university still makes appointments to a number of posts which originated in medieval England, the town, significantly, retains only the position of the pinder from those times. The rights over which the town once arbitrated were much valued: they covered, for example, access to pasture and the right of digging of peat for fuel (turbary); the right of estover governed the collection of wood and that of piscary the access to fish in the Cam. These are strange words to the modern ear; but in a wet fenland, where there was much land on which property could not be built or conventional methods of agriculture practised, such rights over common land were important. These titles and the whiff of medieval Cambridge they conjure up also show that the scholars fleeing from Oxford did not settle on a green-field site: they came to a thriving trading town with its own culture and order, which was then suborned by the success of the university.

In modern times the pinder is responsible for managing the twelve commons; he determines rules for cattle grazing on Coe Fen and Sheep's Green and supervises trading in the Market Square. He was given a new colleague in 2009, when the council appointed a Punting Enforcement Officer; punting operators are to be licensed and the touts who press visitors too hard for business will be curbed. The suggestion that punters should be tested for alcohol abuse has been dismissed, however. The hayward and most of his peers may be forgotten, but the spaces they once protected still provide a valued quality to the urban and suburban lives of local people living in and around Cambridge.

The extent of these open spaces and the college gardens are another of the exceptional features of Cambridge. Their different uses since the thirteenth century tell much about the history of town and university. Practical need always determined their use and appearance, whether it was to make the most of the opportunity to graze between Lammas Day and the next ploughing, or whether the colleges sought to protect themselves from the town and graze the dons' horses. There has been continuity in some parts; not only is a pinder still appointed, but the boundary walls of old colleges still follow those laid out by medieval monasteries. The same species of trees have now been cultivated for centuries on the same ground; honey continues to be collected from the gardens of Christ's and college ducks still live with fish in the same ponds as they did hundred of years ago, although now without the fear of being delivered to the monks' refectory. This mixture of continuity and change in the open spaces makes up much of the charm of Cambridge.

Chapter 11

A Privileged Body

The privileges acquired by the university at the expense of the town were remarkable. The university ran its own gaol and controlled weights and measures and the licensing of printing presses, public houses and theatres. The town's businesses depended on the goodwill of the university; its railway station was banished to the suburbs and people's access to trains proscribed. The university secured the protection of canon law for its members, special tax advantages for its colleges and exceptional political representation in government. Equally remarkable are the privileges that members of the university secured for themselves, both while at university and after their studies had finished.

The ability of Oxford and Cambridge Universities to acquire privilege was immense partly because there were only two English universities until the foundation of Durham University in 1832. The slow unification of countries elsewhere in Europe was reflected in the larger number of regional universities there, which struggled to obtain the privileges won by Cambridge and Oxford. By 1500, Italy had fourteen and France six universities; Cambridge and Oxford were thus in a unique position in Europe.

Most of those securing society's glittering prizes in England had studied at one or other of the universities. They may not all have arrived as members of the country's 'Gilded Youth', but it was certainly possible to leave with the opportunity to join the most privileged and wealthy part of society. This remains the case. Cambridge graduates close to the monarch could also conspire to achieve the closure of competing establishments such as Stamford and Northampton, while extending the privileges of their own university. The situation throughout the latter half of the sixteenth century, when four Cambridge men dominated Elizabethan society, was extreme but not altogether exceptional: the top financial man in the country was then Thomas Gresham of Caius College; Archbishop Parker of Corpus Christi led the Church; the foremost man of medicine and science was Dr Caius himself; while William Cecil, Lord Burghley, who had been an undergraduate at St John's, dominated politics. Furthermore, two of Elizabeth I's tutors when she was a young girl – William Grindall and then Roger Ascham – were fellows of St John's College. It made things easier when the university was faced with some little difficulty, such as over its printing licence, that the university's chancellor, Lord Burghley, was also a St John's graduate.

Illustration 11.1: The Union Debating Chamber: its Speaker's Chair, a Dispatch Box and rising banks of leather seats together with the voting lobbies marked with Ayes and Noes make it quite clear what is expected from the best of those fortunate enough to be educated at the university.

Matters had not changed much by the time of the second Queen Elizabeth. At the time of her coronation in 1953 Trinity College (where her eldest son was educated) had thirty-six of its graduates in the House of Commons. As late as the 1990s remarks could still be made about the Cambridge Mafia in John Major's cabinet and, even in 2005, almost 30 per cent of serving MPs had graduated from Oxford or Cambridge.

The wealth of the undergraduate debating club shows how privilege cascaded down through the ranks from college to fellowship to undergraduate. After centuries when student debates had been banned, three debating societies were permitted in the early 1800s. They merged in 1815 to form the Union – the Oxford Union, at first known as the United Debating Society, was not so named until ten years later. The Cambridge Union, which is legally independent of the university, receives significant funds from rent on the extensive property it owns near its premises behind the Round Church – another illustration of how parts of the university have secured a financial independence which cannot even be dreamt about elsewhere.

The Union's physical structure hints at even greater privilege. After using ill-favoured rooms behind the Red Lion Inn in Petty Cury and then dingy premises in Green Street, the Union was able to commission its present building in 1866. It was designed by a leading Victorian architect, Alfred Waterhouse, and the debating chamber is laid out precisely as is the House of Commons. Leather seats rise up on each side of the chamber in opposing rows. Those leading the debate sit in greater comfort in the two front rows, and stand at a Dispatch Box to address the chamber. The President of the Union sits on a raised chair, just as the Speaker does in Parliament. After the debate the members troop through doors clearly marked Ayes and Noes, as do MPs at Westminster, in order to register their vote.

The Union's architecture and procedures symbolise the expectation that there are places reserved for the best among them at the heart of the establishment. The weight of expectation hangs heavily and none too subtly over the Cambridge student. Magdalene called its college debating society 'The House of Commons' and, since the late 1960s, the old front door of No. 10 Downing Street has been in use at a Cambridge college: when the door of the Prime Minister's home was replaced, a senior civil servant contrived its presentation to his old college, Downing, where it was fitted near staircase D alongside the college dining hall.

Speakers with national reputations come to the Union: the Tory politicians Ken Clarke and Norman Lamont debated there on the Euro and in 2006 Michael Howard proposed the motion of No Confidence in the Government, which was lost by 205 votes to 236. The No Confidence debate takes place each Michaelmas Term and is not considered by its participants to be presumptuous or irrelevant. Such student vanity was indulged right up to the 1970s through the regular broadcast of this annual debate by BBC television.

Some of the Union's debates have been of national significance; in 1938, for instance, the Union voted against the principle of conscription during a national armed conflict. Five years before, the Oxford Union had held a better-known debate on the motion 'This House will in no circumstances fight for its King and Country', which was upheld. Both unions perhaps contributed to Hitler's assessment that the ruling class of Britain would not take a stand against Nazi aggression. Not all the debates are as serious as these; a motion was contested a few years ago on the merits of dunking biscuits in tea, while in 2009 the nightclub owner Peter Stringfellow was invited to oppose the motion that 'This House believes there's more to life than being really really ridiculously good looking'. It is a privileged community which can nurture its young members in this manner.

The university made sure that its privileges carried over into life as a graduate of Cambridge. For almost 400 years, graduates of both Cambridge and Oxford elected university members of parliament. The university had pressed for representation from the 1560s; as substantial landowners, largely of lands once held by the dissolved monasteries, they argued that their colleges merited representation. Elizabethan politicians did not concur, however, arguing that college fellows were merely the equivalent of servants in a domestic household who received wages and were given their food. It was not until the early 1600s that the university achieved this right, when James I allowed both Oxford and Cambridge to elect two of their own representatives to parliament – probably because the Scottish universities had already achieved representation in the Scottish parliament. The Irish and Scottish universities achieved representation at Westminster – two each – only from the 1860s; the combined universities (which comprised at this time Birmingham, Bristol, Durham, Leeds, Manchester, Liverpool and Sheffield) were given two members from 1918. For centuries, Cambridge University graduates could, after voting in the constituency where they lived, vote again to elect the two parliamentary representatives who would sit at Westminster as university members. The university's elections were even held two weeks after the General Election to allow graduates time to reach their second constituency. Clement Attlee's administration abolished this privilege in 1950.

Cambridge graduates had often sent eminent people to Westminster. In the seventeenth century they included Oliver Cromwell's son, Richard, as well as the Protectorate's nemesis, General Monck. In the next generation, the university chose Isaac Newton as one of its representatives; he sat in parliament in 1689 and 1701. This was a period of much national unrest, during which the university must have needed careful representation. Yet this great man's only recorded public utterance within the Commons was when he requested that the chamber's windows be shut. William Pitt the Younger, a graduate of Pembroke, stood for a university seat in 1780; that he came fifth in the poll suggests that these seats were much sought after. He sat for another constituency before representing the university from 1784 up to his death in 1806.

Within five years of the younger Pitt's death, the university chose another colossus of those times as its representative: Lord Palmerston, a graduate of St John's. Like Pitt, Palmerston had also been rejected by the university when he first stood in the by-election following Pitt's death. He was elected for the university seat in 1811. However, the university, clearly a deeply conservative institution, forced him to stand down eleven years later over his support for Lord Grey's electoral reforms. Oxford University was similarly conservative; one of its MPs, Robert Peel, had to resign his university seat in the 1820s owing to his support for Catholic emancipation in Ireland when he was Home Secretary.

Before the electoral reform acts of the nineteenth century, a significant element of an MP's prestige depended on the constituency he represented; least prestige was attached to those representing 'rotten boroughs' like Old Sarum, near Salisbury, which returned two members without having any resident voters. The university members who had won the support of the country's educated elite were, generally, much respected. The memory of the courageous liberalism demonstrated by Oxford University's last MP, the playwright and law reformer A.P. Herbert, is treasured as a lasting rebuke to political parties which flatten the independence of most members. These independent university constituencies had an additional attraction in the rules of conduct which forbade candidates to canvass or to come within ten miles of Cambridge during the election period.

The prestige attached to the university constituencies lasted until their abolition, although some felt that the seats were sometimes used to unnaturally prolong the political life of politicians such as Ramsay Macdonald, who secured the Scottish Universities seat in 1935 after rejection elsewhere. On the other hand, representation by eminent men had ensured that the university's interests received the best possible protection.

Contentment with the status quo was a predictable stance for a place whose members were so privileged. Rarely have the leaders of the university challenged the establishment; the benefits of supporting the Tudor dynasty must have been engrained on its collective consciousness. The colleges were overwhelmingly royalist during the Civil War period and in the nineteenth century the university's representatives in parliament were not encouraged to support the extension of the franchise and Catholic emancipation. The academics' record on the political emancipation of women and their access to higher education in the mid-twentieth century was lamentable. Until well into the nineteenth century they even opposed freedom of speech among their own undergraduates who wished to speak at the Union. However, neither were the students renowned for their liberal behaviour; in 1872 a motion deploring 'any attempt to abolish the special jurisdiction of the vice-chancellor' over the town of Cambridge was passed by 192 votes to 41. Some examples of the university's reluctance to lead any challenge on issues outside academia can still be seen: for instance, fifteen of its colleges still have no guidelines for ethical investment, which puts Cambridge out of step with many other universities, including Oxford.

The university's illiberal position on many issues does not, however, overshadow the revolutionary impact of some of its graduates. So many were involved with the Reformation at the time of Ridley and Latimer that it could almost have been referred to as a Cambridge movement. It was, though, a movement characterised by individuals and not one of the university. Similarly, it was two St John's graduates, Thomas Clarkson and William Wilberforce, who led the anti-slavery movement and Cambridge men who dominated the missionary movement later in the nineteenth century. It is perhaps curious that people as forward-looking as these were nurtured by an institution as conservative as Cambridge University.

The price of privilege

The privileges of the university eventually became so pronounced that rich townsfolk coveted the benefits of university membership. Indeed, the wealthiest among them in the early seventeenth century even purchased this membership to secure exemption from the jurisdiction of the Borough court: the chancellor's court was less severe when punishing its 'clerical' members and better at providing defence from creditors. Another benefit of this manoeuvre was tax avoidance; records of the corporation of Cambridge from 1635 reveal that a noticeable number of rich townsfolk had avoided paying the Ship Money tax through contriving membership of the university. This was not achieved through some sort of false matriculation, but rather required the townsman to purchase the status of a college servant, which itself carried membership of the university.

However, privileges are part of an exchange, one which the state has always expected will take place. In return for the favour shown to it, the university provided people with training and a set of beliefs which supported the state. In this, Cambridge has usually outplayed Oxford at maintaining the support of the Crown, although agility has sometimes been necessary to achieve this. One college master from the 1500s had a particularly deft touch. Andrew Perne, who was the university's vice-chancellor five times, as well as master of Peterhouse, timed his changes of religious faith to coincide with those of the state. He preached the sermon during Queen Mary's reign after which the bodies of the Calvinist thinkers Martin Bucer and Paul Fagius were disinterred and burnt. A few years later, with England back in the Protestant camp, he preached at the rehabilitation of their remains.

Like the Vicar of Bray, Perne appeared 'always faithful to the national religion, whatever it might be'. A weathervane incorporating his initials, A.P., placed in his honour on top of St Peter's church beside the Castle Mound, only stoked the mockery he had endured during his lifetime that his initials stood for 'A Papist' or 'A Protestant', depending from where the wind blew. Although his genuflections to state policy were a source of amusement, they parody the adept manoeuvring often needed at the university to secure the support of the state. The university's privileges have never been obtained unconditionally; such flexibility is still required of the university's leaders.

Charles I's preference between the two universities had been for Oxford and he based his court there during the Civil War. Cambridge, in contrast, had nurtured many puritans and the town (even if initially only by one vote) had elected Oliver Cromwell to the Short and Long Parliaments of the 1640s. Charles II preferred Oxford too and in return Oxford backed the Tories and the Jacobites in subsequent years. In supporting the Whigs and the Hanoverian dynasty, Cambridge once again chose the winning side, leaving the unfortunate royal preference for Oxford as a short-lived interlude; and when the Hanoverians came to England, George I sent a troop of Dragoons to Oxford, while to Cambridge he sent the unique book collection of the late bishop of Ely. These 30,000 books are still referred to as the Royal Collection within the Cambridge University Library. An Oxford man, Joseph Trapp, penned a verse about this exchange:

> To one a troop of horse he sent
> 'cause that learn'd body wanted loyalty
> To th' other he sent books, as well discerning
> How much that loyal body wanted learning.

It took several decades for William Browne to respond for Cambridge:

> The King to Oxford sent a troop of horse
> For Tories own no argument but force
> With equal skill to Cambridge, books he sent,
> For Whigs admit not force but argument.

Behind the humour was the knowledge that significant benefits resulted from supporting the monarch. Allied to this support was the way in which the university moulded those it educated: their special treatment at university – both in terms of privileges and of rules – taught the students the rules of the establishment. Indeed, it is in the context of moulding the state's potential elite that the rules and privileges that flow through the university's culture may best be understood. Where a member of college could sit when dining in hall, the clothes he worn or the patch of grass on which he was permitted to step: each had their source in this background of university privilege. The discipline of following these rules, understanding them, tolerating them, would be a useful skill to take to the outside world in due course. Many of these petty regulations are still enthusiastically imposed on Cambridge students: Gonville & Caius College warns its twenty-first-century students about the rules of graduation and other ceremonies, which are, it is disarmingly stated on the college website, 'archaic, eccentric and strictly enforced by its officers'.

At Gonville & Caius there is a visible symbol of the preparation of its privileged scholars for their intended roles in the establishment. At the time when Dr Caius refounded Gonville College in 1557, three gates were installed in the college: the Gate of Humility, the Gate of Virtue and the Gate of Honour. The

Illustration 11.2: The Gate of Honour from Caius Court. The gate opens on to Senate House Passage. It is before this gate that undergraduates line up before passing through to collect their degrees in the Senate House, shown on the left of this illustration. A portion of the old university library is visible to the right.

first of these was the gate through which the new and supposedly humble untutored student enters the college. The original gate was removed to the master's garden in the 1800s and the gate now framing the entrance in Trinity Street is a replacement dating from the nineteenth century, although it still carries the legend 'HVMILITATIS'. At a crossing point within the college the student, as he acquires more knowledge, passes repeatedly through the second, the Gate of Virtue, which joins Tree Court to Caius Court; this is constructed to Gothic precepts on the Tree Court side but finished within Caius Court in a Classical style. Leading out into Senate House Passage is the extravagantly designed third gate, the Gate of Honour, through which the graduands pass on the way to collect their degrees in the neighbouring Senate House. Moving through these three gates symbolised the path along which the best scholars would pass; with proper humility, virtue could be acquired, leading to honour. Proper work at the university and later in life brings rewards. Gates with symbolic meanings are part of this college's ancient culture. A fourth gate within Tree Court, which opens on to a gentlemen's lavatory, is even referred to as the Gate of Necessity.

Other symbolic privileges survive. For example, a Cambridge Bachelor of Arts may become a Master of Arts six years after the end of their first term of residence, provided the exams of Bachelorship have been passed and a fee of £5 paid. The fee was dropped in the 1960s, but the award of the MA continues, provided a ceremony is attended. With the MA came access to further rights as a voting member of the University Senate. Scholars at lesser universities have to endure a further contest with their examiners to win this title; neither do they have any say as to how their university is run.

Student privilege

Privilege became such a feature of university life that it eventually seeped into the undergraduate body itself and led to artificial divisions which, from the modern perspective, appear outrageous. Initially there had been little social difference in the backgrounds of scholars; the majority would have been the bright children of yeomen, parsons, reeves and others in the lower echelons of the king's administration. The biggest division of all was simply that between the friar-scholars at the monastic houses and the clerks of the more secular colleges. The few who were socially privileged in the Middle Ages were concentrated at King's Hall. Some hint of their background comes from King's Hall's archives, which reveal that in the 1330s its warden felt the country's sumptuary laws, which restricted personal luxuries and extravagant clothes, should be enforced more strictly on the 'Kyngs childer'. The option of living extravagantly was not open to most scholars.

It was the Tudor monarchs' desire for more professional civil servants which persuaded socially privileged families to direct their children to the university. By the end of the sixteenth century, grades of student which reflected those of society were established and scholars were divided into six social groupings: noble fellow commoners, fellow commoners, pensioners, scholars, sizars and sub-sizars. These classifications were used to distinguish students until well into the nineteenth century; some colleges still retain the rank of fellow commoner, although today it is only used to honour such college stalwarts as the archivist or perhaps the director of music.

Different regulations covering food, dress, accommodation and even submission to examination went with each category of scholar. The noble fellow commoners came from families of the nobility and wore a distinctive gold-braided gown. They also wore hats, whereas the fellow commoners of the merchant class wore caps – the biretta which marked them as mere academics. Noblemen retained their right to proceed to a degree without doing battle with the examiners at the Senate House until 1825; members of King's avoided this encounter up to 1851. Nobel fellow commoners ate their food in hall – referred to as 'commons' because the food was eaten 'in common' – with the fellows of the college.

The wealth of the fellow commoners permitted them to live well, as they too shared the fellows' fare. Intellectually they were not always among the most gifted and during the more meritocratic times of the nineteenth century fellow commoners were generally referred to as 'empty bottles'. Even empty bottles had their uses, though; for example, college records at Magdalene in the sixteenth century note far greater expenditure in the college buttery ledger by fellow commoners than by poorer sizars. Similarly, in return for their higher status fellow commoners paid more for their tuition than did the lower grades of student. For centuries rich students have thus provided some cross-subsidy of the poorer students and permitted the fellowship to live in better style than their college endowments might otherwise have allowed.

The third class, who were the most important numerically, were called pensioners (a term from the Latin *pendere*, 'to pay') and were sufficiently well-off to pay for their lodgings. From this etymological root comes also the modern French word for a boarder or paying guest: 'un pensionnaire'. Scholars, in contrast, were bright students from poorer families who had secured scholarships to finance their education.

At the bottom of the hierarchy were the two classes of sizar and sub-sizar. The name 'sizar', like that of the commoners of various ranks, related to food, reflecting its importance in those times: a sizar was a portion of bread or drink. Sizars worked in college in return for their accommodation and instruction. Samuel Johnson grouped sizars with 'lackeys and pages' in his dictionary. St John's and Trinity College introduced the last category of 'sub-sizar', contrasting them with the full rank of sizar, who earned larger allowances. The ambitious sizar often had the clear objective of securing his Bachelor of Arts, followed by ordination and subsequent promotion in the Church. In this sense an education at Cambridge was for many a route to social advancement and not an exclusive preserve for the already socially privileged. Social divisions certainly remain at Cambridge; there are those, particularly at the older colleges, who use their allowances to fund conspicuous consumption and Cambridge has its own version of Oxford's notorious Bullingdon Club in the Pitt Club in Jesus Lane, the high membership cost of which is notoriously split between 'dress, dinners and damages'.

These very vivid social distinctions between students may have disappeared but the university cannot break completely with its penchant for grading and classification. Subtle distinctions in rank are embedded in the university's culture and fellows have acquired as many classifications as the scholars once had. Official fellows make up the majority of the fellowship and each college also has half a dozen research fellows who are usually postgraduates supported by the college endowments. In addition, there are honorary fellows – usually distinguished graduates of a college – and bye-fellows who are invited temporarily to join the fellowship and have the social benefits of fellowship but without full rights (such as voting). There are also life, or emeritus, fellows, who are generally long-standing official fellows. Certain professors or readers (a reader is a grade above a lecturer but beneath a professor) may also be elected to a professorial fellowship, a position largely intended to make sure that each college has a sprinkling of professors. It is worth noting that the head of college is not a fellow; thus announcements by a college come from 'The Master and the Fellows' of such-and-such a college.

Privilege of course has long since drifted down to the student. Despite their cleverness, they receive far more teaching attention than undergraduates at other universities. Most live in ancient buildings set in beautiful gardens and may if they wish belong forever to an exclusive college community. There are feasts to attend in college and servants to look after them. Only at a Cambridge college could undergraduates determine, as they did at Downing in 2006, 'to investigate the efficiency and productivity of bedders'. At the majority of universities a student's room must fend for itself, with cleaners tending to concentrate on communal areas; bedders, their equivalent at Cambridge, do more. At most colleges they make the student's bed – or, these days, shake a duvet – and complete general housekeeping duties within the student's set of rooms. The extent of the service varies by college, but it is still vastly different to the norm at most other universities. At some colleges bedders are encouraged to befriend the students and report any signs of ill-health or unease among their charges to their housekeeper.

Cambridge students have excellent sports facilities within their colleges, even if those at the university level are less impressive. For the typical student there is greater opportunity to play a wider number of sports at significantly less cost than is the case at practically all other British universities. The 900 members of St John's can train in a well-equipped boathouse to secure a place in one of the twelve college rowing

Illustration 11.3: Rowing on the Cam: it remains, by a long way, the leading sport
in terms of undergraduate participation.

eights; in fact, all the colleges either have their own boathouse or share with another college. In contrast, the 32,000 students at Leeds University must make do with two eights and travel some distance in order to train. Even at the university level there are scholarships available to ease the lives of the athletically gifted and direct subsidies for obscure racket sports with which equipment can be purchased and court fees paid. Similarly, actors, singers and musicians have a wide choice of well-equipped theatres, chapels and concert halls in which to perform at Cambridge.

Astonishingly, the student's life at Cambridge is much cheaper in comparison with that at other universities. Students remain in college accommodation for the duration of their undergraduate course – not always in the charming 'Old Courts', but in college accommodation nonetheless. Hence they need only pay for the twenty-four weeks of the year they attend the university. Those at most other universities usually spend only one year in university accommodation before having to rent, for fifty-two weeks rather than twenty-four, in the private sector. Such rented accommodation is usually at some distance from university lecture halls, so there are personal transport costs to contend with. Bicycling around the old town of Cambridge is a much cheaper option. Finally the number of 'contact hours', an issue at all universities since the introduction of tuition fees, greatly exceed those at most other universities.

Even student expenditure on books is less, or at least voluntary, at Cambridge. There is barely a college library which will not promptly obtain a book at the request of an undergraduate, no matter how many copies they already hold in stock. The students' book costs are generally subsidised by up to 40 per cent, providing they are bought with the approval of the Director of Studies. Students elsewhere must compete for the couple of books relevant to their course held at their library and have to buy books themselves at full cost. The Cambridge undergraduate education is simply astoundingly good value for the fees the students, or their families, pay.

To accompany the modest expenditure of the Cambridge student are opportunities to obtain exceptional extra income, mainly through bursary schemes. Funds are available from, among others, the Cambridge Bursary Scheme, whose proud objective is to ensure no one should be put off from applying to study at the university because of financial considerations and, equally, that no one should leave through financial problems. Dons thus feel able to enforce strictly the rule that no undergraduate may seek employment in term time. The university experience elsewhere in Britain is so different, so impersonal, that such an edict would be totally unenforceable. The few Cambridge undergraduates who nonetheless take paid employment do so knowing both that the risk of being caught in the small university town is high and that if caught they will be punished.

However, it is not only penurious students who benefit from bursaries. Colleges reward achievement in exams; certainly, at most colleges those who achieve first-class honours receive financial rewards of up to £500. *The Reporter*, the university's official journal, lists the prizes and grants available; each college has dozens. At Newnham, for example, some have obscure-sounding names, such as the Clothworkers Research Studentship; others, such as the Helen Gladstone Prize (Helen was the daughter of the Liberal prime minister William Gladstone), evoke college history and past scholars. Some prizes simply encourage scholarship through short essay competitions. Neither are the sportsmen overlooked, as the Hawks' Charitable Trust distributes slightly over £20,000 each year between around fifty applicants. Numerous college travel trusts open only to college members make awards against undemanding criteria; hence junior members of King's may each apply confidently for a £500 travel scholarship once before they graduate, while members of Newnham receive anything up to £350 for travelling, depending on the type of overseas trip envisaged. They also have a chance of bidding for an annual $4,000 travel bursary to North America. The extent of these subsidies is unimaginable at institutions other than Oxford and Cambridge.

College privilege

At times, the culture of privilege at the university bred a disregard of rules by college fellowships – or at least the determination to ensure that the rules which applied to society in general held little sway in Cambridge. Until the 1990s college financial reporting, for example, was subject to far less stringent demands of disclosure than was that of listed companies. Similarly, the ancient state monopoly of the postal services was at one time ignored. Three colleges – Selwyn from 1882, Queens' from 1883 and St John's from 1884 – have issued their own postage stamps, decorated with college shields of arms; a fourth college, Jesus, distributed pre-paid return envelopes from 1871 in order, it claimed, to have a more efficient postal service. The money collected from stamp sales financed the delivery of mail by college staff. The system lasted until 1886, when the Postmaster General deemed that the colleges were in breach of the Post Office monopoly. When the colleges did cease producing stamps they managed to extract a superior quality of delivery from the Post Office: it was agreed that postmen would deliver mail to individual rooms within colleges. The immense costs of such a service to the Post Office could not be borne and it was finally suspended in 1911. This particular indulgence of colleges is still reflected in the post boxes which are directly outside the main gates of practically all colleges.

Proximity to the rich or well-bred among their charges has inevitably brushed off on some senior fellows: it would be surprising if it were otherwise. Some live vicariously through their undergraduate 'successes'. The fellowship enjoys elegant rooms into which to withdraw, feasts on exceptional food and wine and lives in elegant old buildings whose appearance would have been familiar to the aristocracy over many centuries. Gardeners and domestic staff are retained to ease their lives and the possibility of securing the keys to the master's lodge is a tempting prospect for many. It must thus have been hurtful when, in the late 1500s, fellows were denied parliamentary representation on the grounds that they were given their food and wages and were therefore little better than retained servants.

Modern privilege

Paul Mellon, the son of a hugely wealthy American industrialist, would in Tudor times certainly have qualified as a fellow commoner; his lifestyle in the 1930s at Clare College must have appeared just as divisive as had those of his predecessors. He remarked of his time at the university:

> I rode constantly. I rowed intermittently. I read occasionally.

The university, particularly the Fitzwilliam Museum and his old college, subsequently benefited enormously from his desire to give away a fortune sensibly. Mellon's aphorism about his time at Clare College may have been inspired by another which was attributed to the renowned master of Trinity Hall in the late 1800s, Henry Latham. Latham, who had a speaking impediment, allegedly informed newcomers to this college with a reputation for excellence in sport that they must either 'weed, wide or wow'.

Although in 1911 the union voted in favour of a motion that it would welcome facilities for the introduction of working men into 'the privileges of the university', it passed by only a small margin. Pure class prejudice permeated the university at that time: Joseph Romilly, the diarist and member of Trinity who was Registrary of the university in the 1850s, recorded his abomination at 'the idea of swamping us with poor beggarly students who ought to be tinkers and tailors'. In another example the snobbish Arthur Benson, renowned Master of Magdalene in the late nineteenth century, wrote of an undergraduate who had 'an accent like a slum' and questioned if there was 'any use in such a man coming here'. Men such as these led the university and influenced many others.

The privileged background of those coming to Cambridge continues in the twenty-first century. Almost half the places at the modern university are taken up by students from public-school backgrounds, who constitute as a body a mere 6 per cent of the country's youth; together with the 4 per cent of the country's youth who go to grammar or faith schools, these two narrow segments of society capture over two-thirds of the places at Cambridge. Expressed in another way, the 90 per cent of the population who are educated in comprehensives take barely 20 per cent of places at the university and those comprehensives sending students to Cambridge will be schools that rank high in the league tables, rather than low-achieving schools in poor areas. Glaringly inequitable as this situation is, the university is not able to solve the problems of state education by discrimination against higher-achieving privately educated students. As Vice-Chancellor Richard pointed out in 2008, it cannot successfully promote its intellectual excellence if it is forced to act as an agent for social justice. Cambridge truly seeks an intellectual, not a social, elite.

It does not say a great deal for the country's state secondary education system that its pupils' share of the Cambridge places in 1967, 60 per cent, fell to 50 per cent by 2007 – albeit it has risen a little since 2007, in part owing to political pressure and positive discrimination. In 2008 the proportion of private sector students was reduced to 41 per cent, a twenty-seven-year low, but it will have to reach far more significant new lows if a Labour administration is to be satisfied. The vice-chancellor's office reports, however, that the immediate prospects of further increasing the proportion from the state sector is slim.

That Cambridge undergraduates do not reflect society is seen through other statistics. The percentage of Cambridge degrees completed by young people from the richest fifth of society has risen since the early 1980s from 9 per cent to 46 per cent. Only 9 per cent, up from 6 per cent over the same period, come from society's poorest quintile. Cambridge remains a place of great privilege. Even if those arriving to study have not come from privileged sectors of society, they are certainly presented with opportunities to become privileged thereafter.

A privileged body

Against this background, it seems only appropriate that the university is in fact recognised legally as a Privileged Body. This status in Britain confers the right of direct access to the monarch, so that if any of the university's rights were abused it could appeal to the Crown. The university's representatives have the legal right to present an address to the sovereign and to receive a personal reply.

This right was last exercised in March 2002, when the university's representatives offered their congratulations on the occasion of the Queen's Golden Jubilee. The titles of those presenting the address symbolise the exclusive culture of the university. The university orator, the registrary, who is the senior university administrative officer, senior and junior proctors, a master, a principal and, finally, two esquire bedells accompanied the vice-chancellor to the Court of St James. These officers of the university took with them their symbols of office, which denoted their privileged positions; these symbols are still used on major ceremonial days at the university. Most of them now appear bizarre. One carries a seventeenth-century mace to symbolise authority, another a measuring device to mark the university's control over weights and measures. Other medieval symbols demonstrate the right of university members to carry arms: a Linstock (once used as a matchholder to fire cannon), a Halberd, which looks like an axe-blade on a long shaft, and its cousin the Partisan, which is a double-headed axe with a spike. Each of these symbols represent rights which had been secured for the university.

In their address these representatives of this venerable university stressed their loyalty to Queen Elizabeth II – 'We are,' claimed the orator, 'half as old as the English Monarchy itself' – and sought to capture the reflected glory that the university had acquired through having educated two of the Queen's sons by referring to them as Cambridge members. The Queen's reply described the role of the university as being 'to instil a sense of duty and service into successive generations'. Such a sentiment could have been expressed by any of the monarchs in the 800 years since the reign of King John, when the university opened. Service has always been expected in return for privilege.

Almost 100 years earlier, in 1910, another address had been made to George V. It also strove to identify Cambridge University with the monarchy, the sensible approach adopted by Cambridge University for centuries. 'We remember with pride,' the university's representatives said, 'that King Edward VII was a Cambridge man.' The new king's reply was another reminder of the monarch's timeless concern with Cambridge: 'I shall watch its progress and expansion with lively interest'.

Every year in the annual commemoration of the university's benefactors at Great St Mary's there is a thanksgiving service for the 'acts of personal munificence which we have received at the hands of our sovereign'. The prime minister may have replaced the sovereign as the source of such munificence, but it is a reminder to the university's members that they are dependent on the powers in the land which lie outside their island of intellectual excellence.

Cambridge University has nurtured a community of scholars in exceptional conditions since its foundation. Other university communities, such as Paris and Oxford, had been known to leave their host cities or country in protest at inadequate support. The academics and students of Cambridge University have neither boycotted their host city nor fled their country; such has been the university's skill at securing its privileges that it has never needed to do so.

Chapter 12

The Monstrous Regiment of Women

John Knox wrote *The First Blast of the Trumpet Against the Monstrous Regiment of Women* in 1558 to express his horror at the rising influence of the female sex in matters political. Mary of Guise and then her daughter Mary Queen of Scots ruled his country, Scotland. Another woman, Catherine de Medici, who was Mary Stuart's first mother-in-law, governed France from the late 1550s, while Mary of Hapsburg reigned in Hungary. Meanwhile, Mary Tudor, followed by Elizabeth I, sat on the throne of England. Women, particularly those of the Catholic faith, had an influence over temporal affairs which Knox thought blasphemous. He claimed the rule of women was punishment from God for the 'Sins of Mankind'; he considered their rule was 'repugnant to nature'. Had he known of their astonishing contribution to Cambridge University at this time and earlier, he might have written more than just an outline of his Second Blast.

The influence of high-born women on the early colleges

Seven of the sixteen colleges that were in existence by the end of the sixteenth century had been founded by women. From 1290, when Edward I's wife Eleanor had bequeathed money for the benefit of poor scholars at Cambridge, women had a remarkable influence on the development of the university. They were involved in the foundation of colleges, in their management and in the endowment of professors' chairs.

Typical of the wealthy and well-connected female college sponsors was Elizabeth de Clare. Her wealth came through inheritance: she was a grand-daughter of Edward I, her brother died without an heir at the Battle of Bannockburn in 1314 and she had buried three husbands before she was thirty. Through her wealth and influence the poorly endowed University Hall was refounded in 1338 as Clare Hall, doubtless to the relief of its founder Richard de Badew, Chancellor of the university. Within her heraldic lozenge, displayed at the college front gate, there is a circle of golden symbols. Some refer to them as tears for her three lost husbands, but they are more likely to represent her wish to spread 'the precious pearls of knowledge' to which she referred in the college's foundation charter.

Illustration 12.1: Trumpington Street, circa 1850, running past the boundary of Pembroke College and the west end of the Wren chapel. The College was one of the seven colleges founded by women.

Although, as so often was the case, there was a Cambridge academic of more modest social standing behind the founder of the college, Lady de Clare stayed closely involved with the funding and direction of the college. College archives reveal that in the early 1350s she was concerned over certain irregularities which later prompted her encouragement of a commission of enquiry to investigate further. These founders, therefore, did more than just lend their name: well-connected aristocrats, who could secure for the college the right of mortmain from a monarch or a bull from a pope to consecrate a chapel, were an essential ingredient in a successful foundation.

Another aristocratic lady, Marie de St Pol de Valence, founded the Hall of Marie Valence, later known as Pembroke College, in 1338. She belonged to the same Anglo-French ruling class as Lady de Clare. Unlike Lady de Clare, she was married only once; it has been suggested that she played the three roles of maid, bride and widow on her wedding day. However, reality is less dramatic: her husband, Aymer de Valence, Earl of Pembroke, died in northern France of apoplexy a few years after their marriage and again the combination of wealth, widowhood and court connections was turned to the university's advantage. Her influence is shown through the college articles, which state that preference was to be given to scholars born in France, 'if such could be found'; she also required that those observed drinking to excess or frequenting brothels were to be reported by their peers.

Although college archives reveal a typical amount of scholarly misbehaviour, they divulge little evidence of Frenchmen as members of college. Indeed, Pembroke was eventually to nurture William Pitt the Younger, who laid the foundations for the defeat of Napoleon's France; his statue has been placed in front of the college library and the Pitt Building stands almost opposite the college's front gate. The name of Marie de Valence lives on in small ways, from remembrance in chapel services and toasts at hall feasts to the moniker 'V' painted, to the mystery of many junior college members, on college bicycles.

After five colleges were set up in the mid-1300s, there was a period of almost 100 years in which no colleges were founded. The reputation of a medieval university depended on the number of scholars it could attract. Henry VI's foundation of King's College in 1441 paid scant attention to the needs of the university; at the outset he planned for there to be only twelve scholars. It was a woman – Margaret of Anjou, the wife of King Henry VI – who met the need of the university to expand at this time. The new college, ultimately to be known as Queens' College, was formed in 1448 from an existing student hostel known as the College of St Bernard. The principal of the hostel, Andrew Docket, became the first head of the new college. The new foundation was charged to conserve 'the Faith'. College articles also directed that daily lectures be held to support 'the magnificence ... of Queen's College ... and to laud and honour of sex feminine ...'.

Queens' has never interpreted the wishes of its first patroness as a requirement to adopt a corporate mission statement which promoted women's interests. Indeed, it does not even have a record of support for women at the university. On formal occasions in college, its presidents sometimes remark on this irony with rueful reference to the 500 years that passed before women were permitted to study there. Their exclusion of women over many centuries would not have surprised Margaret of Anjou, however. Her reference in the college articles to women's honour probably reflected her wish for women to be remembered in the liturgy during chapel, acknowledging that they could be saints and powerful intercessors with God.

Queens' acquired two further queen-patronesses as a result of the Wars of the Roses. Margaret of Anjou was forced out of the country when the Lancastrian fortunes stumbled and was succeeded as college patroness by Edward IV's wife, Elizabeth Woodville. The third queen who became college sponsor was Anne Neville, wife of Richard III. Centuries later this abundance of queens was used to justify the apostrophe shift in the name of the college.

During Richard III's reign the royal couple endowed the college magnificently; indeed, Richard had made his first endowment of the college early in the reign of his brother. After his demise at the Battle of Bosworth in 1485, Henry VII confiscated those gifts, but briefly Queens' had been the richest college of the university. Richard and Anne are remembered twice a year at the college's Commemoration of Benefactors service, apparently to the accompaniment of quiet cheers at the mention of Richard's name and moderate boos for the king who removed the college's wealth. Queens' also adopted as one of its two main shields of arms the silver boar's head used by Richard as his personal badge. On formal occasions the college refers with pride to its three royal patronesses – but, surprisingly in this context, they are usually named as Margaret of Anjou, Elizabeth Woodville and Elizabeth II. Anne is rather overlooked.

It is within the town's landmarks that a memorial to this Yorkist king must be sought out. Great St Mary's contains a small memorial to Richard within a Victorian stained glass window in the north-west corner, marking his support of the church's medieval restoration. The university was well supported by Richard – besides his interest in Queens', he also funded King's College Chapel more promptly and willingly than did either his brother Edward or his Tudor successors. Proper acknowledgement of Richard III is, perhaps predictably given the subsequent success of the Tudors, hard to find in Cambridge.

Queens' college had no official patroness between Anne Neville in 1485 and Elizabeth, the wife of George VI, in 1948, who accepted the role on the occasion of the college's quincentennial celebrations of that year. However, both Lady Margaret Beaufort and Catherine of Aragon probably enjoyed an unofficial involvement with the college. Although all the sixteen oldest colleges have patron saints, only King's and Queens' have secured the support of living patrons. The patrons of the old colleges were usually monastic houses which were not replaced when their direct involvement with Cambridge ended at the time of their repression. Other colleges must make do with 'Visitors', traditionally a person of 'eminence and repute' to whom appeals over unsettled issues within a fellowship may be addressed.

Another rich and widowed aristocratic lady, Anne Neville, the Dowager Duchess Buckingham, refounded a college in the 1470s at the time Queens' was discarding and acquiring its female patrons. There is some doubt as to whether it was she or her grandson, Henry Stafford, the 2nd duke, who supported the foundation of Buckingham Hall (later Magdalene College), but it is now thought most probable that credit should be given to the Dowager Duchess. She was also the mother-in-law of the next great widowed aristocratic lady who assisted Cambridge so much, Lady Margaret Beaufort. Founder of both Christ's and St John's colleges in the early 1500s, Lady Margaret had also given support in the 1490s to John Alcock, the founder of Jesus College.

The involvement of women with St John's continued into Stuart England. Mary, Countess of Shrewsbury, financed the building of Second Court; her statue was placed on the west range above the gatehouse in 1671. She was the daughter of the better-known Countess of Shrewsbury, Bess of Hardwick, who had acquired the wealth which ultimately benefited the college. Bess was married and widowed four times and it was her second marriage, to William Cavendish, that produced Mary, whose descendants helped develop Cambridge as a centre of science. Horace Walpole, the poet and member of King's College, wrote of Bess in the mid-1700s:

> Four times the nuptial bed she warmed
> And every time so well performed
> That when death spoiled each husband's billing
> He left the widow every shilling.

Sidney Sussex College was the last of the oldest colleges which was founded by a woman. Its founder, Lady Frances Sidney, actually died in 1589, seven years before the college's foundation, but funded the college through the terms of her will. She was the widow of the Earl of Sussex.

The contribution from these aristocratic women is remarkable; nothing similar occurred at Oxford. It was clerics, monarchs or chancellors who generally founded medieval colleges, yet at Cambridge women with strong personalities and great wealth wished to be involved in the growth of the university. Furthermore, the academics, determined to expand the university through founding colleges, demonstrated that they could, time and again, attract the support of those at the heart of the regime.

Illustration 12.2: The Shrewsbury Tower, with the effigy of Bess of Hardwick's daughter Mary in its centre.

The exclusion of women from the daily life of the university

Nonetheless, the university remained an extremely male-orientated society, whose chauvinism lingered well into the twentieth century. Although this had much to do with the monastic influence on the university, it also reflected English society. A woman's duty was to focus on her role in the home; this made her unsuitable for the worldly matters on which education was focused. Cambridge University, as so often, conformed to the values of the time.

For centuries women had no place in daily life at the university. Even female visitors to colleges were very rare; they could not pass beyond the communal areas, while often the only person permitted to receive a female non-relative was the head of college. However, the existence long ago of a scale of punishments at Peterhouse for breaking these rules suggests that breaches must have occurred; the college even instructed its medieval fellows to ensure that their heads were washed only by males. As late as 1801 the first British population census recorded the remarkable imbalance of 803 males and 8 females in the university, the latter presumably the spouses of college heads.

At times even service roles within the university have been denied to women. In the 1500s King's College ruled that all its domestic servants had to be male; another university edict in 1635 forbade women under the age of fifty 'to make beds or perform any other service within the scholars' chambers'. Unsurprisingly, laundry remained the responsibility of women, but soiled garments would have been left for collection at the college gate. Women were eventually employed as bedders, but there is no evidence to support the unkind notion that selection was based on their having an unattractive physical appearance. The sentiment of some classics scholar that the women must be 'senex et horrida ex aetate' – 'an old woman who time had rendered hideous' – has no basis in fact. Nonetheless, most of the female college staff were of an age which made sexual misdemeanours between them and the scholars improbable.

The culture which required celibacy and distance from women lasted for centuries. Nevertheless, pretty and less pretty barmaids throughout the many pubs in Cambridge have long received exceptional attention from the university's scholars. Christopher Smart, a friend of Thomas Gray when they were both at Pembroke, wrote a poem in 1740 directed to the 'The Pretty Bar-Keeper' of the Mitre Pub, which still trades in Bridge Street. The poem began:

> Relax, sweet girl, your wearied hand
> And to hear the poet talk
> Gentlest creature of your kind
> Lay aside your sponge and chalk.

It seems hardly necessary to add that women were also excluded from the university as students; but this did not leave them all bereft of education. For centuries leading families, both noble and bourgeois, had arranged private education by tutors at home for both their sons and daughters. In Tudor times, for example, Robert Ascham had taught Elizabeth I, while other women, such as Lady Jane Grey, Katherine Parr and Thomas More's daughter, Margaret, won wide intellectual acclaim. However, the vast majority of less privileged women had no access to education.

The injustice of this situation became more intolerable as the wealth and the population of the country grew. By the mid-1800s colleges for women, such as Queen's and Bedford, had opened in London. Towards the end of the nineteenth century similar pressures led to the creation of the all-female colleges of Newnham and Girton. The small number of women who studied there were technically 'townsmen', as they were not accepted as members of the university. Both colleges nonetheless represented a very significant step towards ending the exclusion of women from higher education at Cambridge.

Passing unnoticed

The critical first breach by women of the male-dominated university came in 1871, when Henry Sidgwick, a liberal professor in philosophy at Trinity College, leased a house for a few women at No. 74 Regent Street. This was the precursor of Newnham College, over which Sidgwick's friend Anne Clough later took charge.

Even Sidgwick remarked of the first five students that they were of 'unfortunate appearance' – they were too attractive and fashionable 'to pass unnoticed', as he chose to express one of the early demands made on women at the university. At that time the idea of young women living away from home was more scandalous than the fact of them being educated – and any whiff of scandal would have delayed the prospect of female education.

The seed which grew into the second college for women at Cambridge had been planted during 1869 in Hitchin, Hertfordshire, by Emily Davies, with the help of the liberal element among Cambridge's dons. This was a safe thirty miles from the university, but the difficulty of studying a wide range of subjects with the limited teaching resources available in Hitchin prompted a move to Girton, within two miles of Cambridge, in 1873. Miss Davies considered her Girton College to be superior to the establishment at Newnham and the two women's colleges rapidly acquired the two characteristics of snobbism and mutual mistrust which some older colleges had spent centuries honing.

Miss Davies mistrusted Miss Clough particularly for her lack of determination in the fight to extract degrees from the university for their young women. Miss Clough, on the other hand, was more concerned to educate women as teachers, seeing cohorts of female teachers as being the best means of challenging the subjugated status of women. Miss Davies condemned the Newnham people as representing 'the serpent eating away at our vitals'. About the students of each college she wrote: 'Girton is for ladies, while Newnham is for governesses'. Doubtless she was happy with the popular contention that the ladies of Girton wore stays while the members of Newnham went about town unlaced.

The foundation of these two colleges was only the beginning of women's struggle to secure fair access to higher education, however, and male prejudice still denied equal treatment to those who had been brave enough to breach the male citadel. Some educational facilities, for example, remained out of bounds to the girls: their use of the university's library was restricted, their presence at lectures was limited and they were excluded from competing for university prizes and scholarships.

Newnham still has a building in its grounds which was originally used as a laboratory. It had been thought inappropriate for their young ladies to spend the long hours required by many scientific experiments in close proximity with the other sex and the well-equipped Cavendish Laboratory was thus out of bounds to women. A perverse benefit of this restriction has been that some of the Newnham science equipment, no longer needed once the sexes could mix more freely, has been preserved. Typical of a late-nineteenth-century laboratory, it is on display at the Whipple Museum of the History of Science in Free School Lane.

Distrust as to the motives of these early Cambridge female undergraduates who wished to receive an education was widespread. Many thought of them, unfairly, as little different to the 'fishing fleet' of middle-class young women who sailed out annually to India looking for husbands among the army officers and business wallahs in the days of the English Raj.

New women and bicycles

From these small beginnings, it took over 100 years to establish full membership, co-educational colleges and then numerical equality between female and male students. The modest progress made by women in the 1870s simply reflected the changing position of women in society, which had been triggered by such legislation as the 1870 Women's Property Act. Those directing the university did not embrace the cause of women's rights; illiberal as ever, they responded belatedly and with reluctance.

Opposition to the advance of women's interests was strong. In a Senate debate in 1865, the eminent geologist Adam Sedgwick referred to the young girls who might be interested in taking the Local Examinations set by Cambridge for the country's secondary schools as 'nasty forward minxes'. Even the Liberal leader W.E. Gladstone, whose daughter was at Newnham in the late 1870s, could speak of how the granting of further rights would 'trespass on the delicacy, the purity, the refinement in the nature of women'. With such opposition from the liberal end of the political spectrum, the path towards equality was destined to progress by painfully slow steps. The conservative academics closed ranks against women's participation in all aspects of university life: as late as 1932, the university's comedians performing at the Footlights were almost forced to close their acting club after employing professional actresses in the female roles of their productions. It was a few more years before the female undergraduates themselves were able to perform.

The prefix 'new' was imposed on the feminist cause in the late 1800s and used in Cambridge because of its pejorative overtones. 'New' has rarely been a flattering prefix for any social or political movement: Catholics at the time of the Reformation had popularised the term 'New Learning' as an abusive description of Protestant theological belief. Conversely, through the importance given to Classical culture and the acceptance that wisdom was acquired with age, 'Old' was a term of respect. The term 'New Woman' was thus an insult. As a term of opprobrium 'New' even caught up with the Labour Party in twenty-first-century Britain, despite having initially been used by the party itself to suggest its own regeneration. *Punch* even portrayed the 'New Women' as bores who were never quiet; in one article of 1894 the magazine referred to them as living off a diet of only 'foolscap and ink'. This insensitive portrayal was even cast into a well-known little rhyme which was doubtless recited in Cambridge:

> There is a New Woman and what do you think?
> She lives upon nothing but foolscap and ink

Interestingly, in a place such as Cambridge, which has shown such an interest in velocipedes, bicycles became a symbol of the New Woman. The birth of the women's emancipation movement coincided with the wider use of these machines and women fully appreciated the greater freedom they brought. When the

Illustration 12.3: The anti-women protest of 1897. A vote in Senate subsequently confirmed women's continued exclusion from the university. An effigy of a woman on a bicycle, the symbol of their liberation, was hung contemptuously from the premises now occupied by the Cambridge University Press, opposite the Senate House.

Senate discussed whether to admit women as full members of the university during 1897, it was an effigy of a woman on a bicycle which protestors chose to suspend from the first floor of the ancient Trinity Street bookshop opposite the Senate. Some men celebrated the denial of full membership on this occasion by an assault on the Newnham Walk entrance of Newnham College.

The life of a female undergraduate long after the late 1800s cannot have been easy. They were isolated through restrictions which had never been imposed on male members of the university even in medieval times. It is telling that the first of the three main entrances which Newnham College used required the girls wishing to leave college to walk some distance in the opposite direction from the town in order to reach its centre: it led across a meadow, now used as a sports field, onto Barton Road. Access through the now-disused Newnham Walk entrance through to Queen's Road and Silver Street was not permitted until the late 1890s.

By then, however, discipline had clearly slipped, as the girls were allowed to invite men to the occasional tennis party on the grass courts to the north of Old Hall. Portions of the tennis pavilion could be booked for teas. Tennis Teas evidently became a bit of a wheeze to entertain favoured male friends, as they were soon referred to as 'Tennis Tea Parties Without Tennis'. The citadel of Girton, two miles away from the dangers of the town, remained more difficult to breach.

Another symbol of the invisibility many men at Cambridge thought appropriate for women resulted from the tragic death in 1893 of the brilliant electrical engineer John Hopkinson in an Alpine climbing accident, along with one of his sons and two of his daughters. His widow funded a new Engineering Building in Free School Lane, which has upon it a commemorative plaque. The inscription, which can be read clearly from the pavement, acknowledges the father and his son, but, astonishingly, excludes his two daughters.

From the beginning there were obviously those among the women who excelled at their studies. A few years after 1881, the year in which the Tripos exams had been unofficially opened to women, a Girton student, Agnata Ramsey, achieved the top Classics degree. It provoked *Punch* to publish another celebrated cartoon: two male railway guards bowing to her as she entered a First Class railway carriage. Similarly, in 1890 Philippa Fawcett, from Newnham College, achieved a higher mark than the top mathematics Wrangler. From 1882, the women of Girton and Newnham could sit mock exams which were marked by the more liberal academics. None, apparently, was more willing to help than Professor Canon Kennedy, once known better to many schoolchildren as the author of the famous *Revised Latin Primer*. Appositely, it seems to have been Kennedy's daughters who transformed his original work – hence the *Revised* – into the popular text still occasionally used in schools offering classics today. Another professor, Henry Sidgwick, permitted women to attend his lectures. The majority, however, resisted the advance of women. The first female lecturer at Cambridge, Ellen McArthur, who taught Economic History at Girton, was not appointed until 1894. An endowment created by her will still funds lectures and research positions.

Progress for women at Cambridge was slow in comparison with the more liberal universities in Scotland and Wales, as well as the English universities of London and Durham. By the 1890s those universities offered full degrees to women. Perversely, some at Cambridge then argued that since women had access to higher education in those places, there was no need for change at their own institution; the further argument that Cambridge would lose 'the best male scholars' to Oxford was also used. Doubtless, the same argument was aired at Oxford.

Homerton, which achieved full college status only in 2009, was the first place of co-education associated with the university. It moved to Cambridge from London's East End in the 1890s, where it had been a mixed college dedicated to the training of teachers. Homerton, as Miss Clough of Newnham had argued, advanced the cause of women's education through addressing the lack of female teachers.

Homerton's initial attempt at co-education in Hills Road was not a success; its records contain references to some of the more proper young ladies complaining both that 'they could not speak freely in front of men' and that some of their own sex 'forgot themselves'. One girl evidently went too far, as a Miss Opie was suspended. Others commented that the men forgot that women did not come to lectures to be 'made eyes at'. Centuries of separation had left huge potential for misunderstanding on both sides. Men had made up 30 of the 130-strong student body at the time of the move from London, but a few years in Cambridge was sufficient for the college to return to single-sex education, choosing to educate only women.

However, the pressure for change continued, particularly as more women joined the university community through marriage. Fellows had been allowed to marry since 1860 at some colleges – the Caius fellowship was the first college to use this freedom, though many of the other colleges retained the statutes which required celibacy for a further twenty years. The Caius fellows were perhaps helped by the fact that their Master, Dr Guest, had himself married in 1859, when the statute revisions were being drafted. The Royal Commission set up in 1877 finally agreed statutes in 1882 which permitted all fellows to marry. Nonetheless, some heads of colleges tried to maintain the ancient exclusion from their fellowship of all matters feminine. Dr George Corrie, Master of Jesus for thirty-six years from 1849, expressed his confidence to the Jesus fellowship that none of them would take advantage of the statute. In a refreshing example of the limitations of a master's authority, it is recorded that one fellow then married after a fortnight, some others within twelve months and virtually the entire Jesus fellowship had taken marriage vows within a few years. Once marriage had been deemed acceptable the prospects for proper co-education must have subtly changed. Furthermore, the centuries-old bachelor accommodation in college, which could not reasonably house new spouses, must have either caused marital disharmony or prompted moves out to the newly built villas to the west of the Backs.

Beyond bringing a much-needed female balance to the often hermetically sealed masculine culture of a college fellowship, the marriage of dons had another impact. For centuries the clever genes of academics had had no legitimate outlet. The celibacy of its staff over centuries must have been of incalculable loss to the nation's gene pool; rich bachelor dons' bequests of their estates to their college hardly compensated. From the late nineteenth century, however, clever academics could produce clever children; Maynard Keynes, for example, was the son of a Pembroke fellow. The Master of Trinity, H.M. Butler, married the Classics scholar Agnata Ramsay and G.M. Trevelyan was another top academic who produced intelligent children, although his daughter Mary Moorman studied at Oxford.

Achievement of full membership

Despite these concessions, the fight for full legal equality lasted until almost halfway through the next century, during which time some demonstrations of their discontent were made by female students. Between 1904 and 1907, for example, 700 women from Oxford and Cambridge travelled ostentatiously to Trinity College, Dublin, in order to receive degrees, their departure from Pierhead Docks in Liverpool securing them the nickname of 'Steamboat Ladies'. It was not until 1921 that women were granted degrees at Cambridge, and even then they were denied full membership of the university, their awards therefore being deemed titular degrees. Academics sheltered from normal mixed society evidently did not appreciate how such nomenclature for women's degrees would be shortened to 'Tit Degrees'.

There were, admittedly, some practical problems concerning the granting of full membership. British women did not win voting rights on a parity with men until 1928. Had full membership been granted in 1921, it would have created a difficult situation in which young female graduates were able to vote for two Cambridge University Members of Parliament while being unable to vote in their domestic constituencies until they were thirty. This was not an insuperable problem, however, as Oxford had by 1920 managed to award full membership to women on the same terms as men.

Full membership of the university for women finally came in 1948, allowing them for the first time to participate in its governance. That it was the first vote in the Senate on this issue since 1897 suggests a distinct lack of interest in female emancipation within the male academic community – indeed, Cambridge was the last university in Britain to correct this inequality. College co-education at Clare, King's and Churchill followed in 1972. St John's, Peterhouse and Magdalene were the last to accept women; Magdalene finally capitulated in 1988, although 45 per cent of its 1,200 resident and non-resident members still voted against co-education. Some of its undergraduates reportedly wore black armbands and fixed a black flag above the porters' lodge to mark the advent of co-education.

Numerical equality between male and female students was achieved in the twenty-first century and, indeed, this was possible only after some specific encouragement in previous years. The key motive in the early 1950s in founding New Hall, known since 2009 as Murray Edwards Hall, had been the shame felt by some in Cambridge at having the lowest proportion of women in undergraduate study of any university in the country. The remaining single-sex colleges, three in all, are those which admit women.

Although the exclusion of women was always indefensible, Cambridge had merely marched more or less in step with, or perhaps a step behind, the rest of Europe. On the continent, the universities of Paris, Berne and Geneva had been the first to educate women, but even here this advance had been achieved only in the 1860s.

Women at the modern university

In relation to the long history of the university, women have studied there in sufficient numbers to make an impact only very recently. By 1969 just 10 per cent of undergraduates were female and even at the end of the 1970s only one-third of undergraduates were women; but by the early years of the twenty-first century they were capturing around 50 per cent of the undergraduate places and 40 per cent of the positions open to postgraduates. The balance of numbers between faculties varies, of course. Women remain under-represented in engineering and also in subjects such as philosophy, where forceful verbal sparring is often an essential part of the course.

The success of women in reaching this parity has, however, come at the expense of students from lower socio-economic groups. The expansion of higher education from the 1980s was meant to serve those with the least wealth, as well as to attract women. However, the disproportionate dominance of the middle classes at Cambridge has continued, as female offspring of the bourgeoisie have simply joined their brothers, who had always been able to secure places. In the forty years since 1970, governments and university administrators have proved unable to tackle simultaneously the two injustices of sexual and social inequality.

Indeed, mixing middle-class women and men at university can be seen as directly hindering the cause of social mobility in Britain, as, unsurprisingly, these privileged graduates frequently marry each other. They then build on the educational advantages of their youth by earning the high incomes typical of graduates.

The children of less privileged families, whose parents were less likely to access either Cambridge or higher incomes, have been kept even further away than before.

Although women now run some key parts of the university in Cambridge, they remain under-represented among academic staff. There are occasional rumblings in parts of the university, such as the History Faculty in 2005, where the number of teaching positions captured by men was thought by some to be very disproportionate. Overall, women hold less than 25 per cent of faculty posts; men retain over 90 per cent of professorships and about 80 per cent of senior lecturer posts. This imbalance at least enabled the university to explain the results of a survey in 2009 which found that male employees of the university were paid 31 per cent more than women: the variance was simply blamed on the higher number of men in senior positions rather than on discrimination.

There is one partial explanation for the lack of women in senior positions. Women win fewer of the top degrees; 18 per cent of men win first-class degrees as against 5 per cent of women. One report in 2007 suggested that men were both cleverer and more stupid than women, who tended to cluster at the level of the upper second while men either excelled or posted only modest achievements. Another study suggested that the format of the final degree examination favoured the male character. Be this as it may, one consequence of the imbalance in the awarding of degrees is that men are able to secure a starting position more easily within the academic career structure; a first-class degree is essential to place the academic career ladder up against the wall, never mind reach the first rung – a funded research post.

This imbalance is also reflected in the international achievements of Cambridge women. Only one among the eighty-three Nobel laureates connected with Cambridge is female: Dorothy Hodgkin, who pioneered the technique of X-ray crystallography, won this prize in 1964. Rosalind Franklin's work, also in the field of crystallography, would surely have earned this prize had she not tragically died so young of cancer – a disease which may have been caused by her research work. Others have thought Jocelyn Bell Burnell should have won the prize in 1969 for her work in astrophysics at New Hall.

Certainly there are still some elderly reactionaries imbibing prejudice and fine wine in the odd senior common room; they are irrelevant. Sexual taunts may still be aimed at those in female-only colleges, as well, but sexual nonconformity at Cambridge is neither a new issue nor only a woman's issue. King's College and Trinity College in the time of Anthony Blunt, E.M. Forster, Dadie Rylands, John Sheppard, Alan Turing and Maynard Keynes provoked similar comments. Maurice Bowra, an Oxford graduate, eloquently captured this confluence of male homosexuality and Communist sympathy at Cambridge with the phrase 'The Homintern'.

Recently, however, female academics have filled some of the university's top positions. Rosemary Murray was the first female vice-chancellor in 1975; since the role became full-time in 2002, another woman, Alison Richard, has been elected. Naturally, she has led the 800th Anniversary celebrations. It is heartening in this regard that of the four themes that have been chosen to give impetus to this fund-raising campaign not one of them concerns women specifically, which suggests at least that sexual equality in education is no longer the issue that it once was. In addition, since 1999 King's and Sidney Sussex have appointed women to lead their colleges. There is even a female esquire bedell, the graduate officer of the university who attends the chancellor on ceremonial occasions; the list of esquire bedell office holders goes back to 1250.

The access of women to Cambridge is assisted through the three women-only undergraduate colleges of Newnham, Murray Edwards Hall and Lucy Cavendish, the college for mature students set up in 1965. Cambridge shows no sign of following the move by all-women colleges at Oxford to co-education; Newnham and Lucy Cavendish have even maintained a single-sex fellowship. The conversion of Girton to co-education was more the result of a special situation: the college's distance from town and single-sex education was proving an unattractive mix for prospective students. Having already experienced the move from Hitchin, it was probably felt easier to accept men than to relocate. Although the concept of all-women colleges has been preserved to protect women, it is clear that female applicants to Cambridge prefer mixed colleges. The force of the argument about young women wanting private space away from young men withers before their opinion that there is more fun to be had in a mixed college. The single-sex colleges no longer attract enough of the brightest women to avoid their descent in the college academic rankings, although a college's reputation in a particular discipline – Newnham's in Classics, for example – can still attract the most talented.

If perceptions of unequal treatment remain, it is more probably now the fault of society beyond Cambridge, rather than lingering misogynism within the university. The barriers are down. There are role models in place. In time women will claim their full share of the senior positions at the university, probably more rapidly than the under-represented socio-economic groups of the nation will win a proportional share of the undergraduate places.

Doubtless the divide between the two sexes will continue to attract attention. A painting within the renowned collection of women's modern art at Murray Edwards Hall fuels women's perception of male prejudice: by Alexis Hunter, it is entitled 'The Fear of the Academic Wife'. It confirms that representations of women in Cambridge still reflect the unreasonable fear which the combination of their sex and intelligence can provoke in men, be they a sexy sixteenth-century devil in the stained glass of King's College Chapel or a female academic in the late twentieth century. The misrepresentation and exclusion of women for so long provided a sad contrast to the immense contribution that they made during the university's vulnerable early days.

Chapter 13

From Beyond the Seas

Since ancient times the beautiful stone lapis lazuli has been crushed to make the brilliant blue pigment known as ultramarine. The stone came from Afghanistan through Venice into Europe. The Venetians gave the dye its name, reflecting the mystery of its source from 'beyond the seas'. The great Italian trading city had found words for new wonders from the east before; they had named porcelain after comparing its translucence and texture to the cowrie shell – *porcellana* in Italian. Both can be found in Cambridge at the Fitzwilliam Museum.

The artefacts, skills and ideas of visitors from abroad have been part of the culture of Cambridge since the very beginning. Within a university fostered under the protection of the supra-national Roman Catholic Church, academics had stronger ties with those they claimed as their intellectual peers overseas than with those among whom they lived. Cambridge has been one of the pre-eminent intellectual trading posts of the world; it has received much from overseas and its own people have travelled widely.

American connections

Links between Cambridge and the United States of America go back to the founding fathers and extend in both directions. Many of those among the leaders of the Pilgrim Fathers, the educated elite of the thirteen colonies, the signatories of the American Declaration of Independence and their soldiers, philosophers and men of business knew Cambridge well. The connections are still being made: Americans visit as tourists, send their children to study at the university and build close business links through research and the enterprises which have made Cambridge such a crucial link in the world's knowledge economy.

The spiritual journey of those Englishmen who felt compelled to migrate to North America began in Cambridge. The notion of a free conscience developed from the religious revolutions of the sixteenth century; to James I, however, such freedom was 'insufferable in any well governed commonwealth'. Forbidden to practise their religion in the manner they wished, many nonconforming puritans left England. Of the first 132 graduate emigrants to New England, 100 came from Cambridge University and 35 of those were from the Protestant college founded in 1584, Emmanuel. John Harvard, after whom the eponymous university was named, had himself graduated from Emmanuel in 1632 and the college's 'Brick Building' has rooms reserved for the annual Lionel de Jersey scholar from Harvard University.

Other Harvard connections include the university's first president, Henry Dunster, who studied at Magdalene from 1627 to 1634. At the other end of the timeline, the 'D' staircase entrance of Benson Court at Magdalene, designed by Lutyens in the 1930s, was funded by members of Harvard in Dunster's memory and carries the Harvard motto 'Veritas'. It was a Harvard graduate, George Downing, who left America to fight for the Parliamentarians in the English Civil War. His timely conversion to the Stuart cause in the late 1650s prompted Samuel Pepys, whose own loyalties had varied, to call him 'a perfidious rogue'. He became a property developer, building the houses in Downing Street, London, one of which was to become the prime minister's residence. It was his grandson who left money to the university for the foundation of Downing College.

The shared religious history of these two countries is also made evident in surprising ways involving Cambridge. Sixteenth-century Protestant reformers met at the White Horse Inn to drink ale and discuss the religious ideas emerging from northern Germany, as the inn's nickname, Little Germany, reveals: both names are recorded on a blue plaque at the junction of Bene't Street and King's Parade. Almost 500 years later the followers of an American religious group meet through the website www.whitehorseinn.org. At their 2009 conference in California, the main topic for discussion was 'Calvin on Law and Gospel'; precisely the same issues had preoccupied the people who gathered half a millennium earlier in the Cambridge inn.

A few hundred yards away, by the north entrance of Little St Mary's Church, is another Cambridge link to America: one of the vicars of the church was Godfrey Washington, the great-uncle of George Washington. A tablet on the wall displays the family shield of arms: red bars below red five-pointed spur rowels on a white background. An eagle is perched above the shield. The same symbols were adopted by the District of Columbia and later used to represent the first thirteen colonies of the new republic – so even America's national totem, the eagle, and its flag were borrowed from England. Their origins are clear in Cambridge. George Washington later claimed that the spurs were stars, suggesting that they transferred God's blessing on to all Americans. Such 'spin' was justifiable, as 'Spurs and Stripes' seems rather less inspiring than 'Stars and Stripes'. Some Americans deny this connection on the grounds that Washington did not sit on the committee which chose the American flag and, indeed, that his noble objection to the cult of personality which some people sought to develop around him was well known. Others, however, such as Winthrop W. Aldrich, Ambassador to the Court of St James in the 1950s, acknowledged when speaking before a similar memorial at Washington Old Hall in Tyne and Wear that the probability of the Washington coat of arms being the true origin of the American flag was overwhelming.

Another piece of early American history is kept within the Old Library of Jesus College. It is a very rare translation of the bible into the language of the Algonquin Indian tribe, by John Eliot, which was published in the 1660s, before any bibles in English had been printed in America. Eliot had graduated from Jesus in the early 1620s and was another of the earliest Cambridge settlers in North America. In a country where the first European settlers were inspired by the bible and the 'Word', these early bibles are greatly revered by Americans.

Illustration 13.1: The eighteenth-century memorial plaque to Godfrey Washington, minister to Little St Mary's and great uncle to George Washington.

A number of the people who were at the centre of momentous events in American history have links back to Cambridge. Several Englishmen who played key roles in the American War of Independence graduated from Cambridge and from Clare College in particular. A Clare man, Charles Townshend, was responsible when Chancellor of the Exchequer for the taxation that so irritated the American colonists. It was the Townshend Acts of 1767 which sparked events such as the Boston Tea Party. Another Clare graduate, Lord Cornwallis (whose grandfather was Charles 'Turnip' Townshend of King's College), played a key part in the 'rebellion'. As second-in-command of the British forces in America, it was Cornwallis who surrendered with 8,000 men to the rebels at Yorktown in 1783. Ironically, he had voted in parliament against the Stamp Act of 1766 out of sympathy for the Americans' cause. Another Townshend at Clare,

Thomas, was an eloquent apologist in parliament for the rebels and spoke out against the conduct of the war. He was later Home Secretary under Pitt. Astonishingly, the man who provoked the war, an apologist for the rebel cause and the losing general were thus each Clare men. Portraits of Cornwallis and Charles Townshend are hung at opposite ends of the Clare College dining hall top table. As if in acknowledgement of the contribution these graduates made to American independence, Clare has been remarkably successful in attracting financial support from the United States. The most generous American support has come from Paul Mellon through the Andrew W. Mellon Foundation – the grandson of Judge Thomas Mellon, who founded the family's fortune, he graduated from Clare in 1931.

Other connections to Cambridge also marked the beginning and end of the war. Three Cambridge graduates signed the Declaration of Independence in 1776: Thomas Nelson of Christ's and Virginia, and Thomas Lynch (Caius) and Arthur Middleton (St John's), who both represented South Carolina. And it was the son of a Jesuan, David Hartley, who signed the Treaty of Paris ending the War of Independence seven years later.

Comrades in arms

During the Great War, American troops spent time at Duxford, to the south of Cambridge, while archives at Fenners, the university's cricket ground, record a visit from the Americans on 4 July 1918, during which a baseball match was played. The Second World War again brought Americans and Britons together in Cambridge. As the town's early trade had grown out of its proximity to the North European coastline, so it was an effective base from which to launch bombing raids in the Second World War. There were over 100 airfields in East Anglia, of which 12 were within ten miles of Cambridge. The US Eighth Air Force ran many of them from places such as Castle Camps, Duxford and Saffron Walden; their pilots came for 'Rest & Recreation' to Cambridge and in particular to the Eagle Pub in Bene't Street. The Eighth Air Force alone bore over 26,000 casualties during the war, practically half of the total USAAF losses; this sacrifice was honoured in 1945 through the granting of the Freedom of Cambridge to the Eighth Air Force.

Cambridge was not only a place of relaxation for American forces, however. As secure from German spies as it was from rioting natives, the Long Gallery in St John's Second Court was used by the Allies to review some of the D-Day landing plans, while the Bull Hotel, between St Catharine's and the screen of King's College, was taken over as an American billet. Demobilised American servicemen were later lodged there while pursuing education courses.

The names of many American servicemen, and perhaps even some of those Eagle customers, are recorded in the American Cemetery at Madingley, three miles west of Cambridge. It occupies thirty acres of land donated to the USA by the university in 1944, and has the peaceful manicured beauty found at other twentieth-century war cemeteries. The only American cemetery in Britain, it is the last established overseas as the bodies of Americans who fall in battle are now repatriated. At Madingley the names of 5,127 missing airmen, soldiers and seamen are recorded; a further 3,812 identified Americans are buried beneath lasa marble headstones. Reminders, both metaphorical and actual, of the United States' presence here are unmistakeable: a circular flowerbed beside the entrance contains a standard rose bush for each state of the

United States, while the US flag is raised every day at sunrise and lowered again in the evening. A hundred thousand people visit the cemetery each year and, since most will be from the United States, it is another means through which Americans maintain contact with Cambridge.

From founders of the United States to funders of the university

As with English aristocrats who married into American money to revive their family fortunes, the old universities benefited considerably from their associations with American plutocrats. Paul Mellon, son of the Pittsburgh industrialist Andrew Mellon, funded part of the Forbes Mellon Library in the centre of Clare College's Memorial Court as well as giving money towards the foundation of Clare Hall in 1966. His generosity also extended to a donation of $8 million to the Fitzwilliam Museum, to which, after his death, a further $12.5 million was added. Cambridge has captured the affections of other Americans, too. Rockefellers contributed generously to the University Library in the 1930s, while Guggenheims supported Pembroke after Harry Guggenheim studied there before the Great War. Individual causes, such as the dismantling of King's College Chapel's glass in 1939, have also often caught their attention.

After enjoying their 'R&R' at the Eagle and elsewhere in Cambridge, members of the US military left one further impression on their host country by returning to the USA with up to 60,000 'GI brides', a large number of whom came from Cambridge and East Anglia more widely. The demographic impact on eastern England of this bride-drain, combined with the death toll of young East Anglian men, was immense.

The strength of ties with America did not weaken after the war. Various schemes, such as the Marshall Scholarships, the Harry S. Truman Scholarship Program and the Fulbright Commission, directed clever Americans to England; initially, most studied at either Oxford or Cambridge. For example, Milton Friedman, the great monetarist who challenged the economic views of King's famous economist Maynard Keynes, was the Fulbright Visiting Fellow at Gonville & Caius in 1954/5. In 1975 Downing College established an annual fellowship reserved for a member of Virginia University and since the mid-1960s funds of the Winston Churchill Foundation support up to fifteen American scholars at the university's Churchill College. In 2000, the Gates family endowed the Gates Millennium Scholars Program with £200 million, an amount which rivals that available to the Rhodes Scholarships. There are over 200 Gates scholars from overseas studying at Cambridge University at any point in time, while the Rhodes Trust funds a mere 70 scholars at Oxford. This influx into Cambridge of the clever and the fortunate from overseas will strengthen international links within the alumni network.

When Churchill College was founded in 1966 the USA was among the many countries which made a symbolic gift to the college. The Americans went one step further by funding the Churchill College Archive Centre, which contains many important political and scientific records. Besides Winston Churchill's records, those of Margaret Thatcher, Neil Kinnock and Lord Young are archived there. The collection receives no direct public support and, like other outstanding treasure houses in Cambridge, such as the Fitzwilliam Museum, the University Library and college libraries, it offers access willingly to those outside the university.

Illustration 13.2: The Brick Building at Emmanuel College, designed by John Westley in the early 1630s, where John Harvard had rooms before leaving for America in 1637.

The Cambridge connection with the United States is recharged regularly in many different ways. James Watson, the American molecular biologist who worked on the structure of DNA, was a fellow at Clare. A large number of US companies have bases in Cambridge and, in addition to those Americans who come to Cambridge to work, many more come on short visits to attend the hi-tech conferences which the university organises. Cambridge continues to be able to attract the support of rich Americans who are motivated either by philanthropy or business objectives. It was through an Englishman, the late Professor Roger Needham, that Microsoft based its European Research Headquarters in Cambridge in 1997 – Bill Gates acknowledged Needham as a crucial mentor and appointed him as the centre's first managing director. The Gates research resource operates from a building named after Needham in J.J. Thomson Avenue, off Madingley Road. Gates has also spent another £10 million supporting start-up technology ventures associated with the university. Similarly, Gordon Moore, the founder of the Intel Corporation, generously financed the library of the Centre of Mathematical Sciences.

German connections

Although links with other countries may not be as all-embracing as those with America, there are nonetheless many which are of great significance. From Germany came the influence of Martin Luther, whose belief in the need to restructure the Catholic Church provoked the English Reformation. Luther never visited Cambridge, but other renowned scholars from the German states, such as the Protestant reformer Martin Bucer, did study at the university. He had been consulted by Henry VIII on the 'Great Matter' of his divorce in the 1530s and then came to Cambridge at the invitation of Thomas Cranmer in 1550, where he was awarded the Regius Professorship of Divinity, which he held until his death in 1551. Bucer had a huge influence on the English leaders of the Reformation and it was because such giants of the Reformation sometimes met at the White Horse Inn in King's Parade that its nickname of 'Little Germany' was acquired.

Albert of Saxe-Coburg, husband of Queen Victoria, was another German who had a great impact on Cambridge. He was chancellor of the university from 1847 until his death in 1861. Aware of the more advanced levels of scientific study on the continent, he worked with the 7th duke of Devonshire to promote science at the university. His memory has not been well tended in Cambridge, however. The sculptor John Foyley, who sculpted the statue of Prince Albert which stands in front of the Albert Hall in London, also completed a sculpture of Albert in Cambridge, which was placed in the magnificent main hall of the Fitzwilliam Museum in the 1870s. However, it was given to Madingley Hall in the 1950s, where it stood unloved for fifty years in the grounds, weathering badly. Reclaimed and brushed up in 2003, it is now inside Wolfson College in Barton Road, although it bears no indication as to its sculptor, its subject or its relevance to the university. The only other memorial to Albert is a faded floor tile in the Round Church recording the visit he made there with Victoria in the 1840s.

The German company Mond continued Albert's support of science by financing the Mond Laboratory behind the Old Cavendish Building in the 1930s for the Russian scientist Pyotr Kapitza, who carried out research in low-temperature physics there. In a Modernist style, its simple form and rotunda entrance make it one of the few attractive Cambridge buildings from the interwar years. Kapitza commissioned Eric Gill to design a striking crocodile into the external brickwork as a tribute to the New Zealander Ernest Rutherford, then director of the Cavendish – his nickname was inspired by *Peter Pan*, as the approach of Rutherford, like that of J.M. Barrie's crocodile, could always be heard.

Germany's contribution to Cambridge has not been exclusively cerebral, however, as their artisans have worked in at least two colleges: the Bavarian craftsman Max Emanuel Ainmiller designed much of the glass in Peterhouse's chapel in the nineteenth century, while stonemasons from the German states worked on the soft French limestone used for the Tudor heraldic symbols within King's College Chapel.

There are also wartime connections between Cambridge and Germany. A young German who fell in battle is remembered in Cambridge. The name of L.H. Jagenberg is inscribed on the Roll of Honour of the First World War within the chapel of St Catharine's College. Beside his name is the touching legend '*Hostis Amicus*' – 'friendly enemy'.

In the Second World War, despite the number of aerodromes in the locality and the importance of Cambridge's railway station to freight movements, the town suffered relatively little damage. Although a number of homes were destroyed and, tragically, a few people were killed, the university itself escaped lightly. The Round Church, the Union building and the Catholic Church near the station were damaged in 1942 and shrapnel scars in the wall of Trinity property at the corner of Jesus Lane and Bridge Street can still be seen clearly from the pavement. More shrapnel scars have been left on some books in the Union's Library.

The books' spines have never been repaired, perhaps being left in disrepair to symbolise the indestructibility of the knowledge Cambridge nurtures. Their condition has reportedly since caused the occasional visitor to express concern as to the Union's finances.

More recently, the West German President Richard von Weizsäcker was awarded an honorary degree by both Oxford and Cambridge. Oxford awarded its degree some years before Cambridge and comment was made at Oxford about the perpetual tardiness of Cambridge when the university finally offered its degree to the elderly von Weizsäcker in 1984. Maintaining the long tradition of Oxbridge spats, a Cambridge don charmingly retorted how comforting it was to appreciate that however old, there was always a chance in life to improve oneself. Helmut Kohl, when chancellor of a reunited Germany, was given an honorary degree in 1998.

Of more recent importance is the re-establishment by a German vet working in Cambridge of the local tradition of grazing cattle on the town commons. The practice had stopped following the outbreak of foot and mouth disease in the early years of this century. However, since 2006 Angelika Von Heimendahl has spread a total of eighty Red Poll cattle, an East Anglian breed, between Midsummer Common, Coe Fen, Stourbridge Common and Grantchester Meadows. The stay of the Red Poll on Midsummer Common is interrupted by the two fairs but otherwise they graze there from the early spring through to November. The meat from these animals, which have been fattened slowly through grazing rather than on grain, is much prized and sold locally.

French connections

French connections to Cambridge also go right back to the beginning of the university. After the university at Cambridge had begun with the arrival of the Oxford scholars in 1209, it received a fillip from the arrival of French scholars fleeing from Paris in the thirteenth century: these were days when a university was often judged by its size and ability to attract scholars, so the Frenchmen would have been made welcome.

The aristocratic cultural background which nurtured the university in the Middle Ages was Anglo-French and Catholic and reminders of this aspect of the university's cultural heritage abound: for example, St John's College is stamped in a number of places with the family motto of Lady Margaret Beaufort, *'Souvent me souvient'* – 'I often remember' – although her impact on the university has ensured that it is she who is often remembered in Cambridge. In a salute to her influence, tiny brass plaques in the shape of the forget-me-not have been set into the pavements which run from the college, along Bridge Street and up past Magdalene. Delightful though this gesture on the part of the local council is – as with the fountain-pen-shaped bollards on the edge of the same pavements, which allude to the literary fame of Magdalene College – it is doubtful that it has made much impact on those wandering through this part of the old town. There are other places in Cambridge where the entwined histories of France and England are physically marked. The fleur de lys, for instance, is shown prominently on the town's own shield of arms on the first-floor balcony of the Guildhall in the Market Square. It has also been repeatedly sculpted in the antechapel of King's College Chapel to witness the English claim to the French throne following Henry VI's coronation as King of France in Paris during 1431, a delusion which was maintained until the coronation of George

IV. Besides the two French ladies who founded colleges, Marie de Valence and Margaret of Anjou, other founders had French blood. The priest Edmund Gonville, of a gentry family of French extraction, founded Gonville Hall, while Henry VI, founder of King's College, was the son of Catherine of Valois.

Pacts of friendship as well as reminders of occasional difficulties between the British and French are marked in Cambridge. In the 1620s the wedding treaty of Charles I to Henrietta Maria, daughter of the French king Henry IV, was signed in the long gallery of St John's Second Court and is commemorated in the glass of the central oriel window. In contrast, the bases of the two fine streetlamps in front of St Catharine's main gates mark one of Britain's many disputes with its neighbour. They are said to have once been cannon on French ships captured at the battle of Trafalgar; the other claim, of course, is that the majority of those cannon were melted down on Landseer's instructions in order to create the lions in Trafalgar Square.

Along with many other European leaders, the French president Charles de Gaulle made a gift to Churchill College in honour of Winston Churchill in the 1960s. The French commissioned a tapestry designed by Jean Lurcat: it is a beautiful work of art named *L'Etoile*, after the area of Paris which contains the Arc de Triomphe, and now hangs in the Churchill College library. It symbolised the Liberation March of the Free French Army through the Arc de Triomphe in 1944. However, de Gaulle used the gift to peddle the French national myth of self-deliverance, as it is boldly embroidered with the inaccurate legend: 'Paris – Libéré soi-même'. As it happens, the tapestry hangs in the college nearest to the American war cemetery, so less than a mile away are remembered the thousands of Americans who died over the North Sea and in northern Europe to free the occupied countries of Europe. Such distortions do little to promote harmony between these two countries, whose relationship is littered with diplomatic rifts.

Italian connections

The people and culture of the Italian peninsular have also influenced Cambridge University. In medieval times the goodwill of the pope was necessary to establish the university. Not only did Pope Gregory IX grant Cambridge status as a 'studium' in 1233, but permission for the establishment of college chapels was repeatedly forthcoming from various of his successors. Popes would have been very aware of the development and success of this university in medieval times. The Catholic Church, much of whose culture derives from Italy, has left a permanent imprint on the university's architecture through the internal architecture of chapels and the ubiquitous cloisters.

Italian universities held an unparalleled intellectual lead in the medieval period and influenced other, less well-established, universities such as Cambridge. Hence it was Padua which attracted Dr Caius, and later William Harvey, because its university was recognised as the centre for Western European medical instruction. Similarly, Bologna maintained a leading reputation in the practice and interpretation of canon law.

In later centuries, English architects returned from their tours around Italy immensely influenced by what they had seen there. The Senate House was designed in the 1730s by James Gibbs, a leading eighteenth-century English architect who had studied in Rome. Stephen Wright designed the façade of the Old Schools Building twenty years later; its recessed windows and the loggia beneath are strongly influenced by the

Venetian style. He also used two Italian artists to complete the internal ceiling plasterwork. The Fitzwilliam Museum, designed by George Basevi in the 1830s, is described by architectural critics as being built in the Baroque style 'with significant Greco-Roman precedents'.

The oak screen of King's College Chapel that separates the choir from the antechapel is decorated in the Grotesque early Christian style that was popular in sixteenth-century Rome, and was completed by Italian craftsmen. The screen is full of Classical allusion, alongside the initials of Henry VIII and other ubiquitous Tudor symbols. Italian artists, too, are well represented in Cambridge. The Fitzwilliam Museum has its share of masterpieces by artists such as Titian, Veronese, Tintoretto and Canaletto. The works of the Italian painters Pittoni, Amigoni, Cipriani and Barocci have been also placed behind the altars in four college chapels, while in the 1770s Giovanni Bastista Cipriani designed the stained glass window of Trinity's Wren Library which features allegorical portrayals of Isaac Newton, George III and Francis Bacon.

Dutch and other north European connections

Other countries, such as the Netherlands, have also had a consistent impact on Cambridge. Dutch influence came through Erasmus of Rotterdam, who was invited by Bishop Fisher to Queens' College in 1511 to retranslate the bible from its Greek sources. The subtle changes Erasmus made to many key parts of the Vulgate edition of the bible inspired reformers to tackle abuses within the Church. As a Catholic, his mission was to promote a sound Christianity through a regeneration of the moral and spiritual life of the Church; but he also provided a philosophical base to the movement of Humanism and, at the university, put life back into the teaching of Greek. At about this time, a Dutchman by the name of Francis van Hoorn established the first major brewery in Cambridge, which must have suited Erasmus, as his letters written from Cambridge often contained complaints about English beer.

It was Dutch wealth which funded the Fitzwilliam Museum. The Viscounts Fitzwilliam, who were members of the Irish peerage, had been kept impoverished and, figuratively at least, beyond the Dublin pale by their devotion to the Catholic cause. Conversion to Protestantism in the late 1600s brought them favour at court. Their wealth was acquired through the marriage of the 6th earl to Catharine Decker, heiress to the wealthy Matthew Decker, who had come from Holland to England with William of Orange. Matthew's grandson, the 7th earl, used his inheritance from his mother's family to endow the museum. This Dutch connection is partly responsible for the museum's renowned collection of Dutch paintings and Delft earthenware.

People from the Low Countries, like the artisans from the German states, have had a practical impact on Cambridge. Grinling Gibbons, whose carvings adorn Trinity's Wren Library, came from the Low Countries, although his parents were English. He learnt his trade over the first twenty years of his life in Rotterdam. Horace Walpole described his talent as being the ability to give 'wood the loose and airy lightness of flowers'. Three of the six leading glaziers who led the installation of the magnificent stained glass in King's College Chapel were from the Low Countries, as was their principal designer Dierick Vellert.

The bricks imported from the Low Countries to build Queens' College were followed by a Dutch influence over the architecture of some college buildings. The Brick Building at Emmanuel, Third Court at St John's and Basil Champneys' buildings at Newnham each show a distinct Dutch style.

A century after King's, Dutch expertise was used to begin the drainage of the fenland north of Cambridge. Cornelius Vermuyden designed the drainage network which lowered the water table in this area sufficiently for the land to be reclaimed for agriculture; by the mid-1700s water extraction was driven by 750 windmills. The fens were drained on the whole successfully, although the main flaw of this system – dependence on the wind – was not addressed until steam and then electrically driven systems were installed in the nineteenth and twentieth centuries.

Danes, too, have spent time in Cambridge and not only under the command of Thorkill the Tall, who led the destruction of Cambridge by fire in 1010. Bertel Thorvaldsen, a Danish sculptor, was commissioned in the nineteenth century by Westminster Abbey to carve the statue of Lord Byron which is now in the Trinity College Library. More recently the Danish architect Henning Larsen designed the Moeller Centre attached to Churchill College, which can be seen on the north side of Madingley Road.

Other connections

As befits the concept of Cambridge as an intellectual trading post, it has not been simply a passive recipient of external influences; there has been an exchange. British students who passed through its educational mould did not just go on to run their own country but much of the Empire as well. Missionaries, too, from John Eliot in the sixteenth century up to Henry Martyn and the followers of Charles Simeon in the nineteenth have set out from Cambridge. As Eliot translated the bible into Alconquin, so Henry Martyn was the first to translate the New Testament into Urdu and Persian before dying in Turkey of fever aged only thirty-one.

Adventurous souls were also inspired at Cambridge. A romantic story tells of how Telegraph Todd, who led the team installing telegraph poles across Australia, met his bride Alice, after whom Alice Springs is known, in Cambridge: her childhood home was a small terraced house in Free School Lane opposite the east end of St Bene't's church, where some of the original black railings by her front door can still be seen. Another adventurer caused Sydney, Australia, to be named in honour of a Clare College man: Thomas Townshend, Viscount Sydney, was home secretary when James Cook arrived on the east coast of Australia in 1770. Cook's wife and one of his sons are buried in Great St Andrew's church, opposite Christ's College.

It is Australians who appreciate best the connection of the shield of arms of Sidney Sussex with the old 'arrowhead' prison uniform. In the early 1700s, William III instructed his Master of Ordnance, Henry Sidney, to find a way of identifying government property. Sidney, whose family had founded Sidney Sussex College, took the symbol known as the 'pheon' from his family shield of arms and had it stamped on government property, hence its use on prison uniforms. The two-tone brown 'magpie' (as it was known in nineteenth-century Australia) convict's uniform was printed with the same arrowheads, although the arrowheads on the uniforms of the Australian convicts pointed upwards, whereas those of the college and of Magwitch in Charles Dickens' *Great Expectations*, as portrayed by Dickens' illustrator Phiz, always point

Illustration 13.3: Hall Court of Sidney Sussex College, where the pheons are moulded into the façade above the entrance to the hall and Master's Lodge.

down. The Royal Navy still stamps its silver-plate with this emblem; after the Second World War it could often be identified on army-surplus items such as binoculars.

Until recently, connections with Japan have been limited. A Japanese aristocrat from the early twentieth century is remembered at Selwyn College; the Marquis Tokugawa Tyesato expressed his thanks for accommodation there by financing the bridge between two buildings in Old Court. A swastika extracted from his family's crest, a symbol of good fortune in the East, is emblazoned on the building. Links with Japan are growing, however, particularly at Pembroke and New Hall: the distinctive round white building alongside Huntingdon Road by New Hall is a design education centre for the Kaetsu Educational Foundation, which promotes Japanese culture, while the University of Nihon has made a large contribution to the building of Pembroke's Foundress Court. The Nihon benefactors also fund the upkeep of a small Japanese garden alongside Tennis Court Lane; to the irritation of Pembroke's college gardeners, Japanese garden experts travel up from London to carry out the maintenance.

Links to the east have been growing over the last century, particularly through the efforts of Professor Joseph Needham, an eminent Sinologist; he was a British biochemist but dedicated much of his life to analysing the scientific contribution of China to human culture. The Needham Institute, behind the grounds of Robinson College, maintains these connections, as does the China Executive Leadership

Programme at the university's Judge Business Institute. The university fosters links to Tsinghua University in Beijing and a total of 600 Chinese students studied at the university in 2006, at a time when there were only 435 citizens of the United States at Cambridge. After that of Britain, the Chinese undergraduate body is now – and is likely to remain – the largest in the university. Groups from other countries are growing, however: through the Dr Manmohan Singh Undergraduate Scholarship programme announced in 2009, it is expected that the number of Indian undergraduates – presently over 200 – will be increased.

It is also from countries such as India and China that the university draws many of its postgraduates. Fifty-three per cent of postgraduates in 2005/6 were non-UK nationals. Almost as significant is the 25 per cent of academic staff who are not British. This contribution from overseas is backed up by the 15 per cent of undergraduates who come from outside the British Isles. However, despite all these treasured contacts with the world's cultures, the university evidently still honours its social contract to educate the youth of Britain: the vast majority of undergraduates are British.

The global reach of the modern university

Although the undergraduate focus of the university remains domestic, its postgraduate programmes support its global ambitions. At this level the university is an institution with a profile which matches the international businesses which have clustered around Cambridge. Many of these students underpin the university's links to business and the exploitation of their latest research achievements.

In a study of the past and the present of the university it is remarkably easy to find links at Cambridge to almost every country; the university has always been an international place. All sorts of treasures of the Fitzwilliam Museum add to the web of international connections; one of its exhibits, for example, strikes at the core of Swiss identity. It is a versatile knife from the Roman occupation of Britannia, which was made many centuries before the Swiss nation provided its army with a similarly multi-purpose knife; found in East Anglia, it is a remarkably exact template for what the Swiss have convinced the world comes from their country.

It contributes much to the vitality of Cambridge that these international links from overseas are constantly renewed. The present vice-chancellor, a Newnham graduate, returned from Yale to take up her post at the same time as the Master of Trinity, who came from the Indian sub-continent, left to study at Harvard. Such international exchange has always been within the bloodstream of Cambridge. Announcements of academic staff leaving or joining are usually accompanied by a synopsis of their career, often covering their previous postings to many of the world's most prestigious universities. Such exchange is encouraged.

Cambridge will seek out the best students in every country in order to maintain its academic pre-eminence, particularly among its postgraduates. This will ensure that the long-established links connecting the world's intellectual cultures remain strong. There are already 41,000 graduates from overseas out of a total of roughly 175,000 and 144 overseas alumni groups, among them ones in Tirana and Phnom Penh, as well as 36 across the United States. Influence from beyond the seas, already as old as the university itself, will grow yet stronger.

Chapter 14

Ball Chasing and Other Pastimes

The monasteries' influence over the university extended beyond the design of its chapels and courtyards. Austerity, discipline and self-denial were the monastic virtues the masters encouraged in their students and there were detailed scales of punishment within college statutes for those who chose to transgress. Much indeed was proscribed, as the colleges embraced an austere approach to leisure that would not have been out of place in a monastery.

Christ's College's statutes of 1505 forbade, for example, the 'keeping of dogs or rapacious birds [and] the playing of dice and cards'. Dons at King's denied entry to dogs, ferrets, birds, monkeys, bears, wolves and stags. The Gonville fellowship ruled out bear and bull baiting, hunting with dogs or hawking. Pembroke chose to state its opposition to tilting on horseback. The manner in which the scholars must have pushed against authority to provoke such a detailed list of proscribed animals and pastimes can only be imagined. In the nineteenth century Lord Byron famously took advantage of Trinity College's restraint in banning only dogs; he wrote to Elizabeth Pigot in 1807 that he had 'a new friend, the finest in the world, a tame Bear, when I bought him here, they asked me what I meant to do with him, and my reply was "he should sit for a fellowship" ... this answer delighted them not'.

Bishop Fisher, Master of Michaelhouse and then of Queens' at the beginning of the sixteenth century, set the tone for colleges when he advised that youth should not be too well fed as a 'low diet is necessary to concentration'. Discipline was severe. Undergraduates were birched for the offence described then, as now, as 'cutting' lectures and for centuries few diversions were permitted. Rather, college life was highly organised, not least because it was feared that the devil would fill idle time; men such as Fisher thus ensured that sport, as well as other pastimes, played an insignificant role in the lives of medieval scholars.

The physical fabric of the college reflected this code of austerity. Corpus Christi still has rooms in its fourteenth-century Old Court which must have been as spartan in the medieval period as any found in a monastery. Several scholars would have shared a room without running water, a fireplace or window glass. Greased cloth would have been stretched across the window during winter, with perhaps ill-fitting wooden shutters, in a forlorn attempt to keep the cold at bay; the stone channels used to secure the cloth are still visible in some windows of this court.

Medieval Europe was essentially a collection of military societies based on feudal ties. The careers of their leaders did not depend on the acquisition of intellectual knowledge. Most medieval members of the university, therefore, came from the middle and lower classes and arrived with neither sophisticated leisure tastes nor an expectation of sporting diversions. Research into the background of scholars in Paris, the only medieval university for which there is reliable evidence, suggests that typically between 15 and 20 per cent of those studying came from poor homes, while the vast majority would have been the sons of lawyers, of yeoman farmers and of those working at modest levels for the state. Cambridge probably had a similar profile. A medieval university was as much an agent of social mobility as were the grammar schools in the twentieth century. A place at Cambridge was not then, as it later became for the children of the merchant class and aristocrats, a rite of passage before the assumption of privileged positions in society.

The majority of medieval students thus had little experience of organised leisure activities. The impromptu kicking of a football, illicit games of dice in the taverns, chasing the local women or fighting with the river workers would have been the illegal pastimes taken up by the wilder element of the scholars. Rioting was another of the scholars' regular occupations: colleges which nurtured 'northerners' fought 'southern' colleges, while at other times they combined together to fight the town's young men.

Colleges did organise some entertainment behind their imposing walls. King's Hall archives from the fourteenth century reveal the hire of minstrels, jugglers and itinerant actors. Some of the minstrels who were hired to play there in the early 1300s are known to have performed for the royal household as well. With plays at the excellent Cambridge Arts Theatre in modern times coming from or going on to London's West End, Cambridge has evidently been on the same thespian circuit for some centuries. King's Hall was not alone: documents at Peterhouse and Corpus Christi also reveal arrangements for visiting entertainers. Such events on Feast Days and High Days had the merit of both entertaining the students and keeping them away from the town's distractions.

The Tudors' need of an educated class of civil servants triggered the interest of the more privileged in attending university. The skills of a 'parfit gentil knyght' were no longer sufficient to maintain the nobility's place in the newly meritocratic state. A new aristocracy was emerging, an aristocracy of talent, which was nurtured by the two universities. The Elizabethan chancellor William Cecil, MA Cantab and grandson of a Stamford innkeeper, was typical of the educated men throughout the Tudor dynasty who filled the highest positions at court. In consequence, aristocrats began to send their sons to university.

Some stayed a mere year in a college and pursued less demanding versions of the Trivium and Quadrivium. Whether or not they were diligent students, colleges welcomed them and the contact they brought with illustrious court families. Family patronage of the sort Magdalene enjoyed from the Buckinghams, or Sidney Sussex from the Sidneys, Pembroke from the Fitzalan-Howards, St John's from the Wriothesleys, Corpus Christi from the Talbots or Emmanuel from the Walsinghams, usually brought money, court connections and prestige by association.

The opportunity to play sport, as is the case in many modern American universities, became a means used by the colleges to attract and retain such students. Tennis and bowls were familiar to young aristocrats and were, therefore, the pastimes that made the first breach in the sports-free culture of Cambridge colleges.

A bowling green was simple to provide; the fellows of Trinity College can still launch their woods towards the Cam along the ancient green which was once kept for the fellows and noble fellow commoners of King's Hall. It is reached through the arch beneath the Clock Tower in Great Court, where a fourteenth-century range from King's Hall survives. Bowls was feared as a distraction which would divert Englishmen from practice at the butts, so in the late medieval period a bowling green could be installed in private grounds only if the freeholder held property with an annual rental value which exceeded the significant sum of £100. The smarter students would have chosen bowls before archery; shooting arrows at the butts was essentially a townsman's pursuit.

However, the pastime which appealed most to the well-born Tudor scholars was tennis – or what is now known as real tennis, as the prefix of 'real' was introduced only in the late 1800s after the alternative game of lawn tennis was devised. In the early 1500s tennis was the sport played by young men of noble birth. The game's impact on Cambridge is borne out by the ten courts which colleges had built by the 1590s, more courts than there were at that time in the whole of London. The game's popularity in Cambridge at this time is a signal of the changing social structure of the university's junior membership.

Tennis courts were expensive. They required stone floors, high brick walls and various other refinements. Yet college accounts show them being rebuilt in new positions when the space they occupied was needed for another purpose. They were clearly considered an essential part of the college fabric from Tudor times until the late nineteenth century: Thomas Fuller's map of 1534 and David Loggan's of 1688 include tennis courts but not, for example, college chapels in their legends. Even the most puritan college, Emmanuel, built a court alongside the low wall which separates the Fellows' Garden from the main gardens, shortly after its foundation in 1584. In an intriguing coincidence, the college has now placed the statue of a jester on the grass where the court once stood: it is unlikely, however, that any of the parties involved in siting the sculpture knew that 'The Jesters' is the world's premier nomadic racket club promoting real tennis and other racket games.

The ubiquity of real tennis in sixteenth-century society was such that Erasmus even used references to the game within his Latin exercises *The Colloquies* to catch the interest of his Paris University students in the 1520s. Erasmus had left Queens' College a few years earlier; his acquaintance with tennis might even have begun in Cambridge. Erasmus wrote about the instruction – still valid – to 'serve the ball onto the penthouse; if anyone serves without warning, that service is not good'. He noted how players will 'sweat less if [they] play with a racquet' as by this time rackets were displacing the use of the hand to hit the ball. His descriptions of the rules of tennis, intended to capture the attention of his students in the manner in which a modern textbook might refer to a soccer star, provides some evidence for the stature of this game within contemporary culture.

Connecting Lensfield Road to Pembroke Road is Tennis Court Road, which earned the name from its place beside the longest-surviving real tennis court in Cambridge. A Pembroke College site plan of 1592 shows a court in an orchard to the back of the college, beyond the college bowling-green. David Loggan's

Illustration 14.1: The St John's real tennis court on the west side of the River Cam,
as shown in David Loggan's 1688 map of Cambridge.

map, made a century later, also shows a timber-built court just to the Pembroke side of the Tennis Court Road–Pembroke Road junction. The court was refurbished in 1734 and finally demolished in 1880. Trinity College built its second court in the meadow across the Cam in 1611, opposite the site which was later used by Christopher Wren for their college library. Its first tennis court, before Great Court was created in the mid-1600s, had been on the south side of Trinity Great Gate behind the houses which ran between the college property and the street itself.

The college courts were often sub-let to professionals to manage. Some at the university complained in the 1600s about the many young men who came in the baggage train of the smarter students 'not to study but to serve as fencing masters, tennis court keepers, riding masters and servants' – eloquent acknowledgement of the changing social structure of the university's members. In modern times the sport is firmly in the grip of the bourgeoisie, but this was not the case in the sixteenth century. There are still two university courts in Grange Road opposite Robinson College; the oldest was built for Trinity College in 1866, while the second was added by Clare College in the 1890s.

The university's puritan tendency fought a somewhat ineffective rearguard action in defence of monastic austerity since pastimes like these appeared at Cambridge. Colleges issued behavioural guidelines in the seventeenth century, with records from Trinity College dating to 1660 revealing warnings given to scholars not to play too much 'time-devouring' chess or, worse, football, as it was 'a boisterous exercise and fitter for clownes than for schollers'. Scarce attention was apparently paid to such edicts, however: in the late 1800s a father penned a charming letter to his son's tutor at Queens' College, evidently replying to the tutor's reproach over his son's inadequate attention to his studies. He wrote: 'I do not understand the tenor of your communication. When I was an undergraduate, it would have been accounted a disgrace to the college, if any man had been present in Hall on a Newmarket [racing] day'. In the late nineteenth century junior members of Magdalene and Queens' ostracised anyone appearing for dinner in hall on any of the eight annual Newmarket days. It must have seemed to those of the 'Bishop Fisher' persuasion as though the Barbarians had triumphed.

The Cambridge influence on sport

Although tennis ruptured the defences of the monastic lifestyle, little other sport developed between the 1500s and the early nineteenth century. Rough football was occasionally played, particularly between St John's and Trinity, although it was generally viewed as an excuse for a fight. Richer scholars would have played tennis, ridden or gone fowling in the fenlands. Poorer students might have shot at the archery butts or walked in the meadowland to the west of the town – indeed, long walks in the afternoon were almost expected of students, as much for the opportunity for academic discussion that they might provide as for any health benefits.

Behaviour at football matches has evidently long been an issue; records of a university match against Chesterton village in 1857 reveal that 'many university representatives had their head broken in by staves and others had to take refuge in the river'. Such match reports made clear the case for a widely accepted set of football rules. The University Football Club had been set up in 1839 but it was not until members of half a dozen public schools met at Trinity College in 1848 that there was an attempt to reach nation-wide agreement on the rules of the game. The 'Cambridge Rules' of football were the result. No full copy of these rules exists, though some diverting extracts are known. 'No player,' they declared, 'may be held and hacked at the same time'. They also introduced a primitive offside rule by forbidding 'loitering' near the opponents' goal. Although it was later widened, the width of the goal was set at fifteen feet, a gap determined by the space between the large lime trees that lined Parkside, which runs along the north-east edge of Parker's Piece.

These 'Cambridge Rules', whose lucidly expressed objective was 'to make the game as simple and natural as possible', did not quite win universal acceptance – there was an alternative version in the north of England – so in 1863 the newly founded Football Association met at the Freemasons' Tavern in Great Queen Street, near Drury Lane, London. It was the Cambridge Rules which provided the base on which football was built. The importance of the university's contribution is reflected by its permanent seat on the FA Council, which is currently filled by a fellow of St Catharine's College. Geoffrey Green acknowledges the university's role in the development of the game in the 1953 official history of the English Football Association: 'Cambridge was clearly the starting point of everything. That fact is beyond argument'. For several years Cambridge entered a team into the FA Cup competition, playing teams like the Sheffield Zulus, which raised money for the widows from the Zulu Wars.

The sporting history of Parker's Piece is not confined to football. Until the 1820s it also hosted the university's cricket pitch, which was moved thereafter to Fenners, where it remains today. The father of the cricketer Jack Hobbs, who was born nearby at River Place in 1882, worked as a groundsman at Fenners. Both town and university originally shared the Piece for their cricket, although the university had on occasion also used a ground alongside Barnwell Chapel: indeed, both Richard Baker's town map of 1830 and Thomas Moule's map of 1837 mark the Barnwell site as the university cricket ground.

Jack Hobbs was later employed as coach at Jesus. To complement the Hobbs Gate at the Oval, Parker's Piece has a Hobbs Pavilion, though it is now used chiefly as a Thai restaurant. As sporting heroes did in those days, he retired from playing to run a retail sports business in Fleet Street. It was Jack's brother, Sidney, who started up the Cambridge shop which bears the family name in 1931. The power of the Hobbs name is not quite vanquished; in the Cambridge City budget for 2005, the annual cost of £3,000 to maintain the cricket square on Parker's Piece was proposed as a saving, but a public outcry foiled this heartless economy.

Another Cambridge sporting hero whose name also retains an echo in modern times is the world rackets champion of 1855, H.J. Gray. Henry Gray started playing the game of rackets in an open court attached to the University Arms Hotel in St Andrew's Street. St John's then employed him for many years as their professional, where he made his first rackets, before he established a shop selling sports equipment. The business Henry Gray started now trades as Gray-Nicolls and owns a number of leading hockey, rugby, and cricket equipment brands. The Gray family ran their retail business from premises in Sidney Street between 1910 and 2006 and celebrated their 150th anniversary as a business in 2005. In comparison, Hobbs, which moved from its smaller premises in Trinity Street to those of Grays in 2006, records a trading history of a mere seventy-five years.

Boxing was another pastime whose rules were established in Cambridge. However, as late as the 1840s, the vice-chancellor had threatened 'suspension, rustication or expulsion' for any student involved with this sport. The first Varsity contest, arranged at the Cambridge Corn Exchange, did not take place until 1897. Initially boxing combined with fencing as an undergraduate club – doubtless in a search for respectability. J.G. Chambers, a Trinity graduate who rowed in the Boat Race in the early 1860s, helped win acceptance for this sport. At the same time as coaching the Blues rowing team in 1865 he drew up a boxing code, the acceptance of which was spread through the use of the name of his friend, the Marquis of Queensberry.

Gradually these new sports won the attention of undergraduates and then colleges. It was the tradition of muscular Christianity, established first at the public schools in the mid-1800s, which changed the approach of the university to sport, breaking down the last vestiges of monastic discipline within the university. The offspring of upper-middle-class families came up with similar leisure expectations to those of the young Tudor aristocrats. The older sports continued, but the merits of having thirty men chasing a leather ball across a grass pitch over entertaining two at a time in an expensive tennis court building were obvious.

It was the 'new' sports of cricket, rowing and athletics that pushed sport from being a minority student pastime to one which all those coming up to Cambridge from the country's public schools could expect to enjoy. Indeed, for some years loyalty to a school outweighed loyalty to a college: at Trinity College, for example, membership of the Third Boat crew was only open to old Etonians and 'Westminsters'. Cricket and rowing were formally introduced in the 1820s and rugby in 1839. Contests between Oxford and Cambridge, known as the Varsity matches, took more time to establish and were not initially annual events – after the first Varsity Boat Race of 1829, seven years passed before the next one and it did not become an annual event until 1856. The Varsity cricket match was played annually slightly earlier, from 1836; the first Varsity rugby match, at Oxford, was played in 1872, when each side fielded twenty players. The next match, on Parker's Piece, was played with fourteen-a-side. It was the third contest, in 1875, that helped establish fifteen as the proper number for all properly constituted rugby teams. In 1921 the contest was transferred to the Twickenham ground. The first Varsity football match was played in 1874 at The Oval; Oxford triumphed by one goal to nil. The match then moved between Queen's Club, Stamford Bridge and Fulham's ground at Craven Cottage. Over the 135 football matches played up to 2009 each side has won forty matches, with a cumulative goal difference of precisely zero.

Boosted by the public schools' games-playing ethos, Varsity matches also began in a variety of other sports: rackets in 1855, with real tennis four years later in 1859, while shooting, athletics and rugby fives followed shortly afterwards. The colleges began to acquire playing fields in order that their members could fill their hours of leisure innocently chasing balls of different shapes. In modern Cambridge a journey westward along Barton Road and its tributary Grantchester Road reveals the huge territory which colleges have acquired for this purpose.

Light Blues

It is widely accepted that light blue was adopted as Cambridge's colour in 1836 at the behest of a rower called R.N. Philipps (not, as is sometimes reported, R.N. Phipps). He matriculated at Christ's in 1835 and, although not in the Boat Race crew, was an enthusiastic rowing supporter. Oxford had already settled on dark blue, which was the colour of Christchurch, who had five men in the Oxford boat at the first Boat Race in 1829. Philipps chose light blue to distinguish the Cambridge boat, possibly because it was the colour of Eton College, where both the leading oarsmen E.H. Stanley and Philipps had been educated. It might have been chosen because it was the colour of Caius College, three members of which rowed in the 1836 boat, or perhaps was simply a random selection of a coloured ribbon from a haberdasher's shop.

Mischievously, in Cambridge's 800th anniversary year, the Vincent's Club (the Oxford Blues' club) website claimed it was an Oxford man, from Christchurch, who chose the light blue colour for Cambridge. They repeated the claim from the writings of Norris McWhirter, a keen athlete and founder of the Guinness

Book of Records, who was at Trinity, Oxford. In this instance his research had been faulty; there was no R.N. Philipps at Christchurch and no mention of him exists in the Alumni Oxonienses.

The award of a Full Blue is granted only following participation in a Varsity match, of which around seventy-seven take place annually. Simple as this sounds, tricky issues arise: one surrounded the matter of whether substitutes, which a number of team games such as football now use, should be awarded a Blue. The committee resolved that as many substitutes as national rules permitted could be used but only the first two substitutes would earn Full Blues; additional substitutes would be awarded only a Half Blue. The substitute need only appear on the pitch for five seconds, but sitting on the subs bench alone is insufficient grounds for an award. It is easy to imagine the reaction of the rowers to this, since they do not have the option of calling on someone with fresh limbs to row the second half of their races. Other apparent iniquities have arisen: in 1988, for example, although the Varsity cricket match was rained off without a single ball being bowled, it was deemed to have been played and Blues were awarded.

The award of Blues is strictly controlled and settled since 1912 on principles determined by the Blues Committee (CUBC). Before that time, other sports requested permission as a matter of courtesy from the rowers to use the colour adopted by the Varsity rowing team. This led to the rowers' ascendancy in all Blues matters. The dominance of rowing is maintained by the fact that the President of the men's Blues Committee, which comprises representatives of the twelve Full Blue sports, is always the President of the Boat Club, while one further Boat Club nominee is permitted on the committee. All the other Full Blue sports have but one vote. The senior sports have always been rowing, cricket and athletics and for almost fifty years (from 1836 until 1884) no sportsmen outside these three games could win Blues. Persistently denied the award by the rowers, both the rugby and football players determined to award themselves Blues in 1884. Shocked by such *lèse majesté*, the CUBC took the issue to the entire university. The vote, by a huge audience, the size of which was itself a testament to the important position sport then held at Cambridge, was decisively won by the footballers and their supporters. By 1912 a further seven sports were granted recognition, although up to this time it was still the rowers alone who determined the sports that were graced with this honour. Members of the university generally valued the Blue very highly. Some of those who were denied this award during the Second World War (as it was thought standards of achievement were then below those of the previous years) still occasionally write to the Blues Committee requesting that this decision be overturned.

In the early twenty-first century there are eight sports played by men and eight by women in which the whole team win Full Blues. Of these, the men's sports are football, cricket, golf, field hockey, lawn tennis, rowing, rugby union and squash; in boxing and cross-country running the captain has the authority to award Full or Half Blues; the grant of Blues to swimmers and athletes depends on the achievement of certain times in the Blues match. The women's Full Blues sports are fencing, football, hockey, lacrosse, lawn tennis, netball, rowing and squash; team captains have the discretion to award Full or Half Blues in athletics, cricket, modern pentathlon and swimming. In a further sixteen sports, all team members receive a Half Blue but the captain may seek permission from the committee, with the expectation of approval, to award a Full Blue to exceptional players. There are another fifteen sports, such as fives, gymnastics and real tennis, when extraordinary sporting achievement is required in order for the committee to grant a Full Blue, while in basketball five team members are awarded Blues automatically and another five receive only Half Blues.

In all, men can win a Blue or a part thereof in forty-six sports, while women can merit this award in forty-seven. The women's branch of the Blues Committee in 2009 considered Half Blue status for a further three sports, while the men pondered the merits of Gaelic Football. In recent years, and not without some dissent, both sexes can win Half Blues through throwing Frisbees, by participating in competitive Salsa and Latin dance, by playing a mixed-sex team ball game called Korfball or by practising Taekwondo, a variety of martial art.

Blues of any fraction, provided they are male, qualify for election to the Hawks', a social club lodged since 1987 in a delightful old building in Portugal Place. The Hawks' Club, which votes each year to nominate a Hawk and a Team of the Year, was established in 1872, at a time when St John's dominated college sports. Sportsmen from other colleges had sought permission to join St John's Eagles Sports Club but, having been turned down, they chose the symbol of another raptor for their club, a tradition which was maintained when the women's Osprey Club was established in 1985. Surprisingly, it is the Hawks' undergraduates who resist giving women membership rights, whereas graduate members would welcome this change.

The modestly priced drink and elegant surroundings at the Hawks' Club attract a lot of students, particularly on Wednesday and Sunday nights – non-members may enter in the company of a member. Many university sports groups hold an annual dinner there, using the occasion to wear proudly their appallingly tailored thick woollen light-blue blazers. There can be very few occasions later in life when it may be worn and its retention in the marital wardrobe doubtless mystifies the graduate's spouse. Although the prestige associated with a Blue is not quite what it once was, there is still some kudos associated with sporting success, particularly in the more traditional sports. Girlfriends of the university's leading rugby players, cricketers or rowers are occasionally referred to, rather unkindly, as Blu-Tacks, after the sticky stationery item. The club remains unfashionably elitist, proud of its claim to accept its members only from the top percentile of the university's sports players.

From the late 1800s to the early 1960s, the era of amateur sports, Cambridge sportsmen competed well with the best clubs in the country. In the interwar years the Varsity rugby match was considered second in terms of quality and interest only to the Calcutta Cup between England and Scotland. However, where the match at Twickenham used to be a certain sell-out barely 30,000 attended the 2008 game – still more than attend some twenty-first-century premiership football matches, but nothing like as many as in the past. Up to the late 1950s and even later it was not unusual for a considerable number of Blues to progress to national sides in several sports. The national cricket team of 1950, for example, contained five members whose skills had been nurtured on the notoriously batsman-friendly square at the university's Fenners ground and as recently as 1971 the triumphant British Lions team included three Cambridge graduates, as well as three from Oxford. The influence that Cambridge has had over the management, as well as the original framework, of a large number of sports as a result of this influx is astonishing. Even into the twenty-first century its graduates have retained immense authority. Their playing days over, many graduate sportsmen,

Illustration 14.2: The Hawks' Club, the sanctuary of the Blues, in Portugal Place. Francis Crick's residence next door is marked by a single helix suspended from the façade of the building.

such as Alistair Hignell and Ian Robertson, became sports commentators, while numerous members of sports' governing bodies met first on the playing fields of the university.

Athletics has also had its heroes, such as David Burghley and Harold Abrahams in the 1920s and Chris Brasher, the pacemaker for Roger Bannister and founder of the London Marathon, in the late 1940s. Although it was Oxford men who broke the four-minute mile, the previous step – breaking the four-minute thirty-second barrier – was achieved by a Cambridge undergraduate, Walter Chinnery, eighty-six years previously. Athletics Blues share membership of the Achilles Club with their peers from Oxford: it is one of many thriving graduate networks, which holds a number of annual events on both sides of the Atlantic.

In the twentieth century it was not exceptional for talented sportsmen to win Blues at two or more major sports. After the Second World War men like Doug Insole or Trevor Bailey, who went on to have very successful careers in test cricket, played football in winter and cricket in summer for the Blues team. In the modern age of specialisation this is now less likely and training for rugby, cricket or tennis, for example, is now a year-round commitment; students must chose one sport. Furthermore, outstandingly talented sportsmen are more likely to be indentured to a sports academy at eighteen, or earlier, rather than pursue academic studies that require their sporting development to be left on one side. Nonetheless, success in university sport does still carry some cachet among peers if not among academic staff and the memory of its past heroes is reinvigorated from time to time by films as well as by the attention paid to the rowing and rugby Varsity matches.

The Great Court Run

One film in particular, *Chariots of Fire* (1981), has fuelled the mystique surrounding sport at Cambridge. Although focused on the success of British athletes at the 1924 Paris Olympics, the film opens with a portrayal of the run around Trinity Great Court. In order to win this race, challengers must run around the court within the forty-three seconds, or thereabouts, that it takes the clock of the King Edward Tower to strike twelve o'clock. The bells strike first a preamble of eight notes, then the hour at a low pitch and finally the hour is struck again at a higher pitch – hence the line in Wordsworth's 'Prelude', 'Twice over with a male and female voice' and from there stemmed the cheap joke that women talk for longer and have the last say.

However, the precise time the striking takes has differed over the years. Comparisons between those who have attempted the run are made even more difficult by a variation in starting points (at the corner or on a straight) by whether the line of outer flagstones or inner cobble stones has been followed and even by whether the challenge was undertaken at midday or midnight. The length of the race varies from 298 metres, if the rectangle is measured hard up against the edging of the grass, to 341.6 metres, if the flagstones are followed; the compromise route of flagstones for much of the straight and cobbles at the corners might amount to around 320 metres. Another variable is the weather, as the runner's ability to grip on wet stone will always make a huge difference. This arcane detail has fascinated many Cambridge people and been the cause of many erroneous claims.

In the nineteenth century magnificent athletes like Alfred Lyttleton (he won five Blues in the 1870s, played cricket for England and was later Secretary of State for the Colonies) reputedly ran round the court on more than one occasion while the clock was still striking. The earliest challengers would have, like Lyttleton, been members of Trinity and run at midnight after the Commemoration Dinner in March, probably in evening dress without jackets. A number of Trinity College members are known to have beaten the clock; for example, W.M. Fletcher, who later became a fellow, did so in the 1890s, as did a number of other Trinity undergraduates after the Second World War. They followed the convention of running at midnight.

It is the triumph of David Burghley, a member of Magdalene, over the clock in 1923 that is best remembered, largely because of *Chariots of Fire*. The film showed scant regard for the truth, however. The race scene was filmed at Eton College instead of Trinity and Burghley did not, as the film portrays, lose in a race against Harold Abrahams of Caius College – Abrahams and Burghley were not even up at Cambridge together. Rather, he challenged the clock alone (at midday in fact, as being a member of another college, Magdalene, he would not have been allowed in Trinity at midnight). Finally, the film sets Burghley's successful challenge of 1927 in the months before the 1924 Paris Olympics instead of just before the Amsterdam games of 1928. Abrahams' appearance in the race reflected the wish of the film producer, David Puttnam, to expose the supposedly anti-Semitic culture at the university. As a result of these misrepresentations Lord Burghley refused to allow his name to be associated with the film – an action which was also taken by the New Zealander Arthur Porritt, who had won the 1924 Olympic bronze medal for the 100-yard sprint in which Harold Abrahams won gold. This subverting of the historical record may explain why both Trinity and Caius Colleges also refused to cooperate with the makers of the film. In fact, Caius is proud of its connections with eminent Jews, such as the Salomons, the Abrahams and the present Head Rabbi, Jonathan Sacks, who is both a Caian graduate and an honorary fellow.

However, the film increased awareness of the run immensely and in 1988 the Olympic athletes Sebastian Coe and Steve Cram restaged the race for charity. Both hired clothes from Angels, the theatrical agency, although they wore modern running shoes. Coe beat Cram by half a second, but whether he actually matched Burghley's achievement in running round the court before the bells completed their tolling was, typically for Cambridge, a matter of debate. His attempt was initially reported as a triumph, but only because television commentators disingenuously claimed that the barely audible dying sounds of the bells could be included in the 'striking' time. In fact, even this Olympian athlete in his prime apparently failed to match Burghley's achievement. The shape of the court makes the run a collection of short sprints and turns, which may have suited Burghley better: his expertise at hurdling – he won the gold medal in the 400m hurdles in the 1928 Amsterdam Olympics – could have been critical in allowing him to leap over the four corners. Coe, in contrast, was a middle-distance specialist, albeit a world-class one. In the opinion of one don at the university in 2009, who himself beat the clock in the mid-1950s, it is almost certain that all those who have succeeded have done a bit of 'cobble-running'. It is also evident that a direct comparison between the races of Coe and Burghley is unreasonable.

The run is now held at the college annually, although so rare are serious contenders that it has become a Fun Run for first-year students. The college banned the midnight run in order to reduce the risk of alcohol-induced injury, and the race is now conducted at midday. In 2007 a Trinity economics student, Sam Dobin, apparently completed the race 0.83 seconds faster than Burghley. National newspapers, to which his success was announced, gave him much publicity. However, his claim has been tossed aside by Trinity College because he had done a touch of cobble-running at the corners, which to those with a more accurate knowledge of the race's background seemed a little harsh. In any event, he had an outstanding publicity agent, as few have heard of Danny Gammell, who recorded the same achievement in the previous year.

The tower whose clock inspired this race was built in 1328 during the reign of Edward III. It is the oldest visible part of Great Court, although a clock was fitted into its south face only in 1610, during the Nevile mastership, when the entire tower was moved back twenty yards to accommodate the grand design of Trinity's Great Court. In the 1720s the Master, Richard Bentley, thought its chime and square clock face too modest; the replacement clock face, larger than the original version, is ill-matched to the tower, as it is out of proportion to the tower's structure and covers a section of the tower's central window. The present clock mechanism, which is similar to the one used for Big Ben, was installed in 1910 and initially took 49 seconds to strike twelve. The first clock mechanism and its square face remain in good order at St Andrew's Church in Orwell, a small village eight miles south-west of Cambridge.

Illustration 14.3: Trinity Great Court, showing, from the left, the early-seventeenth-century hall and Master's Lodge beyond; the fourteenth-century Clock Tower; the sixteenth-century chapel; and the inside of the Great Gate, built in the late 1400s. It is in this court that scholars challenge the clock.

The study of water science

Like the Great Court Race and the Varsity rugby match, the Boat Race is another event which captures the attention of a wide audience outside Cambridge. The 150th anniversary of the race was celebrated in 2004; of these encounters, Cambridge has won a mere half a dozen times more than Oxford. However, the race is no longer an event for undergraduates. The student newspaper *Varsity* even commented in 2009 about 'the unusual number of old somewhat unstudenty people taking places' in the rowing or rugby teams.

Three-quarters of the Cambridge rowing squad in 2006, a typical year, were postgraduates; of the thirty-three in the training squad, less than a third were British. Three of the squad were aged over thirty and Americans outnumbered British, whose own numbers exceeded those of Germany by only one rower. Oxford's team had an almost identical profile, with the added point of interest that two among its ageing squad members were enrolled on a course disarmingly entitled 'Water Science'. Most of both teams had international rowing careers. This has now become a well-established pattern: in 2009 the average age of both rowing teams was twenty-five and only one-third were British; the Oxford team contained five Beijing Olympians.

While the public relations flannel behind the event continues to trade heavily on the ancient heritage of this race, it is clear that the connection to the old races fought between two boats of 'properly aged' undergraduate Oxbridge students from the British Isles is remote. The rivalry between the two universities has sometimes caused some questionable behaviour on the part of each team. Cambridge, for instance, caused a particular outcry on the part of their rivals when Thorsten Engleman, an international German rower, left two weeks after Cambridge had won the 2007 Boat Race without sitting any exams. Oxford claimed the spirit of the race had been broken since a 'bandit' was shipped in and then left without finishing his studies. In truth, though, the spirit of the old contests between undergraduates of each university has long since died in rugby and rowing. In 2008 Oxford imported the New Zealander Anton Oliver to their rugby squad: up to the age of thirty-three he had won fifty-nine caps for the All Blacks. Oxford won the match that year. It is heartening, therefore, that less high-profile sports such as hockey, swimming, football and real tennis do retain the spirit of an earlier age by fielding teams dominated by undergraduates. The average age of the 2009 Light Blues football team was slightly over twenty, with the oldest member being twenty-three.

It would be good to imagine that the mature postgraduates in the Oxbridge boats and rugby squads represent a fortunate confluence of a late-flowering brain and sporting talent. The suspicion must be, however, that some physical attributes do still improve the chance of securing membership of the university – perhaps an outstanding pair of choral scholars' lungs does influence matters when intellectual gifts alone might make admission less sure. In fairness, however, it appears that those performing at these high levels of attainment do have sufficient personal discipline to achieve good academic results.

The Boat Race is watched on television by almost eight million viewers in Britain and millions more overseas. In recent years there has been competitive tendering for the television rights to cover the race; ITV displaced the BBC in 2005, although the latter stepped back in when ITV announced that they no longer wished to cover the event after 2009. The finance of Varsity rugby was also threatened in 2008 when Lehman withdrew its funding, but new sponsorship was secured from the Nomura Bank. This level of commercialisation may be thought inappropriate by some, but the return of rowing and rugby to their proper historic place among undergraduates would deprive the university community of income.

Many sports at the university are not this fortunate. It is the University Sports Syndicate and its subsidiary the Grants Committee that determine how the very modest amount of university financial support allocated to sports is distributed. Most university sports struggle to attract remotely adequate funds for their healthy survival and practically every university sports committee must search for some form of commercial sponsorship to avoid making excessive financial demands on students.

Although a seat in the Blues boat is largely beyond the reach of undergraduates, rowing itself remains far and away the sport with the highest undergraduate participation. Around 2,500 students propel themselves up and down the Cam each year and practically every college employs a boatman, whose costs are put against the head gardener's budget. Undergraduate rowing at Cambridge is focused on the Bumps, in which around 1,500 students row in ten divisions of seventeen eights each; these races are held twice a year and are referred to as 'The Mays' and 'The Lents'. The rules of this ritualistic event derive from the narrowness of the winding Cam, which makes competing side by side impossible. The eights participating in the Bumps line up in single file and set off simultaneously to the sound of a cannon fired from a bridge; 'bumping' occurs when an eight successfully collides with the boat in front. Any 'bump' which does take place is a gentle affair, as the slightest actual or even impending physical contact is sufficient for the cox to concede defeat. A 'bump' against the boat in front moves the team up through a series of heats to claim, in the first division, Head of the River. These races are social occasions, which are well supported from the bank by spectators in marquees and pubs. In common with many Cambridge pastimes, a variety of arcane rituals are associated with them. The rowers of St John's and Trinity Colleges, for example, meet each other in college grounds every morning during Bumps week for a confrontation known as the Stomp, in which the two teams attempt to intimidate one other in similar vein to a Maori Haka. Another tradition requires members of winning boats to attach plants from the riverbank to their heads. The eight rowers who claim the title Head of the River each retain their oar and decorate it with details of their triumph, which, later in life, their spouses are urged to tolerate as an incongruous wall-hanging in their homes. The successful cox acquires an old painted wooden rudder, as the new boats are directed by a tiny fibreglass rudder.

The races themselves are unusual, as some boats pass spectators near the finishing line in splendid isolation, while others may be inches behind the boat in front while being closely chased at the same time. When boats were cheaper, the winning team burnt their craft on the hallowed turf of the college court. Modest replicas or redundant craft are now incinerated; the college garden staff cooperate either by removing turf from the court prior to the bonfire or by finding some less central place for the ceremony.

The pedigree of the Bumps is as old as that of the Varsity rowing match, since the first Bumps contest also took place in the 1820s. Their boat clubs contribute to the myths and traditions of colleges; the first Trinity May Ball, for instance, was held in the 1890s to celebrate victory in the Bumps, and it has been held ever since under the banner of their boat club. The 'First and Third Trinity Boat Club' is so called because the college once ran three separate clubs, the first, second and third. The Second was disbanded in the 1870s and the Third amalgamated with the Firsts in 1946 to save money and as a reaction against its exclusivity. An apocryphal story is told of a fatal accident resulting from a sword attached to the bow of a St John's boat, which led to the banning of the St John's Boat Club and supposedly explains why the college rowers instead employ the club name 'Lady Margaret' – after the famous benefactress Lady Margaret Beaufort. A rowing accident did occur in 1888, sixty-two years after the Lady Margaret Boat Club was founded, but it was a Clare rower who was killed following a bump from the sharp bow of the pursuing Trinity Hall boat. India-rubber balls have since been fixed to the prow of each boat.

The Bumps, like real tennis, is a pastime shared between town and university; the townspeople have conducted their own annual Bumps since 1847. Local businesses and social groups made up crews. Eaden Lilley once had a boat club, as did the printers at the Pitt Press and the Scouts; during the 1930s most colleges ran servants' eights. In 2009 around 400 members of the local community indulged in the pastime. The river is as crowded now as it must have been in the Middle Ages, when the town's international trade was so important.

The decline in sporting achievement

In contrast to the Boat Race, the Varsity rugby match, while an event strongly supported at Twickenham, is far beneath international sporting standards. As a result, the attention the event now captures is much diminished. Neither does the university cricket team attract much attention; the chances of Cambridge again nurturing heroes such as Hignell, Atherton, Dexter, Brearley or May, who were each at Cambridge, are slim. The focus on work for the modern student is too great in general to permit much excellence outside their studies.

Sporting heroes in other arenas since the 1960s have been few. The odd hockey player, swimmer and tennis star have emerged – for example, Mark Cox, who studied at Downing, had some success as a professional tennis player in the 1970s. Perhaps reflecting the past middle-class disdain for the sport, football can claim only an Ipswich Town player, although Daniel Levy, a Sidney Sussex graduate, has been managing director of Tottenham Hotspur since 2001.

In the twenty-first century some undergraduate sportsmen are probably just as good as their predecessors of earlier centuries; however, professionalism outside the university has much increased standards nationally and has opened what was, hitherto, an almost negligible gap between the country's best sportsmen and those of the university. The demise of the gifted amateur has been hastened by the comparative lack of sports facilities at the university. Exceptional sportsmen at the university are now rare. It is telling that the young sporting star Alistair Brownlee, who came twelfth in the triathlon event at the Beijing Olympics and who had initially begun his higher education at Cambridge, left the university so he could train at the better-equipped Leeds Metropolitan University. Those outstanding sportsmen that remain probably do not bother with university sport beyond turning out for the Varsity match in order to secure their Blue. There must be other people like Brownlee who now choose not to come to Cambridge for similar reasons and perhaps sports-inclined international postgraduates may also include the availability or otherwise of facilities for their discipline in their decisions about where to pursue their research.

Professionalism at national level, relatively poor facilities and the passing of the days when the fleet-of-foot or those with exceptional hand–eye coordination could secure a university place regardless of academic ability are the main three factors which have undermined the university's status as a place of sporting achievement. Before the Welsh rugby club Ospreys supplied the largest number of players ever contributed by a single club to a national team in 2008, this record had been held by an Oxford University team from the 1870s. It is safe to assume that the record will not be reclaimed by Oxford – nor won by Cambridge. Nor is it likely that the government-sponsored Talented Athlete Scholarship Scheme, which can provide up to £3,000 annually to outstanding sportsmen, will make much impact. Currently it helps around ten people a year at Cambridge, who are selected by their sport's governing body rather than the university; those helped have so far mainly been sailors, rowers and fencers. Admirable as the scheme is for those sportsmen who wish to continue their education, it will do little to arrest the general decline of undergraduate sporting achievement. It also caused irritation to some that it took the '800 Cambridge Online Giving' website, first set up in 2005, until 2009 to include the option of donating to sporting causes.

However, the performance of Cambridge graduates at the 2008 Beijing Olympics was not undistinguished – nine graduates and one undergraduate (the latter in women's fencing) were in the British squad. The Cambridge University Sports Department proudly claimed that university graduates finished above thirty countries in the medal table; appropriately, most medals were won in rowing. The feeling must be, however, that the university's justifiably narrow focus on academic talent may not provide an opportunity for such claims in future.

The best sport facilities at the university are, as they have always been since the days of the first tennis courts, within colleges. Some obscure corners of Cambridge contain immaculate college sporting arenas, such as those of Caius' at the back of Newnham village. Yet colleges, which have been of such benefit to the university in many ways, have not helped university sport. They rent out their facilities to university teams reluctantly and in the case of the swimming pool at Girton – the only modern one installed by a college – will not rent it out at any price. The only two other college pools, at Emmanuel and Christ's, date back to the seventeenth and eighteenth centuries respectively and fall a little short of modern standards.

The university's sports resources are generally unimpressive. Discounting those used as bicycle sheds, there are, for example, no fives courts in Cambridge; the university team must travel an hour to use those belonging to Oundle School in Northamptonshire. There are no university squash courts. Neither is there a university swimming pool. Since the time when the 120-yard straight stretch of the Cam near Grantchester proved too tough a training venue in 1906 swimmers have had to borrow training premises. The club facilities in Grantchester Meadows had evidently been primitive; the most-prized possession was an old elm tree which had served as a diving board. Perhaps this Spartan background was behind Cambridge's long-established dominance in the swimming Varsity matches, first held in 1892. However, Oxford's installation in 2004 of a twenty-five-metre pool with electronic timing and movable floor has eroded the Cambridge supremacy. The Cambridge team can only afford to train in the town's pool for seven hours a week; Oxford train fourteen hours a week and have been winning the most recent Varsity matches.

With the Cambridge University swimmers obliged to train in borrowed pools, the lament from the 1892 Cambridge Review still holds good over a century after it was written: 'when it is remembered that a swimming bath is now beginning to be considered as a necessity in most of our large public schools, it seems strange that we are still without one'. Doubtless even were a generous swimming-pool donor to appear, the university would be unable to resist the temptation to refocus the philanthropist's attention onto a project which supported more academic pursuits.

It is with relief, therefore, that sportsmen have witnessed the significant investment made in track events and field hockey near Wilberforce Road. Furthermore, the university's Estates Department has so far left alone the many acres of college land used for field games. The signalled intent to build sports facilities at the West Cambridge site with funds raised by the 800th Anniversary campaign is also welcome, although the sports centre was reportedly included only reluctantly and plans have been reworked several times to reduce the original cost estimates. The money is certainly not yet available for this project.

More investment is necessary, however – and this much is made clear by the students themselves. The student newspaper *Varsity* has run articles about the poverty of university amenities, suggesting that they are now so poor that Oxford will become the university of first choice for the clever student who is interested in sport. The Cambridge students' union sold tee-shirts in the 800th anniversary year emblazoned with the legends 'Cambridge University – Second to None – Sports Facilities none' and on the reverse of the shirt: '800 Years … No Sports Centre'.

Although the university must give priority to enhancing its intellectual resources, it must not cease to try to attract those who are fortunate enough to combine intelligence with sporting ability. Sportsmen have for centuries provided a leavening to academic communities. Such young people will be put off Cambridge by its comparative paucity of sports facilities. The future of ball chasing – and of every other recognised sporting pastime – at the university remains in doubt. The successors of those who hit the first tennis balls against the walls of ancient tennis courts and challenged those academics who thought sport had no place at a university will hope that the officially declared intentions to nurture university sport materialise soon.

Chapter 15

Clare Balls and Misbehaviour

The very foundation of the university came about as a result of mischief by scholars in Oxford. Subsequently, misbehaviour by members of Cambridge's academic community quickly became an issue which caused as much concern there as it had in Oxford. Controlling the conduct of scholars has always demanded the attention of those who have governed the university.

The dons' preoccupation with discipline

The university did its best to focus its scholars' attention exclusively on their studies, first ensuring that scholars could be easily recognised when in the town. The Senate complained in 1343 about those of its members who had an 'unclerical appearance in their garments ... disdaining the tonsure' and warned that 'no one shall go forth from his college, except that he be clad in a gown'. They tried also to ensure that scholars returned to college before nightfall; the bells of Great St Mary's were rung when college gates were locked, at 8 p.m. in winter and 9 p.m. in summer time. The university labelled those who ignored this curfew as 'noctivagants', a term more usually used to describe the behaviour of nocturnal animals.

Many activities, such as debating and acting, when organised by the scholars alone, were simply banned as inappropriate pastimes for scholars: it was not until the 1800s that they won toleration. Plays had long been permitted on occasion within colleges, but only under strict supervision: the possibility of students meeting under their own initiative to stage plays independently of their college had been such an unthinkable option that it was not specifically banned until the nineteenth century. However, between 1844 and 1894 the University Senate felt obliged to issue a formal ban of all theatre, for student or the townsman, within fourteen miles of Great St Mary's.

Of course, the ban did not apply on college territory. Trinity College, for instance, had a fifteenth-century Comedy Room beyond the Master's Lodge towards the river. This was abandoned after 1605, as the new Great Hall, designed by Ralph Symons, could be used to both feed and entertain college members.

The college was keen to wrest the reputation for staging the best plays from St John's, which in part it did through staging a play for James I in 1615.

The university's own dramatic society, the Amateur Dramatic Club (ADC) was founded against the wishes of the authorities. In the words of one nineteenth-century Magdalene don, 'Gentlemen don't act'; ironically, theatre was widely considered a hindrance to the proper study of drama. The ADC's early history was, therefore, one of subterfuge and lookouts. From 1855 it camped in rooms rented from the Hoop Inn in Jesus Lane. Elaborate precautions were in place to warn of the proctors' arrival, although from 1861, when the actors' fellow undergraduate the future Edward VII agreed to be honorary president, it secured a degree of toleration from the university authorities. Since then acting has flourished at the university. In 1882 the ADC moved to its present Park Street premises, where it now provides a place where town and gown can mingle. The Footlights began as a drama club in 1883, before specialising in comedy. It was an immediate success. As the ADC was initially dominated by Trinity College, the Footlights spread the interest in acting more widely among other colleges. The student comedians used to meet in a room at the Falcon Inn until the 1970s, when the entire area of central Cambridge around the Red Lion hotel was demolished to make way for Lion Yard. The Footlights' base is now at the ADC, off Jesus Lane.

The university's attitude to theatre has changed over the years. A Cambridge Shakespeare Festival now produces half a dozen plays in college premises. A host of different stages – The Tribune, designed by Wren opposite his library in Nevile's Court, Cloister Court at Queens', or by the sunken Pompeian pond in Clare Fellows' Gardens, with its exits and entrances between the White Flower Walk and trimmed yew hedges – provide perfect settings which only the weather can compromise. Acting is now one of the major pastimes of students, appreciated by many within and outside the university. The live music scene at the university is as vibrant as its theatre; there are over fifty associations, covering musical genres as varied as Chinese orchestra, hip hop and steel band.

Debating societies were also once as contentious as theatres. In the late 1700s, when such activity was still firmly categorised as 'misbehaviour', three debating groups were established, which were eventually amalgamated to form the Union in 1815. These places of debate and free speech were repeatedly closed down both before and after the Union's formation and university records reveal that the proctors, at the behest of the vice-chancellor, broke up a number of debates on the grounds that such activities were contentious and a waste of time for scholars. By 1821, however, the university gave grudging consent to the Union provided that political issues concerning events after 1800 were avoided. The definition of 'political', though left vague at the time, in practice encompassed anything considered contentious. Such restrictions were never really observed. The Union discussed many controversial topics with the barest of subterfuge. Women's rights, for example, were once debated under the cover of a motion on Adam and Eve. Today the students run a short 'emergency debate' before each main event, honing their skills at presenting a debating motion. The guest speakers, who are usually figures from outside the university, dine first at the Union before speaking in the chamber for about ten minutes each. Then the motion is thrown open to the floor.

Like the actors, debaters of the Union first met in an inn, the Red Lion in Petty Cury, near the Market Square. They moved from there to premises near the ADC in the 1830s and then to Green Street; in 1866 they purchased land from St John's for the construction of their present building. The eminent Victorian architect Alfred Waterhouse won the commission in an open competition judged by the Union's members. The Oxford Union, founded two years after the Cambridge club in 1823, subsequently chose the same name for its debating society as had already been adopted in Cambridge and commissioned the same architect to build its premises. Cambridge's Union has 2,000 members, most of whom are undergraduates. Some are more attracted by its nightclub, vast billiards room and restaurant than by the 500-seat debating chamber. Since such sinful practices as belly dancing lessons take place there on Fridays, it is sometimes tempting to think that the proctors of earlier centuries knew where allowing students their liberty would lead.

After controversial beginnings, acting and debating are now pastimes which are lost to those who cherish the thrill of misbehaviour. These are mainstream activities which offer little attraction to the rebellious student.

Night-climbing

Happily, errant scholars developed other opportunities to misbehave. The pinnacles and towers of the university have inspired misbehaviour as well as ambitious dreams, as they proved an irresistible challenge to some students for many years – a challenge made sweeter by official disapproval. The predilection on the part of some students for scaling buildings might even have developed through the need to scale college walls when staying out past curfew, since noctivagant students were locked out of college at night well into the twentieth century. After the Second World War curfew was extended to midnight; college gates are still locked but now every member of college is given a key, thus shifting the porters' role from one of keeping scholars in to one of keeping the *hoi polloi* out.

Padding around the roofs of the university's buildings has long been a pastime of a small number of students known as 'night climbers'. Membership of this group has always been an informal matter; climbers outside their own small band are often not known to each other, as anonymity while at the university helped to avoid the attention of the authorities. A climb up the drainpipes attached to the front of Caius and a jump across the seven-foot gap above Senate House Passage to the neighbouring Senate House secured 'membership' of this elusive group.

The most famous of the 'night climbs' took place on Saturday 7 June 1958. The truth of some climbing tales is uncertain – climbers are, in general, a boastful fraternity – but the outcome of this escapade was very public. Overnight an Austin van appeared on the rooftop of Senate House. Caius students had spent weeks designing a derrick which would hoist the disembowelled vehicle up on to the building's roof and cause no damage to the building in the process. Their achievement won wide acclaim throughout the country and beyond; even newspapers in communist Romania reported this escapade of 'the sons of capitalist Lords'. Removing the vehicle in the glare of publicity proved difficult; to the enjoyment of the students who had accomplished the ascent in only one night, the descent took four days to complete. The Caius fellowship were rather proud of their night climbers; the dean discreetly arranged a case of wine to be given to the suspected miscreants and in 2008, on the fiftieth anniversary of the event, eleven of the original team were fêted in college.

Illustration 15.1: Night-climbing became a pastime which attracted considerable attention from around the 1860s for 100 or so years. Astonishingly, there are no records of any serious injuries. A knowledge of climbers' exploits provokes an interest in the qualities of drainpipes in the old town.

This was not the only time a vehicle was used as a prop by climbers; in the 1960s first an Austin 7 and then on another occasion a three-wheeled car were suspended from St John's Bridge of Sighs. However, compared with hoisting a vehicle onto the Senate House, it is a relatively simple matter to float a vehicle along the Cam on a punt to the bridge. In 1942 a bicycle was suspended from the top of the Old Divinity School opposite St John's. At various times banners have been hung from the east end of King's College Chapel: these proclaimed 'Save Ethiopia' in the mid-1930s and 'Peace in Vietnam' in 1965. On another occasion, in 1932, two umbrellas and then, the following night, two Union Flags were attached to the east end pinnacles of King's College Chapel. The wind removed one umbrella, while the other was shot down. It was thought best to shoot down the flags as well. However, the patriotic scruples of the hired gunman would not permit him to shoot at the Union Flag, so the college had to hire a steeplejack, at considerably greater expense than the marksman, to remove them. After a climb to deposit a lavatory seat on the chapel's roof in 2002, the students considerately wrote an open letter to the vice-chancellor recording their concern for the safety of future climbers should the dangerous state of the crockets along the edges of the main pinnacles not be addressed. Judging from the lower reaches of King's College Chapel, much of the stonework is in a condition that will not support future noctivagants.

Assaults on King's College Chapel were generally undertaken from the west end of the chapel. It was there that special chock-stones designed in the 1930s by Professor Pigou, professor of political economy at that college, were installed to hinder the ascent of the chapel at the most obvious points. Pigou and his Welfare Curve might be well known to economics students, but he was also famous among mountaineers.

St John's was another favourite site for night climbers. Gilbert Scott's chapel tower was considered a fine challenge; Jack Longland, who attempted Everest in 1933 and later became the radio broadcaster of 'My Word', is recognised as the first to have made the climb. The tower of the University Press, at the corner of Silver Street and Trumpington Street, was another provocation to the serious climber. Known climbing corridors such as the 'Lion Chimney' above the lion statues to the side of the Fitzwilliam Museum add another dimension to the appreciation of old buildings; the museum, as a non-college building, had the additional attraction of not having any porters on duty. However, modern security sensors on the outside of the building have ended this particular challenge.

In the heyday of night climbing, during the first half of the twentieth century, an understated style characterised climbs. Rather than place vulgar items like lavatory seats or an item of ladies' underwear in a prominent position, an upturned glass tumbler, discernible only to those who knew it was there, was often the preferred item to leave behind. An astonishing aspect of these ascents is the care that the climbers took to record their achievements; one of the climbers would invariably scale the buildings with all the necessary accoutrements to ensure that there was a photographic record of his intrepid companions, a feat particularly impressive in the days of big flash lamps and heavy cameras. The climbs described here were serious and dangerous; yet there was about them a spirit which personified an era very different to the modern one. One Jonian recalled how, in 1952, he climbed the Gilbert Scott tower in the early morning before taking his final degree. Preparation for exams in these more serious times has changed somewhat.

Henry VIII's regalia and nesting ducks

Less advanced climbing skills are necessary to adjust the accoutrements clasped in the hands of Henry VIII above the main entrance to Trinity College. It is claimed that students replaced the sceptre in his right hand with a chair leg. Edwin Bateman, a Trinity undergraduate in the 1940s, wrote about his challenge to a friend to fly the Red Flag over the Great Gate. The friend completed the dare but broke Henry's sceptre during the escapade and a gilded chair leg, reputedly from the rooms of the White Russian, Prince Obolensky, was then put into Henry's hand to replace the sceptre. However, the CAM magazine, a publication produced for the graduate community, carried a letter in 1999 from the Head of the St John's Maintenance Department,

Clifford Evans. He was asked in the early 1950s to replace the rotten oak stump which Henry held and wrote that this stump had never been a chair leg. Mr Evans replaced the rotten timber with a replica sceptre. Nonetheless, the present 'sceptre' which survives certainly looks like a chair leg. It is also ungilded, in contrast to the smartly maintained orb in the monarch's left hand, as if someone within the college wishes to encourage belief in the tale. The story about this sceptre is yet one more about university life which begs to be believed. The Trinity College archivist declines to reveal the truth of such matters with the *de haut en bas* comment that 'it is not the type of thing that gets recorded in the archives'.

More nerve than is required to meddle with Henry VIII is needed to rearrange the resting place of the once infamous Trinity dining hall Mallard, a duck which nested for some years amid the high trusses of the hall's hammerbeam roof. From time to time college climbers would move it between the rafters, but in 2006 some trespassing pigeons flew into the hall and knocked it to the ground. It proved to have been made in Italy and was inscribed with the nicknames of its first scholarly fanciers; sadly, it was then confiscated by the catering staff.

Ducks and loo seats apart, there is less climbing misbehaviour to record these days. The University Mountaineering club was founded in 1905 and was perhaps encouraged by the university in order to channel their students' exuberance in a more acceptable direction. More recently, female students founded their own climbing club, the Magog Club – although the challenges presented by those modest hills to the east of Cambridge do not compare with those provided by the colleges themselves. Whether these opportunities at Cambridge influenced those of its graduates who later won fame as adventurers is uncertain. The most famous of these is the mountaineer George Mallory, whose college, Magdalene, named a court in his memory. Others include the artist-physician and graduate of Caius Edward Wilson, who died with Captain Scott in 1912, and the Anglo-American astronaut Michael Foale, who studied at Queens' in the late 1970s. Both Wilson and Foale took their college flags with them on their adventures. It is striking that, amid all the careful preparations and restrictions on personal belongings which characterise expeditions such as theirs, both chose to travel with their college flag – and in the case of Foale, his was a full-sized heavy cloth version. These gestures eloquently reveal the deep affection many members retain for their college.

Clare Bridge and other stories

Most colleges can boast their share of fanciful tales. Two of Clare's concern its bridge. There are not quite fourteen stone balls on this, the oldest bridge over the Cam; the second-to-last one on the King's College side has a slice missing. Thomas Grumbold, the mason who built the bridge in the late 1630s, is said to have left it unfinished to express his irritation at the incomplete settlement of his fee by the college. Sadly, a more probable explanation is that the wedge of stone – which is occasionally removed to facilitate the repair of the metal rod securing the ball to the bridge – simply fell out. Much more recently, a Clare student moulded a lightweight copy of one of these balls and carried it to the bridge. When a punt laden with tourists approached the bridge, he adopted a suitably demented look as he struggled to 'separate' the ball

Illustration 15.2: Clare Bridge: the oldest surviving bridge and one of the most attractive of all the river crossings. The heavy stone balls along the coping have provoked some amusing tales.

from the parapet. As the ball was ostentatiously inched free, the tourists abandoned ship and took to the Cam. This innocent diversion led to his suspension from the university, a poor reward for such ingenuity.

Another story involving water is told about the poet Thomas Gray. When a fellow of Peterhouse he had rooms at the top of Burrough's Building, which stands between Peterhouse's chapel and Little St Mary's. A man unpopular in Peterhouse, he also had a well-known fear of fire which some students uncharitably exploited; having placed a large tub of cold water on the ground beneath his window, they made a hue and cry over a supposed fire. Gray descended on a rope from his window into the tub. The episode can be dated to 1756, the year in which he left Peterhouse. He was not amused by the leniency the college master showed to the guilty students and, in consequence, joined Pembroke College, on the other side of Trumpington Street.

Varsity rags and hoaxes are part of the culture, and sometimes the myth, of Cambridge. One such notorious episode was carried out by a Trinity College student, William Horace de Vere Cole. With friends making up his entourage, he impersonated the uncle of the Sultan of Zanzibar when the Sultan himself was visiting London in 1905. To lessen the risk of rustication, they had chosen to dupe the Mayor of Cambridge rather than the university authorities; at one point during his reception by the mayor he declined the opportunity to enter King's College Chapel, mumbling reverently 'What holy men must inhabit here'. He carried out a similar trick on the crew of a Royal Navy Dreadnought in 1910. The prank, however, provoked questions in the House of Commons: making a fool of the Cambridge town mayor was one thing, it was another to mock the Royal Navy.

Neither hoaxes nor the student enthusiasm for climbing brought much contact with the town; the most usual shared misbehaviour of scholar and townsmen was a brawl, particularly in past centuries. Occasional re-enactments still occur. In the summer of 2005, a bout of violence broke out between the sellers of ice cream and the touts who seek out tourists for punting trips on the river. During the summer the touts are often university students earning money through commission; the ice-cream sellers are local townsfolk, often, as they were in this instance, first-generation Italian immigrants. The *Times* devoted its third leader to the dispute under the title of 'Ice Cream Wars', after similar disturbances a few years before in Glasgow. However, the paper overlooked how modern events unwittingly mirror, as is so often the case in Cambridge, an ancient pattern. The modern fracas took place along a short length of the ancient Roman road now known as Bridge Street, just to the south-east of Magdalene College. Precisely the same stretch of road has always hosted the best fights between exactly the same two communities of 'town and gown'. For centuries Magdalene scholars had come out of their college to brawl with the rough young townsmen employed in this quarter of the town's docks. Rioting between scholars and townsmen also took place in other areas of the old town: records of 1824 refer to the Battle of Peas Hill, near the Market Square. Twenty-first-century Cambridge was experiencing nothing new.

Townsmen were not always needed for a riot, however. After the fifteenth century, more scholars were recruited from the north of England. For example, St John's, whose founder Margaret Beaufort had been Countess of Derby as well as of Richmond, was required by its articles to source half its fellows and scholars from the nine northern English counties – that Bishop Fisher's home county was Yorkshire must have helped establish this requirement. King's College, Gonville, Trinity Hall and Corpus Christi recruited primarily from the south. Antipathy to people from other regions was strong in medieval England and manifested itself in Cambridge in riots between 'northern' and 'southern' colleges. It appears that scholars at rival Oxford colleges still fight each other, as in 2009 members of Exeter and Jesus Colleges started a blood-stained brawl during the Turl annual dash, supposedly an innocent bicycle ride around the city. The last decent Cambridge intra-student riot took place in 1921, when a vote in Senate denied women full membership of the university and some less forward-looking male students smashed a cart against the iron entrance gates of Newnham to mark their agreement with the outcome. Well into the 1950s, though, students managed to disrupt the life of the town; for instance, a tradition of misbehaviour grew up around

Guy Fawkes Night, for which the police apparently prepared by donning old uniforms to cope with the abundance of soot and flour thrown by students.

In 1970 rioting students were united in a more serious cause, voicing their antipathy to the Greek military regime during a Greek Tourism week at the Garden House Hotel. Police arrested several students and proctors gave evidence against eight who were widely thought to have been innocent. Their evidence secured their prosecution and dispatch to Borstal. One of them, a third-year student from Clare, graduated *in absentia* with a first-class degree. Another international issue excited student protest in the early 1980s; a debate at the Union, to which the ambassador of the South African apartheid regime had been invited, provoked student protesters to launch bricks through the Union building windows. The most recent protest of this sort took place in 2009, when the Foster Law Faculty building was occupied for a couple of days in protest against Israeli violence in Gaza; the university's threat of rustication quickly brought the students to heel and the building was left undamaged.

Fairs

The fairs held in Cambridge were nationally famous for centuries and, in their heyday, they provided ample opportunities for misbehaviour. They thrived over the long period when water transport was vital to the nation's economy. Their eventual decline with that of Cambridge in the eighteenth century followed the development of the competing road and railway transport networks. The economic relevance of Cambridge was then eclipsed until its remarkable contribution to the knowledge economy emerged in the late twentieth century.

Garlic Fair, dating from 1150, was the town's oldest fair. It was licensed by King Stephen to the Nuns of St Radegund, whose buildings, as well as the right to hold the fair, were taken over by Jesus College in the 1490s. The fair took place in August on land between the college and Jesus Lane, alongside the convent cemetery. When the college enclosed this land, the fair was moved up Jesus Lane to Park Street, which was known as Garlic Lane until the fair's demise in the 1800s.

King John sold licences for three Cambridge fairs, at Reach (from 1201), Stourbridge (from 1199) and Midsummer Common (from 1211). The Angevin kings were particularly popular amongst the merchant class of England, if not the nobility, because they were prepared to sell trading rights such as these in order to finance their Crusades and the struggles against the French. The Reach Fair, ten miles to the north of the town, reflected the monopoly Cambridge had over water trade in the region. It took place during Rogationtide. Timber and iron imported from the Baltic might have been exchanged for Cambridge grain or the local chalk. It has now become a Spring Bank Holiday funfair, but is still opened by the mayor who, as centuries before, distributes newly minted pennies to children.

The best-known of the Cambridge fairs was the Stourbridge Fair, run by the priest of the Leper Hospital and Chapel. The chapel had opened between 1125 and 1150 but the first fair did not take place until 1211. The Cambridge burghers who funded the chapel would have wanted both their charity and, since leprosy was generally thought in the Middle Ages to be a divine punishment, the consequence of sin in Cambridge to be visible: the chapel stands alongside Newmarket Road, close by the Cambridge United football ground.

Whatever the founders' motivations, however, chapels such as these attracted charitable endowments and the right to hold fairs was prized for the revenues it could bring. Lepers have not been treated there since the 1300s and the position of chapel priest became a lucrative sinecure until the Dissolution of the Monasteries. In later centuries the chapel was used as a pub and a storeroom during the fair. The fair itself, which lasted for three weeks during August and September, was so profitable that both university and town vied for its control. After the 1580s the university won the right to determine which traders could attend the fair and to supervise the quality of goods – many of which would have been purchased by its members. The town managed to retain the considerable profits from the fair, as well as responsibility for law and order. There was certainly misbehaviour; one eyewitness in the early 1700s commented on the London men who came 'to drink, smoke and whore' there. The scale of the fair, and of the trouble that could occur at it, required prompt enactment of justice, which was delivered through the delightfully named Pie Powder Courts. In support of those who contend that English is merely badly pronounced French, this name derives from *'pieds poudreux'*, which was the description of those attending such fairs in France. This was the lowest and most expeditious court of English justice, whose last recorded sitting in England was at Bristol in 1870. The last Stourbridge Fair was held in 1933; a modest version of the fair is sometimes re-enacted to raise money for the maintenance of the chapel.

The importance of the Stourbridge Fair was such that it has been immortalised in literature in a variety of guises. Daniel Defoe described it in his *A Tour thro' the Whole Island of Great Britain*, while John Bunyan's Vanity Fair, in his *Pilgrim's Progress*, was inspired by it; he was evidently familiar with the event. 'At all times,' he wrote, 'are seen there jugglers, cheats, games, fools, apes, knaves, and rogues'. His hero, Christian, approaches the town with Faithful from the east down the straight old Roman road now known as Babraham Road. From the Gog Magog Hills the towers and spires of Cambridge beckon. Modern commuters driving down the road from those same hills might sympathise with Bunyan's reference to the 'Valley of Humiliation' which led to the 'Town of Vanity'. In the nineteenth century William Thackeray used Vanity Fair as the title of his famous novel, describing the eponymous town as 'a very vain, wicked, foolish place, full of all sorts of humbugs and falsenesses and pretensions'. His view may have been coloured by the gambling debts which had forced his premature departure from Trinity College in 1830.

An echo of Stourbridge Fair comes through the street names which survive near Newmarket Road and the river. Mercer's Row, Cheddars Lane, Garlic Row, Oyster Row and Swanns Road did not always house the bourgeoisie of Cambridge. The Wrestlers Arms, on the Newmarket Road, also survives into the twenty-first century as a reminder of the entertainment which followed in the wake of the fair; indeed, before the entire road leading east from Cambridge was renamed 'Newmarket Road', the part running through this area was known as Booksellers Row. They are each a reminder that the layout of the fair became sufficiently established for each trading row to earn their names, some of which still survive in the surrounding streets. A description of the fair being opened in 1789 by the university vice-chancellor and his officers, the bedells and proctors, relates that they enjoyed mulled wine, sherry and cakes at the Senate House before travelling in coaches out to the fair, where they consumed a gargantuan feast. So many oysters were eaten that the name of the building near the fair in which they ate was changed from The Tiled Booth to The Oyster House.

Beer was served on the second floor and dancing took place on the third floor. The building, naturally in Oyster Row, was demolished in 1960.

The fourth of these ancient gatherings is Midsummer Fair. The licence was granted in 1211 to the important Augustinian priory at Barnwell, where eminent visitors stayed in the early medieval period before the colleges could offer a suitably sybaritic welcome. King John, Henry III and Edward II are each recorded as visitors. The fair took place at the time of the June solstice and at one time it was renowned for its timber and pottery sales. In the eighteenth century it was actually referred to as the Pot Fair; china can still be brought from stalls at the modern fair. In the past this fair was thought sufficiently important even by the university to be designated a 'Scarlet Day', on which it was customary for all members of the university holding a doctor's degree to wear scarlet. This status was withdrawn after 1855 when the university left responsibility for the fair with the town. The major festivals of the church are still designated by the university as Scarlet Days, as are special occasions such as a royal visit. Some colleges also adopted the practice for college feasts commemorating their founders.

Fairs and markets continue to play a role in modern Cambridge. For the last thirty years Midsummer Common has hosted a funfair known as Strawberry Fair. There is a daily market in the Market Square, while an arts and crafts fair is held at weekends throughout the year in the graveyard of the old All Saints Church, opposite St John's College. Fisher Hall, near the Corn Exchange, hosts a wide variety of traders, while Addenbrooke's Hospital holds a Snow Fair annually to raise money for its Child Development Centre. Outside the town, there is an annual Glass Fair and a Wedding Fair, claimed to be the biggest in the country, at Chilford Hall in Linton. For the last twenty-five years Cambridge has hosted a film festival; a beer festival has been held since 1972. A Winter Fair started in Mill Road in the early 2000s and attracts many visitors to this more socially diverse part of town. This is a significant number of fairs for a county town and is another aspect of Cambridge which links its modern inhabitants to those of earlier centuries.

Dead Bodies

Besides fairs, medical education surprisingly brought another opportunity for misbehaviour to the town. Up to the sixteenth century the study of medical science was a theoretical matter largely derived from the classical texts. When Dr Caius conducted the first recorded practical demonstration in Cambridge of the dissection of a human body in 1557 at Gonville Hall, the supply of bodies did not then seem to have been an issue. However, by the early 1700s demand exceeded supply. This provoked an unappealing, though not illegal, trade in dead bodies. The ownership of bodies, once buried, was for a long time a matter of legal debate.

Cambridge had its first Anatomy Theatre in 1716 at the corner of Silver Street and Queens' Lane on land just opposite the old entrance to Queens' College. St Catharine's College has since occupied the space. Natural distaste for such trade led to inventive methods of smuggling the bodies of London's poor, the prime source, up the Great North Road to Cambridge. The coach traveller's assumption that the malodorous wicker basket on board contained hunted game might often have been mistaken.

There was one particularly macabre 'dead body' incident. A famous Jesus graduate from the 1730s, Lawrence Sterne, ended up on the slab in Queens' Lane. Sterne joined the church, although he remained well known as a political journalist. He won fame through a novel, *The Life and Opinions of Tristram Shandy*, which took until the third of its nine volumes to arrive at the hero's birth. Samuel Johnson's comment that 'Nothing odd will do long' was wide of the mark; Voltaire praised the popular work and it survived to be acknowledged as a great influence by James Joyce and Virginia Woolf. Indeed, it still remains a little fashionable to declare admiration for the novel. Sterne, however, died in extreme poverty. The parish buried his body in 1768 near Marble Arch. After resurrection his cadaver was recognised on the slab in Cambridge and hastily reburied. A painting of him entitled 'Lawrence Sterne and Death', completed shortly after he died, now hangs on the staircase of the Jesus Quincentennial Library.

University archives record the unrest which the dissection of bodies caused. In April 1732 a body was seen being taken into Emmanuel College, though the consequent hue and cry, complete with college search, yielded no body. The incident was a sufficient threat to public order to persuade the Senate to pass a grace ordering that no bodies be dug up in the town. A hundred years later Charles Darwin, who studied at Christ's College, wrote of the riot which had followed the arrest of two body snatchers. In the early 1800s the Anatomy Theatre moved to the unfortunately named Slaughterhouse Lane. It was in a building at the corner of what are now known as Downing Street and Corn Exchange Street. Local people stormed the building in 1833, believing there was a body being dissected illegally. Anatomy is still taught on the opposite side of Downing Street.

Body snatching was a national issue. Following the capture of Burke and Hare in Edinburgh, the Anatomy Act of 1832 was passed in order to reduce the attraction of bodies to thieves. The dead bodies of the Poor House not claimed within forty-eight hours became the property of the state. Tolerable perhaps in anonymous London, the act caused outrage in smaller communities such as Cambridge, where inmates of the Poor House were known. This issue long retained the potential to excite 'misbehaviour' between the town and gown communities.

Cambridge pubs

Pubs and beer provide another meeting point, and a further opportunity for misbehaviour, for the two communities of Cambridge. The town has always supported large numbers of both coaching inns and pubs, partly as a result of the trade generated by the river network; at many of the sluices along the Cam, the ferryman typically increased his toll income by selling beer, a practice reflected in Cambridge pub names such as The Anchor, The Jolly Waterman and The Waterside. East Anglia is well known for the quality of its barley, through which brewing thrived; Greene King is based in Bury St Edmunds, while Adnams, Elgoods, Ridleys and Ruddles, to name just a few brands, are also brewed in the region. The last substantial commercial brewery in Cambridge, which closed in the 1970s, was the Star Brewery run by Tolly Cobbold; there had been five substantial town breweries even up to the 1950s. The city's commercial brewing tradition has since been resurrected through several micro-breweries – for example, The City of Cambridge Brewery is based in Chittering, north of Cambridge, and Milton Breweries operates from near the centre of Cambridge; both were established in the 1990s. As has been the case for centuries, local businesses such as these do what they can to trade on their proximity to the university; City of Cambridge markets its beers under brand names such as Parker's Porter, Atom Splitter, Hobson's Choice and Boathouse Bitter.

King Street, by most standards a short street, once contained as many as thirteen pubs. This extraordinary number gave rise to the King Street Race, the objective of which was to be the quickest to down a pint in each pub without recourse to the lavatory. Once attempted by students, the main participants are now local people. A mere five pubs remain today, so that two pints have to be drunk in three pubs in order to ensure that the target of a gallon of beer is exceeded. Even into the interwar years, pubs were crowded into the quayside area as well, with up to thirty-one in Bridge Street, a street which runs only from the Round Church up to Magdalene. The Pickerel Inn, on the north side of the bridge by Magdalene, is probably the oldest pub in Cambridge and stands beside the building which once housed the Cross Keys, an inn and most probably a brothel. The latter building is almost directly opposite the main entrance to Magdalene College; it now accommodates a ladies' clothing boutique. On its exterior, supporting the jettied first floor, there are five old bracket carvings of male and female gargoyles with exaggerated sexual organs. Surprisingly, it is still possible to meet Magdalene students who have not noticed this advertisement of a trade which flourished in medieval Cambridge. At the crossroads further up the hill towards the castle mound stood the White Horse Inn, which was the first substantial inn encountered by travellers from the north on arriving in Cambridge – its site is now occupied by the Folk Museum. This pub shared its name with the hostelry in Trumpington Street where the men of the Reformation met.

As with the fairs, Cambridge pubs feature in the nation's literature. Samuel Pepys, who was a staunch republican when aged fifteen, recorded his own remark at the king's execution in 1649 that 'the memory of the wicked shall rot'. During a visit to Cambridge fifteen years later he celebrated the Stuart restoration of 1660 at The Three Tunns in the Market Square, noting in his diary that 'we drank pretty hard and [gave] many healths to the King'. He also writes of another night spent in the Rose Tavern, which had forty-two rooms, each individually named; the Spread Eagle was its smartest room. Not drinking hard himself on this occasion, he complained of others who were. He recorded in his diary that he had a bad night's sleep at the Rose Tavern because 'of some drunken scholars making a noise all night'. This pub, which was at the north-east corner of the Market Square, was pulled down in the early 1800s and the area it covered was transformed into Rose Crescent. A small vestige of the Rose Tavern, an iron balcony facing the Market Square, is left at the junction of Market Street and Rose Crescent: it was from this platform that the town's candidates for political office once made their speeches and the victor in parliamentary general elections was announced.

The Hoop Inn, at the corner of Jesus Lane and Bridge Street, was remembered by William Wordsworth in his autobiographical poem 'The Prelude'. He captured the timeless excitement of a student's first arrival in Cambridge, although his time there did not prove to be the happiest period of his life:

> Onward we drove beneath the Castle; caught,
> While crossing Magdalene Bridge, a glimpse of Cam;
> And at the 'Hoop' alighted, famous Inn
> My spirit was up; my thoughts were full of hope.

Illustration 15.3: The medieval brothel in Magdalene Street stands almost directly opposite the college entrance; the bracket carvings supporting the first-floor windows can leave no doubt as to the trade once conducted from its premises.

The pubs, the river and the fairs have each served to mix the townsfolk with the academic community. In twenty-first-century Cambridge, student and townspeople are more likely to meet at the parish churches in the centre of town than in those places. There is generally less mixing than in the past. The two communities row on the Cam separately and the fairs are of little interest to students. Drink in college bars is cheaper than in the town, notoriously so at Emmanuel and Sidney Sussex: it took the combined pressure of the police and the master for the drink prices at Sidney to be increased in 2009. In consequence, there is less drinking together – and less rioting – than there used to be.

The joy of good stories and the sex-weary

Although the truth behind some of the stories of inappropriate behaviour is often a little uncertain, it is sad that hoaxes and climbing appear less of a preoccupation for the modern student. In many ways it does not matter whether it was true that some King's students told workmen digging up King's Parade to ignore the students posing as policemen that were coming to interview them and then immediately informed the police that students pretending to be workmen were ruining the street in King's Parade; it makes a good story.

The recent absence of escapades confirms that modern university life has changed beyond recognition from its medieval origins. So much is permitted to the modern student that disciplinary confrontations with the college dean are rare; night-climbing apart, good behaviour is now defined, practically speaking, by what is legal. Students are also generally more focused on their studies; the prospect of graduating with up to £30,000 of debt concentrates the mind of the student looking for a postgraduate grant as much as much as that of his peer who seeks a lucrative place in the civil service or the City of London.

Today the flourishing pastime, reflecting a trend in other parts of society, is drinking. Part of the explanation for this may lie in the pressures facing the modern Cambridge student: not only is there pressure to excel and live up to their early academic promise, but also to stand out at the dozens of extra-curricula activities which are provided. Escape into an alcoholic haze must seem attractive to some.

The long-established and relatively innocent pastime of 'pennying', a coin dropped into a wine glass obliging its owner to knock the drink back at once, has been eclipsed by a far more serious drinking culture. Student drinking societies are thriving: the Clare Crabs, the Wyverns at Magdalene, the AlleyCatz at St Catharine's, the Patricians of Downing, the Newnham Nuns, the Beefsteaks, the Ferretz and the S.L.A.G.S. are merely the most notorious. At the Blazers & Bikinis party on Suicide Sunday (a day of concentrated drinking after exams have finished) organised by the Wyvern Club, a recent incident following a female jelly-wrestling session ended with police involvement. A Cambridge University spokesman 'deplored' the event. In the circumstances there was little more to be said. In earlier times, however, the official university reaction would surely have been stronger. This fairly constant misbehaviour of Magdalene's junior members long ago fuelled a loose translation of the college motto, *Garde ta foi* – 'Keep constant faith'; the alternative version reads 'Look out for your liver'.

It is telling, perhaps, that in 2009 even a student newspaper denounced these drinking societies, membership of which is secured through, it reported, 'degrading, depraved acts and excessive consumption of alcohol'. That students secure some social standing through membership is a far cry from the times when special attention from ones' peers was reserved for talented Footlights actors, the quick-witted members of the Union or the undergraduate heroes of the sporting arena. Certainly, drinking to excess has always occurred at the university, but its current ubiquity is something new. Doctors at Addenbrooke's comment openly on the increased number of students, particularly women, they treat for alcohol poisoning, while college deans now worry about the health implications for the staff who must clear up student vomit. The hope must be that excessive drinkers remain fewer than the numbers suggested by the publicity they attract and that they do not divert attention from the many more who debate, act and play sport.

Where university disciplinary issues do occur the ultimate court of appeal for junior members is the Septemviri. This body is referred to in Elizabethan statutes of 1570, but by the 1850s its composition had been slightly changed, as it contained only six people. It was therefore referred to as the Sexviri. By the late 1930s the Roman style of pronunciation for 'v' as the modern English phonetic equivalent of 'w' was readopted and thus were the Sexviri joyfully referred to by the irreverent as the Sex Weary. The leaders of the university were sufficiently sensitive about this mockery to readopt the Elizabethan nomenclature of Septemviri.

Their sensitivity was perhaps inevitable after centuries of sexual repression within the single-sex and often misogynist culture which the university had created. However, as this nickname suggests, sexual matters have always fascinated and perhaps it is in reaction to this repressive past that they are now aired with a striking frankness. For a start, provided that it is legal, the university and its colleges no longer classify sexual activity as 'misbehaviour'. Furthermore, unthinkable as it would have been in earlier centuries, sex is now publicly debated. The two main student newspapers *Varsity* and *The Cambridge Student* (weekly publications during term run by the Cambridge University Students' Union) print regular columns with titles such as 'Sex in the (univer) City' (*Varsity*) and 'Prudence Rules of Sex in Cambridge' (*TCS*). Another satirical student publication, called *Vivid*, runs a 'Page Three' on which it prints pictures of scantily dressed female undergraduates in a variety of locations: on Clare Bridge, in the Speaker's Chair at the Union or in a library; the shot on Clare Bridge in particular attracted international publicity. The Debating Union even tried to encourage membership in October 2008 by issuing free contraceptives supported by the slogan 'For A More Perfect Union'. The campaign probably achieved more exposure than might otherwise have been the case because the condoms' lack of a suitable quality kitemark forced them to be withdrawn amid much publicity. The *Independent* ran an article entitled 'A Condom Alert in Cambridge'.

A survey of students' sexual activity undertaken by one of the student publications in 2008 confirmed how the medieval authorities were perhaps right to fear the release of control over their scholars. It revealed a close correlation between sexual activity and poor academic performance. Peterhouse came twenty-fifth in the 2007 Tompkins academic table, yet third in what was referred to as the Promiscuity League; Christ's, second in the academic league, had the highest number of virgins and smallest amount of sexual activity among the colleges. The survey provided further amusement by casting King's as the kinkiest and Downing as the straightest college. Homerton and Fitzwilliam students claimed the most sexual partners. It also drew correlations between sexual activity and academic pursuits; mathematicians, vets and theologians had least sex, while to jokes about the game of 'doctors and nurses', the medics came top. The vets' low position in the sex league, despite the proximity of their studies to medicine, caused surprise, as well as the thought that perhaps their preference for animals extended into the bedroom.

Despite the drinking clubs or the sexual antics to be enjoyed at some colleges, it is still the single-minded pursuit of academic excellence which is the most typical characteristic of the modern Cambridge scholar. It is essential that this continues to be so, as the best among them will reinforce the university's future intellectual pre-eminence. In reaching this conclusion, it is still a little sad to note that of necessity the time has passed when at least a few undergraduates possessed of blue blood or outstanding hand–eye coordination could be squeezed in and left to pursue climbing conquests and sporting triumphs. Inexcusable as their admission may have been to modern meritocratic eyes, their comparatively alcohol-free antics made the place much more fun.

Chapter 16

On the Shoulders of Giants

The media success of Cambridge-educated historians such as Norman Stone, Andrew Roberts, Simon Schama and David Starkey cannot disguise the fact that the modern reputation of Cambridge University has been founded on the strength of its science. Of the eighty-three Nobel prizes won by academics associated with Cambridge, seventy were awarded for research in physics, medicine and chemistry. No other institution in the world has won as many.

In the Middle Ages art flourished through the Church; it provided the artist with both patronage and inspiration. Artists could learn from each other in the great cultural centres of the western world and advances in architecture or in painting were shared. Medieval men of science, on the other hand, faced unique hindrances in their pursuit of discoveries. Few among the elite perceived the relevance of science, so only rarely could patronage be found. In addition, there were no Schools of Science as there were of Philosophy or Law, so those who studied science worked almost alone. There was no network of communication comparable to that of the Catholic Church through which advances in science could be shared. Indeed, men of science often had to be brave, as the Church laid a heavy hand for centuries on those whose advances challenged its theocentric view of the world. The conclusions the Oxford teacher Roger Bacon drew from his empirical research in astrology led to his imprisonment in a French Franciscan monastery during the thirteenth century and, as late as 1632, Galileo was put on trial in Rome for his musings about a heliocentric universe.

Knowledge of metals, the discovery of chemical substances through alchemy and the development of skills to navigate the seas and the heavens were the subjects of medieval science. The mechanical arts were a branch of mathematics. In the medieval university subjects such as geometry, optics and statics (the last concerned with the physical forces which had prompted Aristotle to speculate how a javelin travelled through the air) were part of the curriculum. A place such as Cambridge where the complex, expensive, tools of the trade – astrolobes, quadrants, adjustable maps of the stars known as planispheres and globes made of metal or wood – were collected would have been considered in medieval times as a place of science.

Given the atmosphere surrounding scientific discovery, however, it is unsurprising that Cambridge did not nurture any great scientists before the 1500s. In the wake of the Reformation, and strengthened by the philosophy of Humanism, scientists emerged slowly from the shadow cast by the Catholic Church. Travel improved communication between scientists; it was no longer an outlandish idea to journey to Italy on an intellectual rather than a religious pilgrimage. The university in consequence nurtured two men of outstanding importance to science: in the sixteenth century William Gilbert and, in the following century, William Harvey.

Brave, clever men – Gilbert and Harvey

William Gilbert graduated from St John's in the late 1560s. His main discoveries related to magnetism: he distinguished this force from electrostatic attraction and identified the earth as a giant magnet. His work *De Magnete*, the first significant contribution to the study of physical sciences in Britain, was well received by his academic peers, and contemporary heroes such as Francis Drake and Thomas Cavendish were among his friends. He was the original experimental scientist at Cambridge, his approach being a rejection both of Plato's '*a priori*' approach, where conclusions were drawn from universal principles, and also of the Aristotelian logic of deduction from reason. Gilbert was out of step with his contemporaries at the university's Natural Philosophy School, who he referred to as 'roaches and moths'. He valued the opinions of navigators and farmers, practical men, above those of his peers, whose ability for fresh scientific thought was crippled by adherence to Greek philosophy and the Book of Genesis.

Despite the relevance of his studies on magnetism to a sea-faring nation, the impact of *De Magnete* did not penetrate far into society. For example, it took another 100 years to shake the Royal Navy's belief that garlic demagnetised a ship's compass. Helmsmen caught chewing garlic were still being flogged on board His Majesty's ships at the turn of the eighteenth century. Nevertheless, Gilbert was certainly one of those giants on whose shoulders later men of science stood and St John's acknowledges this through a statue on the south-facing wall of its college chapel.

William Harvey has also been captured in stone by his college, Gonville & Caius. Twelve feet from the Trinity Street pavement, his statue portrays him with a heart in the palm of his left hand to acknowledge his work on the circulation of the blood. Up at Cambridge in the 1590s, Harvey studied anatomy through the dissection of animals and of human corpses; in so doing he observed valves working in the heart and veins. He was unable to identify capillaries, as the microscope had yet to be invented, but concluded correctly despite the lack of this crucial piece of evidence that blood circulates around the body. Harvey's discovery did not result just from his own observation of how the body worked, however. He could rely on studies already completed by others and travel to more advanced places of study than Cambridge. Although the university can claim to have imbued Harvey with a thirst for discovery it was, tellingly, necessary for him to move to Padua in order to develop intellectually. At that time Cambridge University was certainly not numbered among the leading places in Europe to pursue the study of science. In Padua he found an invaluable mentor in Girolamo Fabricius, a pioneering anatomist from Lazio sometimes referred to as the 'father of embryology'.

Illustration 16.1: William Harvey has been captured in stone in Trinity Street opposite his college, Caius. He holds a heart in
his left palm and the *Anatomical treatise on the motion of the heart and blood in animals*
in his right hand. Many Cambridge heroes have been similarly honoured,
making it worthwhile for visitors to stretch their necks upwards in the old town.

Whether the motive of the modern scientist is to forestall competing researchers, secure funding or win
fame, publication of significant discoveries occurs quickly. Harvey, however, took ten years to announce his
findings; such delay puts the position of these early Cambridge men of science in the context of their times.
He feared the impact of his findings on himself; it was barely ten years since Galileo had been found guilty of
heresy. Harvey wrote of the potential consequences of his own discovery: 'so much do I fear harm to myself
from other people's ill-will, so much does custom and doctrine once received and deeply rooted prevail with
everyone'. The Greek physician Galen had explained matters to the satisfaction of doctors centuries earlier

through his theory of two systems of blood, one carried by the veins, the other by the arteries; this new theory of blood circulation was thus mocked.

Harvey lived in London from 1602, becoming the court physician to James I and then Charles I. He did not publish his work until 1628, three years after the accession of Charles. Although his peers objected to the condemnation of their bloodletting skills, he retained his position at court; indeed, he was a supporter of the Stuart monarchy and socially conservative, despite the radical implications of his work.

Harvey and Gilbert command admiration and epitomise the first phase of Cambridge science. They were clever, courageous and usually worked without patronage. In those days fame and patronage flowed more readily to architects, for example, than to men who studied science; the loss to science of Christopher Wren (he had first been an astronomer who had, like Gilbert, studied terrestrial magnetism) could well be explained by the obscurity which generally faced scientists.

Individual men of science – Newton, Babbage and Darwin

Although the next pinnacle of scientific achievement in Cambridge occurred after the Restoration, when circumstances were easier for scientists, the full range of support available to modern scientists was certainly not yet available. From this period three men stand out: Isaac Newton, who came up to Trinity College in 1661; Charles Babbage, who entered the same college in 1810; and Charles Darwin, who joined Christ's College in 1827.

Newton and Darwin shared one similarity with modern scientists: they achieved immense fame in their lifetime, but there the parallels end. Newton worked alone without much assistance from his academic contemporaries; only his genius protected him from severe penalties for his religious nonconformity. Scientists like John Ray, the outstanding classifier of plants, had been forced from the university for similar independence a few years earlier.

Newton was the first and greatest of the pure scientists of Cambridge – those whose work was carried out without immediate consideration for its application. He was initially a Trinity College sub-sizar, which was the lowest of the six social grades of undergraduate, and so would have been expected to complete menial tasks for the college fellowship in return for his board and instruction. Newton's family was far from impoverished, in fact, but family circumstances apparently dissuaded them from paying for his education. He was thought a little odd by his fellow scholars; a contemporary there referred to him as 'a prickly, dishevelled recluse so serious upon his studies that he ate very sparingly'. His brilliance secured a scholarship within three years, then a fellowship in 1667 and finally the Lucasian Chair of Mathematics in 1669. The £200 annual income from the post came with the undemanding requirement to give one lecture course each year. The post is awarded for life; Stephen Hawking, the current holder, is only the seventeenth incumbent. Unlike many of the great scientists claimed by Cambridge, whose brush with the university was sometimes ephemeral, Newton was to spend twenty-eight years in Cambridge.

The achievements for which Newton is best remembered actually crystallised when he was absent from the university. Memories of the Black Death, which had devastated Cambridge, prompted the closure of the university when the plague reached East Anglia in 1666. It remained closed for two years. While at his country home in Woolsthorpe, Lincolnshire, Newton worked on his theory of universal gravitation and wrote three papers on calculus, or fluxions, as he termed his discovery. At the age of twenty-four he was the leading mathematician in Europe. In Saxony, Gottfried Leibniz was developing similar theories, and a bitter dispute as to which of them had been the plagiarist followed. The outcome was probably a draw; Newton's original notation is still used but Leibniz's work is equally regarded. In any event, Newton had uncovered a method of measuring the non-linear world through his work on tangents and planetary motion. Measurement of the non-linear uncovered the mysteries of the non-constant universe. His invention of calculus permitted the exploration of nature and the heliocentric universe.

These dramatic discoveries did not flow from a moment of epiphany, but were the culmination of years of thought. His most famous work, *Principia Mathematica*, first published in Latin during 1687, established the framework for all subsequent progress in physics, mathematics and indeed mechanics, and dramatically accelerated man's ability to exploit nature. Newton moved on from calculus and gravitational theory to the phenomenon of colours. His approach to experimentation with light, reputedly provoked by his purchase of a prism at the Stourbridge Fair, fits aptly into the new age of empirical discovery; the simple experiments he carried out displaced the prevalent view that colour was a mixture of light and darkness. The French sculptor Louis-Francois Roubiliac portrayed Newton holding a prism in the 1730s; the statue stands in the antechapel of Trinity Chapel.

By the end of the 1660s he had invented a new form of telescope, based on the principles of reflecting dishes, which was much more powerful than any previous telescope. Modern telescopic technology still uses the advances which he pioneered. The range of his immense achievements stunned his contemporaries; in the late 1660s the French mathematician Guillaume de l'Hôpital wrote 'Does he eat and drink and sleep? Is he like other men?'

The rest of his long life – he died aged eighty-four in 1727 – held no further such dramatic discoveries; academic disputes distracted him a good deal. To the battle over plagiarism with Leibniz was added an ill-tempered dispute with Robert Hooke, who regarded optics as his own province. Unsurprisingly, given his awe-inspiring genius, he remained difficult company for lesser mortals. He only just won a contested election as President of the Royal Society in 1703; cantankerous brilliance makes difficult 'club material'. Late in his life Newton became obsessed with biblical prophecy; he believed it was through mathematics and physics that the secrets of God's works could be understood. He was knighted in 1705 in a ceremony held at the Trinity master's lodge during a visit of Queen Anne.

Newton's achievements were immense; despite this, he remained modest, borrowing Bernard of Chartres's early-twelfth-century phrase, which heads this chapter, when writing to his rival Robert Hooke in 1676: 'If I have seen a little further, it is by standing on the shoulders of giants'. In a phrase which matches this eloquence, he described his life to a nephew as if he had been 'only a boy playing on the seashore ... while the great ocean of truth lay all undiscovered before me'. Where the natural philosophers of the Renaissance world, men such as Harvey and Gilbert at Cambridge, left cracks in the mould which constrained medieval scientific knowledge, Newton smashed the mould. He had demonstrated where the scientific method, which the Trinity College scholar Francis Bacon had popularised in the early 1600s, could lead. Voltaire, as a keen admirer of Newton, did much to help the achievements of this scientist reach a wider audience.

When Newton died in 1727, Voltaire was in England during one of his periodic displacements from the autocratic France of Louis XV. He attended the state funeral, marvelling at the country which 'honours its scientists as other countries honour its kings'.

Part of Newton's legacy was that the study of science became so complex that its inclusion within a general curriculum became impossible. After Newton only a specialist could absorb the quantity and complexity of scientific knowledge necessary to make further advances. By 1750 the university had established the first specialised tripos in mathematics. A few years later, in 1768, Robert Smith founded the Smith Prize for the leading theoretical physicist at Cambridge. This prize is still awarded and counts Lord Kelvin, James Clerk Maxwell, J.J. Thompson and Alan Turing among its winners. The prize was funded by stock held in the South Sea Company, as it happens a company in which Newton had invested. When the speculative bubble around its share price famously burst in 1720, he lost the enormous sum of £20,000. Apparently mystified by his loss, the experience provoked his rueful comment: 'I can calculate the motions of heavenly bodies, but not the madness of people'.

Newton is perhaps the ultimate example of scientific genius at Cambridge. He had no patronage and his work had little apparent relevance to society; in spite of his modest protestations, he received little assistance from those who had passed before him. Despite all these disadvantages he was able, almost alone, to push forward the sum of human knowledge.

The work of Charles Babbage was, in contrast, nothing if not immediately relevant. Babbage, the great pioneer of computing, bypassed the conventional curriculum of an undergraduate after moving to Peterhouse, studying only those things which interested him; he took the Lucasian Chair in 1828, but never gave a lecture. His work was intended to replace eighteenth-century computers, also known as reckoners – the people who calculated numerical tables. The profession did not enjoy a reputation for precision; inaccuracies in navigational tables were thought to have often caused shipwrecks and more reliable tables would reduce the number of ships lost at sea. Babbage's idea was to design a machine which would calculate mathematical data more accurately and faster than was possible with men using tables. His project attracted interest because of its relevance to contemporary concerns and by the 1820s he had earned the patronage of the Duke of Wellington. The Difference Engine he designed was intended to produce mathematical tables for scientific and commercial use.

Disputes with his manufacturer and the withdrawal of government patronage ensured the Difference Engine was never finished. Like most scientists of those times Babbage was wealthy, but the development costs exceeded his resources and neither Prime Minister Melbourne nor his successor Peel valued the machine as highly as had Wellington. Pure research, then as now, was hindered by the paymaster's vision of the speed at which the science could be applied. The conundrum facing modern scientific progress, the need for theoretical science to precede applied science, has a long pedigree. The Difference Engine was finally constructed in the 1990s, using Babbage's drawings; it was accurate to thirty-one digits. Sections of this machine are on display at the Whipple Museum in Free School Lane. After funding was withdrawn in the 1850s, Babbage abandoned his engine to start a second project, his Analytical Engine, which was designed to be programmed by punch cards. From Babbage came the idea of a program that, once created, could drive other computers.

Illustration 16.2: Christ's College commemorated the bicentenary of Charles Darwin's birth by commissioning a statue of him as a young scholar perched on a bench. It is placed in a garden containing plants he discovered; Denys Lasdun's 1960s building 'the Typewriter' is in the background.

When he died in 1871, the Royal Society virtually ignored his death; it was left for *The Times* to comment that 'in spite of organ-grinding persecutors', Babbage was 'one of the most active and original thinkers'. That such a farewell could be written of a great scientist places nineteenth-century British science in its context as an unfashionable pursuit; indeed, Babbage had even written a work entitled *Reflections on the Decline of Science in England*. At least mockery, or indifference, was an improvement on the persecution which the giants of earlier times had endured. The acclaim won by Newton and Babbage's contemporary Charles Darwin were exceptional.

Charles Darwin, on the other hand, became a universally acclaimed and successful scientist in his own lifetime. After an aborted period of studying medicine at Edinburgh, he came to Christ's College in 1827. He studied theology, but achieved only an ordinary degree because his mathematics, a compulsory subject at that time, was weak. In fact, he was not a particularly diligent student: in the *Life and Letters of Charles Darwin* he admitted to being part of 'a sporting set, including some dissipated and low-minded young men', and he recorded that no other pursuit at Cambridge gave him 'so much pleasure as collecting beetles'. His modest achievements at university could not contrast more greatly with those of his later life. By the time Darwin died in 1882, aged seventy-three, he had collected all such prizes as there then were for British scientists – the Royal, Wollaston and Copley medals. Above all, his work provoked immense interest through its devastatingly simple conclusion that if man was descended from the ape, he could not be descended from Adam.

At Cambridge he was deeply influenced by three professors. The first of these was William Whewell, scientist and Master of Trinity, who provided a modern framework of inductive reasoning for the study of science. The second was the geologist Adam Sedgwick, who, despite his traditionalist Christian views, ultimately had to conclude that there had been a number of Divine episodes of creation. Finally, Professor John Henslow, the driving force behind the new Botanic Garden, stimulated Darwin's interest in the systematic study of variation. Darwin, too, stood on the shoulders of giants.

It was Henslow who secured for Darwin the role of ship's naturalist and gentleman's companion to Captain Fitzroy on HMS *Beagle*. During Darwin's five years on board the *Beagle*, it was Professor Henslow to whom he sent, among his other specimens, the Galapagos finches with their variety of chiselled and pointed beaks. These birds and other field material which so dramatically demonstrated the laws of evolution are displayed at the university Zoology Museum off Downing Street.

The *Beagle* returned to England in 1836; after a brief stay in Cambridge, at a house in Fitzwilliam Street opposite the museum (now marked with a blue plaque, as is his undergraduate accommodation above a shop in St Andrew's Street), Darwin lived in London before moving to Kent, from where he published his geological observations. However, it was not until the early 1840s that he introduced some colleagues to his theories of genetic mutation and evolution. His notebooks from this busy period of consolidation are now at the University Library. He published a number of books after his return to England, yet a short summary of his most revolutionary work, *On the Origin of Species*, did not appear until 1859, twenty-three years after he had stepped off the *Beagle*. Its publication was probably prompted by the imminent distribution of a similar study by another scientist.

During the 1850s, as Darwin worked on his theory of evolution, he was painfully aware of its conflict with Christian belief; society's pressure on scientists, particularly from the Established Church, had not disappeared. The publication of *On the Origin of Species* thus renewed the battle to free science from the grip of the Church. While Darwin did not have to be as brave as those scientists who lived during the era of Tudor and Stuart monarchs, he still faced ridicule, and one of his supporters, the biologist T.H. Huxley, famously rebuked Bishop Wilberforce during a debate at Oxford in 1860. Wilberforce had asked Huxley on which side of his family he was related to a monkey. Huxley, well deserving his nickname of 'Darwin's Bulldog', declared that he was not ashamed to have a monkey for his ancestor; but he would be ashamed to be connected with a man who used his great intellectual gifts to obscure the truth.

Some challenge the originality of Darwin's work and, indeed, there is evidence that Islamic scientists had recognised the principle of evolution during the European Dark Ages. However, his concept of species adapting to a changing environment through natural selection was an inspired and revolutionary conclusion. Equally, a crucial part of his achievement was the assembly of a huge amount of evidence which supported and explained his theory, a crucial factor in the acceptance of his work by contemporaries. He became fascinated with the contrast between the results of his own fieldwork and the artificial animal husbandry of his times and himself became a pigeon fancier as a means of understanding the extent of variation within a single species. It was the ultimate demonstration of the inductive approach to science, promulgated at Cambridge since the days of Francis Bacon.

A continuing need for bravery – Turing and Hawking

Other giants of science at Cambridge, Alan Turing and Stephen Hawking, are linked to Darwin through bravery as well as brilliance; the treatment of Turing demonstrated that prejudice could still drive out individual scientists. However, in more recent years banishment was more likely to result from the scientists' personal qualities, rather than punishment by the Established Church for inconvenient discoveries: Alan Turing chose not to conform during an age of convention and suffered in consequence.

Turing was a student of King's in the 1920s and a fellow there in the 1930s, although the university never offered him any paid employment and he worked at the National Physical Laboratory and Manchester University after the Second World War. During the war itself he worked at Bletchley Park, where his brilliant mathematical mind was instrumental in the breaking of the Enigma machine code; he had put his immense intellect to the service of the state in wartime, where others, such as Bertrand Russell and another Cambridge man of science, the mathematician G.H. Hardy, had refused to do so. In the late 1940s, when he worked for the National Physical Laboratory, he supervised the building of ACE (the automatic computing engine), which was one of the first examples of a large-scale computer. It conformed to the principles he laid down for the 'Turing Machine' in the 1930s at Cambridge.

At Manchester University he developed the first working electronic digital computer and announced the prospect of artificial intelligence in the early 1950s; but his research was then interrupted by his arrest for homosexuality. His huge contribution to victory over the Nazis counted for naught; his security clearance was removed amid contemporary fears over the defection to the Soviet Union of spies who were known homosexuals. He was obliged to undergo chemical castration which doubtless contributed to his suicide. Turing never won any of the world's glittering prizes; rather, he has been posthumously rehabilitated. The Turing Prize for Computing, established in the 1960s, awards an annual prize of $100,000; its prestige in academic circles approaches that of the Copley, Fields and Nobel prizes.

Also deserving inclusion among the Cambridge scientists who have shown extraordinary bravery in the pursuit of their work is Stephen Hawking, the physicist whose disabilities as a result of motor neurone disease have not prevented his immense scientific achievement. Like Newton, he has achieved a fame more widely based than in mere academic circles. He won the Copley Medal in 2006, the Royal Society's oldest award; other winners with Cambridge connections include Charles Darwin, Paul Dirac, Francis Crick and Captain James Cook.

Hawking, like the heroes of old, stood on the shoulders of his predecessors. His first major work in theoretical physics was completed with Roger Penrose, who took his PhD at St Johns in 1958; together they built on the research of Albert Einstein. This research led to his work on black hole mechanics within a framework of quantum physics and theoretical cosmology. Hawking's studies have had a unique impact because of his ability to introduce cutting-edge scientific debate to all manner of people: his book *A Brief History of Time* had sold nine million copies by 2002. *A Briefer History of Time*, published in 2005, will probably reach an even wider audience, among them perhaps some of those who brought the earlier book but who have yet to understand, or finish, it. He plans to write an even simpler version, which he has described as 'like Harry Potter, but without the magic'.

The significance of the Cavendish

Just as it is interesting to understand why the medieval university first came to Cambridge and thrived there, so it is intriguing to know why it was Cambridge which emerged as one of the leading centres of science in the world. Leaving aside the chance that brought isolated geniuses such as Newton to the university, it was, remarkably, two aristocrats who provided the patronage which led to the nurturing of so many scientists at Cambridge. Prince Albert, the husband of Queen Victoria and university chancellor from 1847 to his death in 1861, was aware of the greater strength of science in the German states at that time. He encouraged the development of science at the university. This intent was pursued by another aristocrat and Albert's successor as chancellor of the university, William Cavendish, the 7th Duke of Devonshire, whose ancestor Henry Cavendish had measured the earth's density and discovered hydrogen – christened inflammable air – at Peterhouse in the 1750s.

One result of the involvement of these eminent men was the construction of the Cavendish Building in Free School Lane, which opened in 1874. It marked a decisive step in the transformation of the university into a powerhouse of science. The building was dedicated to experimental physics and was open to anyone with sufficient intellect to keep pace. Thus scientific inquiry was moved from the preserve of rich men such as Robert Boyle, Henry Cavendish and Charles Babbage, who had been able to fund much of their work through private wealth. Scholarship boys now replaced the gentlemen scientists. Relatively poor students from overseas, such as Ernest Rutherford, the son of a New Zealand sheep farmer, could contribute to the advancement of scientific knowledge. Above all, physicists, recognised as a separate breed for almost the first time, could now benefit from working in close proximity to each other.

A statue of the 7th duke of Devonshire above Free School Lane holds up a model of the building for a blessing from God, a gesture copied from the older colleges. There were clearly some, then as now, for whom God and science were not incompatible. The statue stands between large windows with exceptionally wide sills which were fitted with reflective material, bringing more light into the building. Inside the long room is laid out in the classic style of a physics laboratory: a long, wide rectangular wooden table three feet high fills most of the room. However, it took more than just the building of the Cavendish to push Cambridge forward to the level of continental competitors in science: research students were also required. The university did not admit this grade of student until 1894 – any later and Cambridge would not have provided a base for Ernest Rutherford, the future Cavendish director, who won the '1851 Exhibition Science Scholarship' in that year. In 1935, two years before he died, Rutherford wrote of his own time at Cambridge: 'The opening of the doors ... to research students ... had a great influence on the progress of research both in England and in the Dominions ... one cannot rate too highly the wisdom of those pioneers who recognized that the University must open its doors more widely to qualified students of outside universities if it was to play its part as a great center of research and learning.'

The brilliant achievements of those who have worked at the Cavendish have caused scientists throughout the world to consider the very building itself an inspiration. Men at the Cavendish took the first key step towards the discovery of atomic energy through the artificial disintegration of the atomic nucleus in 1932; twenty-one years later the structure of DNA was uncovered. Since J.J. Thomson's Nobel Prize of

Illustration 16.3: The Old Cavendish Building. It was constructed between 1874 and 1908 in Free School Lane, a few yards from where the Perse School was founded in 1615. So many of the most important discoveries in physics have been made within this building that the word Cavendish is known to scientists throughout the world.

1906, a further twenty-eight have been awarded for research carried out in this building. It is no wonder that the name 'the New Cavendish Laboratory' was chosen for the place on the West Cambridge site where researchers of the twenty-first century from the departments of physics, biochemistry, chemical engineering and clinical medicine now meet.

Since the time of Prince Albert, a huge number of scientists of the greatest pre-eminence studied and worked at Cambridge. The Victorian physicist William Thomson (later Lord Kelvin) studied electricity, was instrumental in developing the first and second laws of thermodynamics and devised the Kelvin temperature scale. His contemporary George Stokes worked on the physics of fluids. J.J. Thomson discovered the electron in the late 1890s and Ernest Rutherford studied atomic and nuclear physics, discovering the proton in 1919 and theorising about the existence of the neutron, a theory proved by James Chadwick in 1932. This discovery prepared the way towards the fission of uranium and the nuclear bomb.

Ranked by many at the head of all the Cavendish scientists is James Clerk Maxwell, the first Cavendish Professor. Some argue that his discoveries merit a place alongside those of Newton. Clerk Maxwell died from cancer in 1879, at the early age of forty-six. By that time, he had developed the kinetic theory of gases, later deciphering the four basic equations of electromagnetism, from which he could predict the electromagnetic spectrum. The development of this theory was a fitting tribute to that other Cambridge scientist of so many centuries earlier, William Gilbert. It was Clerk Maxwell, rather than Einstein, who first introduced the term relativity into physics. He also found time to study optics and cinematography and is credited with taking the world's first coloured photograph: it was of a tartan ribbon, symbol of the country of his birth, Scotland.

The influence of Cambridge scientists has been wide. Many are justly famous, such as Frank Whittle, who was at Peterhouse in the 1920s; he developed the jet engine through using a gas turbine for jet propulsion. In his honour a gas turbine fan is mounted on a building on the West Cambridge Site and since 2004 there has been a blue plaque dedicated to him on the gates of the University of Cambridge Engineering Department in Trumpington Street.

Similarly well-known are the two scientists who unravelled one of the mysteries of human life through their work on the structure of DNA, James Watson and Francis Crick, who completed their research in Cambridge in the early 1950s. They were not required to be brave; indeed, the immediate relevance of their research to mankind was clear and relatively uncontroversial. Conditions in which a Cambridge scientist worked had evidently changed considerably since the days of Gilbert and Harvey. Unlike some of their Cambridge predecessors, however, Watson and Crick did not so readily acknowledge their debts to others; they took credit for having found the 'secret of life', despite that the contribution of Rosalind Franklin through her vital research into X-ray crystallography techniques received little credit from them. It is also unlikely that their elucidation of the structure of DNA could have been completed without the analytical capability of modern computing. The younger partner in the team, James Watson, began his description of their revelation of DNA's structure with the line 'I have never seen Francis Crick in a modest mood'; of the immediate fame, which most other Cambridge scientists either never saw or waited years to receive, Crick remarked 'rather than believe that Watson and Crick made the DNA structure … the structure made Watson and Crick'. There are a number of representations of the DNA helix around Cambridge: a single helix stands over the home of Francis Crick at No. 19 Portugal Place and Clare College, where James Watson studied, has a statue of a double helix in Clare Gardens, while a blue plaque adorns the wall of the Eagle Pub in Bene't Street, where the pair celebrated their discovery.

Others, a little less famous, have made significant advances: for example, Christopher Cockerill, who studied at Peterhouse in the 1930s, invented the hovercraft and worked on the development of radar during the war. Joseph Needham did pioneering research into chemical embryology, identifying the chemical process by which the fertilised ovum developed into a fully formed organism, before changing direction to study the history of Chinese science. The Needham Institute, which studies east Asian science and medicine, is based in Sylvester Road off Grange Road. The Chinese-inspired architecture of the building is matched by an oriental garden.

The role of Cambridge in modern science

The increased relevance of science to the economy is now the single strongest factor in the university's maintenance of its pre-eminence. The scale of commercial development around Cambridge as a result of the university's science prowess is astonishing. Within ten miles of the city there are more than 1,000 high-tech companies employing 30,000 people in the generation of over £2 billion annual revenue. Chance, too, played a part in linking the university to the commercial exploitation of science; where Oxford University had become surrounded by industries associated with car manufacture, the land around Cambridge remained farming territory, with no competitive industry to divert resources and manpower from the growing high-tech sector.

The commercialisation of the university's science knowledge started in the 1960s with the information technology for which Clive Sinclair, through the manufacture of the first affordable computers, was the figurehead. Sinclair himself was not a university man and it demonstrates well the pull that Cambridge exerts, through the science conducted at the university, that his businesses have been based around the town. Over the last thirty-odd years multitudinous new technologies have come to, or begun in, Cambridge. Examples of the breadth of research and innovation within the Cambridge area are easily found. The Cambridge Nanoscience Centre was built next to the New Cavendish Building on the West Cambridge Site in 2003; studies of reduction in particle size and the manipulation of material on the nanoscale there have attracted cooperation from other British universities and prompted the government to focus its research into nanotechnology at Cambridge. CAPE, the Centre for Advanced Photonics and Electronics, opened in 2007. Photonics, the study of the technical applications of light, will maintain the Cambridge reputation for science through the fields of, for example, laser manufacturing, optical computing and communications. As the discovery of electrons unleashed the era of electronic technology, so the impact of photons will be enormous: Cambridge will be at the forefront of this new technology. Plastic Logic, the company at the forefront of the design of flexible electronic 'paper', was spun out of research undertaken at the Cavendish Laboratory and is supported by the university's venture capital fund, reflecting the encouragement the university gives to mixing intellectual pursuits with business. Cambridge proved as attractive to the Wellcome Trust as it has done to Microsoft. Wellcome established the Sanger Institute a few miles to the south of Cambridge in 1992; further investment since 2005 is exploiting data from the human genome sequence. This will ensure the position of Cambridge as the world centre of genomics. The St John's Innovation Centre, established by St John's College in 1987, organised its ninth Enterprise Conference, 'Tigers of Tomorrow', in 2008 at Churchill College: the university is keen for its kittens to grow into the big beasts of high-tech industry.

Cambridge's role within applied science and its economic exploitation is of great national importance. It is the university which has ensured that Cambridge has emerged as one of the four leading hubs of scientific research in the world, along with the east coast of the United States, California and the Tsukuba

Science City outside Tokyo. Cambridge has become an important base for networking and research, where the relationship between academic research and its commercial exploitation is referred to as the 'Cambridge Phenomenon'. The nature of scientific research generally is changing through the ability of groups to come together virtually to collaborate on the most complex issues. Simultaneously, solutions to these challenges are no longer as readily available to individual researchers, or perhaps even to their departments, as they once were. The concentration of so much varied scientific expertise in the university will thus help to ensure that its community stays at the forefront of research and makes further dramatic discoveries, which the businesses of Silicon Fen will remain able to exploit.

At times the success of science at Cambridge has threatened the balance between academic disciplines. Yet theology, whatever the difficulties it once threw in the path of science, also thrives; the atheism expounded by the Oxford academic Richard Dawkins has had no spectacular success in this place of science. College chapels are vibrant places, while students worship enthusiastically at some of the city's central churches. Westcott House, the Anglican Seminary in Jesus Lane, is so well subscribed with students that it has to borrow its magnificently restored 'redundant' neighbour, All Saint's Church. Undergraduates enrolling for theology courses increased from 1,085 in 2002 to 1,224 in 2005 and by 40 per cent over the last ten years. Both science and religion are in balance with each other and prosper in this place of learning.

Cambridge's journey to science excellence

It was only after the Reformation, when the Church's grip on society was significantly loosened, that the university could start its journey towards its scientific destiny. The barriers which held up the advance of science crumbled before the bravery of the university's scientists. Armed with the growing weight of accumulated scientific knowledge, they challenged established beliefs. When there was a clear relevance to their research, as Elizabeth I had perceived in the work of William Harvey and the Duke of Wellington noticed in the computing studies of Charles Babbage, patronage was possible. Others, such as Newton, armed with genius, defied the normal conditions necessary for progress and stepped out on their own.

Then the interest of two great patrons, William Cavendish and Prince Albert, triggered an astonishing explosion in scientific achievements in Cambridge from the mid-nineteenth century onwards. The success of Cambridge scientists attracted still more scientists to study or research at the university. The area has now claimed a – presently unassailable – place at the heart of the country's knowledge economy. The legacy of the great scientists who studied at Cambridge has ensured that there is far more to the university than just teaching. It is because of them that 70 per cent of the university's activity is not in teaching but in research. The extent of scientific progress in Cambridge is astonishing. It is fair to assume that more giants of science will emerge from the university in the future.

Chapter 17

The Cultural Legacy of Cambridge

The impact the university has made beyond the confines of Cambridge is not restricted to science. So many of the country's leaders have had the shared experience of an education at the university that its customs have been carried into the heart of the country's culture, as was noted by Sir Humphrey Appleby, the permanent secretary in the 1980s television series *Yes, Prime Minister*: he defined the important things within British cultural life as being 'the Opera, Radio Three, the Law, the Universities ... both of them'.

The story of the university and town also teaches well the first rule observed by historians that there is nothing much new about the human condition. Many things have stayed essentially the same, while ancient themes have been given new twists. Bishop Latimer complained in 1549 that there was 'a tendency for gentlemen's sons to take over the university and exclude poor men's sons'. Equally, a Labour politician complained in the 1990s about access by those attending state schools after Laura Spence, an applicant from a Tyneside community school to an Oxford college, was not given a place; her rejection was used as a stick to beat both Oxford and Cambridge. The university's present administrators must attend to the wishes of the state as did their predecessors.

The Times wrote in the twenty-first century of the most recent eruption of violence near Magdalene Bridge as if it were novel, ignoring the fact that there have been such altercations in exactly the same place for centuries. Similarly, the university must still struggle with those who would share its beautiful buildings; efforts to contain the townsfolk have been replaced by the battle to manage millions of tourists. Porters control the grand entrance gates of colleges, but now their duty is to keep tourists out rather than to keep scholars in.

Books still dominate the same corners of Cambridge as they have for centuries; long after Latimer and Ridley discussed the printed works of Luther at St Edward's, the written word flourishes in bookshops in the alleys around that same church. College fellows still irritate each other; colleges maintain disputes and covet each other's land. As the university shifts its focus to the west of the old town the Backs are resuming their ancient role as the Fronts, as they were when the focus of the town was on the docks opposite Magdalene College and at the Silver Street mill pond.

Cambridge is a timeless sort of place, a good place from which to understand enduring features of this country's culture. It also contains a huge part of Britain's heritage. From ancient manuscripts and the earliest printed books through the innumerable artefacts of the museums to the resources of the modern Mathematical Sciences site, there is a feast available for those who wish to partake.

Idioms gleaned from university life

Many of the nation's idiomatic phrases can find illustration at the university. Where better to learn the root of the word stationery than by Great St Mary's on King's Parade in front of the country's oldest bookshop? Similarly, the origin of the phrase 'costing an arm and a leg' can be explained with reference to Joseph Wright's portrait of the 7th Viscount Fitzwilliam in the main gallery of the Fitzwilliam Museum; Wright covers the young Fitzwilliam's hands beneath the gilded gown of a noble fellow commoner, the depiction of which was substantially easier and cheaper than that of lifelike limbs. Directly opposite hangs a portrait of Archbishop William Laud, whose exquisite hands were expensively completed a hundred years earlier by the court painter, Sir Anthony van Dyck. This is not the only artefact in the Fitzwilliam which may explain a popular English idiom: on the ground floor a tiny selection of ancient coins from the museum's huge collection is displayed, in which a large coin from the reign of Genghis Khan's son, Ogedei, is always present. Owing to its weight, a square hole was cut into its centre so that it could be carried on a strap. Such coins may account for the English expression 'strapped for cash'.

When standing in front of almost any of the beautiful illuminated manuscripts at the Fitzwilliam Museum, the expression 'a red-letter day', denoting a day of special importance, can also be readily understood; the colour red was particularly expensive and thus was saved for the first letter of the page on saints' days within the ecclesiastical calendar. Yet another phrase springs to life when standing in the huge antechapel of King's Chapel – it is simple to imagine the medieval sidesman in an act of charity letting 'the weak go to the wall', where the original chapel benches survive; there would have been no other seating for the vulnerable.

There are also many English idioms which are used directly because of the airing given them at Cambridge. The Mathematical Tripos, a contest with the examiners that lasted several days and was as much a test of stamina as of intellect, left behind two expressions absorbed by the rest of the country; the winner was declared Senior Wrangler, with others ranked in order as Second, Third, Fourth Wrangler and so on. The term 'wrangler' is now beloved by journalists seeking to make their point that an advanced knowledge of mathematics is not required to understand some simple point involving figures about the economy. Meanwhile, the student who came bottom was awarded the Wooden Spoon, and won a certain sort of prestige among his peers. It actually required some judgement to secure the spoon. If performance was too weak the student could be excluded from the list altogether, and be required to resit the exam; the Wooden Spoon would then have been taken by a less weak candidate. There is something peculiarly British about a prize for coming last: many British amateur sportsmen still treasure moments of gentle humiliation by their peers as they grasp a wooden spoon.

Illustration 17.1: The Wooden Spoon: There are a number of late-nineteenth-century photographs depicting the winners of this trophy – in one a policeman poses with an inane-looking 'empty-bottle' scholar.

A student of St John's won the last sumptuously decorated six-foot-long spoon; it is pinned to the wall at the end of the St John's College Combination Room. The choice at Cambridge of a wooden spoon to symbolise this position does not relate to some cranial analogy about 'wooden tops'; it is most likely to have originated in the Middle Ages when, after the harvest festival, coins would be collected from those present in a wooden scoop shaped almost like a table spoon, which symbolises a plough. Crisps, a carver, gilder and frame-maker which once occupied No. 16 King's Parade, decorated the spoons with college shields of arms. The Senior Wrangler award was officially ended in 1909, as eminent mathematicians at the university felt that the system was encouraging exam-passers rather than people who could think for themselves.

In fact the term has not been lost to the university; an undergraduate awarded a first-class degree in mathematics is referred to as a Wrangler, while someone with an upper second becomes a Senior Optime and someone with a lower second a Junior Optime. Indeed, alone among the faculties, the mathematicians conduct a special ceremony in the Senate to distribute their esoteric nomenclature a few weeks before the graduation ceremonies. This ceremony, unique among faculties, reflects the time from the early 1700s through to the educational reforms of the late 1800s when mathematicians controlled the curriculum of the university; through the influence of Newtonian philosophy, mathematics was considered the most elevated academic pursuit and its dominance was equal to that of Logic in medieval times. At the Wrangler ceremony, the head of the mathematics faculty reads out the exam results from the balcony within the Senate chamber, starting with those who have won Wrangler status. The names of the Wranglers are read out alphabetically and the identity of the Senior Wrangler is made known only through a doff of the professor's hat, to cheers from the massed students below. It remains a prize which is sought after both by individuals and by the more competitive college fellowships.

There are other expressions whose origin Cambridge can claim. 'Nosey Parker' derives from Archbishop Parker, once Master of Corpus Christi, who was noted for his energetic investigation into his clergy's behaviour in the late 1500s. Another Cambridge graduate, Oliver Cromwell, was on occasion given the nickname of 'Nosey' due to his prominent proboscis. In modern Cambridge 'Hobson's Choice' would bring a locally brewed pint of beer to the pub bar, but more widely it refers to a choice that is no choice at all. Thomas Hobson, an astute sixteenth-century Cambridge businessman who hired out horses, gave his customers no choice as to the horse they rented, in order that his good horses were not be over-used: thus it was 'this horse or no horse'.

Cronies, chums, men of intelligence and other matters of tradition

Mere words as well as phrases have passed into common use through Cambridge. Fittingly for environments in which there are many opportunities for friendship, the two oldest universities have each provided a well-known term for companionship, serving as a reminder that an university education is as much a social experience as an intellectual one. 'Crony', from the Greek *khronios* ('long lasting'), is the term once used with perfectly inoffensive connotations to describe a Cambridge student's roommates. Oxford claims the more innocent-sounding 'chum', clipped from 'chamber companion' in the seventeenth century.

Claims for sartorial elegance do not belong to Oxford alone; both the blazer and a new tie knot, the Cavendish, originated in Cambridge and go well on top of Oxford Bags. The term 'blazer' passed into English use after the Lady Margaret Boat Club of St John's College chose a scarlet jacket trimmed with braid and gold buttons as their club uniform. Typically of Cambridge, the Cavendish knot was one result of a mathematical model built in 1999 by Thomas Fink and Yong Mao to establish how many ways a tie could be worn: the answer was eighty-five.

'Dunce', 'ignoramus' and 'silly billy', oddly enough, also have connections to this place of generally clever people. 'Dunce' was the term applied to a follower of John Duns Scotus, a thirteenth-century Franciscan who spent some time at his order's friary on what was to become Sidney Street. His theological arguments earned him the nickname of 'Doctor Subtilis'; he was beatified by Pope John Paul II in 1993. However, many contemporaries, who thought his arguments a little abstruse, ridiculed his writings. The common meaning of the word 'ignoramus', a legal term denoting that a jury is unconvinced about an accusation, comes from the chief character in a satirical play mocking the common lawyer which was written by George Ruggle, a fellow of Clare Hall; it was performed in the theatre of Trinity College to entertain James I during his visit in 1615. The king apparently much enjoyed the play. The term 'silly billy' was probably first used in reference to an elder cousin of William IV, the dim-witted William Frederick, Duke of Gloucester, who nonetheless was chancellor of the university for twenty-three years from 1811.

Appropriately in a place which has proved so successful at accumulating wealth, Cambridge people have contributed well-known phrases to the world of economics and finance. Maynard Keynes remarked, in the context of his macro-economic theory, that 'in the long run, we are all dead'. A few centuries before, while in the employ of Elizabeth I, the financier Thomas Gresham (Gonville & Caius) made the observation that 'bad money drives out good'. Later known as Gresham's Law, this statement expressed the tendency for debased coins to circulate more freely than 'good' coins where legal tender laws applied: where the face value of coins differed from their bullion value, the coin of higher value will be melted down or retained and so put out of circulation. Gresham is remembered by his college with a statue near the corner of Trinity Lane and Trinity Street. A contemporary of Gresham, the poet and gardener Thomas Tusser, who entered King's College in the 1540s, is credited with an even better-known proverb about wealth – 'a fool and his money are soon parted'. Another saying which has provided some amusement was probably coined by Dr Samuel Ogden, the eighteenth-century fellow of St John's (though some attribute it to his contemporary Samuel Johnson), who, with a personal reputation for heavy eating in college and everywhere else, referred to a goose as 'a silly bird – too much for one and not enough for two'.

Other phrases, once more widely used than they are now, had their origins at the university. Samuel Johnson defined 'commons' or 'half-commons' in his dictionary 'as so called from colleges where it is eaten in common'. At one time being placed on 'half commons' or 'short commons' denoted punishment, but the phrases have passed from general use.

A wide variety of arcane expressions used at the university are incomprehensible to most people, but this is the key part of their charm to some others, perhaps snobbishly so, as an understanding of them almost signifies membership of a superior stratum of British society. Command of such a vocabulary also makes the solving of the more cerebral newspaper crossword puzzles easier. The 'Senate House', the ceremonial centre of the university, is a place, while 'Regent House' exists only as a body of people which votes on matters relating to the university's governance. 'Supervisions' are the term Cambridge students use to describe what are known as tutorials at most universities. 'Gyps' are college servants, possibly so named through the Anglicisation of the medieval French word *jupeau*, for the tunics which they habitually wore. Colleges have 'courts', shortened from courtyards, though Oxford prefers the term 'quad', abbreviated from quadrangle. 'Bumps' describe the biannual competitive rowing ritual on the Cam. The term 'pollmen' describes the students at the opposite end of the scale to the high-achieving Wranglers; it is derived from 'hoi polloi'.

These expressions are summarised in a charming book, *Bedders, Bulldogs and Bedells*, written by the Emmanuel College classics academic Frank Stubbings. The author only had to go as far as 'B' to find appropriate alliteration for the title of his book, as it could equally have been entitled 'Fellows, Freshers and Fenners', 'Gowns, Graces and Gyps' or perhaps 'Proctors, Praelectors and Pensioners': all are Cambridge words laced with esoteric significance. Oxford, of course, has its own variation of arcane 'Varsity language'.

Cambridge has played its part in keeping the country's heralds employed, as shields of arms can be found emblazoned in many places around the old town. Most colleges, particularly the older ones, fly different heraldic flags depending on the occasion and display badges on cornices and above door mantels. Many of them are those of past patrons, famous alumni or important donors. Jesus College, for example, uses a 1575 version of its shield of arms, a variant relating to Bishop Alcock himself and also the arms of the see of Ely. All of them can be seen around the college. The ceiling and side walls of King's College Chapel are, of course, a herald's dreamland, decorated as they were in the cause of Tudor propaganda.

Most of the old colleges were awarded arms by the particularly active Clarenceux King of Arms Robert Cooke in the last quarter of the sixteenth century. Modern colleges have also played their part in keeping Cambridge's link with heraldry strong, with the result that pageantry and display remain deeply embedded in the culture of the university. The College of Arms even chose to hold their annual dinner at Clare College in 2007; it can be presumed that its members walked round Cambridge with their necks stretched backwards, examining the many heraldic displays, carvings of shields and other insignia, which are not confined to the university, of course: the town's Guildhall displays two large seahorses from the town shield of arms.

There are a number of amusing conceits within colleges in the form of rebuses. Besides the cock on top of the globe commemorating Alcock at Jesus, St John's has symbols of a tree and a tun of beer to commemorate Hugh Ashton, a lifelong servant of Lady Margaret Beaufort and benefactor of the college. Around the same college, even on new buildings, carvings of a fish and ears of corn can be found as a reminder of the college founder, Bishop Fisher. It has been suggested that the Tudors were persuaded to adopt the portcullis symbol of the Beaufort family because of the twist that could be made from Tudor to 'two door' and the fact that it was generally a pair of portcullises which protected castles. Those sceptical of such explanations need only turn to the nearby Essex town of Saffron Walden, twenty miles to the south of Cambridge. Its coat of arms, acquired in 1960, displays the *crocus sativus* inside a curved wall, as if the flowers were 'walled in'. The College of Arms has long been a source of appalling puns.

Through church bells, Cambridge has made another surprising impact on British national consciousness: the chimes of Big Ben in Westminster are actually those of Cambridge. This tune, which rings from the tower of Great St Mary's, was written in the 1790s by a Professor of St John's called Joseph Jowett and a young student of King's, William Crotch, who was the assistant organist at King's from the age of eleven. It is derived from an aria in Handel's *Messiah*, 'I know that my Redeemer liveth', and was borrowed by Westminster Palace during its rebuilding under the direction of Charles Barry and Augustus Pugin in the 1860s; its subsequent broadcast through radio and television has caused it to be known as the chimes of Big Ben, but in Cambridge it had long been known as 'Jowett's Jig'. It is now probably the most commonly used chime for all striking clocks, but Cambridge is rarely given credit for this contribution to national identity. In an odd exchange, the mechanism of the clock in Trinity Great Court, installed in 1910, is copied from the one which drives Big Ben in London.

Handel's work also inspired another Cambridge man at this time, the 7th Viscount Fitzwilliam. He was a great lover of Handel's music and played a key part in organising one of the first centenaries held in the country: the 100th anniversary of Handel's birth was celebrated in 1785 and was so successful that it triggered the enduring cult of centenary celebrations. Through Fitzwilliam's bequest to the university, the Fitzwilliam Museum has an outstanding collection of Handel memorabilia.

Words, as well as men, of science

Scientific discovery, the outstanding strength of Cambridge, has been reflected in the new words of science which have cascaded out of Cambridge. Some even attribute the word 'scientist' to a Trinity man, William Whewell, who was a scientist and Master of Trinity in the mid-nineteenth century; science before the end of the eighteenth century had merely meant the fact of knowing or the acquisition of knowledge by study. Although the Oxford English Dictionary supports this view, others maintain it was coined in the eighteenth century. Four hundred years before, William Gilbert had begun this feast of words by appending 'north pole' and 'south pole' to the two ends of a bar magnet. He also introduced the term 'electricity', through the Greek word *elecktron* (amber); subsequently, Cambridge men generated new words at a remarkable rate in order to keep pace with the strides they made in science: to name just a few examples, 'anode', 'cathode', 'ion', 'proton', 'neutron', 'photographic negative' and 'synapse' were added to the dictionary. The phrase 'double helix', stemming from the discovery of DNA, represents more recent scientific achievement, as does the word 'pulsar', to describe a pulsating star. The latter discovery was initially coded as 'LGM', when its discoverers, Jocelyn Bell and Anthony Hewish, initially feared that they might have unearthed other life in the solar system. At the point when humour replaced anxiety over what they might have uncovered, they chose the acronym LGM to represent Little Green Men.

Inventions which came out of Cambridge also required names: hence Frank Whittle wrote of gas-turbine and turbojet engines in the 1940s, as Christopher Cockerill did of hovercrafts ten years later. Cambridge inventions were not always so grand; Isaac Newton, allegedly prompted by the irritation which his cat caused him when it wished to come back into his rooms at Trinity, designed it a small hinged entrance– which came to be known centuries later as the cat flap. Typically of a Cambridge scholar, he then proceeded to use its swinging movement to describe an important scientific law, in this case the Third Law of Motion, which states that every motion has an equal and opposite reaction. A Cambridge physicist, Dr N. Hill, strode further down this particular Newtonian path in 2006 when he set up a business called Sureflap: using radio frequency identification technology, his cat flap recognises a pet's chip implant and therefore prevents the entry of unwanted feline visitors.

Other great men of Cambridge have also added to the minutiae of life; in the mid-1800s Charles Babbage briefly turned his considerable attention from the invention of the first computer to the problem which wandering cows and other such objects caused to the new railways and came up with the pilot, or cow-catcher, a metal frame which fitted onto the front of the engine to clear the railway line.

Smaller in size but perhaps no less significant to the advance of humankind was the toothbrush, popularised, if not invented, in Cambridge by the dentist George Cunningham. He did not study at Cambridge but chose to live and practise almost opposite King's College's main entrance, at No. 2 King's Parade. A small plaque marks his home, which is now occupied by a wine merchant. He was the earliest exponent of mass oral hygiene; consequently, Cambridge was the first local authority in the country to establish dental clinics. Bad teeth were a national problem; in the first quarter of the twentieth century, four out of every five men rejected by the British Army were declared unfit because of bad teeth. In consequence, Cunningham founded a chain of toothbrush clubs, taking the radical step of advertising to the public at the cinema, where slogans declared 'You can't fight if you can't bite' and, less convincingly, 'Oral hygiene can be fun'. The 1893 World Dental Congress awarded Cunningham their Gold Medal; sadly, he died in poverty at the end of the First World War.

Another practical invention of great impact by a Cambridge man was the flushing loo. A godson of Elizabeth I, Sir John Harington, who graduated from King's in 1578, is credited with having introduced the first modern version of this convenience in the 1590s. One of his devices, known as the Ajax, was installed in Richmond Palace for the Queen's use, while another was fitted at Robert Cecil's Hertfordshire home, Theobalds. Harington published details of his invention, which included a primitive mechanism to release water, in a satirical treatise entitled *New Discourse upon a Stale Subject, called the Metamorphosis of Ajax*. Ajax was a pun on the medieval nickname, a Jake, for the 'place of retirement' and was also then the familiar version of the Christian name John. This connection may possibly have been the source of the modern meaning in America of a 'John'.

Certainly, the choice made by Palmolive Colgate in the 1950s to market their lavatory cleaner under the brand name of 'Ajax' prompts respect for the erudition of their marketing executives. In a small twist on this story, during the restoration of Christ's dining hall in the late 1800s under George Gilbert Scott's supervision, 'Harrington' was incorrectly claimed as a Christ's graduate – probably because at some point he was a pupil of a Christ's fellow. He was considered 'glass-worthy' and his name, misspelt with two r's, was inserted into the west oriel window in their college dining room. The college history of 1900 by John Peile admitted to this error but the glass dedication remains in place.

Cultural signposts – literal and metaphorical

More esoteric aspects of British culture have perhaps unexpected links to Cambridge. Generally unaccredited to the university, in common with the chimes of Great St Mary's, is the return of milestones to British highways in the eighteenth century. The route south to London from Cambridge is still marked with milestones placed by a master of Trinity Hall, William Warren, in that century. These useful roadside features had generally disappeared from these islands after the Roman retreat from the province, although some were reintroduced on turnpikes or as status symbols on the land of the gentry. Warren prompted their reintroduction. He wished to guide his fellows, who were sought throughout the country for their legal expertise, to and from Cambridge and used money left to his college a century earlier by an improbably named pair of graduates, Dr Mouse and Mr Hair. The original white stones, decorated with Trinity Hall's shield of arms in black, still stand on several roads leading out of Cambridge; one of them, for example, is placed at the junction of Brooklands Avenue and Trumpington Road.

Through a variety of cultural events, literature and filmed productions Cambridge's culture has seeped into the entire nation's consciousness. The Boat Race, the Festival of Nine Lessons and Carols and the Varsity rugby match capture a nation-wide interest far beyond those with a direct link to the university.

Illustration 17.2: Trinity Hall milestones. There are still a number near Cambridge, particularly on the road south towards Royston and London.

More recently, thoughts of Harry Potter have caused the eyes of young visitors to light up when confronted with college dining halls similar to the hall at Christchurch, Oxford, which inspired Hogwarts Hall. The country's literature is filled with references to the university. Chaucer's reeve tells of a student on his way to 'S(c)oler Halle', in reality King's Hall, one of Trinity College's predecessors. The dramatic background of the huge Stourbridge Fair inspired John Bunyan to have Christian and Faithful face danger at Vanity Fair, the phrase borrowed by William Thackeray for his greatest novel *Vanity Fair*. William Wordsworth wrote much about St John's and the Inns of Cambridge in his poem 'The Prelude', some lines from which have been quoted here. The film version of Alan Bennett's play *The History Boys* featured scenes filmed at Cambridge – although its author himself read history at Oxford. An even more irreverent look at Cambridge by Tom Sharpe, author of *Porterhouse Blue* and *Grantchester Grind*, parodies the internal workings of college life to brilliant comic effect and inspired a TV series. Giants of literature whose work stands at the heart of the country's culture grew up in this place – a list naming but a few of them who passed through Cambridge would include Spencer, Marlow, Milton, Dryden, Pepys, Defoe, Gray, Macaulay, Wordsworth, Coleridge, Tennyson, Thackeray, Housman, C.S. Lewis, E.M. Forster, A.A. Milne, Siegfried Sassoon and J.G. Ballard.

C.P. Snow, a fellow of Christ's, based some of his books in Cambridge; in *The Masters*, he captures the intense rivalries that can smoulder within a college fellowship.

Films or television programmes with settings in Cambridge can be confusing for viewers who know Cambridge as they are often not filmed in the old town and a passing shot of cyclists on King's Parade is evidently thought sufficient to capture the town's spirit. The race in *Chariots of Fire* was not filmed at Trinity, while *Porterhouse Blue* was filmed neither at Peterhouse, nor Pembroke opposite – from where the author had graduated – but had scenes from Sidney Sussex. The recent television series *Cambridge Spies*, about the lives of the Cambridge Five, also contained very few genuine Cambridge scenes.

Spies, of course, are another famous speciality of Cambridge, although this pedigree reaches further back into history than is generally realised. Around the time in the sixteenth century when the Christ's College alumnus Christopher Marlowe was on Her Majesty's secret business, and about to pay the price with a dagger to his eye in a Southwark hostelry, another agent from Cambridge, one Dr Dee, worked for Elizabeth I. His work on navigation had attracted the attention of the court – a skilled astrologer, he had accurately forecast the storm which scattered the Spanish Armada; his forecast might have even inspired Drake's sang-froid on the bowling green. It is him, and not Ian Fleming, to whom Britain ultimately owes the moniker '007'. The Queen's favourite, Leicester, already signed his letters to the Queen with two noughts containing dots, as a reference to her nickname for him as 'Her Eyes'; to sign his own reports, Dee merely added the seven after the '00'. The pedigree of 007 stretches back further than most might think, to a Tudor Cambridge man.

To an educated scholar such as Dee, seven had immense significance. God spent seven days creating the world; rest was permitted to man on the seventh day; there are seven deadly sins and virtues; seven colours could be discerned in the rainbow; seven planets are visible to the naked eye: the number seven had enormous importance in medieval and early modern numerology. It also had some more local significance at Cambridge: seven years was necessary to complete the Trivium and Quadrivium courses, which together contained seven subjects. William Shakespeare knew this: in *As You Like It* the second age of man, his years of education, began at fourteen and ran through to twenty-one.

Dr Dee, as a founding fellow of Trinity College and a spy with irreproachable loyalties, would have been horrified by the antics a few hundred years later of the Cambridge Five: Anthony Blunt, Kim Philby, Don Maclean, Guy Burgess and John Cairncross. All apart from Maclean, who was at Trinity Hall, were members of Trinity College and all came from socially privileged backgrounds; perhaps their initial success can in part be explained by the reluctance of the Establishment to suspect those of its own class.

Spying connections continue at Cambridge. Richard Tomlinson, who graduated from Caius in 1984, was imprisoned briefly in 1997 after breaking the Official Secrets Act. In 2004 Sir Richard Dearlove, who directed MI6 as 'C', was made Master of Pembroke College; it is assumed that he was initially recruited, as so often is thought to be the way, while a student at Queens' in the 1950s. Another spy-chief, Stella Rimington, who led MI5, was also acquired by Cambridge when she was made an honorary fellow of Lucy Cavendish College in 1997. It is fair to assume that some secret service recruits still join in the manner that it is assumed Richard Dearlove did; indeed, some claim that each college had its own MI6 recruiting fellow – apart , it is mischievously claimed, from Trinity, whose track record in producing spies for the wrong team perhaps led to its exclusion from recruitment matters. It was even a Trinity man, Arthur Wynn, who set up the ring of Soviet spies at Oxford. He came up to Cambridge from Oundle School in the late 1920s to read Natural Sciences. After graduation he studied at Oxford and married the communist Peggy Moxon. As so often with these spies from the core of the establishment, he was not definitively identified as Agent Scott until after his death in 2001.

In a twist to the centuries during which sex had been officially banned from Cambridge colleges, the Cambridge spies spanned the sexual gamut, from rampant heterosexuality through bisexuality to homosexuality; within this spectrum, behaviour ranged from unrequited love to sexual predation. It is one among many Cambridge ironies that so many centuries of determined sexual repression within colleges should end with such a demonstration of sexual variety. The novelist E.M. Forster, who was both a scholar and, at the end of his life, an honorary fellow at King's, also challenged the centuries-old collegiate repression of sexuality. The consequences of repressed sexuality and the need for true love form the main theme of *A Room with a View*; his novel *Maurice*, published posthumously in 1971, is also a plea for emotional and sexual honesty.

Cultural movements

The assault on the establishment by the Cambridge spies is not the only influence that the university has had on British society – and, indeed, further afield. The impact on religion of Cambridge's Protestant revolutionaries of the sixteenth century has already been mentioned, but such influence re-emerged in the late 1700s through the Protestant missionary movement, as many of the pioneer missionaries set out to distant parts after an education in Cambridge. The first chaplains in New England came from Emmanuel College, the first three chaplains to the earliest penal settlement in Australia were from Magdalene and other men from that college worked as missionaries in New Zealand and for the East India Company on the sub-continent.

These missionaries made a huge impression throughout the world. Their inspiration, although he remained in Cambridge, was Charles Simeon. A fellow of King's College, he preached at Holy Trinity Church, by the Market Square, for fifty years. Henry Martyn, from St John's, was the most famous of these missionaries; a meeting hall between the church of the Holy Trinity and the shops along Market Street is named after him. Many of the university's evangelicals joined Magdalene College, which was actually nicknamed the 'Simeonites College' in the late 1700s. Tea was a symbol of their religious passion – the Magdalene college boat was even known as the 'Tea Kettle' – but their tea-drinking earnestness did not always endear them to their more licentious peers.

The anti-slavery movement was another cause which derived its early inspiration from Cambridge. Not only were Thomas Clarkson and his younger Jonian acolyte, William Wilberforce, at the forefront of this political movement, but a Clare man, Lord Cornwallis, also stood up against the evil of slavery in a practical way: as Governor General of India from 1787, he helped liberate slaves brought to India from the east and banned slavery from the provinces controlled by the British. His career had evidently survived the British surrender to the rebels at Yorktown, Virginia, in 1781.

It was the Master of Magdalene, Peter Peckard, who first stimulated Clarkson's passionate concern with slavery. When Peckard was university vice-chancellor in 1784, he set the university's Latin Prize essay on the morality of slavery, posing the question as to whether it could be right to make men slaves against their will. The prize was won by the young Thomas Clarkson. In Eamon Duffy's history of Magdalene College, published in 1994, he refers to Clarkson as 'a gifted scholar who had never given a moment's thought to slavery until he decided to try for the prize'. Inspired by what he learnt in researching his essay, Clarkson shaped the English anti-slavery movement, while his younger brother, John, led the sixteen ships of the Liberty Fleet which took more than 1,000 freed slaves from Nova Scotia to Sierra Leone in 1792. This was forty years before the laws which gave slaves their freedom were passed. It is strange to conjecture that the end of the grotesque Atlantic trade in slaves began with an obscure academic prize at the university.

Even though many leading politicians passed their formative years at the university, the impact of Cambridge on the British political structure has been less direct than on religion. However, a case can be made for the first national political structure being set up through the influence of a Cambridge man, William Pitt the Younger. Pitt had never derived sufficient support from parliament and had relied more on the king's support to maintain his political career. After his premature death, those who had supported him chose to extend the country's adherence to his principles through setting up a network of political clubs, known as the Pitt Clubs; one survives in Jesus Lane. Above the entrance, which now leads to a rather grand pizza restaurant, is a profile of Pitt; while the statue outside the Victorian library of his old college, Pembroke, portrays him looking suitably exhausted, despite his young age, through the burdens of high office.

For over 100 years from the 1840s, Cambridge played a key role in the cultural movements of the country. In some, such as the Pre-Raphaelite movement, it may have been Oxford which led, but Cambridge was nonetheless an immense source of patronage. The chapel at Jesus, the dining halls of Queens' and Peterhouse, All Saints Church and the Pre-Raphaelite paintings and books from the Kelmscott Press held at the Fitzwilliam Museum make Cambridge a treasure trove for those who admire the work of the movement. The medieval buildings of Cambridge, of course, provided the ideal background for these advocates of medieval culture.

Another influential group interested in medieval buildings was formed by Cambridge graduates. The Cambridge Camden Society was established in 1839; its members studied medieval church architecture with a passion that led them to a position of great influence over the bricks and mortar of the Church of England. They saw church architecture as inspiration for a return to the purity of ancient religion and defended their adoration of medieval architecture with the argument that it was no sign of weakness to copy perfection. Influenced by A.W. Pugin, who restyled Jesus College's chapel in the 1840s, the Cambridge Camden Society restored the Round Church in the same decade; the original medieval architecture of both the Round Church and Jesus Chapel was considered by them to be superior to the additions and alterations of the intervening centuries.

Their selection of 'a golden age' of church architecture, in preference to a medley of building styles which had emerged over centuries, had an immense impact throughout the country. The internal structures of many of the churches known to twenty-first-century Anglicans conform to principles laid down by this group of Cambridge intellectuals, who acted as consultants on the design of old churches. Ceilings, pews and rood screens in parish churches all over the country were reworked to suit the taste of these arbiters of Victorian culture. Ancient – but not ancient enough, according to the Camden members – structures and items of furniture were frequently ripped away. By the 1870s the Cambridge Camden Society changed its name to the Ecclesiological Society; it still thrives as a group for those who love churches. There are few churches in England left unaffected by the influence of this group and its passionate followers of late medieval architecture.

The Cambridge Conversazione Society – more commonly known as the Apostles – though hardly making a cultural impact of national significance, had an influence which nonetheless reached beyond Cambridge. The group began in the 1820s essentially as a debating club based at King's and Trinity College and acquired its nickname because there were twelve original members. Supposedly selected from among the most brilliant students at the university, the Apostles met, and perhaps still meet, each Saturday evening during term to debate and consume sardines on toast, or 'whales'. Touchingly, past members who had, as Lytton Strachey put it, 'taken wings', are referred to as 'Angels', while members being considered for election are called 'Embryos'. Many eminent men have been members, among them Maynard Keynes, E.M. Forster, Ludwig Wittgenstein, G.M. Trevelyan and Rupert Brooke; interestingly, Blunt and Burgess were also among this group. The society is said to maintain a leather diary of its debates dating back to its founding.

A number of 'Angels' went from Cambridge to form the Bloomsbury Group, which had a wide cultural impact on the arts and society from the early 1900s up to the Second World War. Individual members of this group have an even wider significance: the influence of Keynes' writings on how the macro-economy should be handled was immense, though insufficient to avert the economic depression of the 1930s; Virginia Woolf is recognised as an inspiration for the Feminist movement; the writer Clive Bell is credited as having distilled the intellectual argument for the dismantling of the British Empire.

More recently, those who passed through the Cambridge University Footlights have made enormous contributions to modern British drama and comedy. Throughout the twentieth century Footlights members represented the elite in English comedy. The key characters within such well-known entertainments as Monty Python, *Fawlty Towers* and *Blackadder* were played by Cambridge graduates. A list of past players would contain a large number of well-known figures, among them Cecil Beaton, Jimmy Edwards, Julian Slade, Derek Jacobi, Trevor Nunn, Michael Frayn, John Cleese, David Frost, Tim Brooke-Taylor, Bill Oddie, Clive James, Clive Anderson, Griff Rhys Jones, Stephen Fry, Hugh Laurie, Emma Thompson and Sacha Baron Cohen. Four out of five of the artistic directors who have run the National Theatre have come from Cambridge. No matter that a number of the Footlights actors emerged with third-class degrees, or, in the case of Cecil Beaton of St John's, with no degree at all; their talents, nursed in Cambridge, have brought pleasure to many. However, little widely acknowledged acting talent, Sacha Cohen apart, has emerged since the 1980s. It might just be that an emphasis on serious intellect effort in the colleges' admissions procedures will affect the quality of Cambridge comedy as it has decimated the ranks of the night climbers and sports teams

Clubs are a trademark of undergraduate university life; among such diversity kindred spirits can always be found. The impact of some of these groups was immense, while the mark of others has been more

Illustration 17.3: King's College Chapel. This view from across the Front Court of King's is not the most familiar to those from outside college, but it displays the dramatic architectural of the chapel at its best.

ephemeral. Joseph Addison, who ran the *Spectator* magazine, wrote in May 1711 about the newly formed Cambridge 'Club of Ugly Faces', which admitted only men who were distinctly ugly; they met in the then-new and, possibly to some, ugly hall of Clare College. In the 1980s the Authenticators were formed to deride the Peterhouse Master, Hugh Trevor Roper, after his erroneous verification for the *Sunday Times* of the Hitler Diaries. Clubs have been a means of expression at the university for centuries, and it can only be hoped that the present high profile of drinking clubs is transitory and will not overshadow the many other activities which are still pursued by students.

Pastimes which have remained in Cambridge

Some things, which are integral to Cambridge, simply remain there. Punting is not quite exclusive to Cambridge, but against the local background of fowling and angling in the watery fens it is certainly an appropriate pastime. A few private companies do well from renting out punts; the cheapest renting station has long been at the back of Trinity, in the lee of Garret Hostel Bridge. Tourists play their own version of the Bumps on the Cam during crowded summer weekends, but it is disappointingly rare to see the navigator, separated from his craft, clinging to a punting pole stuck in the mud. Cambridge punters stand on the flat 'till' at the rear of the punt; those in Oxford also stand to the stern, but their feet are inside the boat, with the till at the bow end. Just as the ancient college buildings lend an aura of antiquity to college gardens, so the fenland background suggest an ancient history to punting in Cambridge, but it is in fact an early-twentieth-century addition to the charm of the town.

Punting along the backs in Cambridge is easiest from the centre of the Cam. The canny coxswain of a punt can still locate parts of a paved ridge a few feet beneath the water along the edge of the river, which was once used by horses to tow the commercial craft using the river. The fellows of grand colleges along the Backs would not tolerate such a vulgar symbol of commerce as a towpath disturbing their view of college property, so the horses were forced to approach the wide pool by the King's Mill under the water. This scene was captured in Ackermann's 1815 history of Cambridge; the engraver was A.C. Pugin, father of the more famous son. His colour plate shows three wherries tied together being towed by a horse in mid-river just to the south of Clare Bridge; the barge horse's rider is standing high on its back in an attempt to stay dry. The languid river of modern times was not always the preserve of the pleasantly idle.

The colleges maintain their hostility to river traffic through signs with severe messages which forbid punters from landing on their river banks. The dons, whose predecessors complained about the noise of river commerce, have not gained the peace and quiet for which they yearned. In another turn of the wheel, leaving things more or less as they were, the disturbance of dons' ruminations by the noise of tourists must equal any that bargemen made urging on their horses a century or two ago.

Like punts, the 30,000 bicycles used around the old town are a symbol of modern Cambridge. It is the bicycling capital of the country; seemingly, no other city challenges for this honour. The culture of bicycling led recently to a curious experiment which suggests that the otherworldliness of the university has rubbed off a little onto the town: the city council's Green Bike Scheme distributed bicycles around the city centre in 1993 for the use of anyone, without charge. The idea was not a success. The fifty released on the first day vanished within forty-eight hours. A month later the immediate disappearance of the second batch caused the scheme to be permanently abandoned, amid much mockery of the local politicians. Surprisingly, the council raised the issue of a free bicycle scheme again in the summer of 2007. Before the Second World War a similar scheme did operate among the undergraduates.

Punting and bicycling around towns are two aspects of the Cambridge culture which have not had a significant impact beyond the town. In all manner of other ways, Cambridge has played a huge part in building the national identity of the country. Apart from its intellectual impact in so many spheres, it has entrenched itself into British culture in such a way that those who have never been near the place know of its customs and sights; the famous views along the Backs towards King's College Chapel or of the Senate House at the end of King's Parade, for example, are amongst the best-known of the nation's iconic views. Cambridge has played an integral part in this country's cultural, religious and political evolution. In consequence those far beyond its boundaries take pride in its achievements and express an interest in what it does.

Chapter 18

'For the Increase of Learning'

In his will of 1816 Lord Fitzwilliam bequeathed pictures, books and manuscripts to the Fitzwilliam Museum. Commending that they be used 'for the increase of learning and other great objects of that noble foundation', he captured the essence of the university. Lady de Clare had expressed the same wish in 1338. She had directed that her wealth be spent so that 'the world of learning should be replenished and that the precious pearls of knowledge should be disseminated for the greater service of Church and state'. Those at the heart of the university are still motivated by such fine sentiments.

As Lady de Clare implied, the pursuit of learning alone is never enough to secure the success of the university. It has also to benefit those who live beyond Cambridge. The exchange of service in return for privilege was among the earliest lessons the university community learnt. Maintaining the balance between learning and 'greater service' to the state remains a key objective to those directing this great institution.

Although the university's focus on religion has slipped a little since the days of de Clare, it still runs several theological colleges. Some of them, like Westcott House and Ridley Hall, are flourishing; Cambridge has educated five of the seven archbishops of Canterbury since 1945. It still serves the state in other ways, too: it challenges the intellect of the country's cleverest young people; scholars raise their game to win a place at Cambridge and the college-based education system is an unparalleled means of provoking excellence. The university does something further – it sets a benchmark to which other institutions of higher education aspire. It fulfils its role in the world of learning superbly.

Furthermore, its contribution to the knowledge economy is immense – even if much of its service is, in consequence, to Mammon. The importance of these contributions will ensure that the country's leaders continue to take a close interest in the university, which indeed is not unreasonable since the state provides half its income. However, the wish of the state to interfere and of others to pass judgement shows how relevant this university has become: the university matters to twenty-first-century Britain. When the university slept deeply in the eighteenth century and was largely an irrelevance to the country it was untroubled by outsiders.

The university's achievements are a source of national pride in which every Briton may express an interest, particularly as it still receives more generous funding and enjoys more privileges than are available to most other British universities. The activities of this privileged community attract the interest of outsiders. Indeed, the state, educational experts, newspapers and the 'chattering classes' each believe they have the right to be consulted, to advise, and to warn – as well as, in the case of the state, to interfere. The university belongs to the nation and not to those who happen to be ensconced there momentarily.

Thus the behaviour, or more usually the misbehaviour, of its students attracts the attention of national newspapers. Furthermore, politicians involve themselves in who has access to the university – and just as the steps up to the altar in the east end of King's College Chapel were removed, returned and removed to reflect change in the nation's official religion, so the university must respond to pressure in the twenty-first century for its undergraduate profile to reflect the social structure of modern Britain. Its management is also a topic which provokes national debate. In May 2007 the university approved only a slight increase in the number of outsiders on its council – from two in twenty-three to four in twenty-five. The broadsheet newspapers lambasted its complacency and forecast a miserable future, even though the benefits from more 'outsiders' running other great institutions, such as the NHS, have not always been clear. This is the price for being so relevant to Britain.

The university must overcome huge challenges if its relevance and success is to be sustained. Ever since Edward II determined to educate the 'King's childer' in Cambridge, the state has interfered in the colleges and the university. Access to a Cambridge education was regulated in various ways. Yet despite the shadow of rigid Church doctrine and absolute monarchs, there was a freedom for its academics to pursue the dictates of their intellects. Oaths of allegiance or signing up to Test Acts and Acts of Uniformity have long since ceased; entry to the university is based on ability, not religious faith. However, the dominance of hypothesis-driven research within the university raises the risk of inadvertently restricting the freedom to roam which the great intellectuals of the past enjoyed.

Today's academics bidding for research contracts are skilled at making submissions as vague as they imagine is compatible with the securing of funds. The system, however, still limits their freedom to move outside the tramlines agreed with the supplier of funds. The growing cohort of post-doctoral researchers must work for the body which finances them and complete the project which has attracted finance. It is only the small number of research fellows financed by college endowments who remain in the fortunate position of having to answer to no one intellectually for the duration of their fellowship. Thus the sort of freewheeling, barely financed intellectual effort that led Rutherford's team towards the first artificial splitting of the atom may be compromised by this modern method of funding. Those who control the purse strings perhaps risk inhibiting the blue-sky thinking which Newton, Rutherford, Thomson and Clerk-Maxwell employed to such devastating effect.

The university's past would have been less impressive without such intellectual freedom. It is a challenge to the university to ensure that proscriptive funding does not dim the brightness of its future. The procedures employed to secure cash contain a further threat; they risk becoming so complex and time-consuming that some of the world's best scholars spend the majority of their time battling for short-term finance rather pursuing their research. Those who venture into the university from the 'real world' of business to lecture or to manage the university's wealth are invariably surprised that money is so often a topic of debate in academia.

The emphasis on research at Cambridge also raises the challenge of its reconciliation with the requirement to teach. Talents for discovery and for teaching are rarely found in one person. If its role as a place of education is not to be undermined, fellows must be encouraged through greater remuneration and respect for the art of teaching to spend time educating junior members of the university. The problem is that the international ranking of the university – second only to Harvard in recent years – as well as the personal prestige of its staff and the acquisition of further research grants depends on research success. The vice-chancellor has drawn attention to this quandary; awareness is at least the first step in dealing with an issue about which some undergraduate students, who can feel neglected, already comment.

Obtaining adequate funds remains another huge challenge for the university; new sources of wealth must be found because government funding, in particular of undergraduate teaching, is inadequate and the dependence on state finance must be reduced. Its own assets must also be managed to the highest standards. The enforced openness about college and university wealth since the late 1990s will in any case provoke change; a few years of poor returns on college investments will ensure that the wealth management of at least the poorer colleges will pass to the vice-chancellor's new Chief Investment Officer. Indeed, those colleges may come to welcome such loss of responsibility.

The size of the higher education sector has also become a political issue which has caught the university in its slipstream. Those who run the state are convinced that there is a direct relationship between the quantity of higher education and economic success; over the last fifty years the development of education has been framed with this objective. Almost every European country has set high targets for the proportion of its youth it wishes to pass through higher education – 50 per cent in England and Sweden, 40 per cent in Germany – with a similar motivation. A further challenge has thus come from Cambridge's requirement to play a full part in this expansion. It has indeed done so. There were 1,000 undergraduates in 1800 and 2,027 in 1869/70; at the end of the 1890s numbers had increased to 2,983. In 1909 there were 3,700. Almost a century later, by the year 2000/1, there were 16,075, a number which increased to 18,077 in 2008/9. There is talk of 21,000 by 2025. So far this has been managed without a dilution of the college experience for undergraduates through increasing the number of colleges from twenty-four in 1950 to the present number of thirty-one. It has been a further challenge to ensure that the increased numbers of fellows and research postgraduates also have a chance to share in collegiate life.

Some now question whether education policy is an effective tool to achieve economic growth, arguing that universities should be left free to focus on quality rather than quantity. It has certainly been the quality of the Cambridge education, not its quantity, which created the research nexus of the 'Cambridge phenomenon'. It would be a shame, too, if the university's role in transmitting cultural values from one generation to the next, until now so ably fulfilled, were to be overwhelmed by vast numbers of students who could not be absorbed into its college-based culture.

There are other political issues to be negotiated. The extent of the university's role in broadening social access remains unresolved. Never mind that the best means of representing the nation's socio-economic groups proportionally in the make-up of the undergraduate body is to lift the standards of the public sector to those of the private sector; Cambridge is pressed to accept candidates with lower grades if they come from an impoverished background. It is a pressure which extends to the alteration of its college-based entrance system: politicians could more easily influence a central admissions process.

Sensitive as Cambridge must be to its political masters, the signals sent from government can be impossibly confusing. Within twelve months of the Education Secretary, Charles Clarke, commenting in 2003 that 'Education for education's sake is a bit dodgy', the Higher Education Minister, Kim Howells, was exhorting students to learn for learning's sake, rather than simply to get a job.

Cambridge must compete internationally for the best academics, researchers and, increasingly, under-graduates if it is to retain its international pre-eminence. The benefits to the higher education system, to successful research and to the national economy of running one of the very best universities in the world are clear. Cambridge will suffer if politicians seek to spread research funding more evenly between British universities and reduce its income to match those of its domestic competitors. Indeed, it needs to continue to have a disproportionate share of resources if it is to compete successfully with the world's very best universities: leaving Oxford to one side, its significant rivals are Harvard, Yale and Stanford, each of which have multiples of the wealth which Cambridge commands.

Despite these challenges and changes, Cambridge retains much charm. The colleges, as the guardians of the university's cultural traditions, are almost all outstandingly lovely places to live. College membership is an immense privilege. Beautiful college buildings put a roof over members' heads and capture the souls of those who pass through; any resistance to capture by the sheer wonder of the physical environment may be broken down by the influence of a kind tutor who has seemingly spent an entire lifetime in college. As a means of securing the loyalty of undergraduates – and ultimately their financial support – colleges are crucially important in an era when new sources of funds must be found. However, they stand for far more than a sentimental attachment to the past.

It is probable in future that the impact on society of Cambridge's graduates will change. Selection procedures now focus almost exclusively on intellectual excellence; as a result fewer of this country's non-academic garlands may be won by Cambridge graduates. There are more clever students than ever, but many perhaps are less well-armed than some of their predecessors with the wider set of skills which are needed to triumph outside academia and the knowledge economy. It is more certain that its future graduates will win Nobel prizes than they will the positions of prime minister, archbishop and other of society's glittering prizes. The time in late Elizabethan England when Cambridge men simultaneously dominated the Church, finance, medicine and politics is unlikely to be repeated.

Another change has occurred in the last twenty years: the university now welcomes those from the local community who wish to share its treasures. Visitors are invited to chapel services, colleges participate in the National Gardens Scheme and unlock their courts to Fun Runs, the Fitzwilliam Museum offers a huge variety of free lectures and Madingley Hall provides a riveting array of subjects for study to all-comers. Colleges cooperate generously with the knowledgeable Blue Badge guides who provide a taste of university life to the many thousands who visit the modern city. The university also now looks into the local community, as well as among the great and good, to find recipients for its awards; hence Allan Brigham, local historian and council road-sweeper, was awarded an honorary MA in 2009. No longer can anyone speak, as did Professor Fox of the archaeology faculty at the opening of the Folk Museum in 1936, of a university where 'more is known of Papua than of Pampisford' (a village a few miles away). The university wishes to be involved with the local community in a way that it never did in earlier centuries.

Furthermore, where once the university pulled down much of central Cambridge, its colleges now assist the town's enchanting ancient churches. Heads of colleges and their spouses involve themselves in local causes, setting an example for their fellowships to follow. This support now provides some compensation for the behaviour of their distant predecessors, who so often had lived in isolation from the town. The hardship once caused to the medieval townsfolk through displacement by King's College or the incarceration of the town's nineteenth-century girls suspected of prostitution should on occasion be remembered, but, whatever the past, the university is now an excellent neighbour to those who live around Cambridge.

The university has a fine record in adapting to the needs of society; it served the medieval Catholic monarchy and then the needs of the Protestant religion. In the nineteenth century it embraced the natural sciences in a manner which laid the foundations for its astonishing scientific excellence. In the twentieth century it coped with converting its colleges to meet the demand for higher education on the part of women. Recently it has engaged with business to create the Cambridge Phenomenon. It has also embraced the more recent political mantra of inclusion, be that of more children from the state sector as members or as an excellent neighbour to the townspeople. These are huge achievements.

The university's leaders now work on its image and take trouble to ensure that its inclusion of as many sections of society as possible is noticed. It also rightly wishes to be seen as a place of the future, whose past is of less concern: hence the book the university sponsored to mark its 800th anniversary in 2009 paid little attention to its history. Instead it gave a fascinating summary of the relevance of the manner in which the university's members occupy themselves in the twenty-first century. The same desire to look forward could be noticed in the lamp-post banners put up throughout the old town in 2009; historical dates were included but most space was dedicated to the legend 'Cambridge University – Transforming Tomorrow'.

England has benefited from having just two universities for over 600 years during the medieval and early modern periods. These two institutions, so remarkably similar in terms of achievement and style, have provoked each other to excellence. The rivalry expressed through witty snatches of verse, or even the occasional serious sporting dispute, obscures neither the great respect the one has for the other nor the acknowledgement that competition has helped them each to thrive. In the twenty-first century the possession of two of the world's top universities within 100 miles of each other is a considerable British achievement. Indeed, according to the 2008 ranking of the respected THE-QS survey of the world's universities Britain has four universities in the top ten, the 'other' two being UCL and Imperial College. The Shanghai Jiao Tong index of 2008 also placed the same four universities in its top twenty. Furthermore, King's College and the University of Edinburgh were ranked 22nd and 23rd respectively in the same year. There are inevitably criticisms of these indices, not least that they weigh past research too heavily (Nobel prizes score highly but the research to which they relate has usually long since been completed) and undervalue current research. Nonetheless, for Britain to have six of the world's top universities in the top twenty-five – the United States has fourteen – when no other member state of the European Community

Illustration 18.1: The University Chest, kept within the Registrary's Office in the Old Schools behind the Senate House. For many among the university's senior staff, the chest is symbolic of their duty of care to guard the community's wealth and treasures.

has any is an outstanding achievement. Britain presently 'does' universities well and that achievement must in part be due to the high standards set by its two leading institutions.

Whether they can each retain their dominance when competing in the modern age for scarce resources with the other hundred or so British universities is another matter. Much of the international success of Oxford and Cambridge has depended on the blatantly unequal distribution of privilege and financial support within Britain. However, the cultural, educational and economic contribution of Cambridge to the country is huge – as, it could reasonably be argued, it should be, given the advantages and privilege that it has secured over the centuries. It has been an outstanding investment for the state.

As the 'fabrick' of the university remains unfinished so does the task of meeting these new challenges. Intellectual independence, the balance between teaching and research, fair access, changing political priorities, the constant search for funding and the need to compete with the world's best universities are each huge challenges. Certainly, one challenge has been met and conquered – the ancient animosity between town and gown has been replaced by a cooperation that enriches the lives of those outside the university.

At least it seems the senior members at the university are heeding the advice of Tancredi in Giuseppe de Lampedusa's novel *The Leopard*: if things are 'to stay as they are, things will have to change'. The change that the university has repeatedly embraced over the last 800 years has formed a beautiful and fascinating place. As the Fitzwilliam Museum is the treasure house of this community, so the university has created an entire island of treasure at Cambridge. It is now an island with accessible shores, open to change, and will for a long time yet remain an outstanding place 'for the increase of learning'.

Selected Reading

Among the books the author has found most pleasure in reading and has used as sources are:

University histories

Benstead, C.R. (1968) *Portrait of Cambridge*, Robert Hale, London

Benstead, C.R. and Norfield, E. (1944) *Alma Mater: a profound study of a great university*, Frederick Muller, London

Boyd, S. (2005) *The Story of Cambridge*, Cambridge University Press, Cambridge

Brooke, C.N.L. gen. ed. (1988–2004) *A History of the University of Cambridge*, 4 vols, Cambridge University Press, Cambridge

Bury, P. (1952) *The College of Corpus Christi and of the Blessed Virgin Mary: a history from 1822 to 1952*, Cambridge University Press, Cambridge

Bury, M.E. and Winter, E.J. (2003) *Corpus: within living memory*, Third Millenium Publishing, London

Clark, J.W. (1929) *A Concise Guide to the Town and University of Cambridge in an Introduction and Four Walks*, Bowes and Bowes, Cambridge

Clark, J.W. (1946; 12th edn, revd) *A Concise Guide to the Town and University of Cambridge in an Introduction and Four Walks*, Bowes and Bowes, Cambridge

Collinson, P., Rex, R. and Stanton, G. (2003) *Lady Margaret Beaufort and her Professors of Divinity at Cambridge, 1502–1649*, Cambridge University Press, Cambridge

Cunich, P. *et al.* (1994) *A History of Magdalene College Cambridge, 1428–1988*, Magdalene College Publications, Cambridge

Eden, R.J. (1998) *Clare College and the founding of Clare Hall*, Clare Hall in the University of Cambridge, Cambridge

Garrett, M. (2004) *Cambridge: a cultural and literary history*, Signal, Oxford

Glazebrook, P. ed. (2007) *Jesus: the life of a Cambridge college*, Book Production Consultants, Cambridge

Guest, G.H. (1994) *A Guest at Cambridge*, Parclette Press, Orleans, Mass

Johnson, G. (2008; 2nd edn) *University Politics*, Cambridge University Press, Cambridge

Leedham-Green, E. (1996) *A Concise History of the University of Cambridge*, Cambridge University Press, Cambridge

Pagnamenta, P. gen. ed. (2008) *The University of Cambridge: an 800th anniversary portrait*, Third Millennium, London

Reynolds, D. ed. (2005) *Christ's: a Cambridge college over five centuries*, Macmillan, London

Sager, P. (2005) *Oxford and Cambridge: an uncommon history*, Thames & Hudson, London

Scott-Giles, C.W. (1951) *Sidney Sussex College: a short history*, Cambridge University Press, Cambridge

Sealy, G. and Gray, R. (1996) *Emmanuel College: buildings and gardens*, Emmanuel College, Cambridge

Simms, T.H. (1979) *Homerton College, 1695–1978*, Trustees of Homerton College, Cambridge

Steegman, J. (1940) *Cambridge*, B.T. Batsford, London

Stubbings, F.H. (1991) *Bedders, Bulldogs and Bedells: a Cambridge glossary*, Cambridge University Press, Cambridge

Trevelyan, G.M. (1990) *Trinity College: a sketch*, privately published by the Master and Fellows of Trinity College

Watson, N. (2002) *The Opportunity to be Myself: a history of Lucy Cavendish College, Cambridge*, James & James, London

Williamson, R.R. (1951) *Ackermann's Cambridge*, Penguin, London

Architectural history

Clark, K. (1928) *The Gothic Revival*, John Murray, London

Gregory, N. (2006) *Cambridge Inscriptions Explained*, Fern House, Haddenham

Hill, R. (2007) *God's Architect: Pugin & the building of Romantic Britain*, Allen Lane, London

Mount, H. (2008) *A Lust for Window Sills: a lover's guide to British buildings from portcullis to pebble-dash*, Little, Brown Book Group, London

Pevsner, N. (1943) *An Outline of European Architecture*, Pelican, Harmondsworth

Pevsner, N. (1954) *The Buildings of England: Cambridgeshire*, Penguin, Harmondsworth

Rawle, T. (1985) *Cambridge Architecture*, Trefoil Books, London

Ray, N. (1994) *Cambridge Architecture: a concise guide*, Cambridge University Press, Cambridge

Reeve, F.A. (1976) *The Cambridge that Never Was*, Oleander Press, Cambridge

Howard, P. and Webster, H. (1999) *Cambridge: an architectural guide*, Ellipsis, London

Willis, R. and Clark, J. (1886) *The Architectural History of the University of Cambridge, and of the Colleges of Cambridge and Eton*, 4 vols, Cambridge University Press, Cambridge

Medieval and religious history

Chrimes, S.B. (1964) *Lancastrians, Yorkists and Henry VII,* Macmillan and Co Ltd.

Chrimes, S.B. (1972) *Fifteenth Century England, 1399-1509.* Manchester University Press.

Cobban, A. (1999) *English University Life in the Middle Ages*, UCL Press, London

Erlande-Brandenburg, A. (1995) *The Cathedral Builders of the Middle Ages*, Thames & Hudson, London

McCullough, D. (2004) *The Reformation: Europe's House Divided, 1490–1700*, Penguin, London

Collinson, P., Rex, R. and Stanton, G. (2003) *Lady Margaret Beaufort and her Professors of Divinity, 1502–1649*, Cambridge University Press, Cambridge

Zutshi, P. gen. ed. (1993) *Medieval Cambridge: essays on the pre-Reformation university*, Boydell, Woodbridge

Cambridge town

Craft, S., Elliot, K. and Simmons, E. (1999) *Cambridgeshire Voices*, Tempus, Stroud
Gray, R. and Stubbing, D. (2000) *Cambridge Street-Names: their origins and associations*, Cambridge University Press, Cambridge
Fellows, R.B. (1978) *Railways to Cambridge: actual and proposed*, Oleander Press, Cambridge
Payne, S. (1983) *Down Your Street: Cambridge past and present*, Pevensey Press, Cambridge
Taylor, A. (1999) *Cambridge: the hidden history*, Tempus, Stroud
Taylor, K. (1994) *Central Cambridge: a guide to the university and colleges*, Cambridge University Press, Cambridge
Ward, P. (1978) *Cambridge Street Literature*, Oleander Press, Cambridge

Fiction

Faulks, S. (2008) *Engleby*, Vintage, London
Follett, K. (1989) *The Pillars of the Earth*, Pan Macmillan, London
Gregory, S. (1998) *The Matthew Bartholomew Chronicles*, Warner Books, London
Snow, C.P. (1963) *The Masters*, Penguin, London

Gardens

Batey, M. (1989) *Historic Gardens of Oxford & Cambridge*, Macmillan, London
Bird, R. (1994) *The Gardens of Cambridge*, Covent Garden Press, Cambridge
Brown, J. (1988) *The Making of the Gardens, Newnham College Cambridge*, Newnham College, Cambridge
Gray, R. (1984) *Cambridge Gardens*, Pevensey Press, Cambridge
Lyons, U. (2000) *Lucy Cavendish Gardens*, Cavendish
Pearce, A. and Pearce, D. (2005) *A Cambridge Keepsake*, Fotogenix Publishing, Cambridge

Sport

Garnett, M.P. (2006) *A Tennis Miscellany*, Historical Publications, Romsey, Vic., Australia
Morgan, R. (2001) *Real Tennis in Cambridge: the first six hundred years*, Cambridge University Press, Cambridge
Powell, W.A. (2001) *Varsity Cricket*, Tempus, Stroud

Science

Darwin, F. ed. (1887) *The Life and Letters of Charles Darwin*, 3 vols, John Murray, London

Harman, P. and Mitton, S. eds (2002) *Cambridge Scientific Minds*, Cambridge University Press, Cambridge

Rouse Ball, W.W. (1889) *A History of the Study of Mathematics at Cambridge*, Cambridge University Press, Cambridge

Stained glass, churches and chapels

Halliday, S., Archer, M., Lockhart, A. and Lushington, L. (1994) *Stained Glass*, Pitkin Guides, Andover

Binns, J. and Meadows, P. eds (2000) *Great St. Mary's, Cambridge's university church*, Cambridge University Press, Cambridge

Chainey, G. (1987) *In Celebration of King's College Chapel*, Pevensey Press, Cambridge

Hayman, R. (2005) *Church Misericords and Bench Ends*, Shire Publications, Botley

Hicks, C. (2007) *The King's Glass*, Chatto & Windus, London

Humphery-Smith, C.R. (1985) *The Cambridge Armorial*, Orbis, London

Remnant, G. (1969) *A Catalogue of Misericords in Great Britain*, Clarendon Press, Oxford

Rouse, C. (1991) *Medieval Wall Paintings*, Shire Publications, Botley

Smart, C.H.L. (1996) *The Christmas Story as Told by the Great Windows of King's College*, King's College, Cambridge

Smart, C.H.L. (2005) *King's College Chapel, Cambridge: the great windows*, Scala Publishers, London

Tibbs, R. (1970) *King's College Chapel Cambridge: the story and the renovation*, Lavenham Press, Dalton

Wayment, H. (1972) *The Windows of King's College Chapel, Cambridge*, Oxford University Press for the British Academy, Oxford

Woodman, F (1986) *Architectural History of King's College Chapel*, Routledge, London

Other

Chainey, G. (1985) *A Literary History of Cambridge*, Pevensey Press, Cambridge

Cheason, D. (1983) *Cambridge Connections: a literary guide*, Waterbeach

Pallis, E. (2003) *Oxbridge Entrance: the real rules*, Tell Books, London

Reeve, R.A. (1977) *Varsity Rags and Hoaxes*, Oleander Press, Cambridge

Sargood, L. (2004) *Literary Cambridge*, Sutton, Stroud

Yeates, G. (1994) *Cambridge College Ghosts*, Jarrold, Norwich

Appendices

1. The world's oldest universities – generally accepted dates of foundation

The accuracy of foundation dates of universities is disputed, as indeed are the criteria as to what constituted a university. An esoteric debate over these dates could start with Salerno; there was a Benedictine monastery there by 794, from which instruction most probably began; some, however, would argue for an even earlier date. Indeed, those in charge of fund-raising at Cambridge University in twenty years' time may well argue that 2009 was all a mistake – the claim might then be made that the granting of studium status through the papal decree of Pope Gregory IX in 1233 was the real foundation date, unless, of course, the studium generale status granted in 1318 is preferred. That ten of the earliest fifty universities were within 200 miles of Rome emphasises the role which the Catholic Church played in education. The large number of universities in areas which later became the nation states of Italy, France, Spain and Germany helped to embed cultural diversity on the European continent. Universities transmit cultural values; they reflect, for instance, the immense cultural diversity of France, that drew from de Gaulle the lament 'Comment voulez vous gouverner un pays où il existe 258 variétés de fromage?' England was united as a kingdom long before its continental neighbours, and had only two universities as a result.

Date	University	Founding power
850	Salerno	Sicily
859	Fes	Idrisid (Fatamid Caliph.)
972	Al-Azhar (Cairo)	Egypt (Fatamid Caliph.)
1088	Bologna	Emilia-Romagna, Papal St
1150	Paris	French Kingdom
1160	Montpellier	Kingdom of Burgundy
1167	Oxford	Kingdom of England
1209	Cambridge	Kingdom of England
1218	Salamanca	Kingdom of Castile
1222	Padua	Lombard League
1224	Naples	Kingdom of Sicily
1228	Vercelli	Lombard League
1229	Toulouse	Count of Toulouse
1229	Angers	2nd House of Anjou
1240	Siena	City state of Siena
1276	Perugia	City state of Perugia
1290	Lisbon	Kingdom of Portugal

1290	Coimbra	Kingdom of Portugal
1300	Lleida	Principality of Catalonia
1303	Rome	The Papacy
1308	Perugia	City state of Perugia
1336	Camerino	City state of Camerino
1343	Pisa	City state of Pisa
1346	Valladolid	Kingdom of Castile
1348	Prague	Kingdom of Bohemia
1361	Pavia	Lombard League
1364	Krakow	Kingdom of Poland
1365	Vienna	Dukes of Hapsburg
1367	Pécs	Kingdom of Hungary
1386	Heidelberg	Palatinate of Heidelberg
1391	Ferrara	City state of Ferrara
1402	Würzburg	Bishop Prince of Wurzburg
1404	Turin	Duchy of Savoy
1414	St Andrew's	Kingdom of Scotland
1419	Rostock	Duchy of Mecklenburg
1425	Louvain	Duchy of Brabant
1431	Poitiers	Poitou, province of Fr.
1432	Caen	Henry VI of England
1447	Palermo	Kingdom of Sicily
1450	Barcelona	County of Barcelona
1451	Glasgow	Kingdom of Scotland
1453	Istanbul	Ottoman Empire
1457	Frieburg	House of Hapsburg
1460	Basel	Prince-Bishop of Basel
1472	Munich	Duke of Bavaria
1477	Uppsala	Kingdom of Denmark
1479	Copenhagen	Kingdom of Denmark
1481	Genoa	City state of Genoa
1495	Aberdeen	Kingdom of Scotland

2. THE-QS World University Rankings: 2008 world rankings of the world's top universities based on research achievement, teaching quality and employability of graduates

The rankings of these universities have not varied much in recent years; 14 of the top 20 are American, 4 are English. Of those below the top twenty, the highest European universities were King's College, London (22nd), followed by Edinburgh (23rd) and ETH Zurich (24th).

1	Harvard
2	Yale
3	Cambridge
4	Oxford
5	California
6	Imperial
7	UCL
8	Chicago
9	Massachusetts
10	Columbia
11	Pennsylvania
12	Princeton
13	Duke
14	John Hopkins
15	Cornell
16	Australian Nat University
17	Stanford
18	Michigan
19	Tokyo
20	McGill

Universities ranked by an assessment of their teaching ability

A group of Scottish academics led by a director of research at Napier University ranked British universities on the quality of their teaching in 2006. Sheffield Hallam was judged the best, followed by Middlesex, Oxford, Leeds and the University of the West of England. Cambridge did not merit a place in the top ten, according to this study.

3. Nobel prizes by university

There is sometimes disagreement as to which centres of learning deserve accreditation, but the following summary is generally accepted.

Cambridge	83	Cornell	40
Columbia	82	Yale	33
Chicago	79	Gottingen	32
Harvard	76	John Hopkins	21
MIT	63	Zurich	31
Berkeley	61	Princeton	29
Grand écoles	50	Berlin	29
Stanford	50	New York	23
Oxford	47	Manchester	21
Paris	41	Rockefeller	20

Cambridge Nobel prizes were divided as follows

Physics	29	Economics	7
Medicine	22	Literature	2
Chemistry	19	Peace	2

The Oxbridge rivalry

Much of the Oxbridge rivalry is conducted through statistics: for example, Cambridge claims 83 Nobel Laureates, Oxford 47; Oxford has had 9 Poet Laureates, Cambridge only 7; there have been 25 prime ministers from Oxford and 14 from Cambridge; Cambridge has had 11 heads on postage stamps, Oxford only 6. Of the 37 primates of the Church of England since 1533, 19 attended Oxford and 14 Cambridge (though of the seven since 1945, 5 were at Cambridge and 1 at Oxford). It could be argued that this leaves Cambridge ahead by 129 to 106.

4. University positions

Chancellor	Head of the university, who is elected by the Senate; though the holder takes no part in running the university, they attend major ceremonial occasions, particularly to confer honorary degrees.
Vice-chancellor	Administrative head of the university; the position is held for seven years, though it is confirmed annually by a vote in Senate. It has been a full-time role since 1992. The vice-chancellor normally awards undergraduate degrees.
Proctors	Two proctors, elected annually, have represented the graduate body since the early thirteenth century; they handle order and discipline within the university. The university also appoints a Motor Proctor who is responsible for the undergraduates who have cars within ten miles of Gt St Mary's. They retain an office in St Mary's Passage.
Constables	Long since referred to as Bulldogs, they support the proctors; on formal occasions they carry the ancient insignia of the university, which include a linstock, a halberd and a butter measure.
Esquire bedells	These two graduate officers walk in front of the chancellor or the vice-chancellor on ceremonial occasions, carrying silver maces given to the university by the Duke of Buckingham in 1616.
Marshal	Stands as a mace-bearer in addition to the two esquire bedells; also recruits the Constables.
Orator	Ceremonial role which handles tasks such as exercising the university's right to make an address to the monarch. He also introduces honorary degree candidates to the Senate.
Professor	There are over 150 professorships in the university, ranging from the Regius Professorships down to the lesser positions of Ad hominem, which are held for a fixed term by a named individual.
Reader/lecturer	A reader is a grade of teacher between a professor and lecturer.
Registrary	The senior administrative post, whose holder oversees a budget of £30m, manages 750 staff and controls the university chest; other similar ancient roles include the positions of Treasurer and Librarian.

5. College positions

College heads	Variously referred to as master, mistress, provost, president, warden, principal.
Fellows	Fellows of different classes share the management of a college; there are research, official, professorial, emeritus, honorary and bye fellowships. The shared characteristic of the first three grades is their teaching role.
Tutor	More a guardian than a teacher; each student in college is assigned a tutor, who does not in fact teach the student.
Supervisor	A supervisor in the student's tripos will be appointed by the college; at the weekly meetings, known as a supervision, the student traditionally submits the weekly essay.
Dean	The dean, usually in holy orders, is responsible for college chapel services; there may be a chaplain at college chapel.
Praelector	A senior member of college who ensures proper matriculation into the college and who oversees graduation ceremonies.
Bursar	The college bursar looks after the college's financial affairs; until the late 20th century most bursars were academics, though the positions are now filled by professionals with various assistant bursars in support.
Manciples	Some colleges have a manciple who is responsible for domestic management, though they might be called marshalls.
Others	Head porters and porters man the college gatehouses, handling basic administrative tasks and keeping tourists at bay. Other medieval-sounding job titles are gyps – college manservants – though they generally disappeared in the 1960s. Bedders still exist as room cleaners, though Girton perversely refers to its bedders as gyps.
Scholars	This is historically the generic term for an undergraduate. Scholarships as an entrance award ceased in 1985, together with the lesser award of Exhibitioner; they were replaced by awards made during an undergraduate's career.
Grades of scholar	The grades of scholars, which mostly date from Tudor times, have died out: they were fellow noble commoners, fellow commoners, pensioners, scholars, sizars and at some colleges, sub-sizars. The wealth of fellow commoners often purchased distractions from study; hence the sobriquet 'an empty bottle' became at one stage an interchangeable expression with 'fellow commoner' among their less privileged contemporaries.

6. College junior members

The figures vary slightly from year to year; those below are based on the academic year 2005/6. Clare Hall and Darwin College take only postgraduates. Oxford University has the same number of students spread among 39 colleges.

	u/grads	p/grads	Total
Homerton	596	453	1049
Trinity	704	260	964
St John's	587	258	845
Queens'	526	274	800
Gonville & Caius	547	169	716
Girton	543	133	676
Jesus	524	215	739
Fitzwilliam	496	195	691
King's	412	192	604
Churchill	479	185	664
Wolfson	100	377	477
St Catharine's	467	147	614
Trinity Hall	386	182	568
Downing	439	180	619
Clare	484	187	671
Pembroke	446	159	605
Emmanuel	493	130	623
Newnham	400	123	523
Robinson	424	69	493
Selwyn	383	106	489
Sidney Sussex	370	131	501
Magdalene	371	120	491
New Hall	373	53	426
Christ's	409	73	482
Corpus Christi	264	129	393
Peterhouse	257	104	361
St Edmund's	132	183	315
Hughes Hall	101	305	406
Lucy Cavendish	104	88	192
Clare Hall	1	168	169
Darwin	8	488	496
Totals	**11,826**	**5,836**	**17,662**
Other students (writing up/under exam.)			**1,438**
Grand total			**19,100**

7. College academic rankings

Source: the Tompkins Table

Students score 5 for a first, 3 for a 2:i, 2 for a 2:ii and 1 for a 3rd. The Oxford equivalent is the Norrington table.

	2008	2006	2004
Selwyn	1	7	11
Emmanuel	2	1	1
Trinity	3	5	3
Gonville & Caius	4	2	5
Magdalene	5	20	22
Churchill	6	13	19
Jesus	7	10	9
Christ's	8	6	2
Corpus Christ	9	8	10
Pembroke	10	4	6
St Catharine's	11	3	7
Downing	12	11	17
Clare	13	12	4
Sidney Sussex	14	9	18
Trinity Hall	15	16	12
Queens'	16	14	8
Robinson	17	18	16
Peterhouse	18	21	21
King's	19	17	20
St John's	20	15	14
Fitzwilliam	21	19	15
Girton	22	22	25
New Hall	23	24	23
Newnham	24	23	13
Homerton	25	25	24
Hughes Hall	26	29	27
Wolfson	27	27	28
Lucy Cavendish	28	26	26
St Edmund's	29	28	29

(Clare Hall and Darwin College, as graduate collages, are omitted.)

8. College foundation dates

A number of the oldest colleges were absorbed by later foundations; names in bold are those of colleges still existing in the twenty-first century. There are 29 undergraduate colleges with two more (Clare Hall and Darwin) which take only post-graduates; however, in practice Wolfson, St Edmund's and Lucy Cavendish are also primarily focused on the mature, and usually postgraduate, student.

College	Foundation	Founder
Peterhouse	1284	Bishop of Ely
King's Hall	1317	Edward II
University Hall	1326	Richard Badew
Michaelhouse	1324	Hugh de Stanton
Clare Hall	1326	Lady de Clare
Pembroke Hall	1347	Marie de Valence
Gonville Hall	1348	Edmund Gonville
Trinity Hall	1350	Bishop Bateman
Corpus Christi	1352	Town guilds
Buckingham College	1428	Duchess of Buckingham
Godshouse	1438	William Bingham
King's College	1441	Henry VI
St Bernard's College	1446	Andrew Dockett
Queens' College	1448	Margaret of Anjou
St Catharine's College	1473	Robert Woodlark
Jesus College	1496	Bishop Alcock
Christ's College	1505	Lady Margaret Beaufort
St John's College	1511	Lady Margaret Beaufort
Magdalene College	1542	Lord Thomas Audley
Trinity College	1546	Henry VIII
Emmanuel College	1584	Walter Mildmay
Sidney Sussex College	1596	Lady Sidney
Downing College	1800	George Downing
Girton College	1869	Emily Davies
Newnham College	1871	Henry Sidgwick & Anne Clough
Cavendish College	1873	
Selwyn College	1882	Committees are credited with founding
Fitzwilliam Hall (college 1966)	1892	colleges from the 1870s onwards
Homerton College (full status 2008)	1894	
St Edmund's Hall (College 1965)	1896	
New Hall	1954	
Churchill	1960	
Darwin College	1964	
University Hall (later Wolfson College)	1965	
Lucy Cavendish College	1965	
Clare Hall	1966	
Hughes Hall	1968	
Robinson College	1977	

9. Triposes open to Cambridge undergraduates

There are presently 28 degree courses, each of which constitutes a Tripos.

Anglo Saxon, Norse & Celtic
Archaeology & Anthropology
Architecture
Chemical Engineering
Classics
Computer Science
Economics
Education Studies
Engineering
English
Geography
History
History of Art
Land Economy

Law
Linguistics
Management Studies
Manufacturing Engineering
Mathematics
Medicine
Modern & Medieval Languages
Music
Natural Sciences
Oriental Studies
Philosophy
Social & Political Sciences
Theology & Religious Studies
Veterinary Medicine

10. Cambridge professorships founded between 1502 and 1800

Date	Name
1502	Lady Margaret Professorship of Divinity
1540	Regius Professor of Divinity
	Regius Professor of Civil Law
	Regius Professor of Physic
	Regius Professor of Hebrew
	Regius Professor of Greek
1632	Sir Thomas Adams Professor of Arabic
1663	Lucasian Professor of Mathematics
1683	Knightbridge Professorship of Moral Sciences
1684	Professor of Music
1702	Professor of Chemistry
1704	Plumian Professor of Astronomy
1707	Professor of Anatomy
1724	Regius Professor of Arabic
1724	Regius Professor of Modern History
1724	Professor of Biology
1728	Woodwardian Professor of Geology
1749	Lowndean Professor of Astronomy & Geometry
1777	Norris Hulse Professor of Divinity
1783	Jacksonian Professor of Natural Philosophy
1800	Downing Professor of the Laws of England

Index